MW01076974

image® COMICS PRESENTS

DEEP SLEEPER™

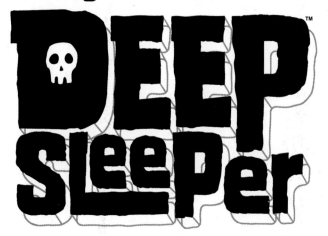

DEEP SLEEPER ™

written by
phil hester

illustrated by
mike huddleston

book design
by
k.seda

covers and
logo by
mike huddleston

lettering by
sean konot

IMAGE COMICS, INC.

Erik Larsen - *Publisher*
Todd McFarlane - *President*
Marc Silvestri - *CEO*
Jim Valentino - *Vice-President*
Eric Stephenson - *Executive Director*
Missie Miranda - *Controller*
Brett Evans - *Production Manager*
B. Clay Moore - *PR & Marketing Coordinator*
Allen Hui - *Production Artist*
Joe Keatinge - *Traffic Manager*
Mia MacHatton - *Administrative Assistant*
Jonathan Chan - *Production Assistant*
www.imagecomics.com

NIGHT INTO DAY

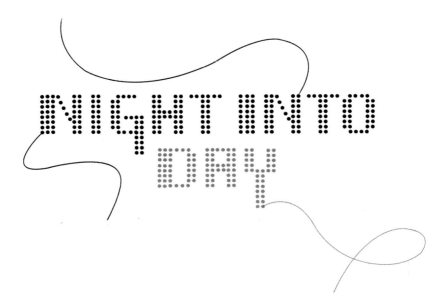

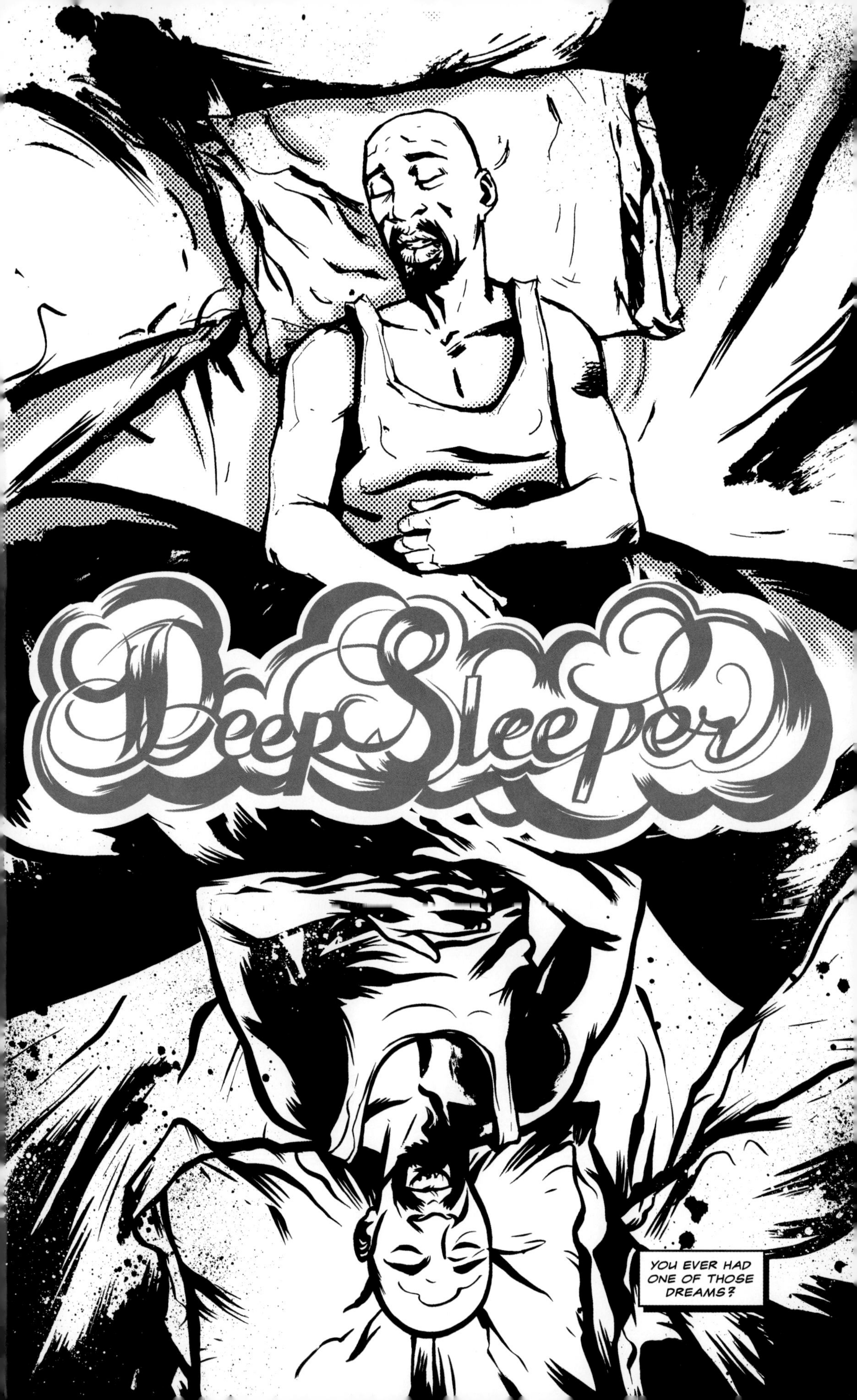
Deep Sleeper
YOU EVER HAD ONE OF THOSE DREAMS?

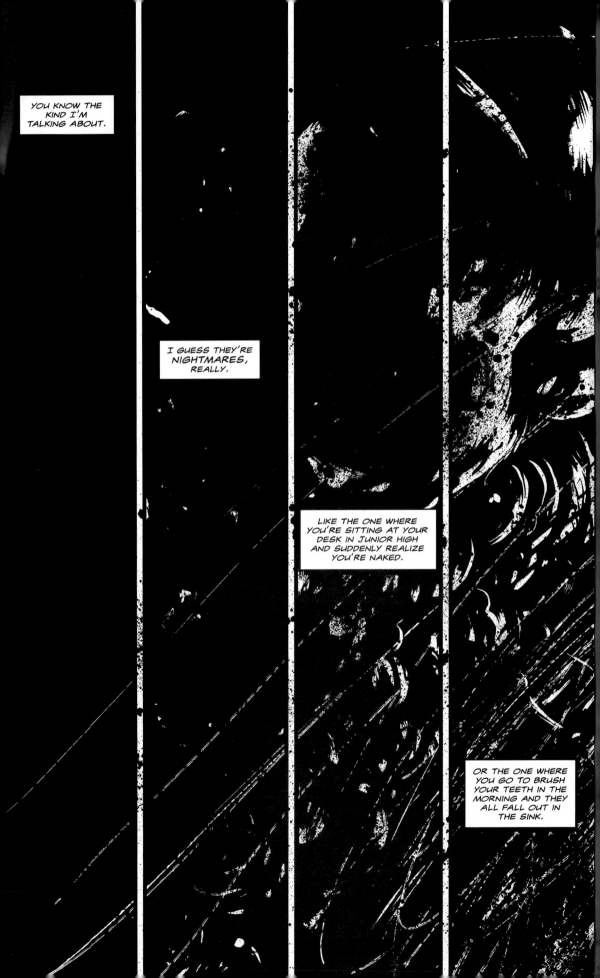

YOU KNOW THE KIND I'M TALKING ABOUT.

I GUESS THEY'RE NIGHTMARES, REALLY.

LIKE THE ONE WHERE YOU'RE SITTING AT YOUR DESK IN JUNIOR HIGH AND SUDDENLY REALIZE YOU'RE NAKED.

OR THE ONE WHERE YOU GO TO BRUSH YOUR TEETH IN THE MORNING AND THEY ALL FALL OUT IN THE SINK.

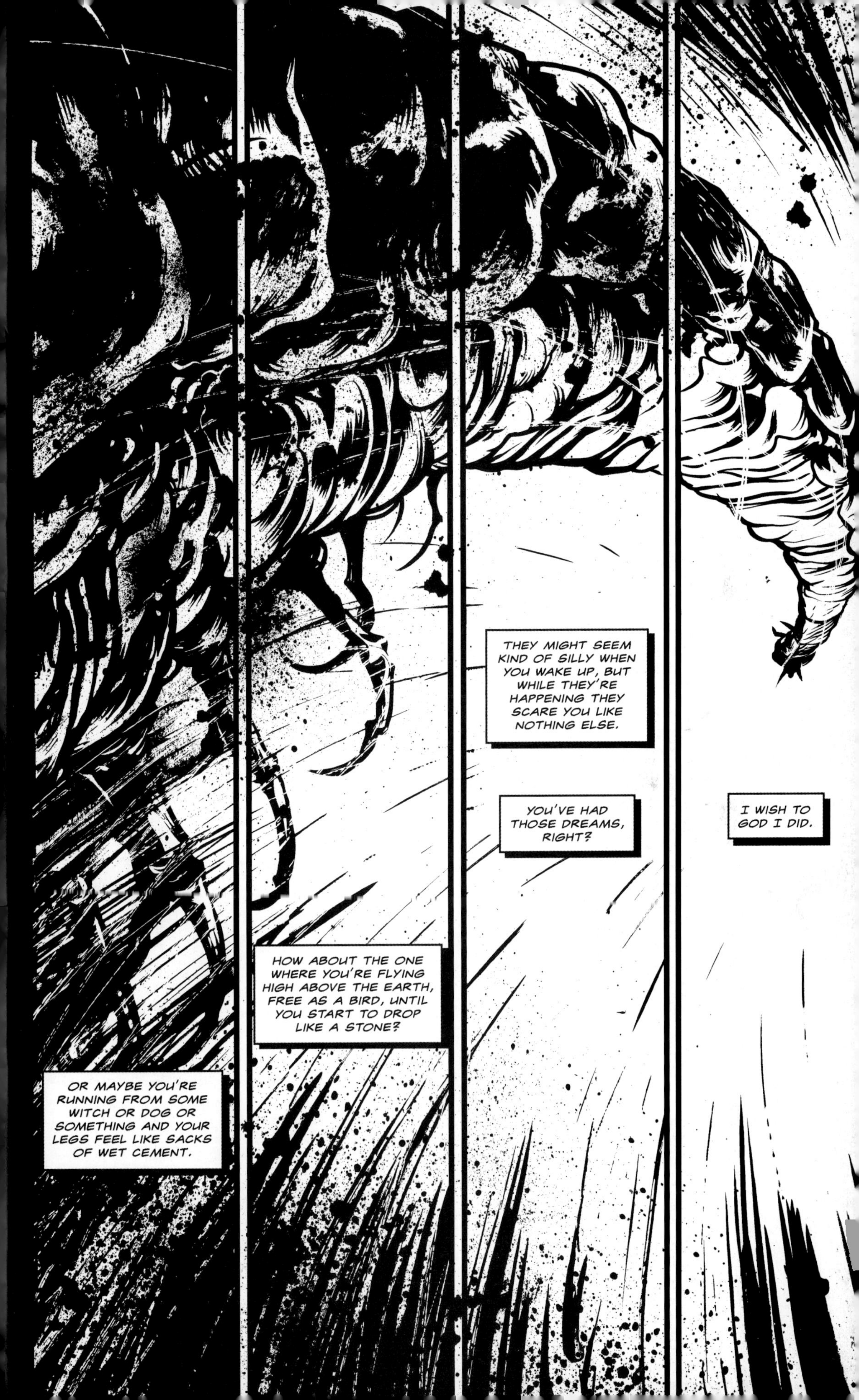
OR MAYBE YOU'RE RUNNING FROM SOME WITCH OR DOG OR SOMETHING AND YOUR LEGS FEEL LIKE SACKS OF WET CEMENT.
HOW ABOUT THE ONE WHERE YOU'RE FLYING HIGH ABOVE THE EARTH, FREE AS A BIRD, UNTIL YOU START TO DROP LIKE A STONE?
THEY MIGHT SEEM KIND OF SILLY WHEN YOU WAKE UP, BUT WHILE THEY'RE HAPPENING THEY SCARE YOU LIKE NOTHING ELSE.
YOU'VE HAD THOSE DREAMS, RIGHT?
I WISH TO GOD I DID.

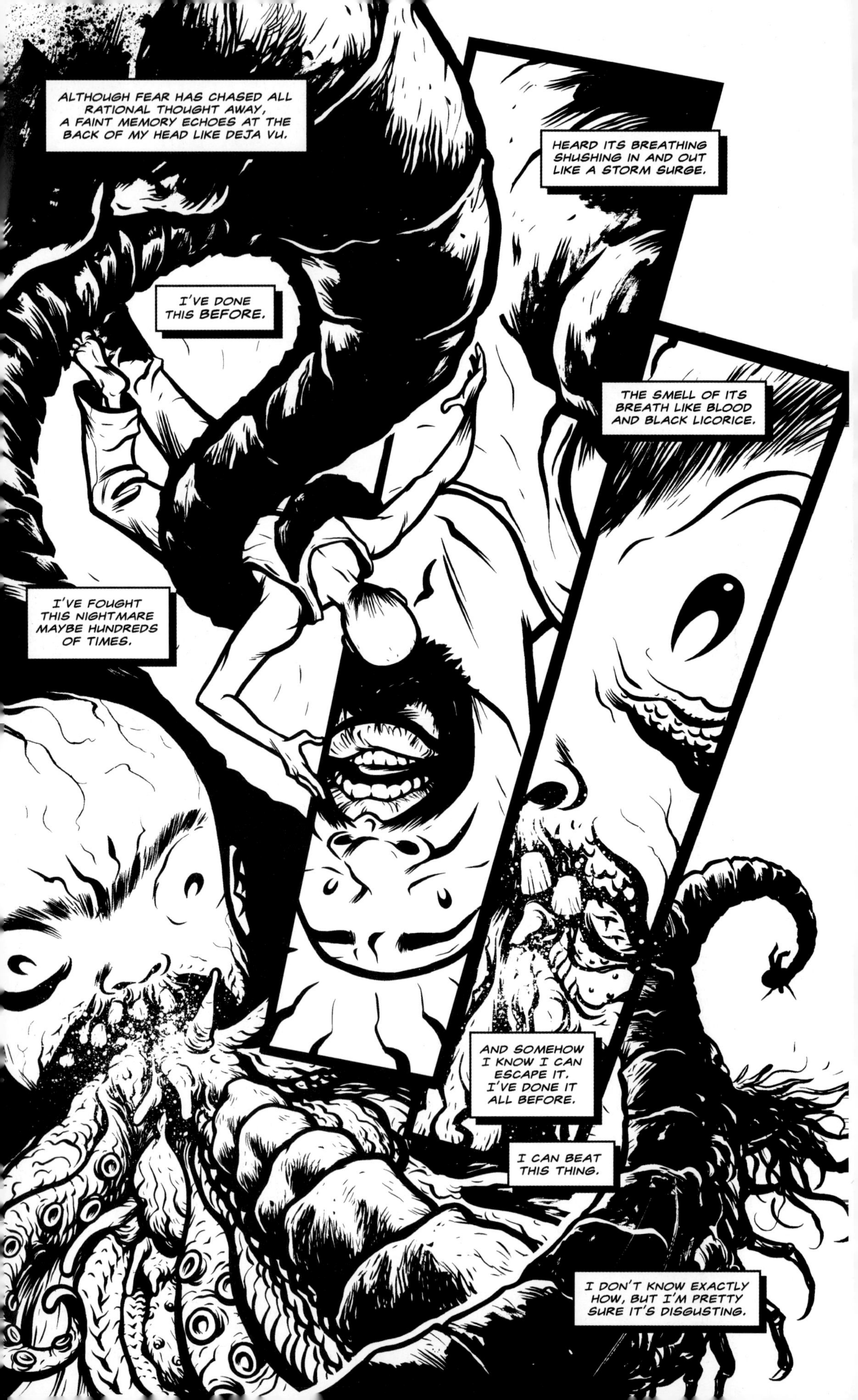
ALTHOUGH FEAR HAS CHASED ALL RATIONAL THOUGHT AWAY, A FAINT MEMORY ECHOES AT THE BACK OF MY HEAD LIKE DEJA VU.
HEARD ITS BREATHING SHUSHING IN AND OUT LIKE A STORM SURGE.
I'VE DONE THIS BEFORE.
THE SMELL OF ITS BREATH LIKE BLOOD AND BLACK LICORICE.
I'VE FOUGHT THIS NIGHTMARE MAYBE HUNDREDS OF TIMES.
AND SOMEHOW I KNOW I CAN ESCAPE IT. I'VE DONE IT ALL BEFORE.
I CAN BEAT THIS THING.
I DON'T KNOW EXACTLY HOW, BUT I'M PRETTY SURE IT'S DISGUSTING.

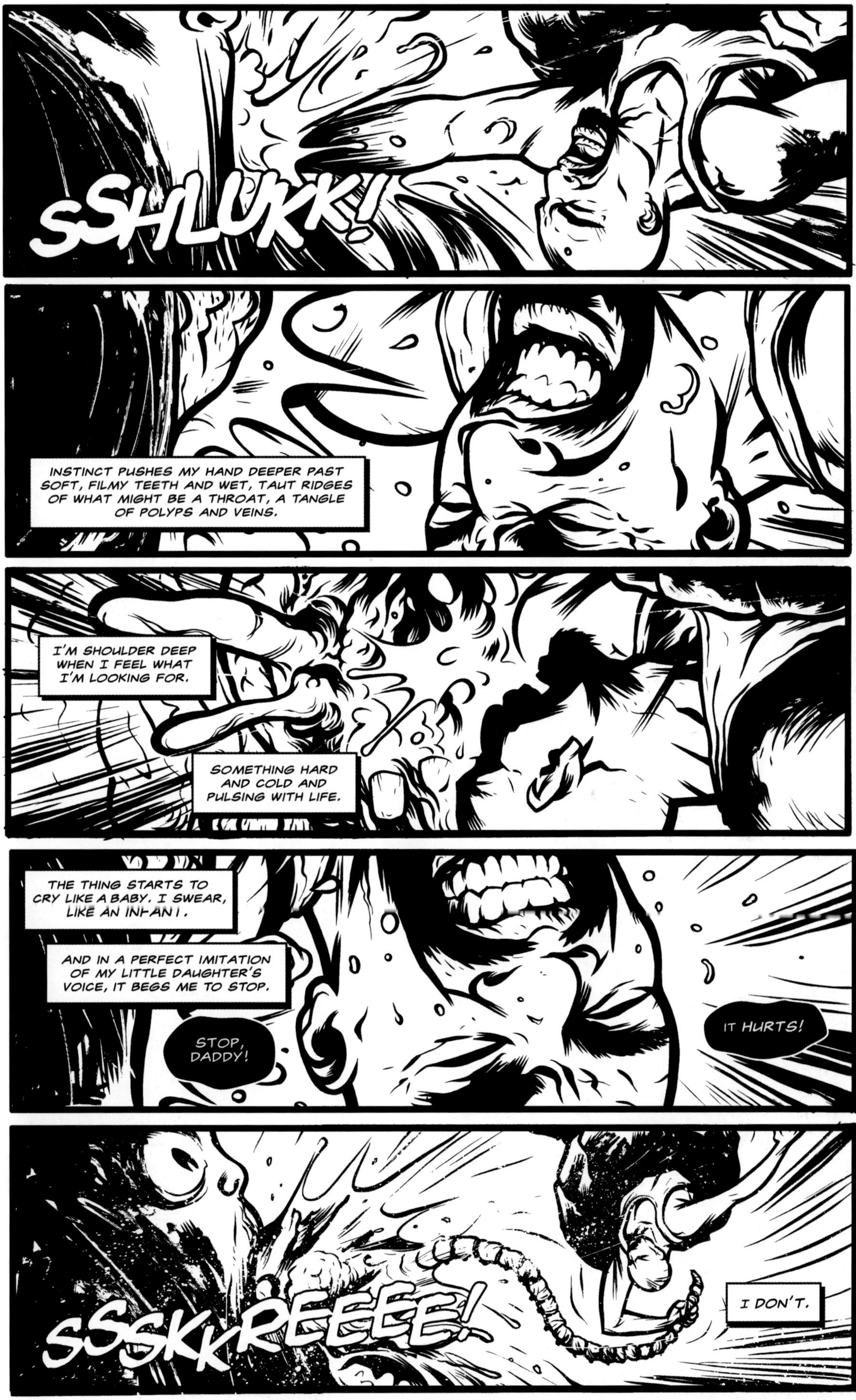
SSHLUKK!
INSTINCT PUSHES MY HAND DEEPER PAST SOFT, FILMY TEETH AND WET, TAUT RIDGES OF WHAT MIGHT BE A THROAT, A TANGLE OF POLYPS AND VEINS.
I'M SHOULDER DEEP WHEN I FEEL WHAT I'M LOOKING FOR.
SOMETHING HARD AND COLD AND PULSING WITH LIFE.
THE THING STARTS TO CRY LIKE A BABY. I SWEAR, LIKE AN INFANT.
AND IN A PERFECT IMITATION OF MY LITTLE DAUGHTER'S VOICE, IT BEGS ME TO STOP.
STOP, DADDY!
IT HURTS!
SSSKKREEEEE!
I DON'T.

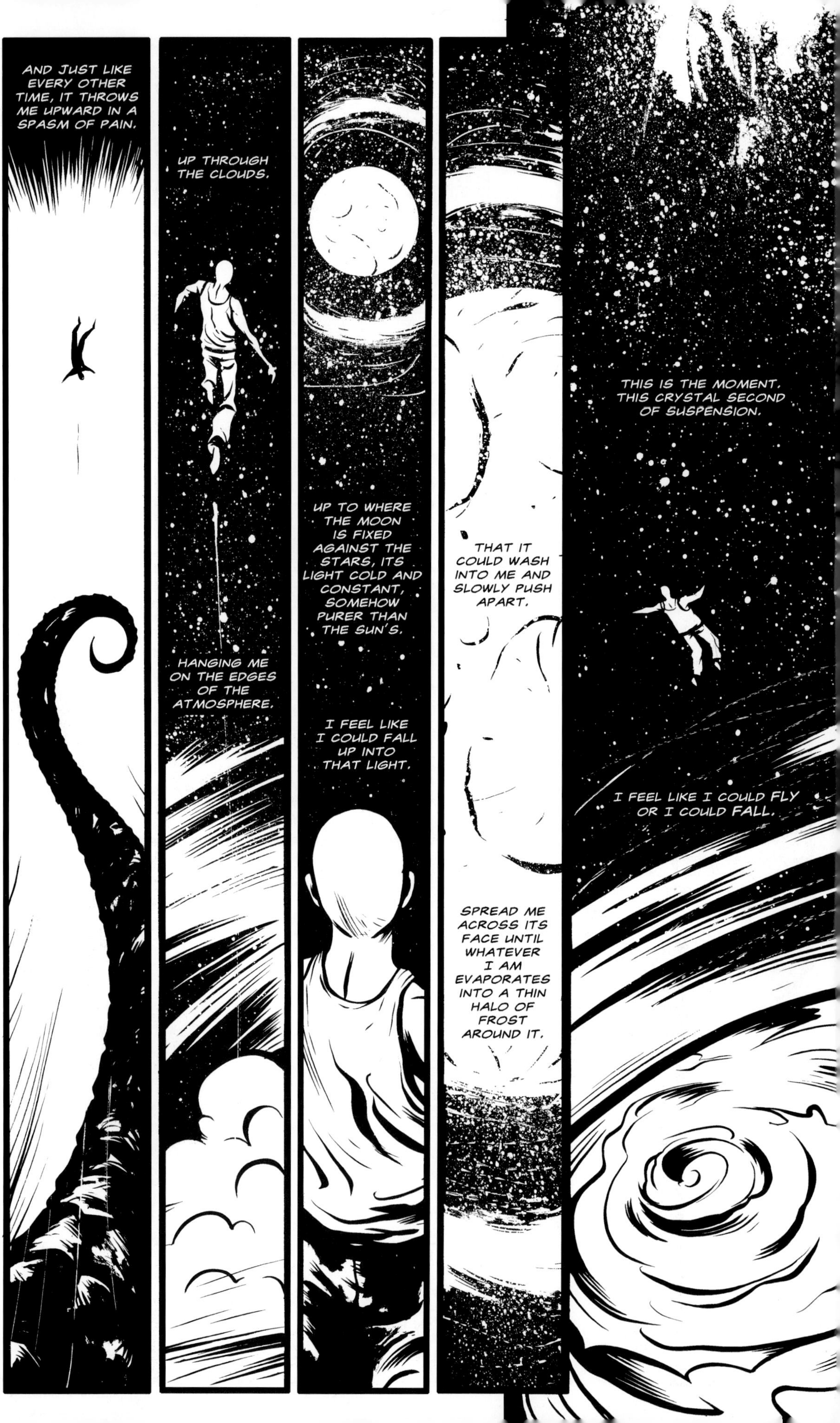
AND JUST LIKE EVERY OTHER TIME, IT THROWS ME UPWARD IN A SPASM OF PAIN.
UP THROUGH THE CLOUDS.
HANGING ME ON THE EDGES OF THE ATMOSPHERE.
UP TO WHERE THE MOON IS FIXED AGAINST THE STARS, ITS LIGHT COLD AND CONSTANT, SOMEHOW PURER THAN THE SUN'S.
I FEEL LIKE I COULD FALL UP INTO THAT LIGHT.
THAT IT COULD WASH INTO ME AND SLOWLY PUSH APART.
SPREAD ME ACROSS ITS FACE UNTIL WHATEVER I AM EVAPORATES INTO A THIN HALO OF FROST AROUND IT.
THIS IS THE MOMENT. THIS CRYSTAL SECOND OF SUSPENSION.
I FEEL LIKE I COULD FLY OR I COULD FALL.

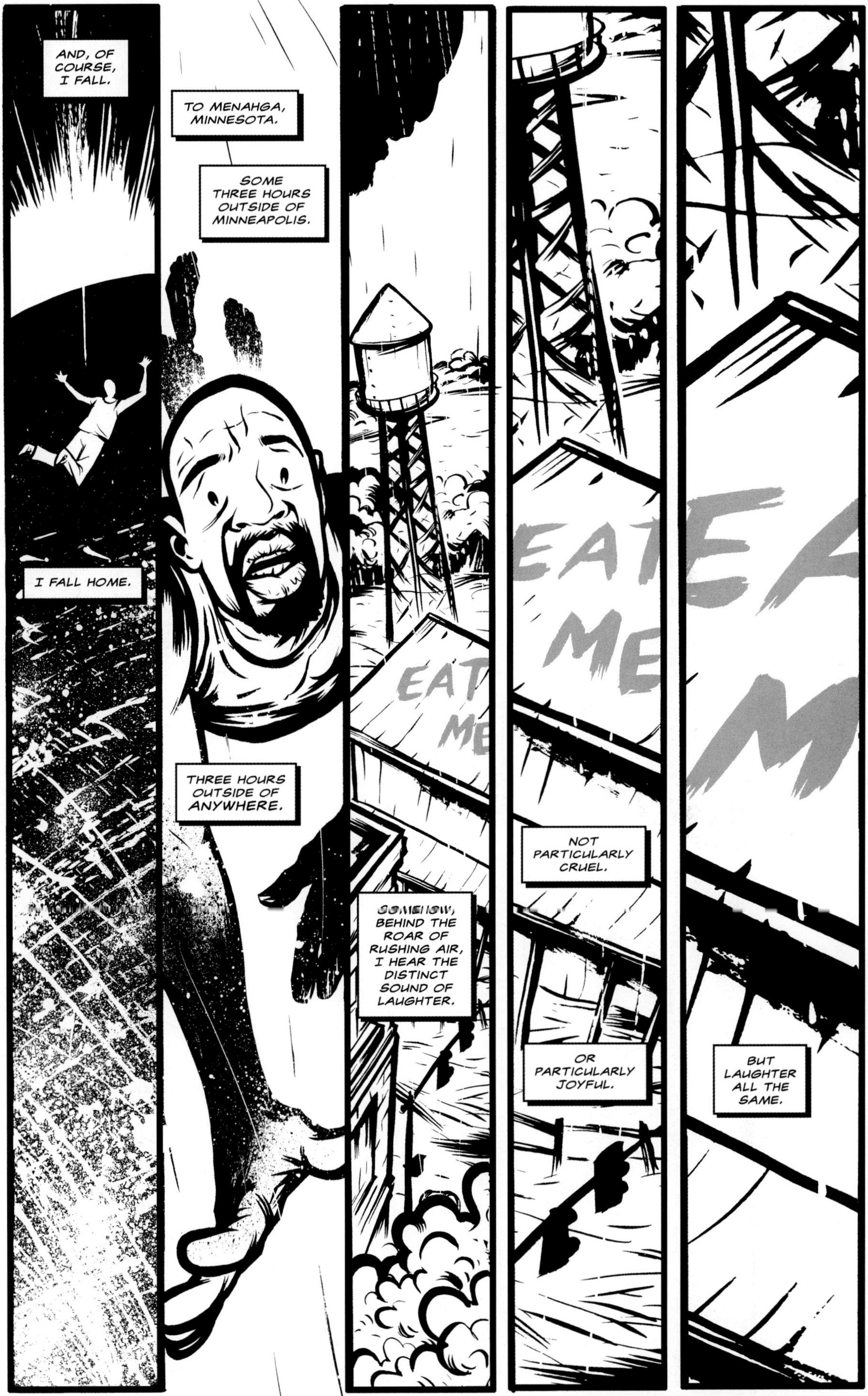
AND, OF COURSE, I FALL.
I FALL HOME.
TO MENAHGA, MINNESOTA.
SOME THREE HOURS OUTSIDE OF MINNEAPOLIS.
THREE HOURS OUTSIDE OF ANYWHERE.
SOMEHOW, BEHIND THE ROAR OF RUSHING AIR, I HEAR THE DISTINCT SOUND OF LAUGHTER.
EAT ME
NOT PARTICULARLY CRUEL.
OR PARTICULARLY JOYFUL.
BUT LAUGHTER ALL THE SAME.

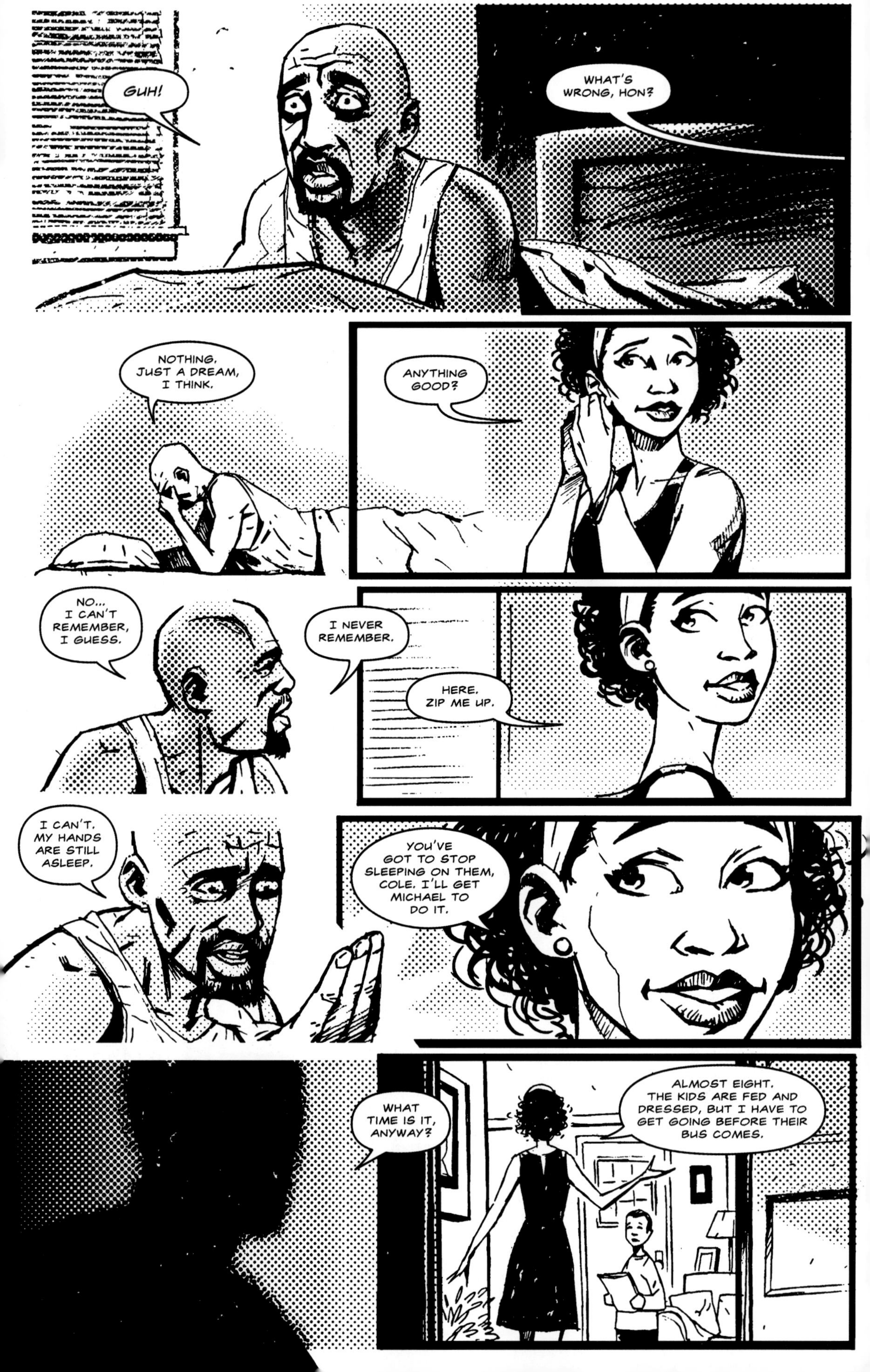
GUH!
WHAT'S WRONG, HON?
NOTHING. JUST A DREAM, I THINK.
ANYTHING GOOD?
NO... I CAN'T REMEMBER, I GUESS.
I NEVER REMEMBER.
HERE. ZIP ME UP.
I CAN'T. MY HANDS ARE STILL ASLEEP.
YOU'VE GOT TO STOP SLEEPING ON THEM, COLE. I'LL GET MICHAEL TO DO IT.
WHAT TIME IS IT, ANYWAY?
ALMOST EIGHT. THE KIDS ARE FED AND DRESSED, BUT I HAVE TO GET GOING BEFORE THEIR BUS COMES.

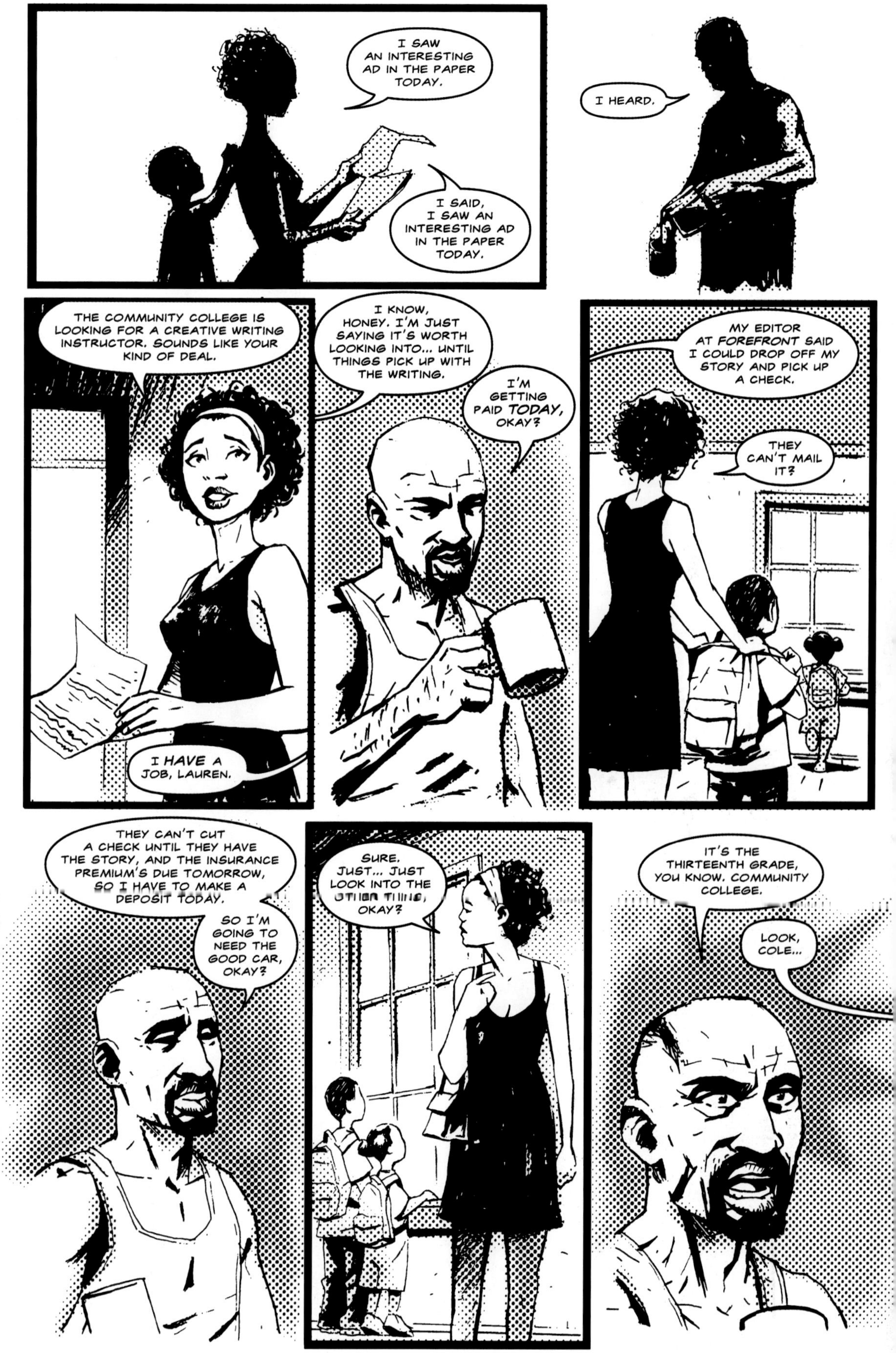

I SAW AN INTERESTING AD IN THE PAPER TODAY.
I SAID, I SAW AN INTERESTING AD IN THE PAPER TODAY.
I HEARD.
THE COMMUNITY COLLEGE IS LOOKING FOR A CREATIVE WRITING INSTRUCTOR. SOUNDS LIKE YOUR KIND OF DEAL.
I *HAVE* A JOB, LAUREN.
I KNOW, HONEY. I'M JUST SAYING IT'S WORTH LOOKING INTO... UNTIL THINGS PICK UP WITH THE WRITING.
I'M GETTING PAID *TODAY*, OKAY?
MY EDITOR AT *FOREFRONT* SAID I COULD DROP OFF MY STORY AND PICK UP A CHECK.
THEY CAN'T MAIL IT?
THEY CAN'T CUT A CHECK UNTIL THEY HAVE THE STORY, AND THE INSURANCE PREMIUM'S DUE TOMORROW, SO I HAVE TO MAKE A DEPOSIT TODAY.
SO I'M GOING TO NEED THE GOOD CAR, OKAY?
SURE. JUST... JUST LOOK INTO THE OTHER THING, OKAY?
IT'S THE THIRTEENTH GRADE, YOU KNOW. COMMUNITY COLLEGE.
LOOK, COLE...

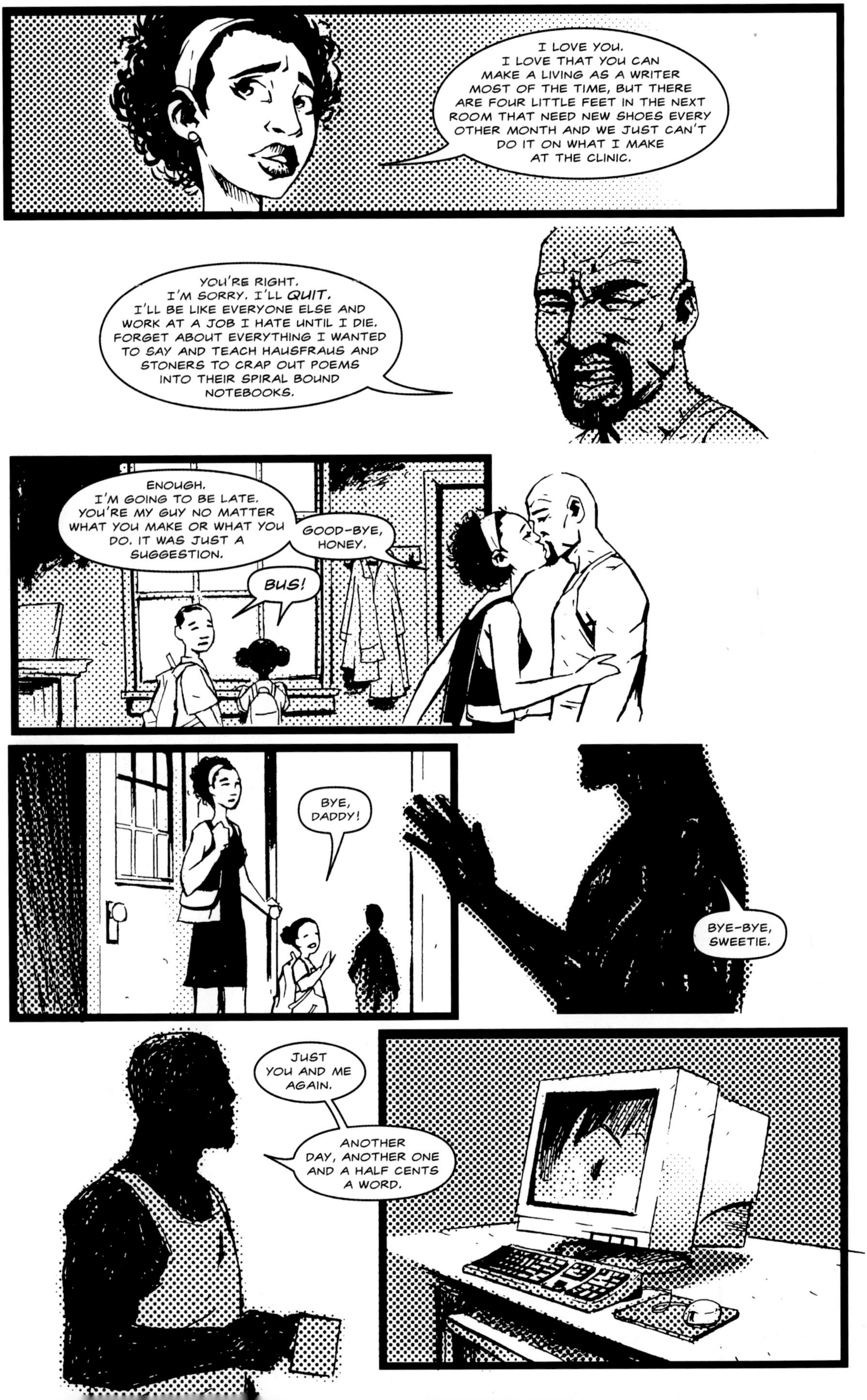
I LOVE YOU. I LOVE THAT YOU CAN MAKE A LIVING AS A WRITER MOST OF THE TIME, BUT THERE ARE FOUR LITTLE FEET IN THE NEXT ROOM THAT NEED NEW SHOES EVERY OTHER MONTH AND WE JUST CAN'T DO IT ON WHAT I MAKE AT THE CLINIC.
YOU'RE RIGHT. I'M SORRY. I'LL QUIT. I'LL BE LIKE EVERYONE ELSE AND WORK AT A JOB I HATE UNTIL I DIE. FORGET ABOUT EVERYTHING I WANTED TO SAY AND TEACH HAUSFRAUS AND STONERS TO CRAP OUT POEMS INTO THEIR SPIRAL BOUND NOTEBOOKS.
ENOUGH. I'M GOING TO BE LATE. YOU'RE MY GUY NO MATTER WHAT YOU MAKE OR WHAT YOU DO. IT WAS JUST A SUGGESTION.
GOOD-BYE, HONEY.
BUS!
BYE, DADDY!
BYE-BYE, SWEETIE.
JUST YOU AND ME AGAIN.
ANOTHER DAY, ANOTHER ONE AND A HALF CENTS A WORD.

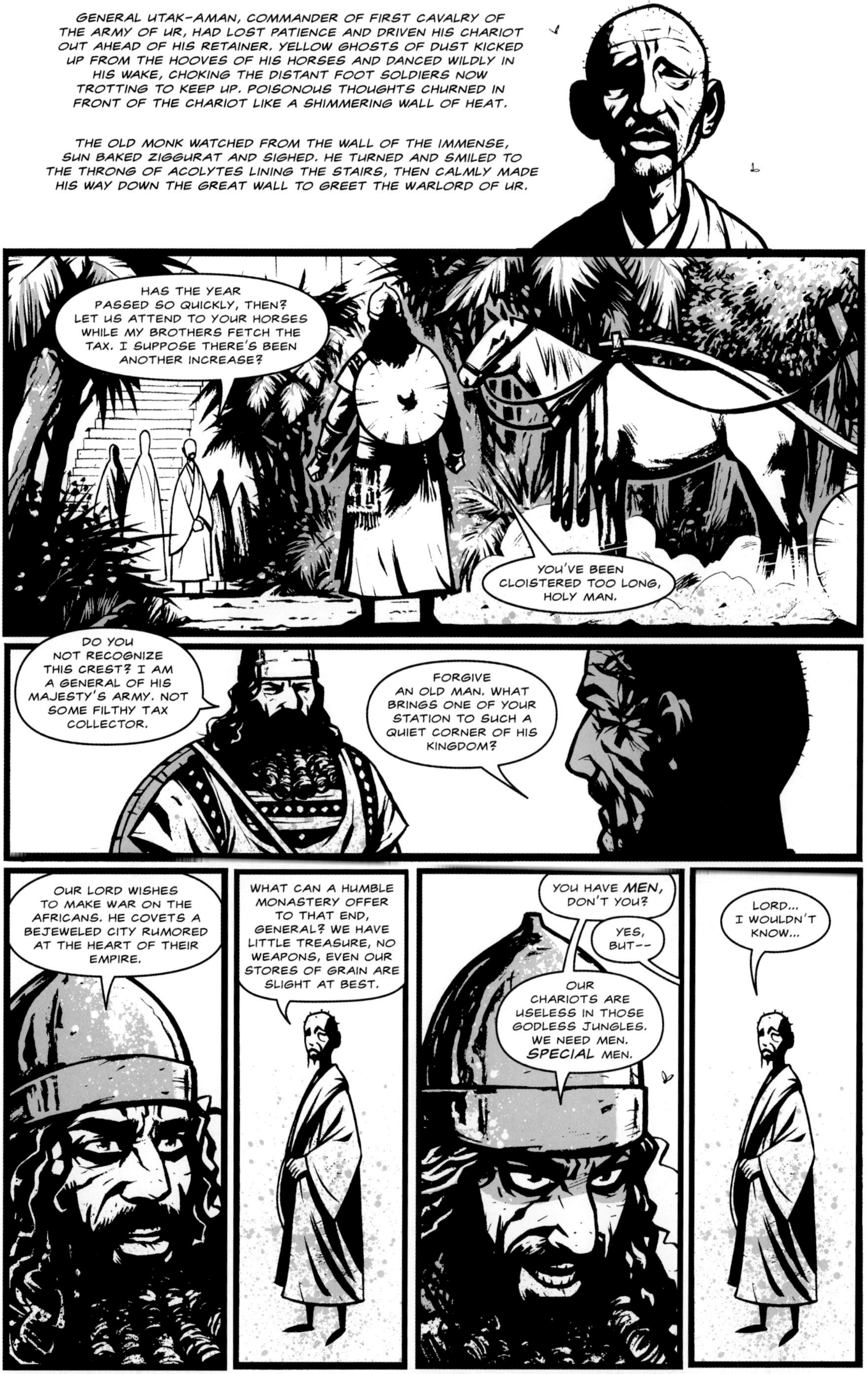
GENERAL UTAK-AMAN, COMMANDER OF FIRST CAVALRY OF THE ARMY OF UR, HAD LOST PATIENCE AND DRIVEN HIS CHARIOT OUT AHEAD OF HIS RETAINER. YELLOW GHOSTS OF DUST KICKED UP FROM THE HOOVES OF HIS HORSES AND DANCED WILDLY IN HIS WAKE, CHOKING THE DISTANT FOOT SOLDIERS NOW TROTTING TO KEEP UP. POISONOUS THOUGHTS CHURNED IN FRONT OF THE CHARIOT LIKE A SHIMMERING WALL OF HEAT.
THE OLD MONK WATCHED FROM THE WALL OF THE IMMENSE, SUN BAKED ZIGGURAT AND SIGHED. HE TURNED AND SMILED TO THE THRONG OF ACOLYTES LINING THE STAIRS, THEN CALMLY MADE HIS WAY DOWN THE GREAT WALL TO GREET THE WARLORD OF UR.
HAS THE YEAR PASSED SO QUICKLY, THEN? LET US ATTEND TO YOUR HORSES WHILE MY BROTHERS FETCH THE TAX. I SUPPOSE THERE'S BEEN ANOTHER INCREASE?
YOU'VE BEEN CLOISTERED TOO LONG, HOLY MAN.
DO YOU NOT RECOGNIZE THIS CREST? I AM A GENERAL OF HIS MAJESTY'S ARMY. NOT SOME FILTHY TAX COLLECTOR.
FORGIVE AN OLD MAN. WHAT BRINGS ONE OF YOUR STATION TO SUCH A QUIET CORNER OF HIS KINGDOM?
OUR LORD WISHES TO MAKE WAR ON THE AFRICANS. HE COVETS A BEJEWELED CITY RUMORED AT THE HEART OF THEIR EMPIRE.
WHAT CAN A HUMBLE MONASTERY OFFER TO THAT END, GENERAL? WE HAVE LITTLE TREASURE, NO WEAPONS, EVEN OUR STORES OF GRAIN ARE SLIGHT AT BEST.
YOU HAVE MEN, DON'T YOU?
YES, BUT--
OUR CHARIOTS ARE USELESS IN THOSE GODLESS JUNGLES. WE NEED MEN. SPECIAL MEN.
LORD... I WOULDN'T KNOW...

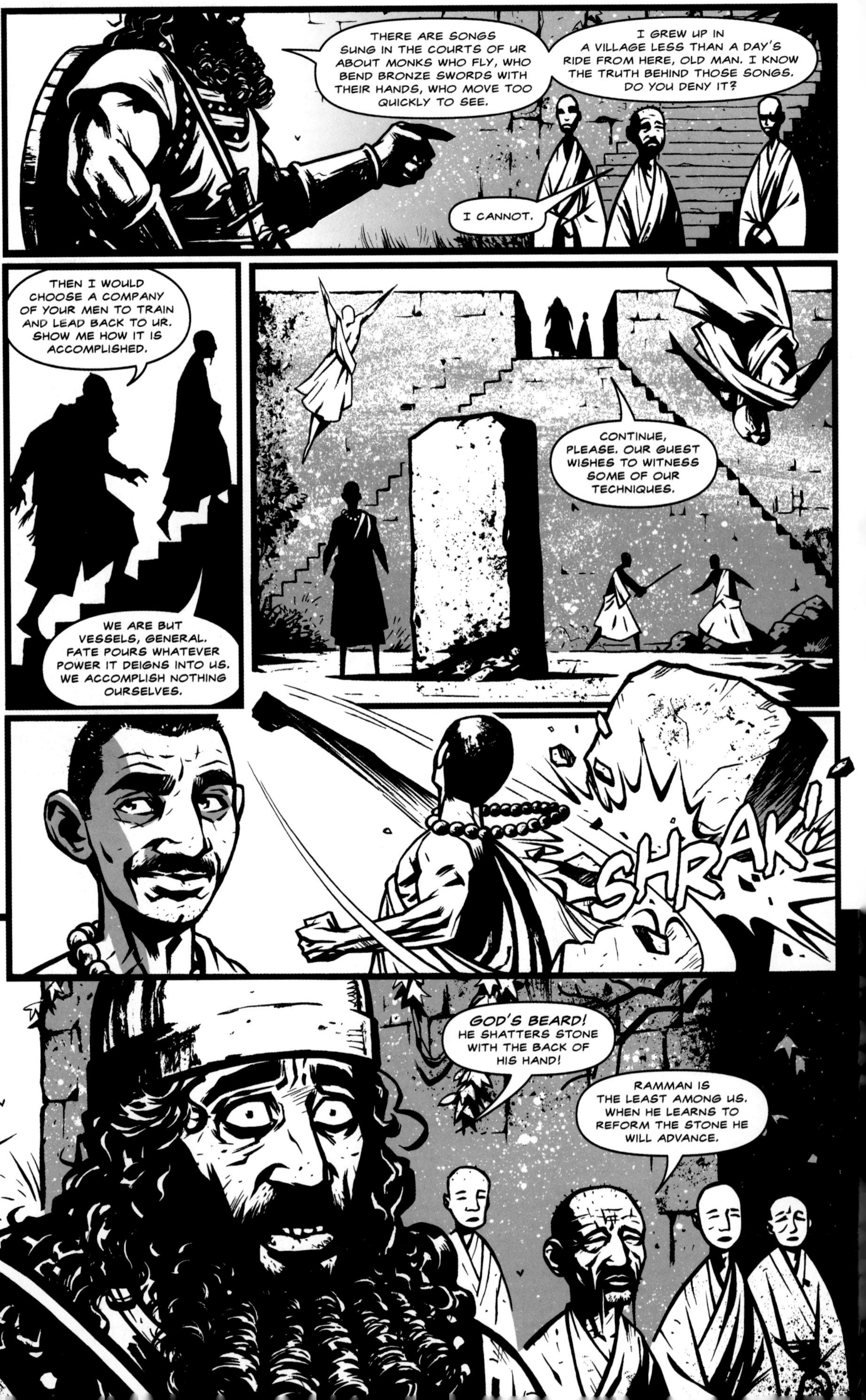
THERE ARE SONGS SUNG IN THE COURTS OF UR ABOUT MONKS WHO FLY, WHO BEND BRONZE SWORDS WITH THEIR HANDS, WHO MOVE TOO QUICKLY TO SEE.
I GREW UP IN A VILLAGE LESS THAN A DAY'S RIDE FROM HERE, OLD MAN. I KNOW THE TRUTH BEHIND THOSE SONGS. DO YOU DENY IT?
I CANNOT.
THEN I WOULD CHOOSE A COMPANY OF YOUR MEN TO TRAIN AND LEAD BACK TO UR. SHOW ME HOW IT IS ACCOMPLISHED.
WE ARE BUT VESSELS, GENERAL. FATE POURS WHATEVER POWER IT DEIGNS INTO US. WE ACCOMPLISH NOTHING OURSELVES.
CONTINUE, PLEASE. OUR GUEST WISHES TO WITNESS SOME OF OUR TECHNIQUES.
SHRAK!
GOD'S BEARD! HE SHATTERS STONE WITH THE BACK OF HIS HAND!
RAMMAN IS THE LEAST AMONG US. WHEN HE LEARNS TO REFORM THE STONE HE WILL ADVANCE.

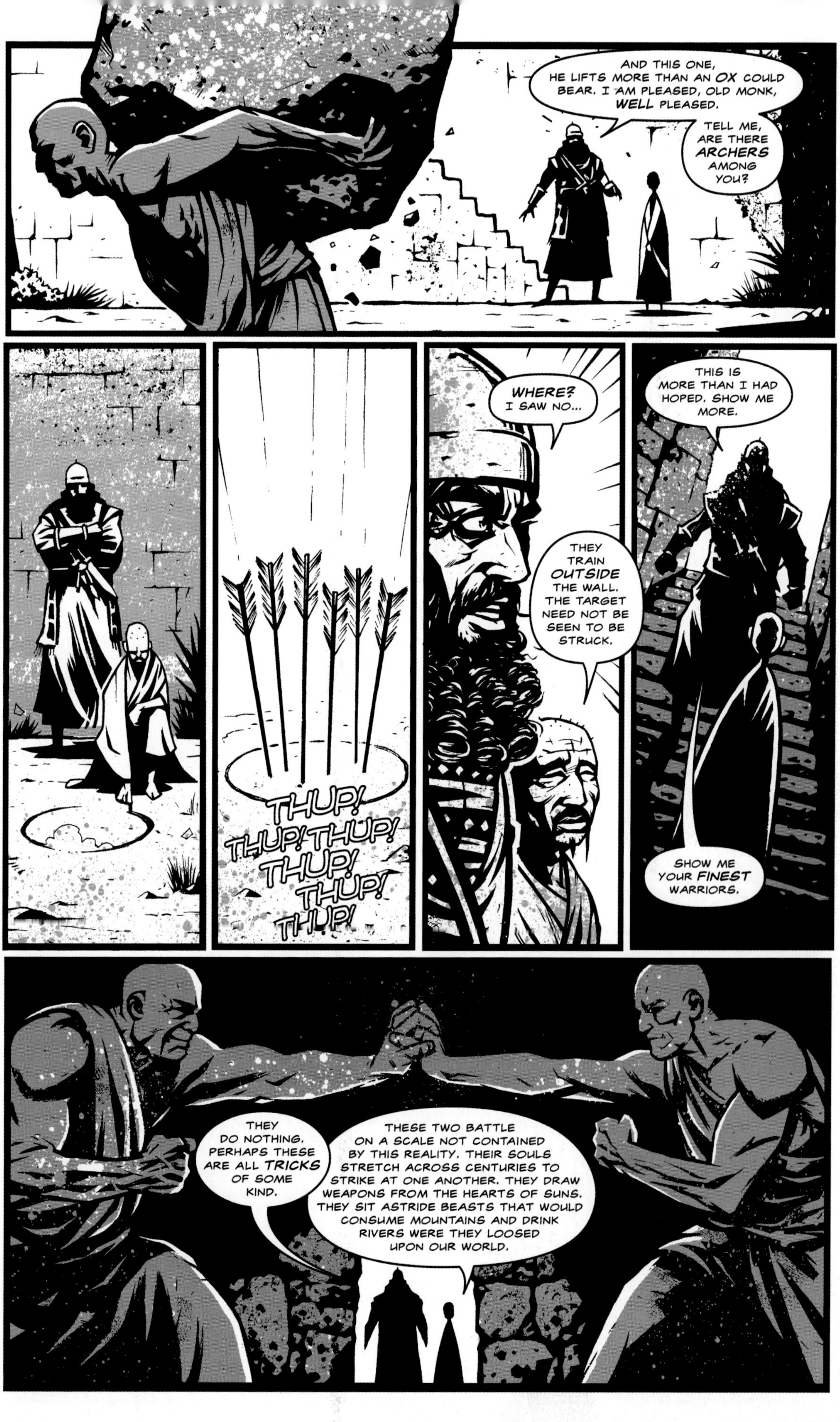

AND THIS ONE, HE LIFTS MORE THAN AN OX COULD BEAR. I AM PLEASED, OLD MONK, WELL PLEASED.
TELL ME, ARE THERE ARCHERS AMONG YOU?
THUP! THUP! THUP! THUP! THUP! THUP!
WHERE? I SAW NO...
THEY TRAIN OUTSIDE THE WALL. THE TARGET NEED NOT BE SEEN TO BE STRUCK.
THIS IS MORE THAN I HAD HOPED. SHOW ME MORE.
SHOW ME YOUR FINEST WARRIORS.
THEY DO NOTHING. PERHAPS THESE ARE ALL TRICKS OF SOME KIND.
THESE TWO BATTLE ON A SCALE NOT CONTAINED BY THIS REALITY. THEIR SOULS STRETCH ACROSS CENTURIES TO STRIKE AT ONE ANOTHER. THEY DRAW WEAPONS FROM THE HEARTS OF SUNS. THEY SIT ASTRIDE BEASTS THAT WOULD CONSUME MOUNTAINS AND DRINK RIVERS WERE THEY LOOSED UPON OUR WORLD.

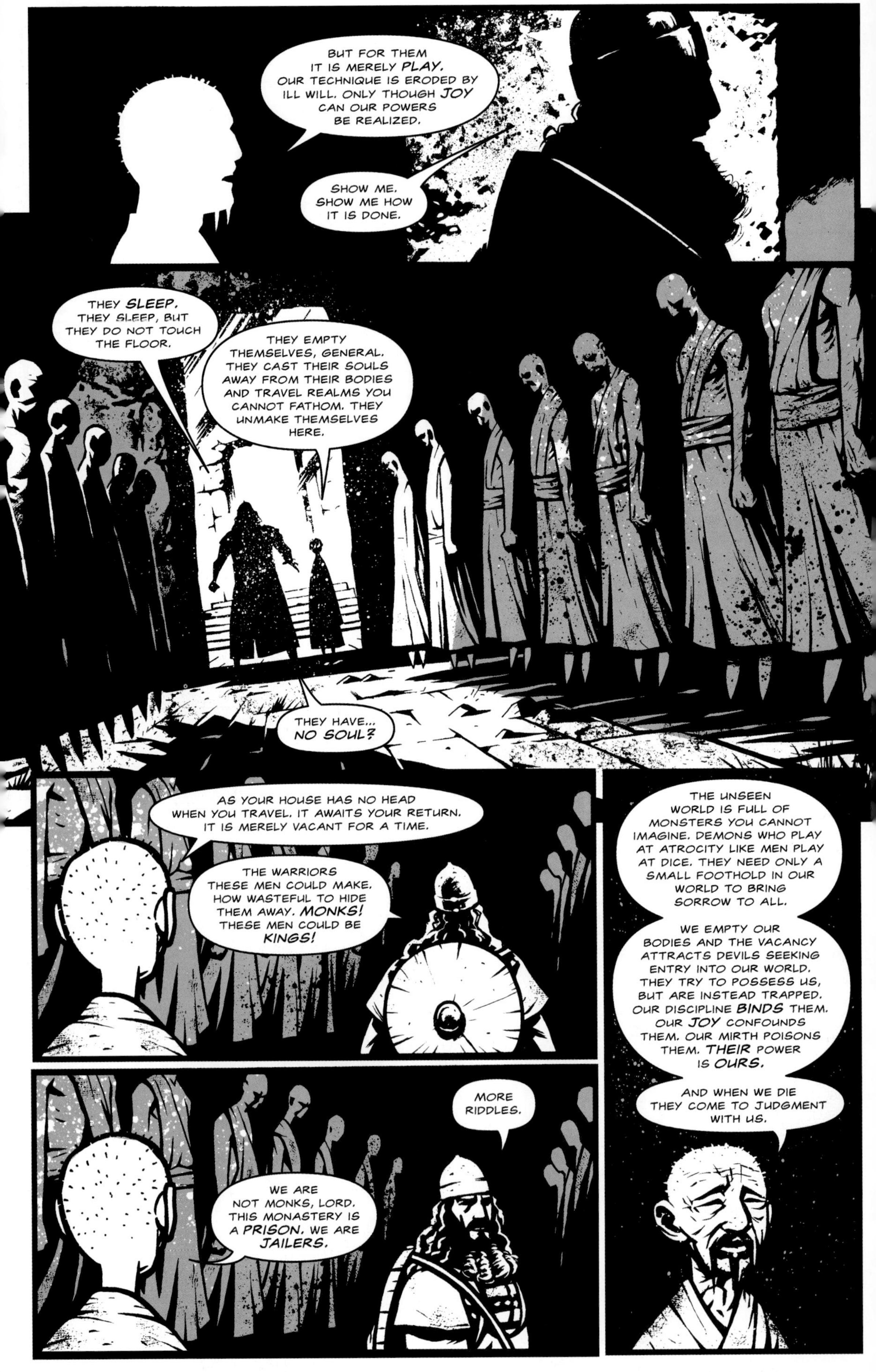
BUT FOR THEM IT IS MERELY PLAY. OUR TECHNIQUE IS ERODED BY ILL WILL. ONLY THOUGH JOY CAN OUR POWERS BE REALIZED.
SHOW ME. SHOW ME HOW IT IS DONE.
THEY SLEEP. THEY SLEEP, BUT THEY DO NOT TOUCH THE FLOOR.
THEY EMPTY THEMSELVES, GENERAL. THEY CAST THEIR SOULS AWAY FROM THEIR BODIES AND TRAVEL REALMS YOU CANNOT FATHOM. THEY UNMAKE THEMSELVES HERE.
THEY HAVE... NO SOUL?
AS YOUR HOUSE HAS NO HEAD WHEN YOU TRAVEL. IT AWAITS YOUR RETURN. IT IS MERELY VACANT FOR A TIME.
THE WARRIORS THESE MEN COULD MAKE. HOW WASTEFUL TO HIDE THEM AWAY. MONKS! THESE MEN COULD BE KINGS!
MORE RIDDLES.
WE ARE NOT MONKS, LORD. THIS MONASTERY IS A PRISON. WE ARE JAILERS.
THE UNSEEN WORLD IS FULL OF MONSTERS YOU CANNOT IMAGINE. DEMONS WHO PLAY AT ATROCITY LIKE MEN PLAY AT DICE. THEY NEED ONLY A SMALL FOOTHOLD IN OUR WORLD TO BRING SORROW TO ALL.
WE EMPTY OUR BODIES AND THE VACANCY ATTRACTS DEVILS SEEKING ENTRY INTO OUR WORLD. THEY TRY TO POSSESS US, BUT ARE INSTEAD TRAPPED. OUR DISCIPLINE BINDS THEM. OUR JOY CONFOUNDS THEM. OUR MIRTH POISONS THEM. THEIR POWER IS OURS.
AND WHEN WE DIE THEY COME TO JUDGMENT WITH US.

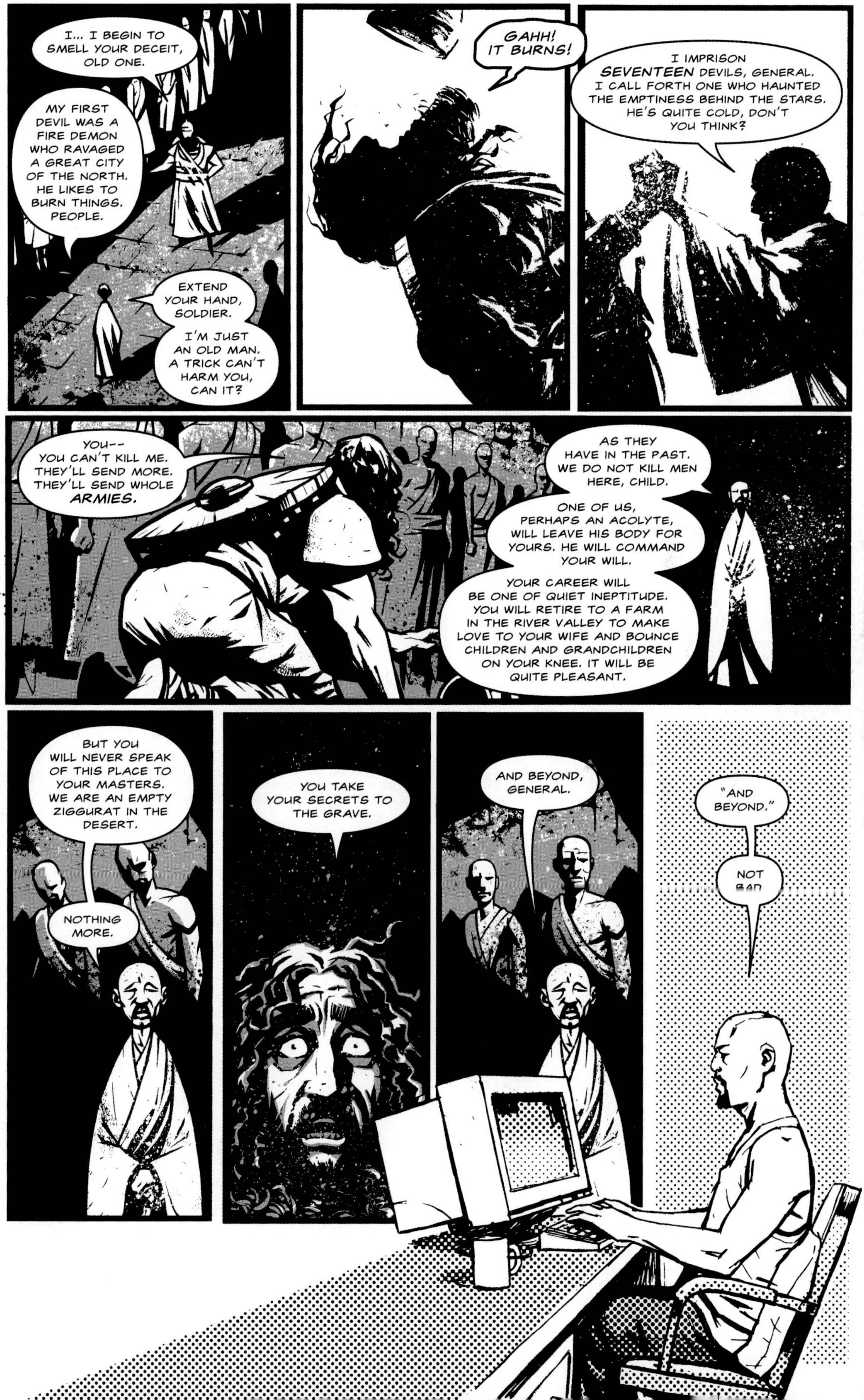
I... I BEGIN TO SMELL YOUR DECEIT, OLD ONE.
MY FIRST DEVIL WAS A FIRE DEMON WHO RAVAGED A GREAT CITY OF THE NORTH. HE LIKES TO BURN THINGS. PEOPLE.
EXTEND YOUR HAND, SOLDIER.
I'M JUST AN OLD MAN. A TRICK CAN'T HARM YOU, CAN IT?
GAHH! IT BURNS!
I IMPRISON SEVENTEEN DEVILS, GENERAL. I CALL FORTH ONE WHO HAUNTED THE EMPTINESS BEHIND THE STARS. HE'S QUITE COLD, DON'T YOU THINK?
YOU-- YOU CAN'T KILL ME. THEY'LL SEND MORE. THEY'LL SEND WHOLE ARMIES.
AS THEY HAVE IN THE PAST. WE DO NOT KILL MEN HERE, CHILD.
ONE OF US, PERHAPS AN ACOLYTE, WILL LEAVE HIS BODY FOR YOURS. HE WILL COMMAND YOUR WILL.
YOUR CAREER WILL BE ONE OF QUIET INEPTITUDE. YOU WILL RETIRE TO A FARM IN THE RIVER VALLEY TO MAKE LOVE TO YOUR WIFE AND BOUNCE CHILDREN AND GRANDCHILDREN ON YOUR KNEE. IT WILL BE QUITE PLEASANT.
BUT YOU WILL NEVER SPEAK OF THIS PLACE TO YOUR MASTERS. WE ARE AN EMPTY ZIGGURAT IN THE DESERT.
NOTHING MORE.
YOU TAKE YOUR SECRETS TO THE GRAVE.
AND BEYOND, GENERAL.
"AND BEYOND."
NOT BAD

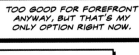
TOO GOOD FOR FOREFRONT ANYWAY, BUT THAT'S MY ONLY OPTION RIGHT NOW.

I NEED THIS GIG JUST A LITTLE WHILE LONGER, UNTIL I CAN CATCH THAT BREAK THAT'S BEEN JUST AROUND THE BEND ALL MY ADULT LIFE. EVEN A TINY CHECK GOES A LONG WAY TOWARDS CALMING LAUREN.

TRAVELING TO THE TWIN CITIES IS A GAMBLE, THOUGH. AT ANY TIME OUR ELEVEN YEAR OLD SEDAN COULD BREAK DOWN AND EAT UP THE VERY PAYCHECK I'M DRIVING IN TO PICK UP.

BUT IT'S WORTH THE RISK.

THE CONTRAST WITH MENAHGA IS SHARP AND SATISFYING.

THE SOUNDS. THE SMELLS.

THE PEOPLE.

OOF!

JEEZ, I'M SORRY, MAN. I SHOULD WATCH WHERE I'M GOING.

MY FAULT AS MUCH AS YOURS, FRIEND.

BUT YOU REALLY SHOULD BE MORE CAREFUL. FOR YOUR OWN SAFETY, AT LEAST.

ESPECIALLY IN THE FUTURE.

UH... YEAH.

DAR! PUT THAT THING AWAY.

TIME ENOUGH FOR THAT LATER.

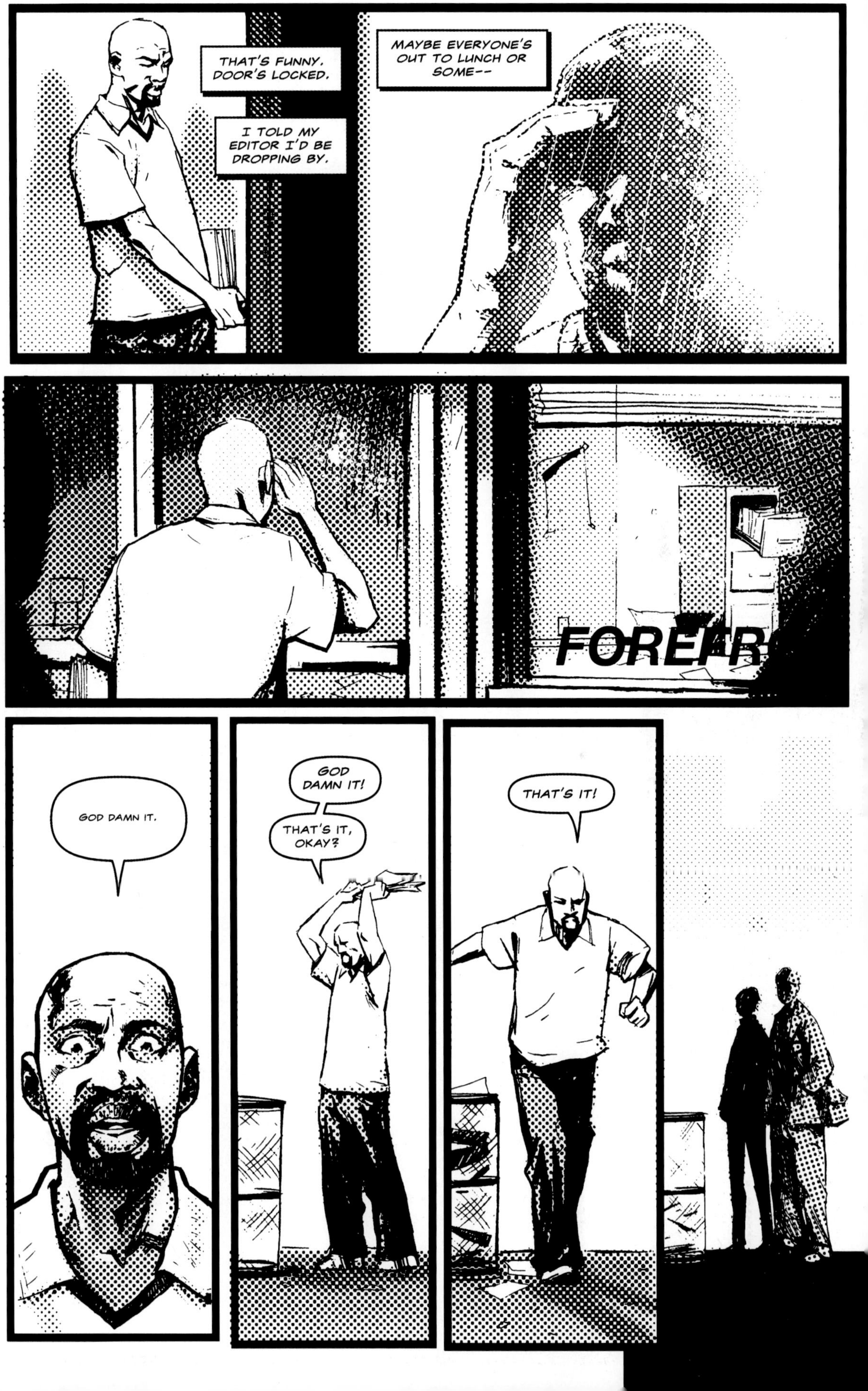
THAT'S FUNNY. DOOR'S LOCKED.
I TOLD MY EDITOR I'D BE DROPPING BY.
MAYBE EVERYONE'S OUT TO LUNCH OR SOME--
GOD DAMN IT.
GOD DAMN IT!
THAT'S IT, OKAY?
THAT'S IT!

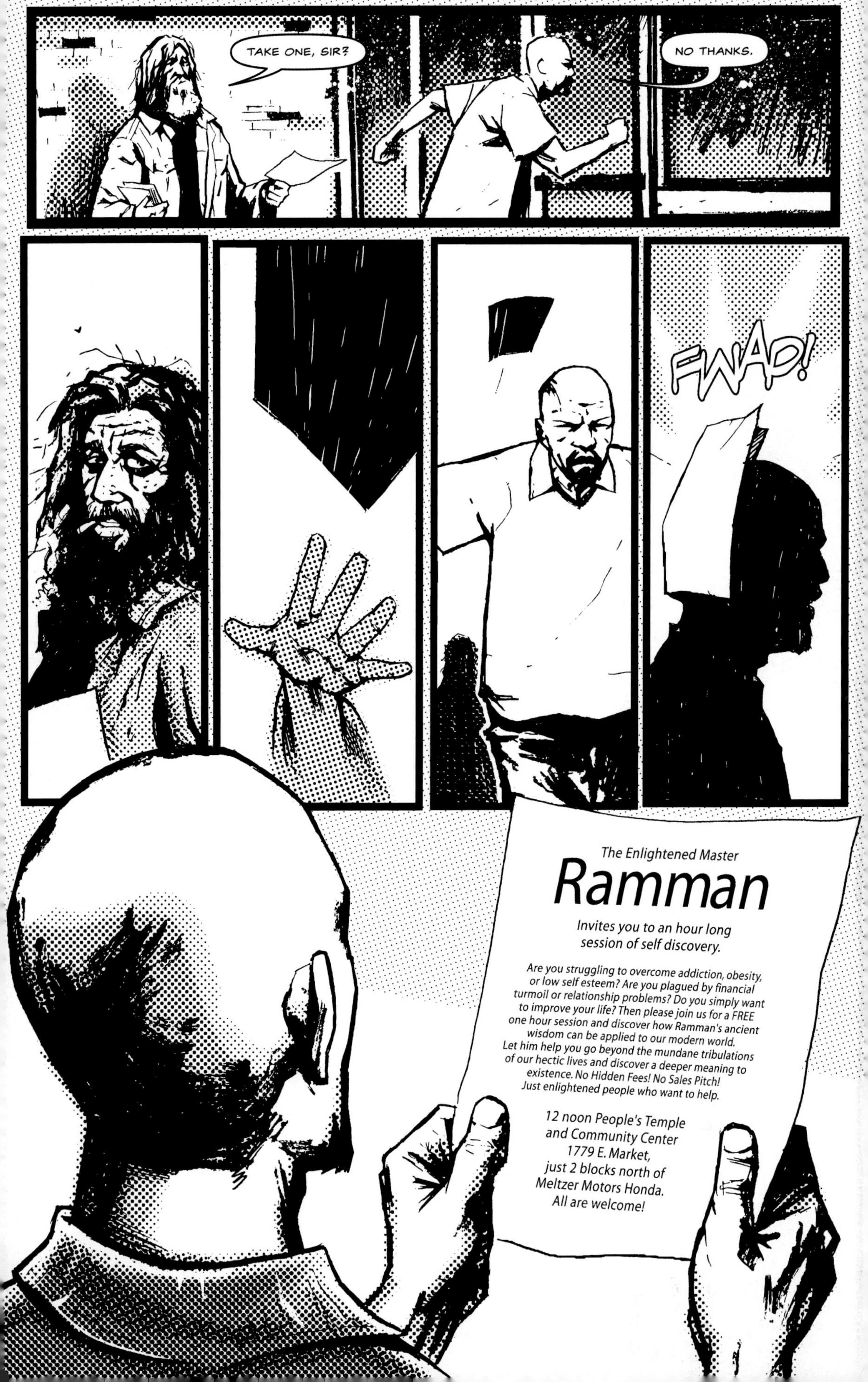
TAKE ONE, SIR?
NO THANKS.
FWAP!
The Enlightened Master
Ramman
Invites you to an hour long session of self discovery.
Are you struggling to overcome addiction, obesity, or low self esteem? Are you plagued by financial turmoil or relationship problems? Do you simply want to improve your life? Then please join us for a FREE one hour session and discover how Ramman's ancient wisdom can be applied to our modern world. Let him help you go beyond the mundane tribulations of our hectic lives and discover a deeper meaning to existence. No Hidden Fees! No Sales Pitch! Just enlightened people who want to help.
12 noon People's Temple and Community Center 1779 E. Market, just 2 blocks north of Meltzer Motors Honda. All are welcome!

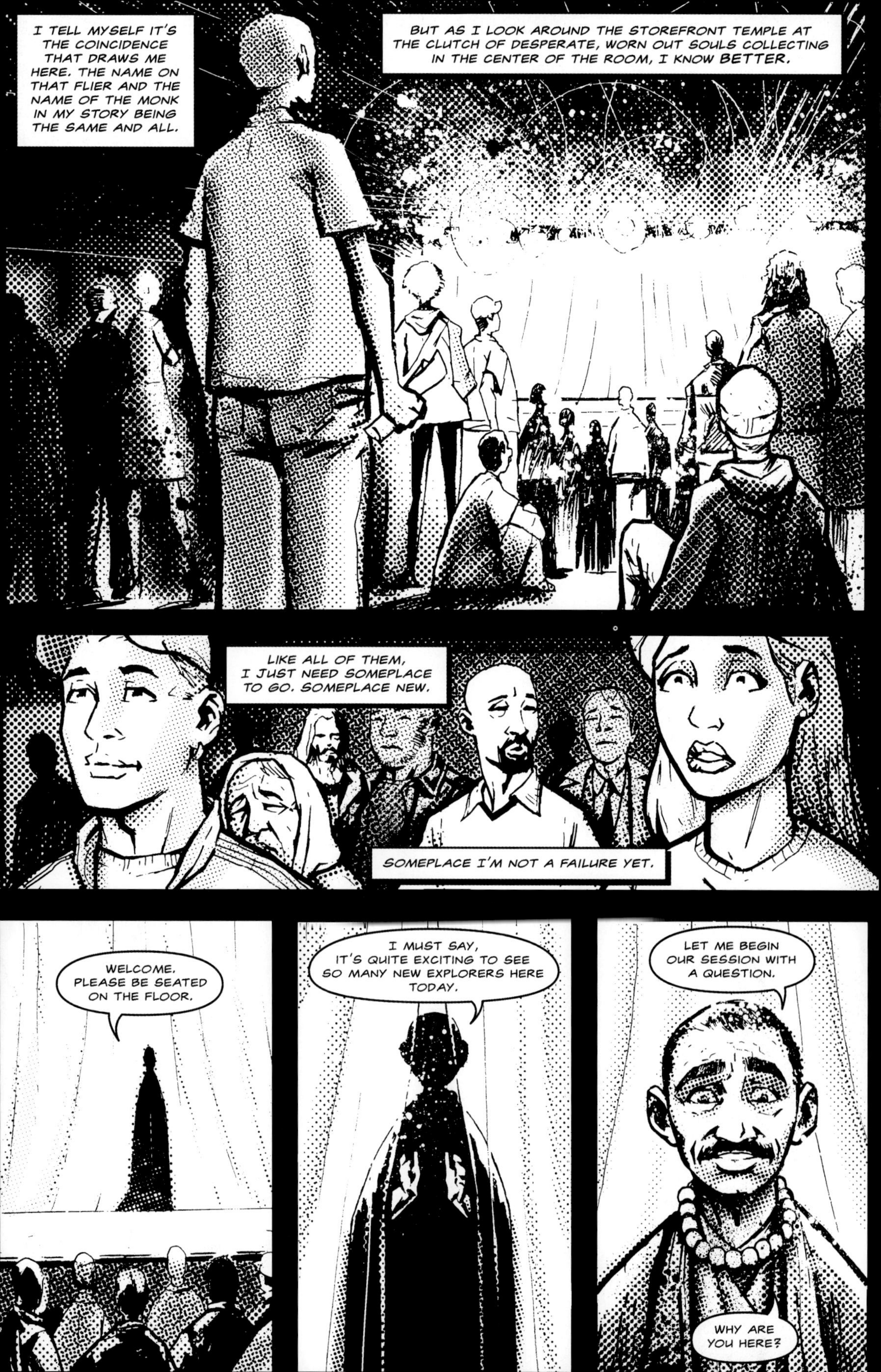
I TELL MYSELF IT'S THE COINCIDENCE THAT DRAWS ME HERE. THE NAME ON THAT FLIER AND THE NAME OF THE MONK IN MY STORY BEING THE SAME AND ALL.
BUT AS I LOOK AROUND THE STOREFRONT TEMPLE AT THE CLUTCH OF DESPERATE, WORN OUT SOULS COLLECTING IN THE CENTER OF THE ROOM, I KNOW BETTER.
LIKE ALL OF THEM, I JUST NEED SOMEPLACE TO GO. SOMEPLACE NEW.
SOMEPLACE I'M NOT A FAILURE YET.
WELCOME. PLEASE BE SEATED ON THE FLOOR.
I MUST SAY, IT'S QUITE EXCITING TO SEE SO MANY NEW EXPLORERS HERE TODAY.
LET ME BEGIN OUR SESSION WITH A QUESTION.
WHY ARE YOU HERE?

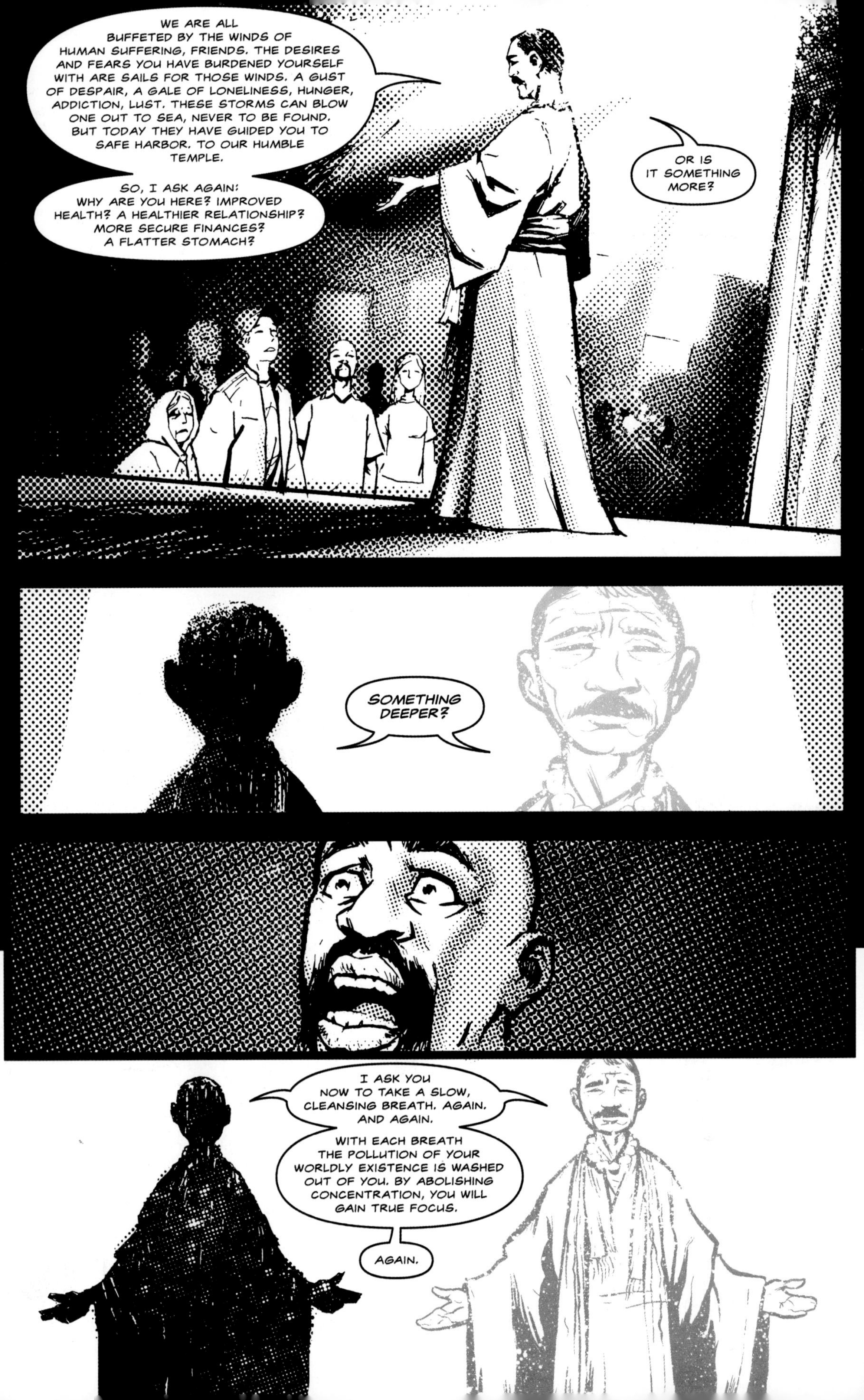
WE ARE ALL BUFFETED BY THE WINDS OF HUMAN SUFFERING, FRIENDS. THE DESIRES AND FEARS YOU HAVE BURDENED YOURSELF WITH ARE SAILS FOR THOSE WINDS. A GUST OF DESPAIR, A GALE OF LONELINESS, HUNGER, ADDICTION, LUST. THESE STORMS CAN BLOW ONE OUT TO SEA, NEVER TO BE FOUND. BUT TODAY THEY HAVE GUIDED YOU TO SAFE HARBOR. TO OUR HUMBLE TEMPLE.
SO, I ASK AGAIN: WHY ARE YOU HERE? IMPROVED HEALTH? A HEALTHIER RELATIONSHIP? MORE SECURE FINANCES? A FLATTER STOMACH?
OR IS IT SOMETHING MORE?
SOMETHING DEEPER?
I ASK YOU NOW TO TAKE A SLOW, CLEANSING BREATH. AGAIN. AND AGAIN.
WITH EACH BREATH THE POLLUTION OF YOUR WORLDLY EXISTENCE IS WASHED OUT OF YOU. BY ABOLISHING CONCENTRATION, YOU WILL GAIN TRUE FOCUS.
AGAIN.

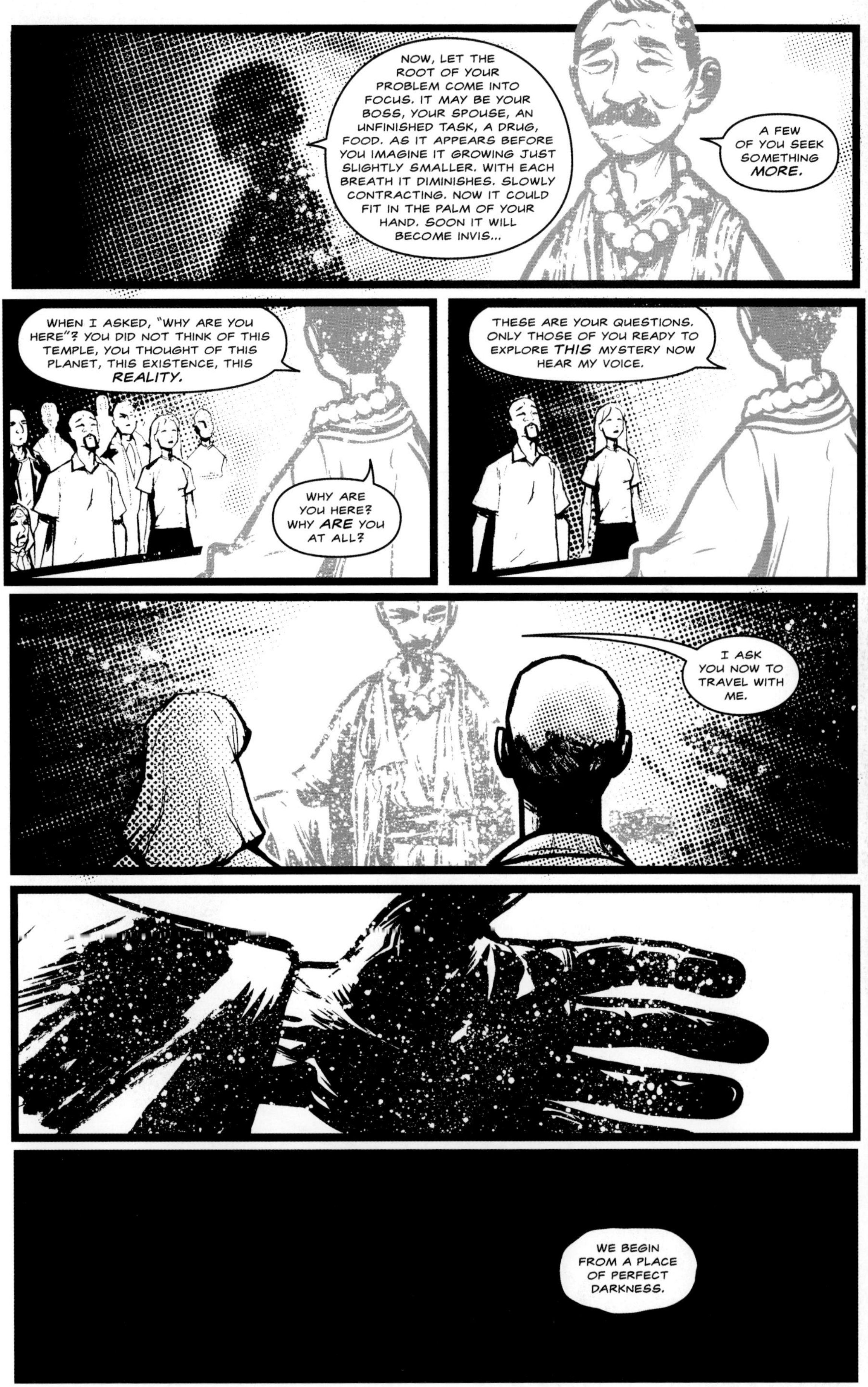
NOW, LET THE ROOT OF YOUR PROBLEM COME INTO FOCUS. IT MAY BE YOUR BOSS, YOUR SPOUSE, AN UNFINISHED TASK, A DRUG, FOOD. AS IT APPEARS BEFORE YOU IMAGINE IT GROWING JUST SLIGHTLY SMALLER. WITH EACH BREATH IT DIMINISHES. SLOWLY CONTRACTING. NOW IT COULD FIT IN THE PALM OF YOUR HAND. SOON IT WILL BECOME INVIS...
A FEW OF YOU SEEK SOMETHING MORE.
WHEN I ASKED, "WHY ARE YOU HERE"? YOU DID NOT THINK OF THIS TEMPLE, YOU THOUGHT OF THIS PLANET, THIS EXISTENCE, THIS REALITY.
WHY ARE YOU HERE? WHY ARE YOU AT ALL?
THESE ARE YOUR QUESTIONS. ONLY THOSE OF YOU READY TO EXPLORE THIS MYSTERY NOW HEAR MY VOICE.
I ASK YOU NOW TO TRAVEL WITH ME.
WE BEGIN FROM A PLACE OF PERFECT DARKNESS.

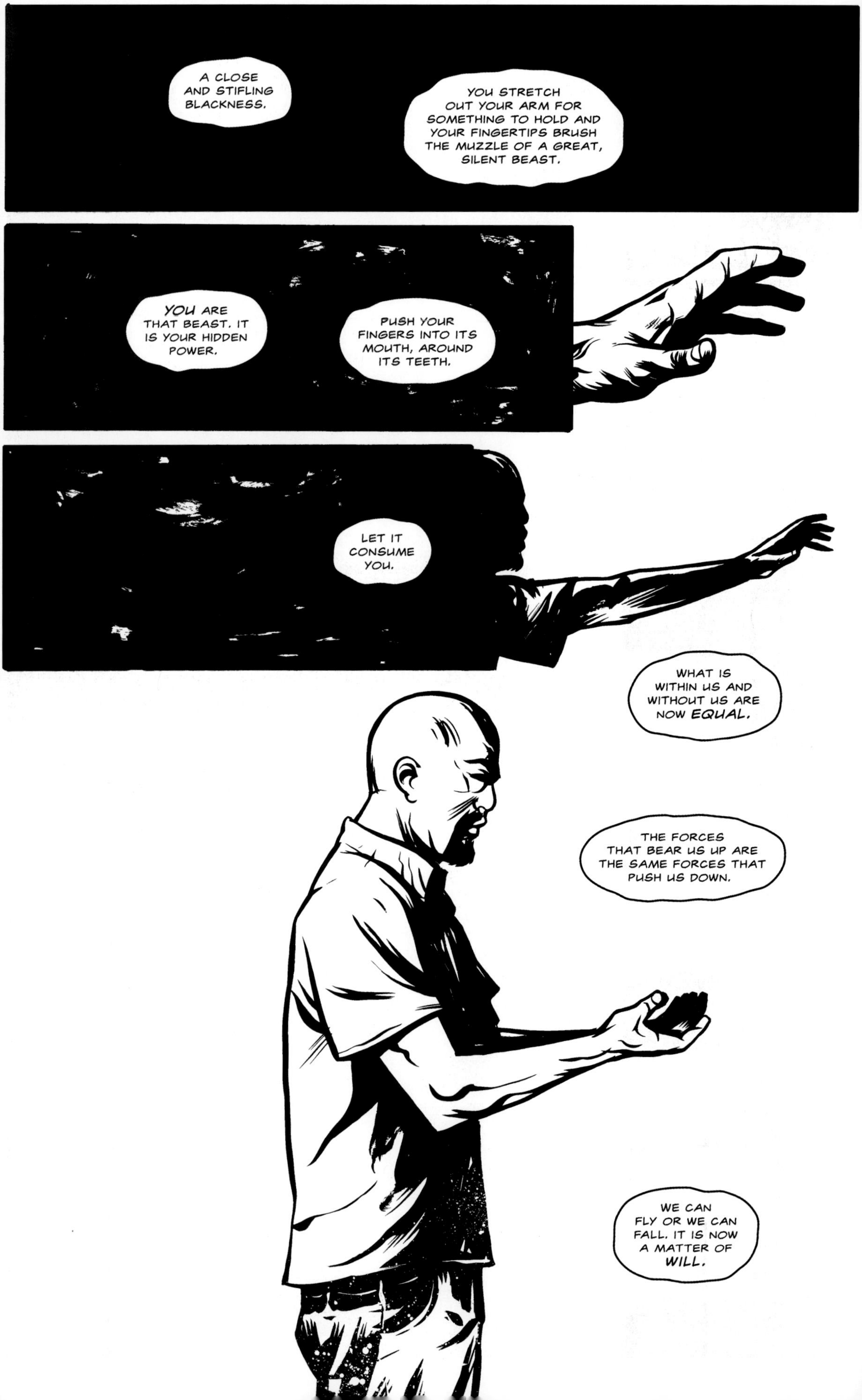
A CLOSE AND STIFLING BLACKNESS.
YOU STRETCH OUT YOUR ARM FOR SOMETHING TO HOLD AND YOUR FINGERTIPS BRUSH THE MUZZLE OF A GREAT, SILENT BEAST.
YOU ARE THAT BEAST. IT IS YOUR HIDDEN POWER.
PUSH YOUR FINGERS INTO ITS MOUTH, AROUND ITS TEETH.
LET IT CONSUME YOU.
WHAT IS WITHIN US AND WITHOUT US ARE NOW EQUAL.
THE FORCES THAT BEAR US UP ARE THE SAME FORCES THAT PUSH US DOWN.
WE CAN FLY OR WE CAN FALL. IT IS NOW A MATTER OF WILL.

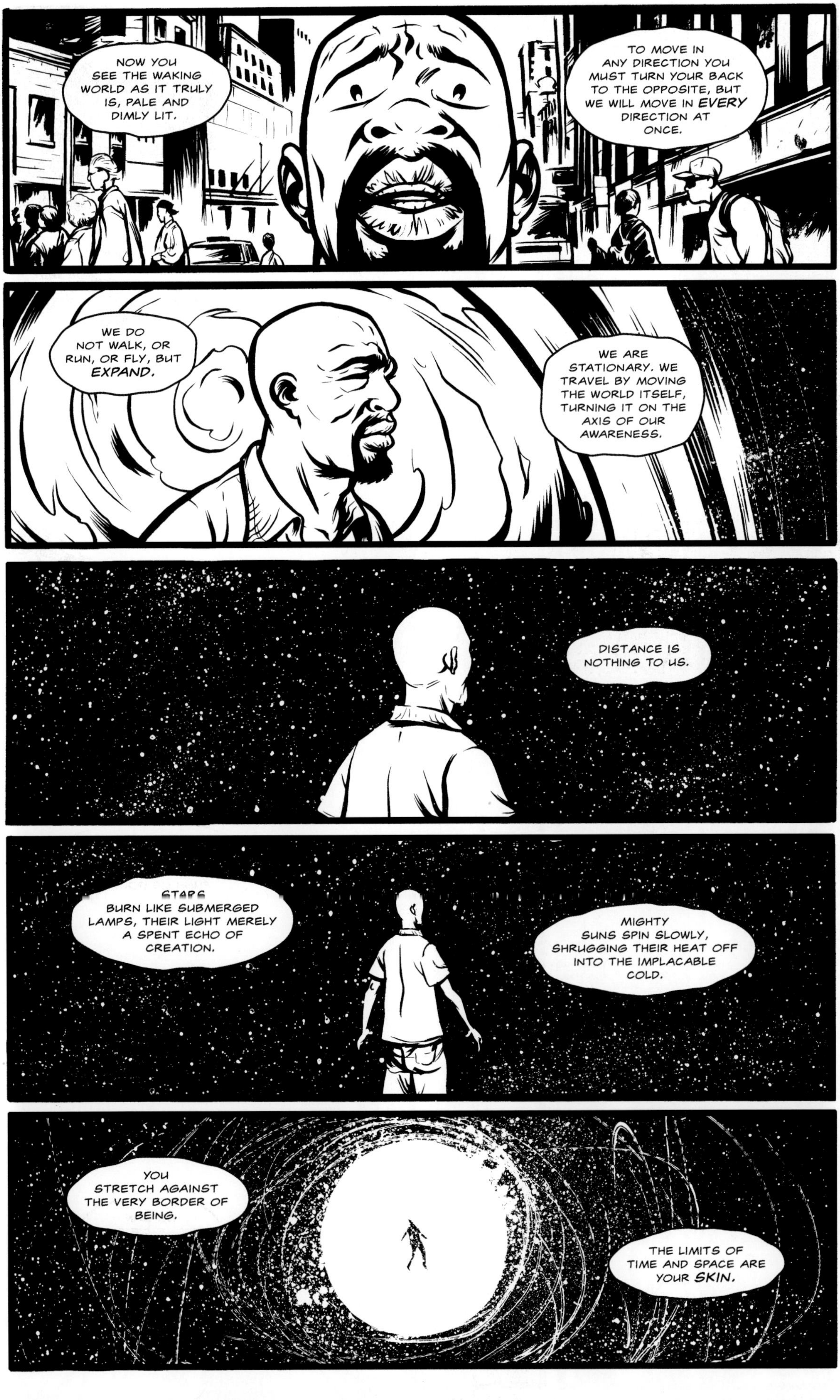
NOW YOU SEE THE WAKING WORLD AS IT TRULY IS, PALE AND DIMLY LIT.
TO MOVE IN ANY DIRECTION YOU MUST TURN YOUR BACK TO THE OPPOSITE, BUT WE WILL MOVE IN *EVERY* DIRECTION AT ONCE.
WE DO NOT WALK, OR RUN, OR FLY, BUT *EXPAND.*
WE ARE STATIONARY. WE TRAVEL BY MOVING THE WORLD ITSELF, TURNING IT ON THE AXIS OF OUR AWARENESS.
DISTANCE IS NOTHING TO US.
STARS BURN LIKE SUBMERGED LAMPS, THEIR LIGHT MERELY A SPENT ECHO OF CREATION.
MIGHTY SUNS SPIN SLOWLY, SHRUGGING THEIR HEAT OFF INTO THE IMPLACABLE COLD.
YOU STRETCH AGAINST THE VERY BORDER OF BEING.
THE LIMITS OF TIME AND SPACE ARE YOUR *SKIN.*

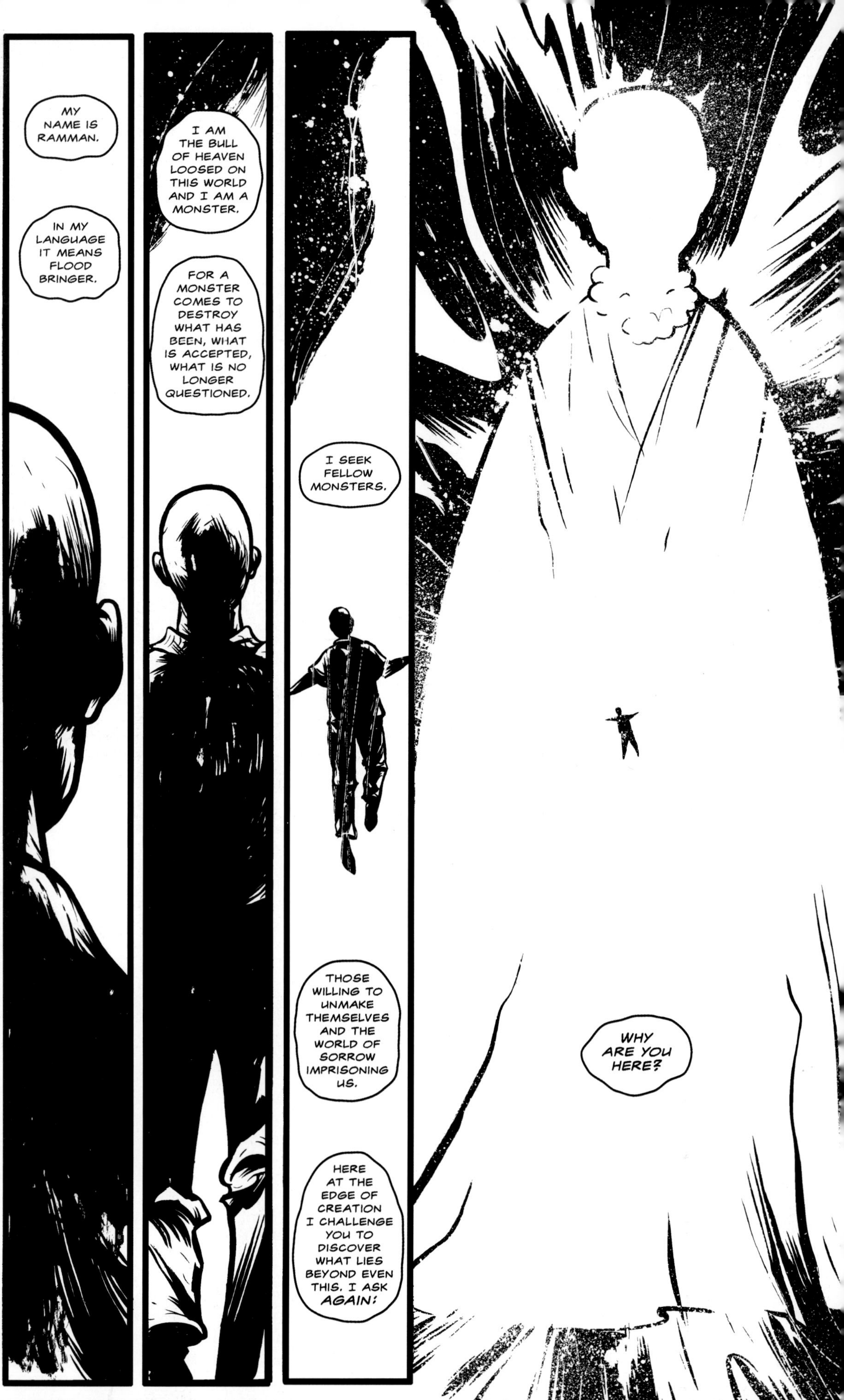

MY NAME IS RAMMAN.
IN MY LANGUAGE IT MEANS FLOOD BRINGER.
I AM THE BULL OF HEAVEN LOOSED ON THIS WORLD AND I AM A MONSTER.
FOR A MONSTER COMES TO DESTROY WHAT HAS BEEN, WHAT IS ACCEPTED, WHAT IS NO LONGER QUESTIONED.
I SEEK FELLOW MONSTERS.
THOSE WILLING TO UNMAKE THEMSELVES AND THE WORLD OF SORROW IMPRISONING US.
HERE AT THE EDGE OF CREATION I CHALLENGE YOU TO DISCOVER WHAT LIES BEYOND EVEN THIS. I ASK AGAIN:
WHY ARE YOU HERE?

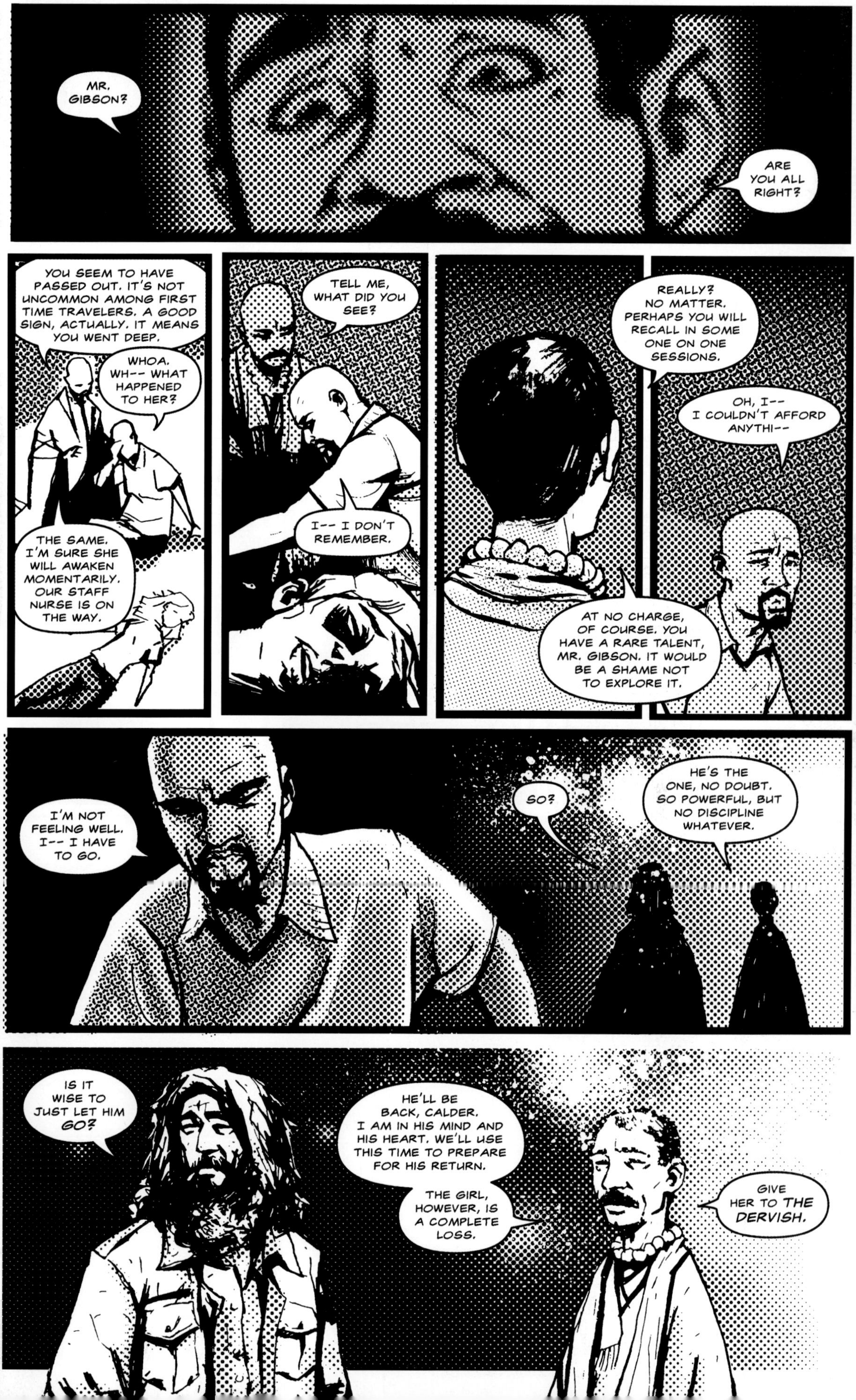
MR. GIBSON?
ARE YOU ALL RIGHT?
YOU SEEM TO HAVE PASSED OUT. IT'S NOT UNCOMMON AMONG FIRST TIME TRAVELERS. A GOOD SIGN, ACTUALLY. IT MEANS YOU WENT DEEP.
WHOA. WH-- WHAT HAPPENED TO HER?
THE SAME. I'M SURE SHE WILL AWAKEN MOMENTARILY. OUR STAFF NURSE IS ON THE WAY.
TELL ME, WHAT DID YOU SEE?
I-- I DON'T REMEMBER.
REALLY? NO MATTER. PERHAPS YOU WILL RECALL IN SOME ONE ON ONE SESSIONS.
OH, I-- I COULDN'T AFFORD ANYTHI--
AT NO CHARGE, OF COURSE. YOU HAVE A RARE TALENT, MR. GIBSON. IT WOULD BE A SHAME NOT TO EXPLORE IT.
I'M NOT FEELING WELL. I-- I HAVE TO GO.
SO?
HE'S THE ONE, NO DOUBT. SO POWERFUL, BUT NO DISCIPLINE WHATEVER.
IS IT WISE TO JUST LET HIM GO?
HE'LL BE BACK, CALDER. I AM IN HIS MIND AND HIS HEART. WE'LL USE THIS TIME TO PREPARE FOR HIS RETURN.
THE GIRL, HOWEVER, IS A COMPLETE LOSS.
GIVE HER TO THE DERVISH.

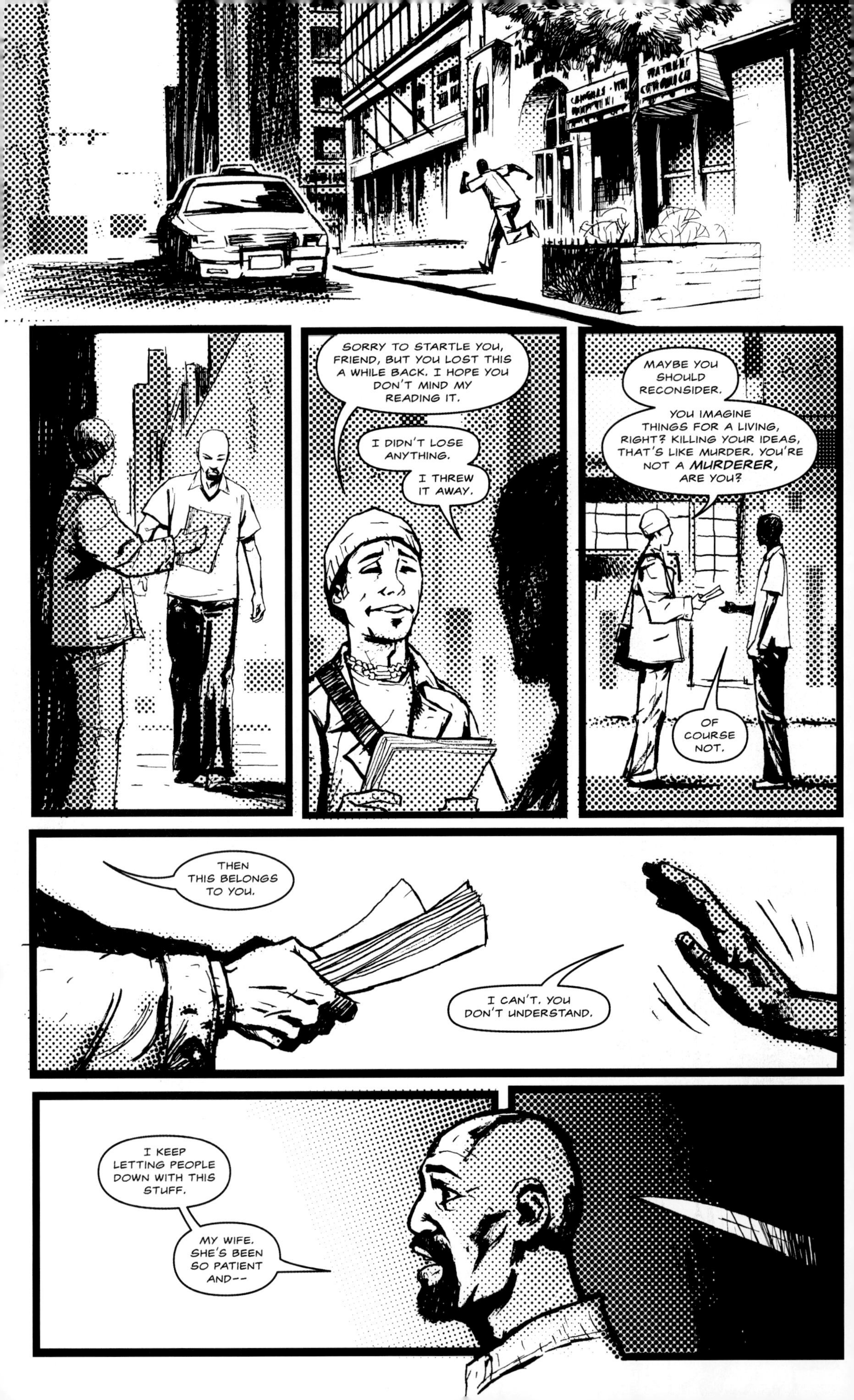
SORRY TO STARTLE YOU, FRIEND, BUT YOU LOST THIS A WHILE BACK. I HOPE YOU DON'T MIND MY READING IT.
I DIDN'T LOSE ANYTHING.
I THREW IT AWAY.
MAYBE YOU SHOULD RECONSIDER.
YOU IMAGINE THINGS FOR A LIVING, RIGHT? KILLING YOUR IDEAS, THAT'S LIKE MURDER. YOU'RE NOT A MURDERER, ARE YOU?
OF COURSE NOT.
THEN THIS BELONGS TO YOU.
I CAN'T. YOU DON'T UNDERSTAND.
I KEEP LETTING PEOPLE DOWN WITH THIS STUFF.
MY WIFE. SHE'S BEEN SO PATIENT AND--

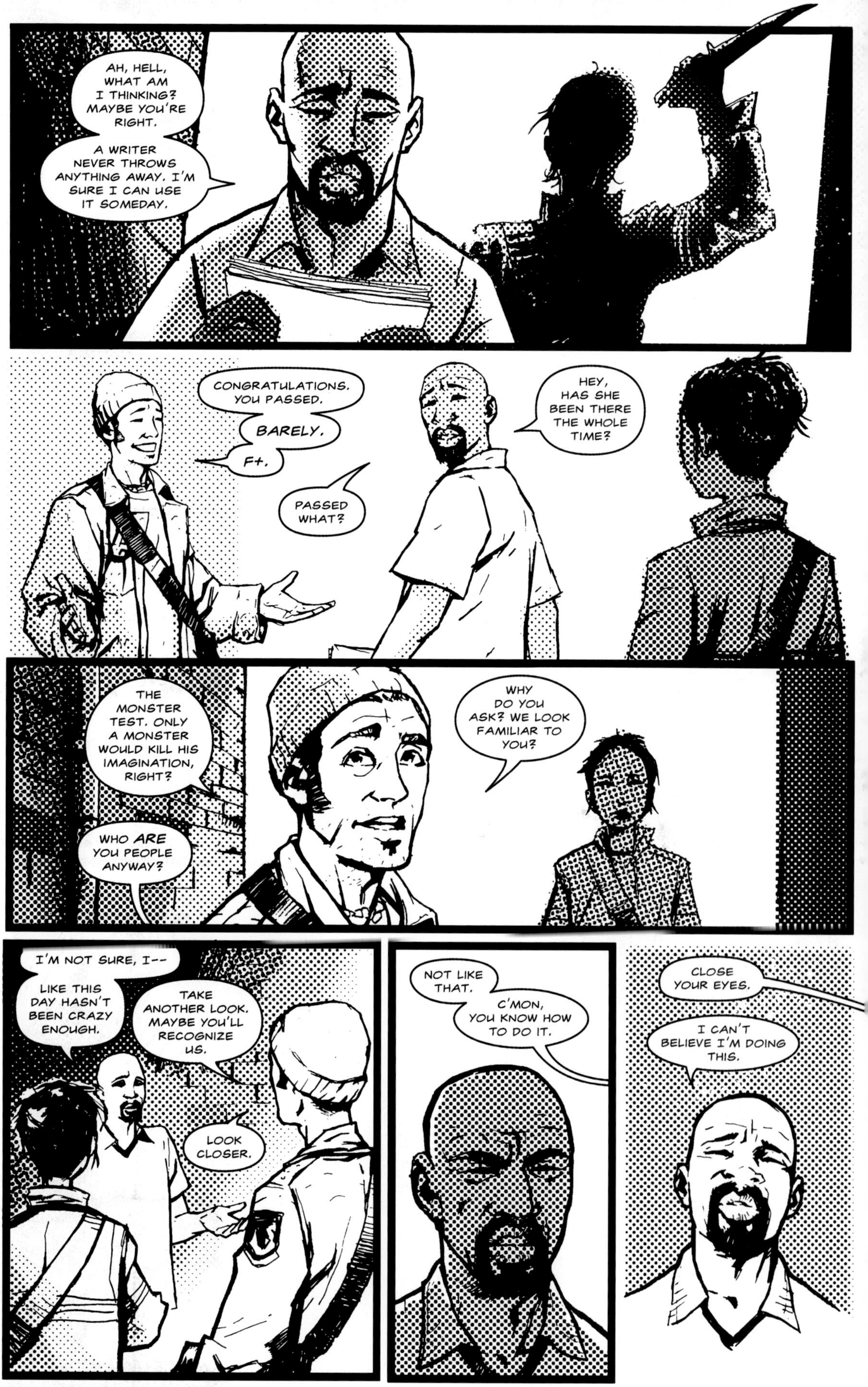

AH, HELL, WHAT AM I THINKING? MAYBE YOU'RE RIGHT.
A WRITER NEVER THROWS ANYTHING AWAY. I'M SURE I CAN USE IT SOMEDAY.
CONGRATULATIONS. YOU PASSED.
BARELY.
F+.
PASSED WHAT?
HEY, HAS SHE BEEN THERE THE WHOLE TIME?
THE MONSTER TEST. ONLY A MONSTER WOULD KILL HIS IMAGINATION, RIGHT?
WHY DO YOU ASK? WE LOOK FAMILIAR TO YOU?
WHO ARE YOU PEOPLE ANYWAY?
I'M NOT SURE, I--
LIKE THIS DAY HASN'T BEEN CRAZY ENOUGH.
TAKE ANOTHER LOOK. MAYBE YOU'LL RECOGNIZE US.
LOOK CLOSER.
NOT LIKE THAT.
C'MON, YOU KNOW HOW TO DO IT.
CLOSE YOUR EYES.
I CAN'T BELIEVE I'M DOING THIS.

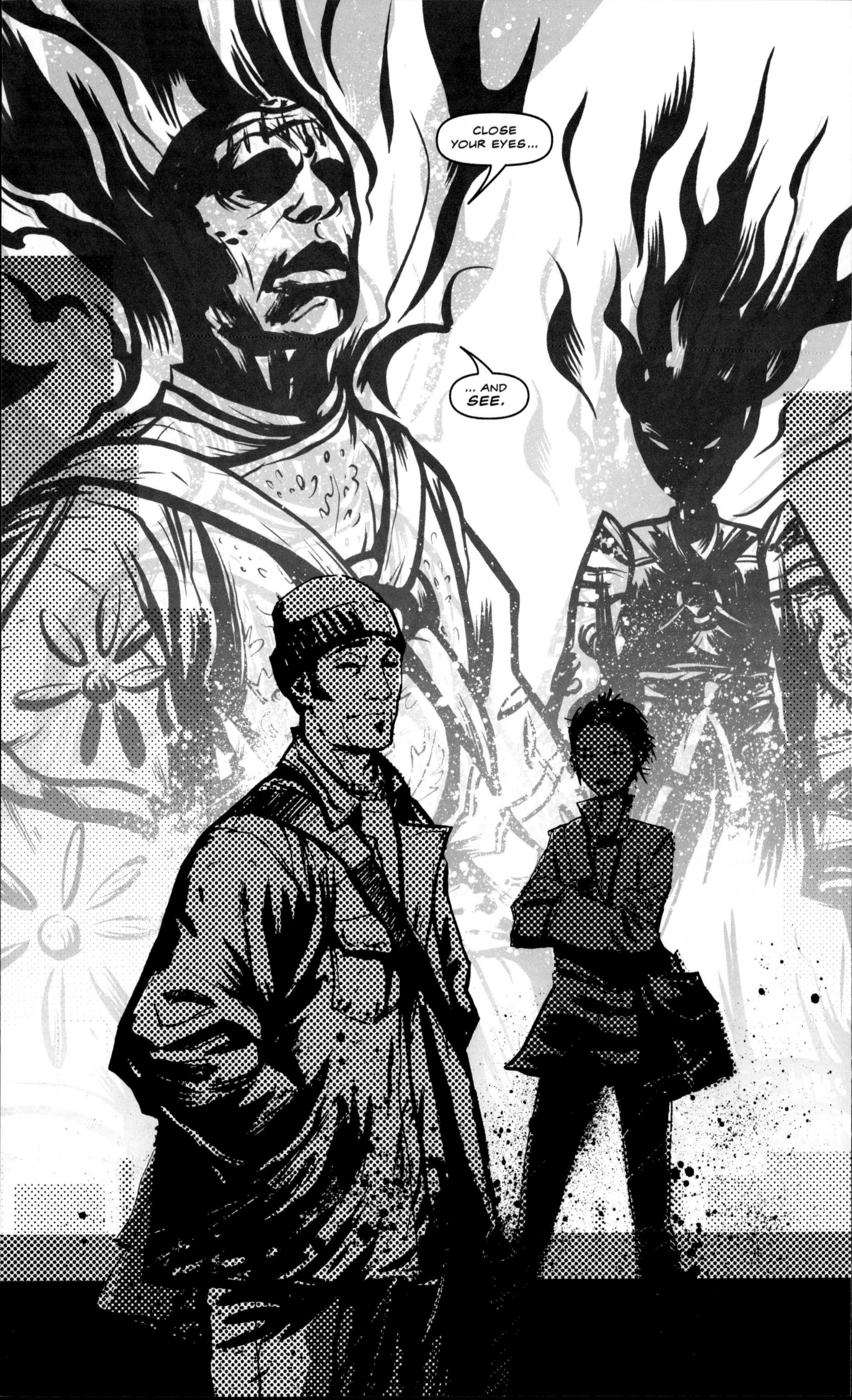
CLOSE YOUR EYES...
... AND SEE.

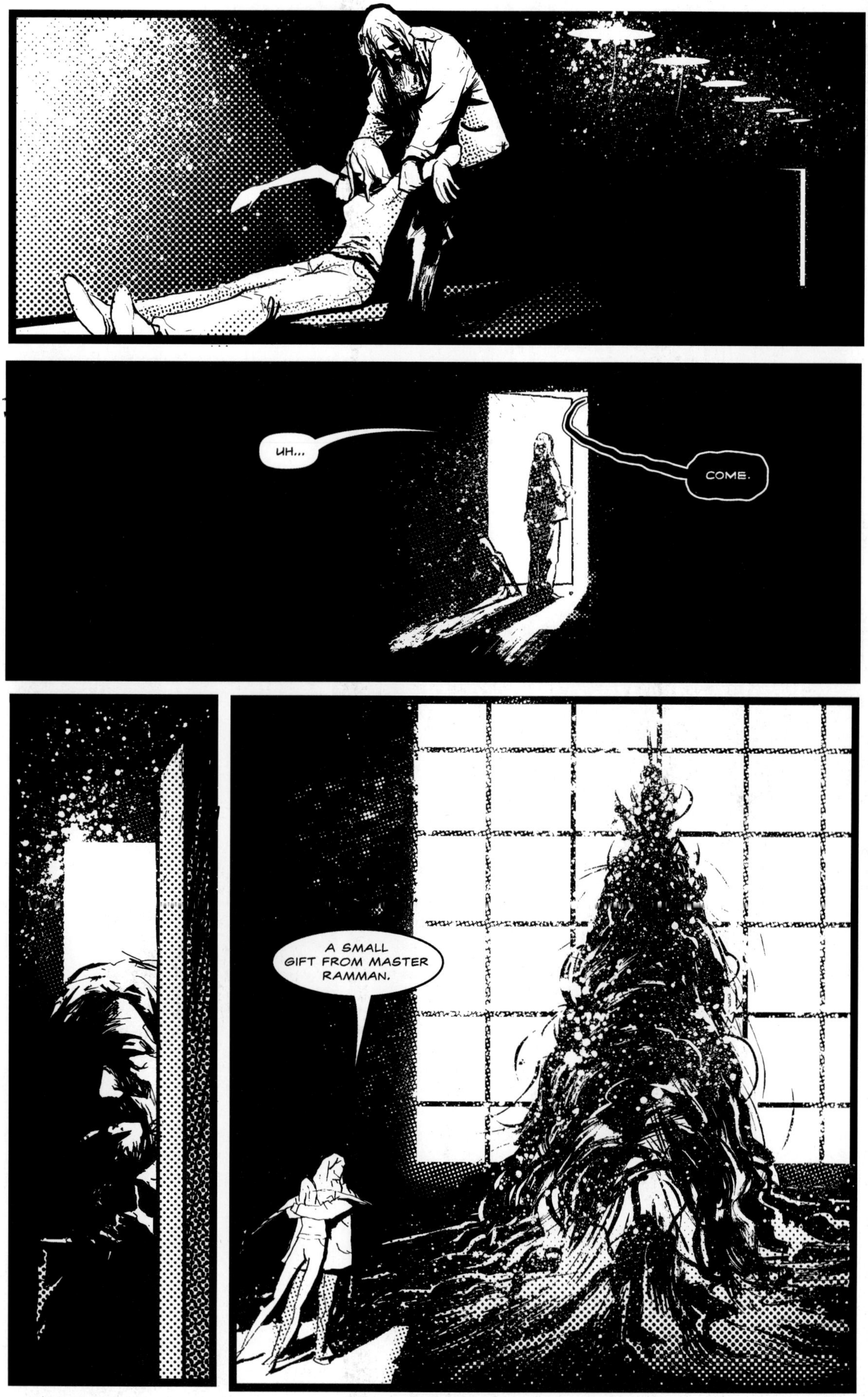

UH...
COME.
A SMALL GIFT FROM MASTER RAMMAN.

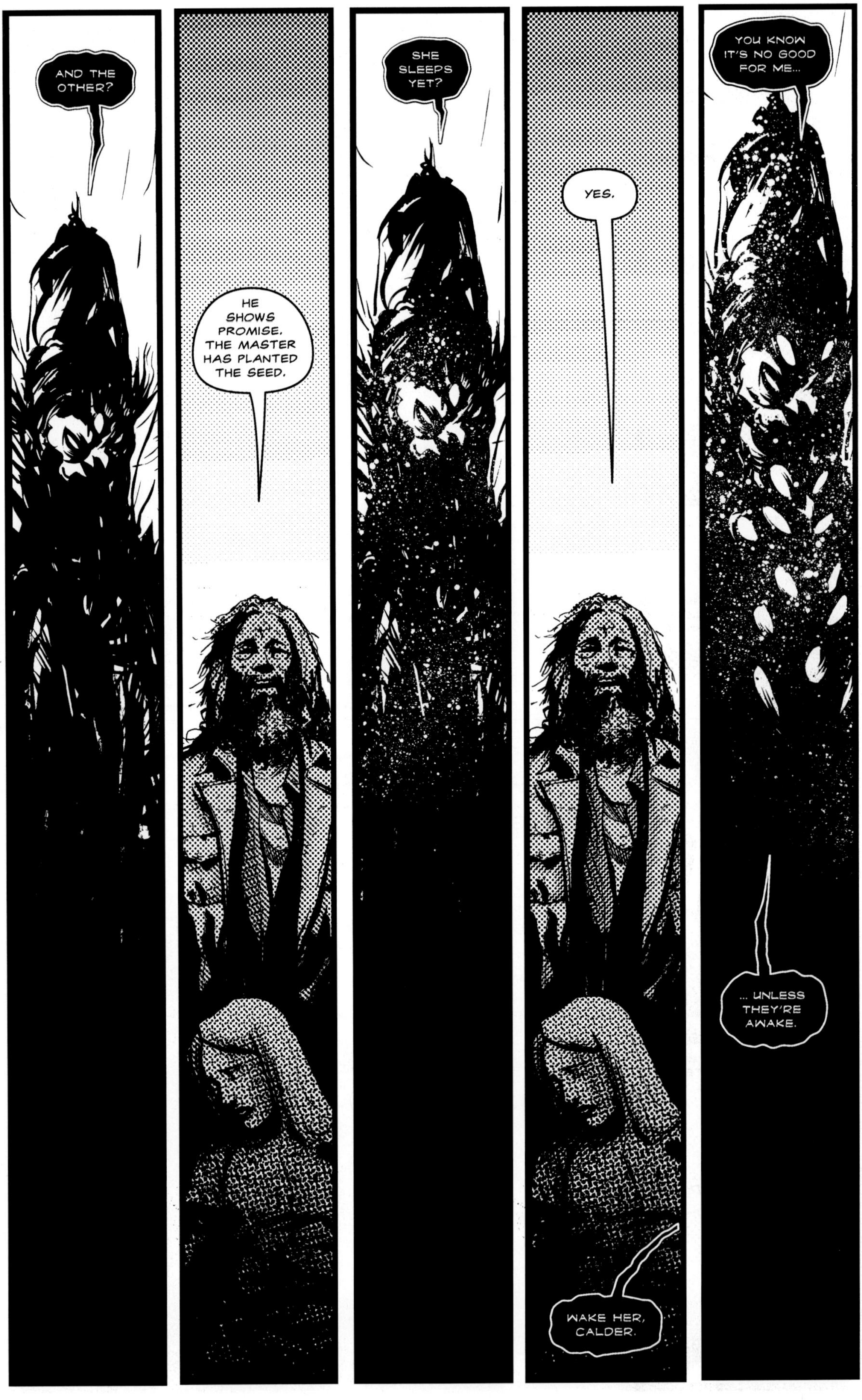
AND THE OTHER?
HE SHOWS PROMISE. THE MASTER HAS PLANTED THE SEED.
SHE SLEEPS YET?
YES.
WAKE HER, CALDER.
YOU KNOW IT'S NO GOOD FOR ME...
... UNLESS THEY'RE AWAKE.

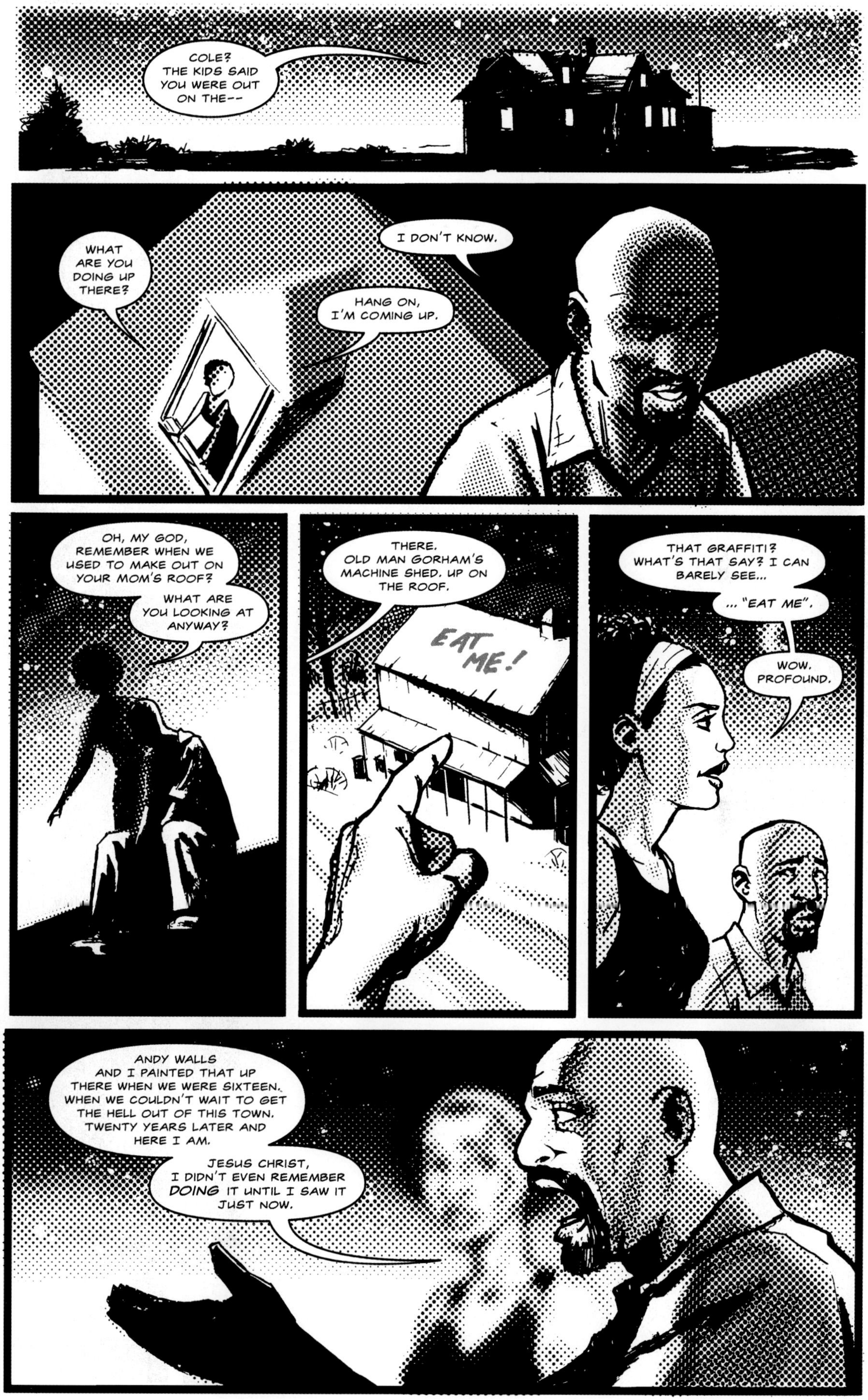
COLE? THE KIDS SAID YOU WERE OUT ON THE--
WHAT ARE YOU DOING UP THERE?
I DON'T KNOW.
HANG ON, I'M COMING UP.
OH, MY GOD, REMEMBER WHEN WE USED TO MAKE OUT ON YOUR MOM'S ROOF?
WHAT ARE YOU LOOKING AT ANYWAY?
THERE. OLD MAN GORHAM'S MACHINE SHED. UP ON THE ROOF.
EAT ME!
THAT GRAFFITI? WHAT'S THAT SAY? I CAN BARELY SEE...
... "EAT ME".
WOW. PROFOUND.
ANDY WALLS AND I PAINTED THAT UP THERE WHEN WE WERE SIXTEEN. WHEN WE COULDN'T WAIT TO GET THE HELL OUT OF THIS TOWN. TWENTY YEARS LATER AND HERE I AM.
JESUS CHRIST, I DIDN'T EVEN REMEMBER *DOING* IT UNTIL I SAW IT JUST NOW.

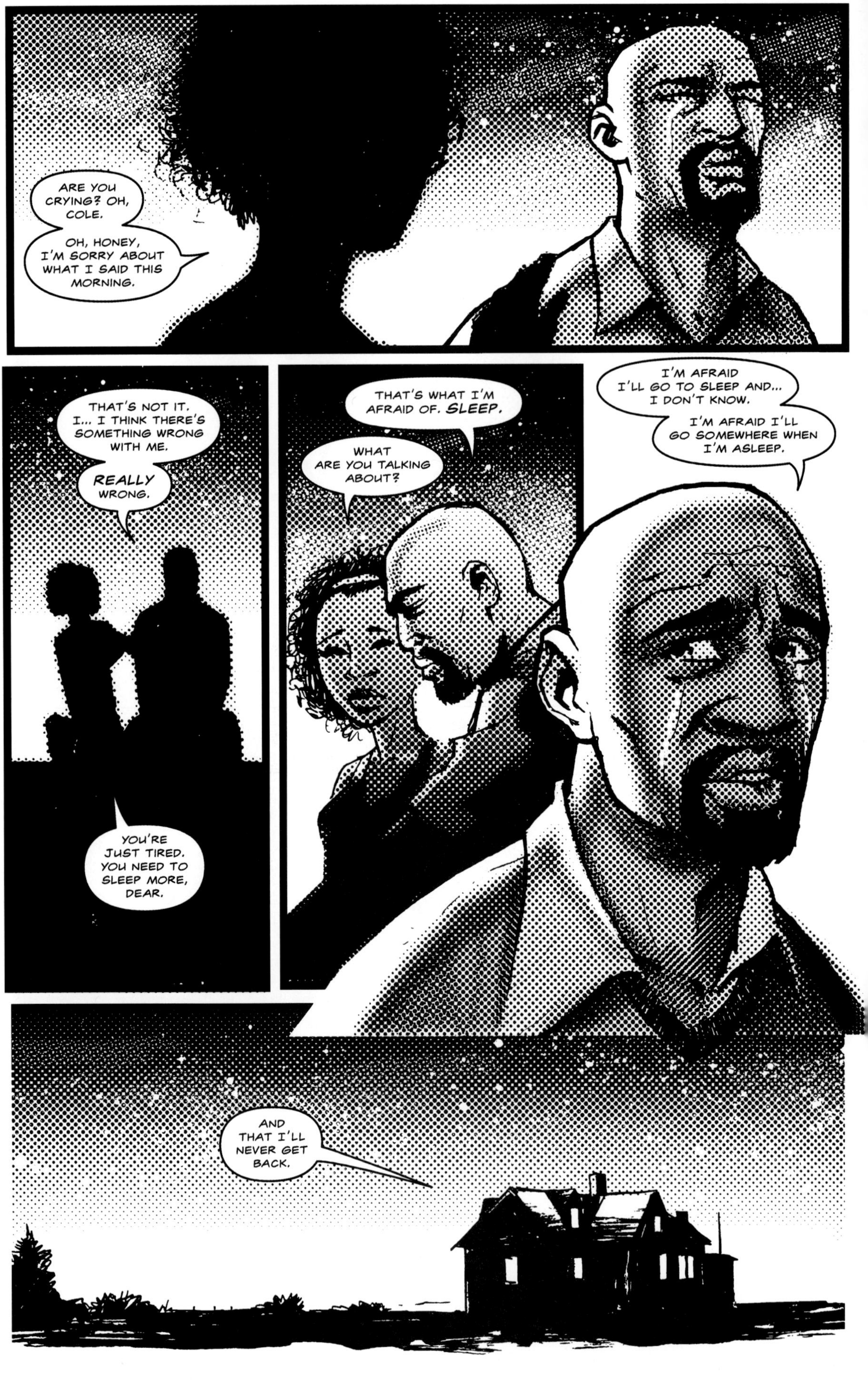
ARE YOU CRYING? OH, COLE.
OH, HONEY, I'M SORRY ABOUT WHAT I SAID THIS MORNING.
THAT'S NOT IT. I... I THINK THERE'S SOMETHING WRONG WITH ME.
REALLY WRONG.
YOU'RE JUST TIRED. YOU NEED TO SLEEP MORE, DEAR.
THAT'S WHAT I'M AFRAID OF. SLEEP.
WHAT ARE YOU TALKING ABOUT?
I'M AFRAID I'LL GO TO SLEEP AND... I DON'T KNOW.
I'M AFRAID I'LL GO SOMEWHERE WHEN I'M ASLEEP.
AND THAT I'LL NEVER GET BACK.

THAT
BRIGHTER
WORLD

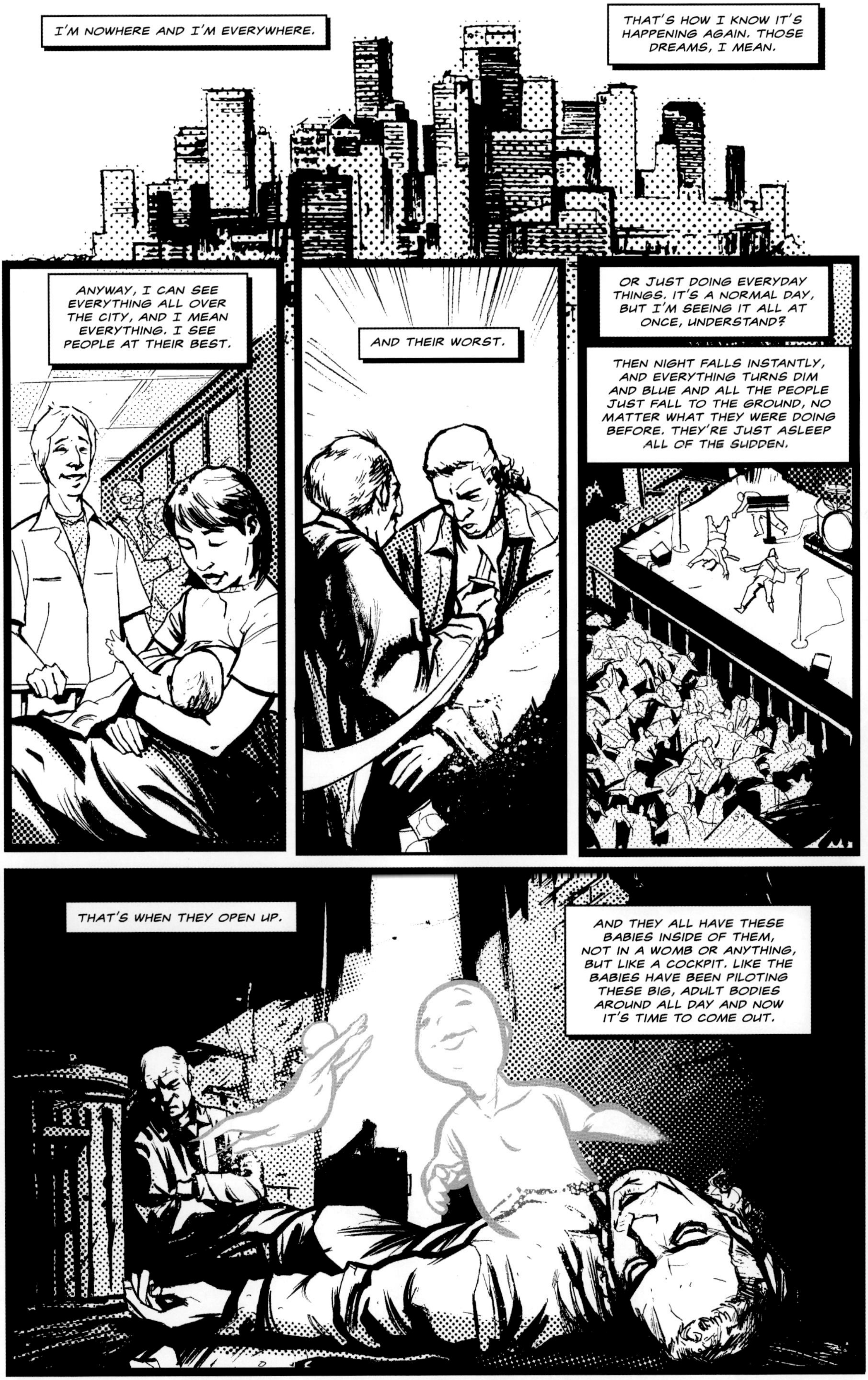
I'M NOWHERE AND I'M EVERYWHERE.
THAT'S HOW I KNOW IT'S HAPPENING AGAIN. THOSE DREAMS, I MEAN.
ANYWAY, I CAN SEE EVERYTHING ALL OVER THE CITY, AND I MEAN EVERYTHING. I SEE PEOPLE AT THEIR BEST.
AND THEIR WORST.
OR JUST DOING EVERYDAY THINGS. IT'S A NORMAL DAY, BUT I'M SEEING IT ALL AT ONCE, UNDERSTAND?
THEN NIGHT FALLS INSTANTLY, AND EVERYTHING TURNS DIM AND BLUE AND ALL THE PEOPLE JUST FALL TO THE GROUND, NO MATTER WHAT THEY WERE DOING BEFORE. THEY'RE JUST ASLEEP ALL OF THE SUDDEN.
THAT'S WHEN THEY OPEN UP.
AND THEY ALL HAVE THESE BABIES INSIDE OF THEM, NOT IN A WOMB OR ANYTHING, BUT LIKE A COCKPIT. LIKE THE BABIES HAVE BEEN PILOTING THESE BIG, ADULT BODIES AROUND ALL DAY AND NOW IT'S TIME TO COME OUT.

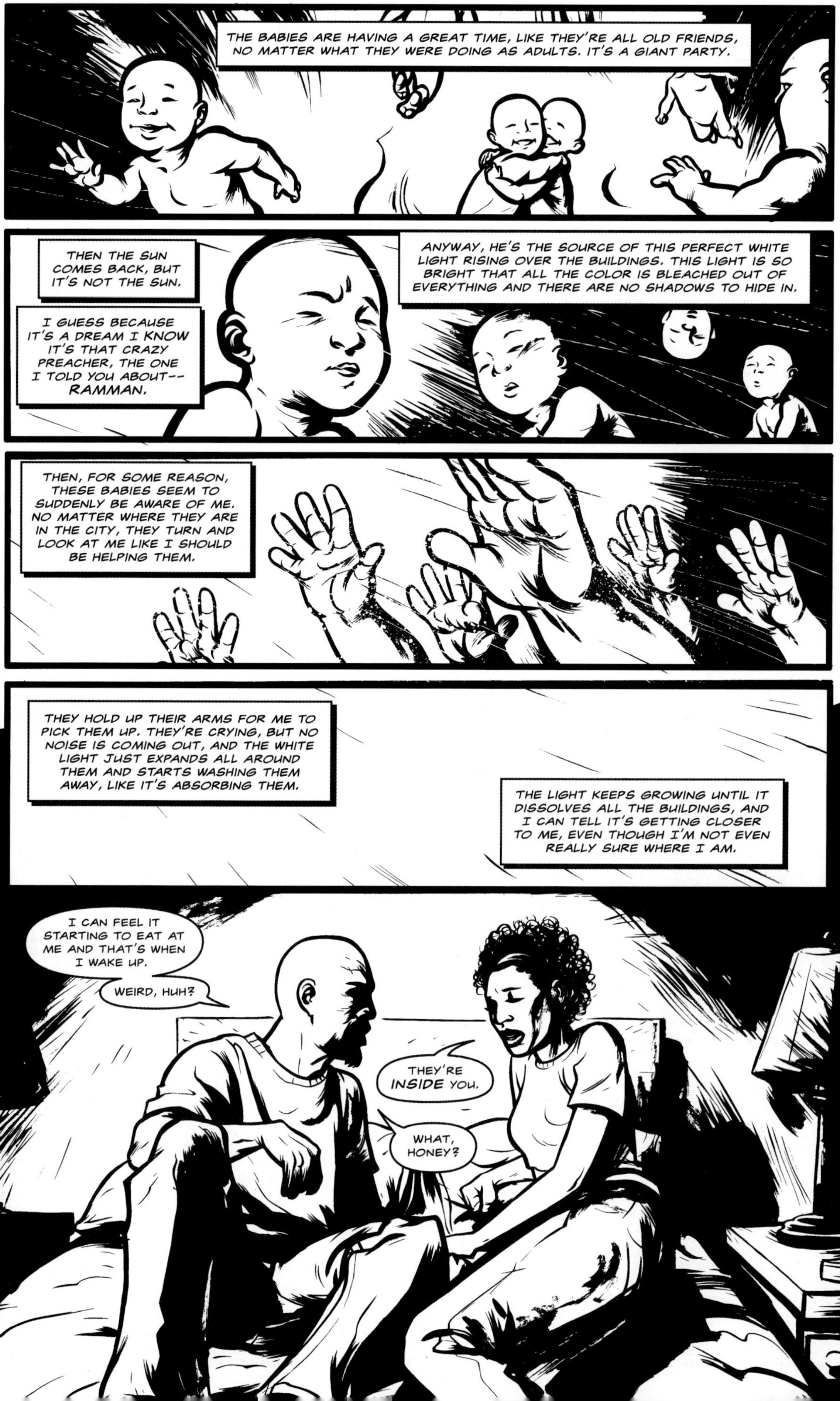
THE BABIES ARE HAVING A GREAT TIME, LIKE THEY'RE ALL OLD FRIENDS, NO MATTER WHAT THEY WERE DOING AS ADULTS. IT'S A GIANT PARTY.
THEN THE SUN COMES BACK, BUT IT'S NOT THE SUN.
I GUESS BECAUSE IT'S A DREAM I KNOW IT'S THAT CRAZY PREACHER, THE ONE I TOLD YOU ABOUT-- RAMMAN.
ANYWAY, HE'S THE SOURCE OF THIS PERFECT WHITE LIGHT RISING OVER THE BUILDINGS. THIS LIGHT IS SO BRIGHT THAT ALL THE COLOR IS BLEACHED OUT OF EVERYTHING AND THERE ARE NO SHADOWS TO HIDE IN.
THEN, FOR SOME REASON, THESE BABIES SEEM TO SUDDENLY BE AWARE OF ME. NO MATTER WHERE THEY ARE IN THE CITY, THEY TURN AND LOOK AT ME LIKE I SHOULD BE HELPING THEM.
THEY HOLD UP THEIR ARMS FOR ME TO PICK THEM UP. THEY'RE CRYING, BUT NO NOISE IS COMING OUT, AND THE WHITE LIGHT JUST EXPANDS ALL AROUND THEM AND STARTS WASHING THEM AWAY, LIKE IT'S ABSORBING THEM.
THE LIGHT KEEPS GROWING UNTIL IT DISSOLVES ALL THE BUILDINGS, AND I CAN TELL IT'S GETTING CLOSER TO ME, EVEN THOUGH I'M NOT EVEN REALLY SURE WHERE I AM.
I CAN FEEL IT STARTING TO EAT AT ME AND THAT'S WHEN I WAKE UP.
WEIRD, HUH?
THEY'RE INSIDE YOU.
WHAT, HONEY?

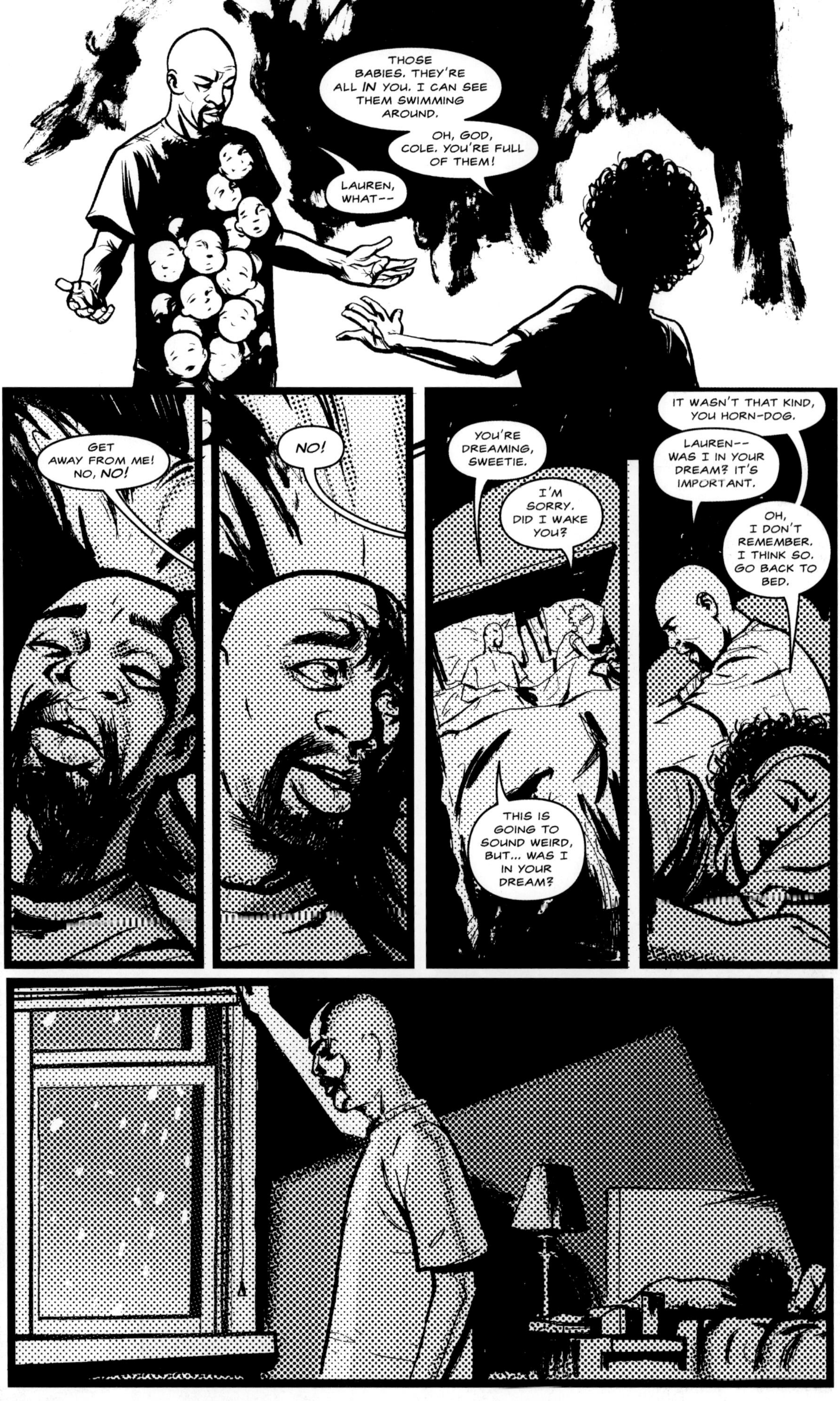
THOSE BABIES. THEY'RE ALL IN YOU. I CAN SEE THEM SWIMMING AROUND.
OH, GOD, COLE. YOU'RE FULL OF THEM!
LAUREN, WHAT--
GET AWAY FROM ME! NO, NO!
NO!
YOU'RE DREAMING, SWEETIE.
I'M SORRY. DID I WAKE YOU?
THIS IS GOING TO SOUND WEIRD, BUT... WAS I IN YOUR DREAM?
IT WASN'T THAT KIND, YOU HORN-DOG.
LAUREN-- WAS I IN YOUR DREAM? IT'S IMPORTANT.
OH, I DON'T REMEMBER. I THINK SO. GO BACK TO BED.

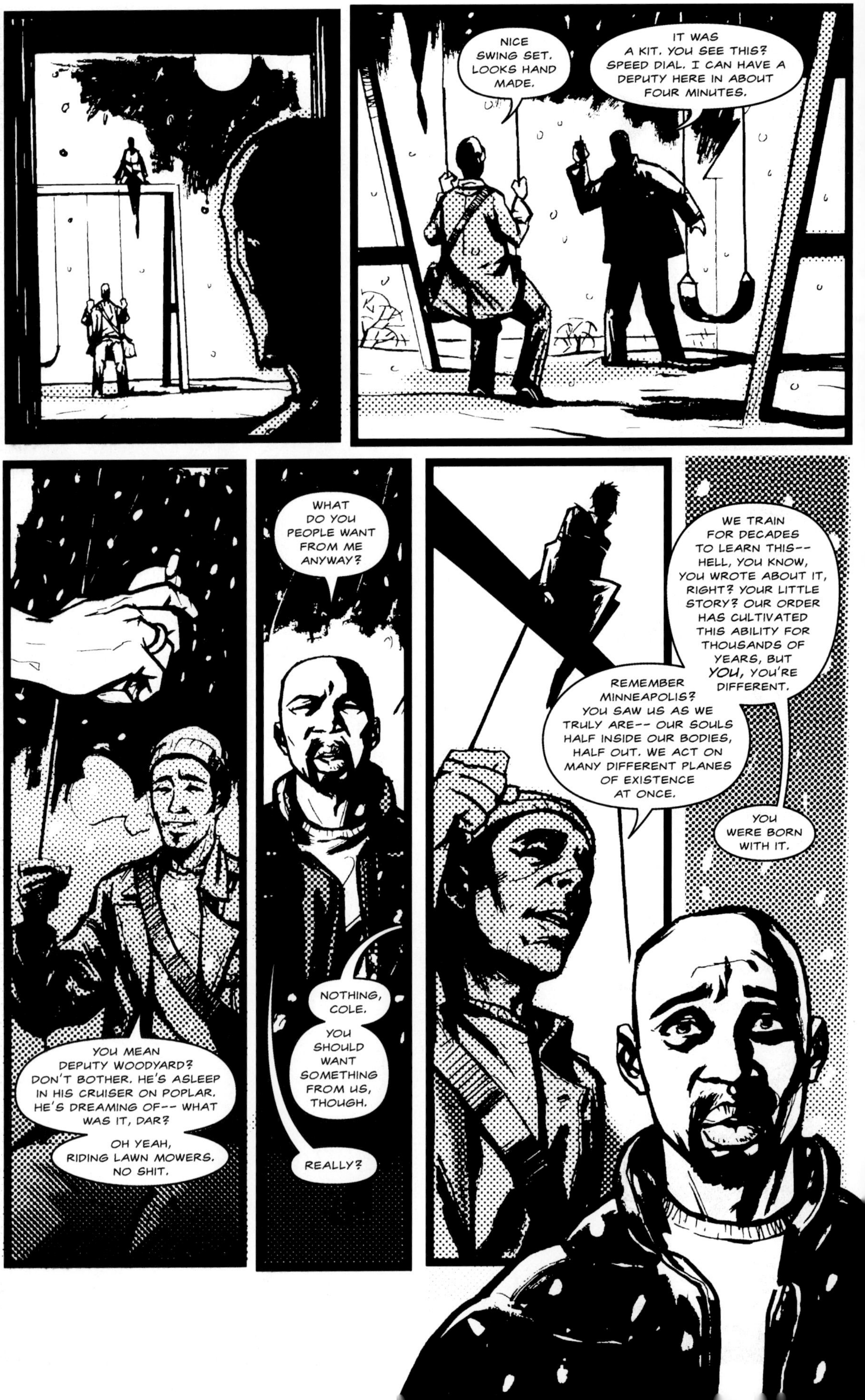
NICE SWING SET. LOOKS HAND MADE.
IT WAS A KIT. YOU SEE THIS? SPEED DIAL. I CAN HAVE A DEPUTY HERE IN ABOUT FOUR MINUTES.
YOU MEAN DEPUTY WOODYARD? DON'T BOTHER. HE'S ASLEEP IN HIS CRUISER ON POPLAR. HE'S DREAMING OF-- WHAT WAS IT, DAR?
OH YEAH, RIDING LAWN MOWERS. NO SHIT.
WHAT DO YOU PEOPLE WANT FROM ME ANYWAY?
NOTHING, COLE.
YOU SHOULD WANT SOMETHING FROM US, THOUGH.
REALLY?
REMEMBER MINNEAPOLIS? YOU SAW US AS WE TRULY ARE-- OUR SOULS HALF INSIDE OUR BODIES, HALF OUT. WE ACT ON MANY DIFFERENT PLANES OF EXISTENCE AT ONCE.
WE TRAIN FOR DECADES TO LEARN THIS-- HELL, YOU KNOW, YOU WROTE ABOUT IT, RIGHT? YOUR LITTLE STORY? OUR ORDER HAS CULTIVATED THIS ABILITY FOR THOUSANDS OF YEARS, BUT YOU, YOU'RE DIFFERENT.
YOU WERE BORN WITH IT.

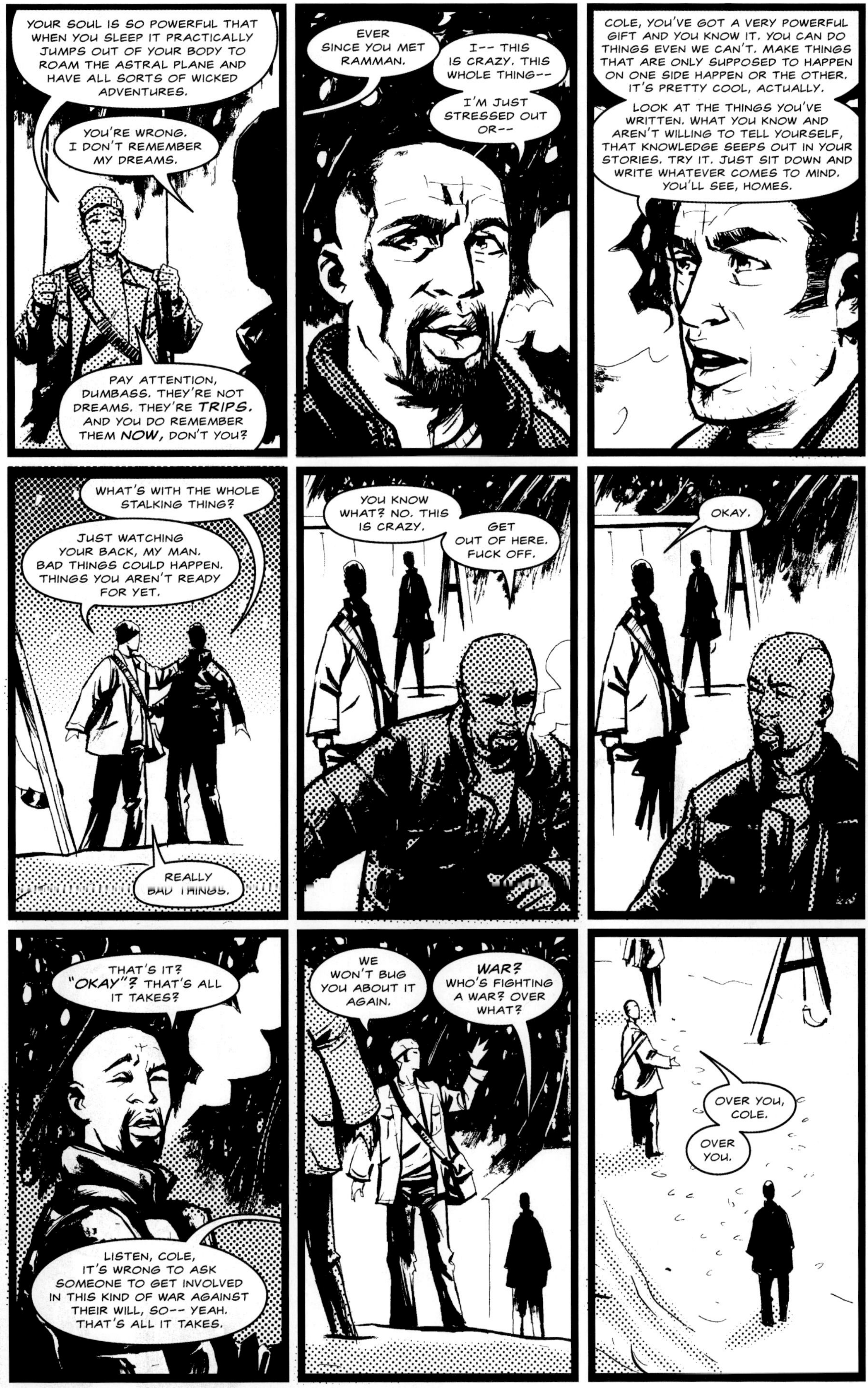
YOUR SOUL IS SO POWERFUL THAT WHEN YOU SLEEP IT PRACTICALLY JUMPS OUT OF YOUR BODY TO ROAM THE ASTRAL PLANE AND HAVE ALL SORTS OF WICKED ADVENTURES.
YOU'RE WRONG. I DON'T REMEMBER MY DREAMS.
PAY ATTENTION, DUMBASS. THEY'RE NOT DREAMS. THEY'RE TRIPS. AND YOU DO REMEMBER THEM NOW, DON'T YOU?
EVER SINCE YOU MET RAMMAN.
I-- THIS IS CRAZY. THIS WHOLE THING--
I'M JUST STRESSED OUT OR--
COLE, YOU'VE GOT A VERY POWERFUL GIFT AND YOU KNOW IT. YOU CAN DO THINGS EVEN WE CAN'T. MAKE THINGS THAT ARE ONLY SUPPOSED TO HAPPEN ON ONE SIDE HAPPEN OR THE OTHER. IT'S PRETTY COOL, ACTUALLY.
LOOK AT THE THINGS YOU'VE WRITTEN. WHAT YOU KNOW AND AREN'T WILLING TO TELL YOURSELF, THAT KNOWLEDGE SEEPS OUT IN YOUR STORIES. TRY IT. JUST SIT DOWN AND WRITE WHATEVER COMES TO MIND. YOU'LL SEE, HOMES.
WHAT'S WITH THE WHOLE STALKING THING?
JUST WATCHING YOUR BACK, MY MAN. BAD THINGS COULD HAPPEN. THINGS YOU AREN'T READY FOR YET.
REALLY BAD THINGS.
YOU KNOW WHAT? NO. THIS IS CRAZY.
GET OUT OF HERE. FUCK OFF.
OKAY.
THAT'S IT? "OKAY"? THAT'S ALL IT TAKES?
LISTEN, COLE, IT'S WRONG TO ASK SOMEONE TO GET INVOLVED IN THIS KIND OF WAR AGAINST THEIR WILL, SO-- YEAH. THAT'S ALL IT TAKES.
WE WON'T BUG YOU ABOUT IT AGAIN.
WAR? WHO'S FIGHTING A WAR? OVER WHAT?
OVER YOU, COLE.
OVER YOU.

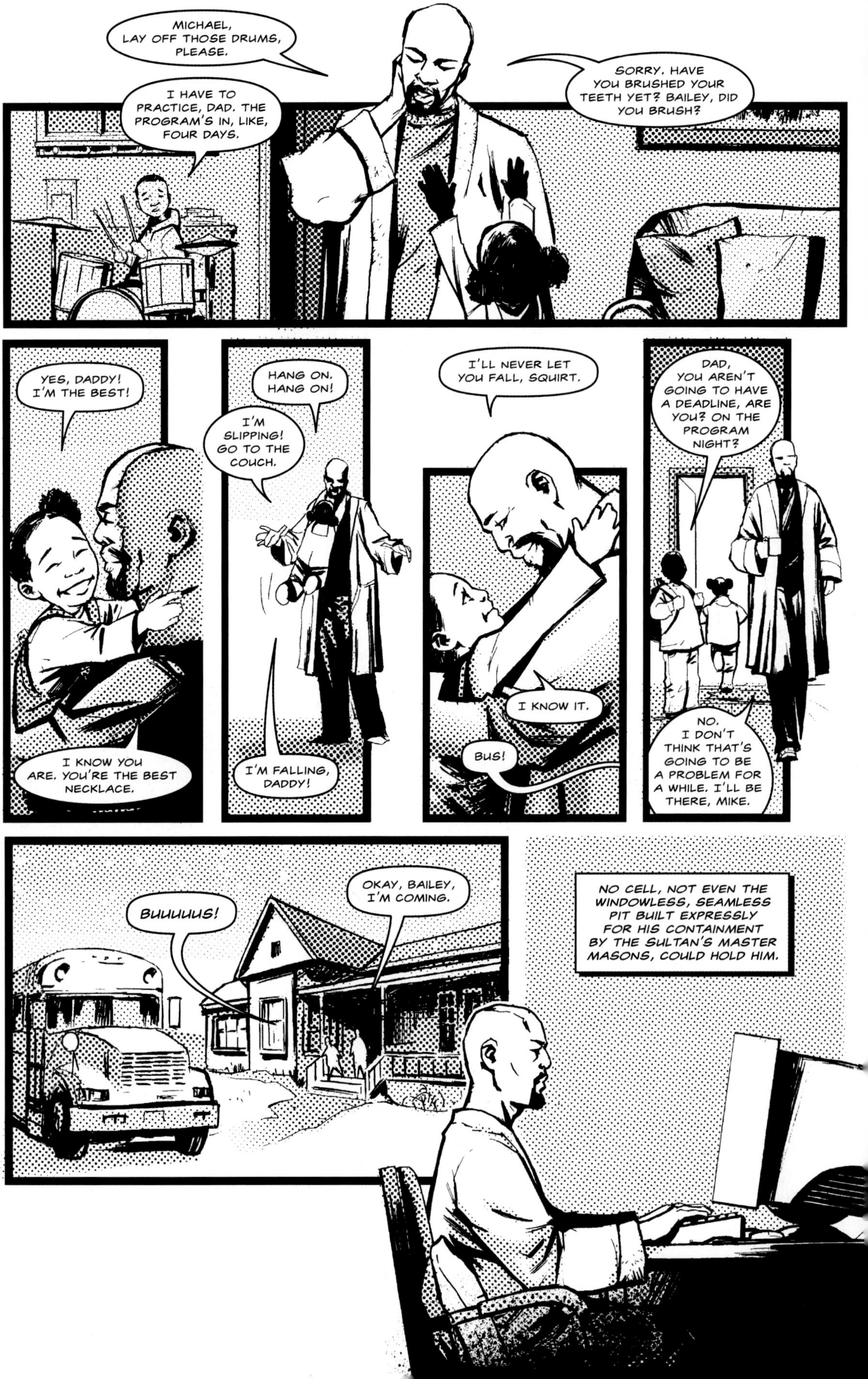
MICHAEL, LAY OFF THOSE DRUMS, PLEASE.
I HAVE TO PRACTICE, DAD. THE PROGRAM'S IN, LIKE, FOUR DAYS.
SORRY. HAVE YOU BRUSHED YOUR TEETH YET? BAILEY, DID YOU BRUSH?
YES, DADDY! I'M THE BEST!
I KNOW YOU ARE. YOU'RE THE BEST NECKLACE.
HANG ON, HANG ON!
I'M SLIPPING! GO TO THE COUCH.
I'M FALLING, DADDY!
I'LL NEVER LET YOU FALL, SQUIRT.
I KNOW IT.
BUS!
DAD, YOU AREN'T GOING TO HAVE A DEADLINE, ARE YOU? ON THE PROGRAM NIGHT?
NO. I DON'T THINK THAT'S GOING TO BE A PROBLEM FOR A WHILE. I'LL BE THERE, MIKE.
Buuuuus!
OKAY, BAILEY, I'M COMING.
NO CELL, NOT EVEN THE WINDOWLESS, SEAMLESS PIT BUILT EXPRESSLY FOR HIS CONTAINMENT BY THE SULTAN'S MASTER MASONS, COULD HOLD HIM.

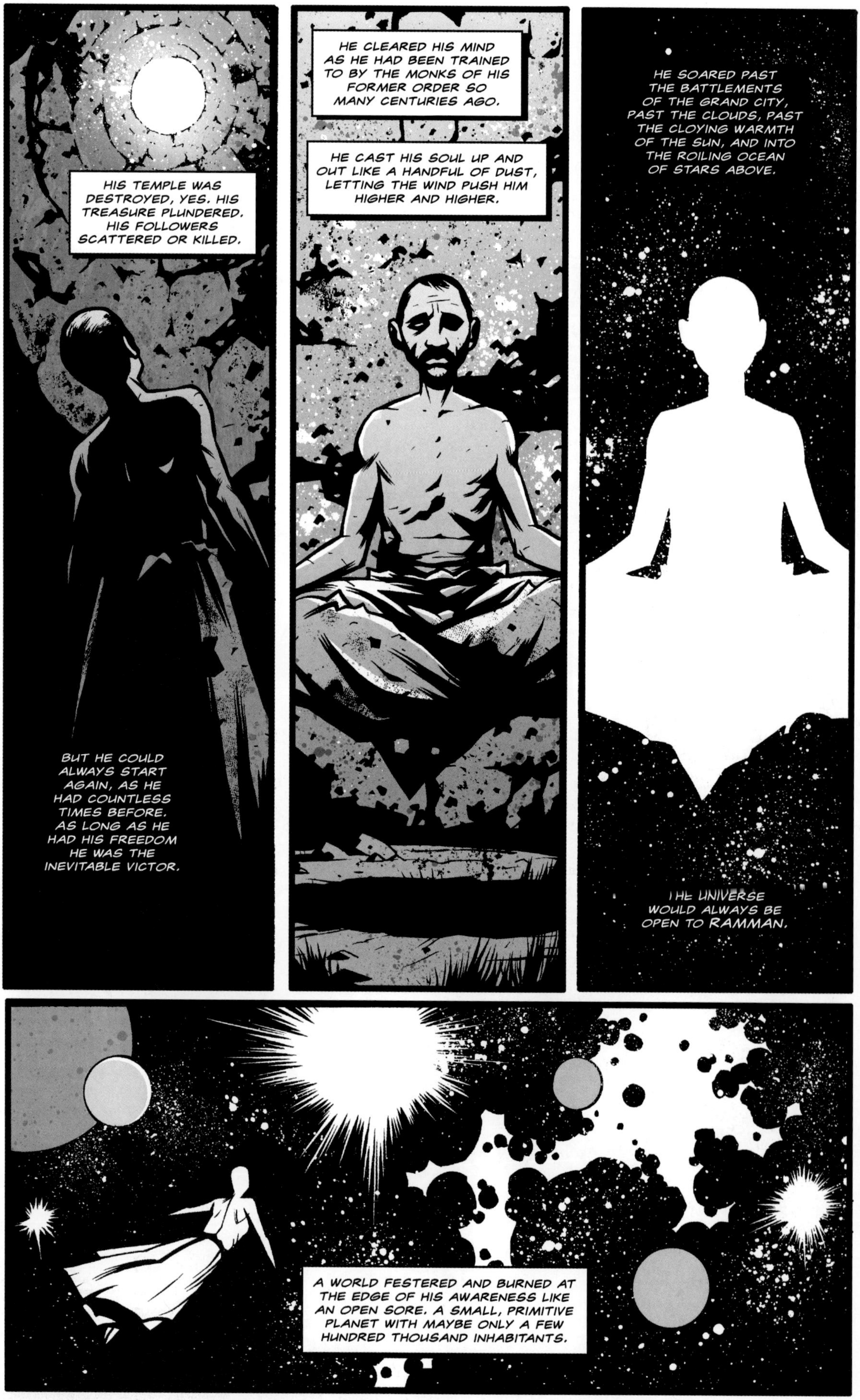
HIS TEMPLE WAS DESTROYED, YES. HIS TREASURE PLUNDERED. HIS FOLLOWERS SCATTERED OR KILLED.
BUT HE COULD ALWAYS START AGAIN, AS HE HAD COUNTLESS TIMES BEFORE. AS LONG AS HE HAD HIS FREEDOM HE WAS THE INEVITABLE VICTOR.
HE CLEARED HIS MIND AS HE HAD BEEN TRAINED TO BY THE MONKS OF HIS FORMER ORDER SO MANY CENTURIES AGO.
HE CAST HIS SOUL UP AND OUT LIKE A HANDFUL OF DUST, LETTING THE WIND PUSH HIM HIGHER AND HIGHER.
HE SOARED PAST THE BATTLEMENTS OF THE GRAND CITY, PAST THE CLOUDS, PAST THE CLOYING WARMTH OF THE SUN, AND INTO THE ROILING OCEAN OF STARS ABOVE.
THE UNIVERSE WOULD ALWAYS BE OPEN TO RAMMAN.
A WORLD FESTERED AND BURNED AT THE EDGE OF HIS AWARENESS LIKE AN OPEN SORE. A SMALL, PRIMITIVE PLANET WITH MAYBE ONLY A FEW HUNDRED THOUSAND INHABITANTS.

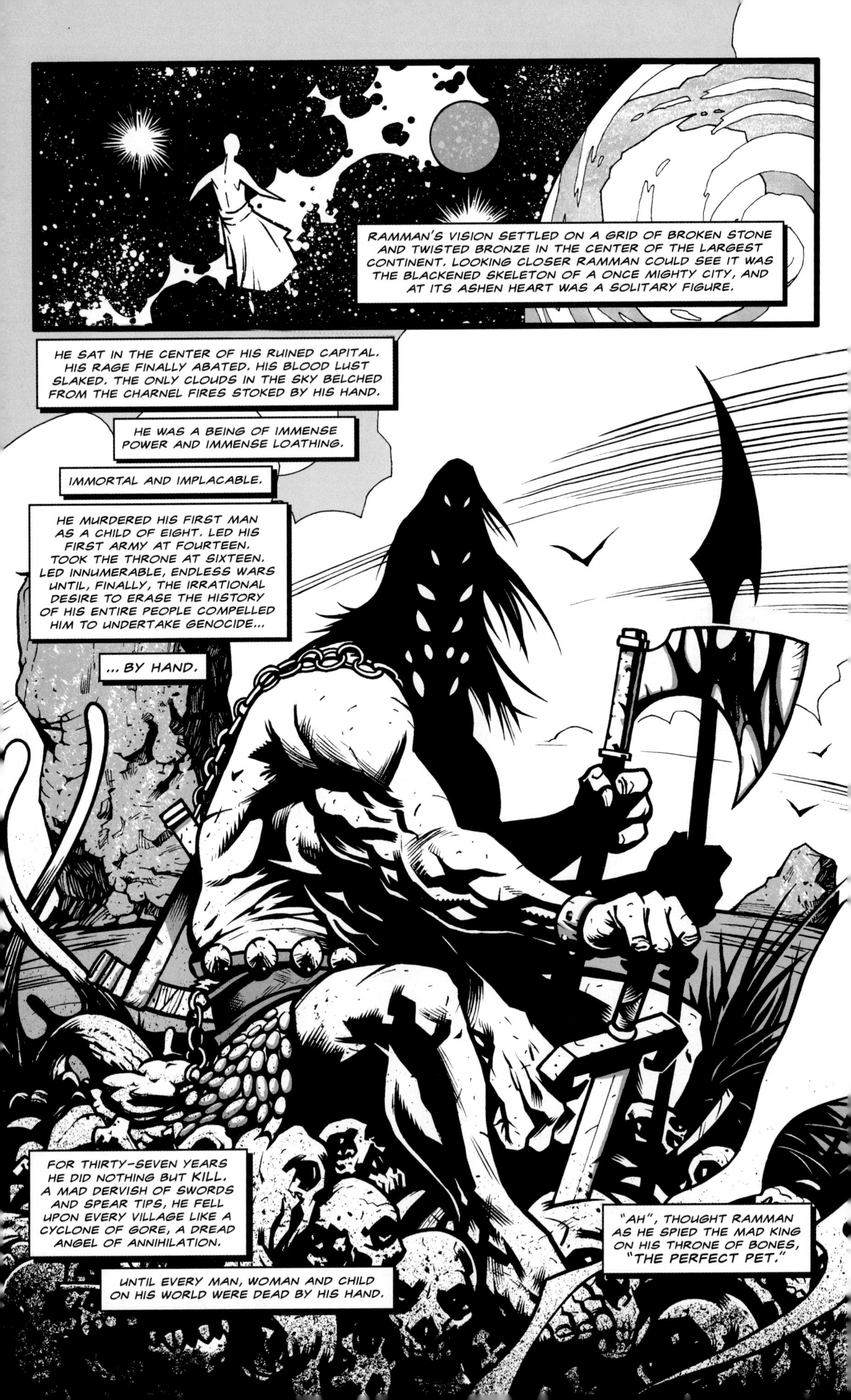
RAMMAN'S VISION SETTLED ON A GRID OF BROKEN STONE AND TWISTED BRONZE IN THE CENTER OF THE LARGEST CONTINENT. LOOKING CLOSER RAMMAN COULD SEE IT WAS THE BLACKENED SKELETON OF A ONCE MIGHTY CITY, AND AT ITS ASHEN HEART WAS A SOLITARY FIGURE.
HE SAT IN THE CENTER OF HIS RUINED CAPITAL. HIS RAGE FINALLY ABATED. HIS BLOOD LUST SLAKED. THE ONLY CLOUDS IN THE SKY BELCHED FROM THE CHARNEL FIRES STOKED BY HIS HAND.
HE WAS A BEING OF IMMENSE POWER AND IMMENSE LOATHING.
IMMORTAL AND IMPLACABLE.
HE MURDERED HIS FIRST MAN AS A CHILD OF EIGHT. LED HIS FIRST ARMY AT FOURTEEN. TOOK THE THRONE AT SIXTEEN. LED INNUMERABLE, ENDLESS WARS UNTIL, FINALLY, THE IRRATIONAL DESIRE TO ERASE THE HISTORY OF HIS ENTIRE PEOPLE COMPELLED HIM TO UNDERTAKE GENOCIDE...
...BY HAND.
FOR THIRTY-SEVEN YEARS HE DID NOTHING BUT KILL. A MAD DERVISH OF SWORDS AND SPEAR TIPS, HE FELL UPON EVERY VILLAGE LIKE A CYCLONE OF GORE, A DREAD ANGEL OF ANNIHILATION.
UNTIL EVERY MAN, WOMAN AND CHILD ON HIS WORLD WERE DEAD BY HIS HAND.
"AH", THOUGHT RAMMAN AS HE SPIED THE MAD KING ON HIS THRONE OF BONES, "THE PERFECT PET."

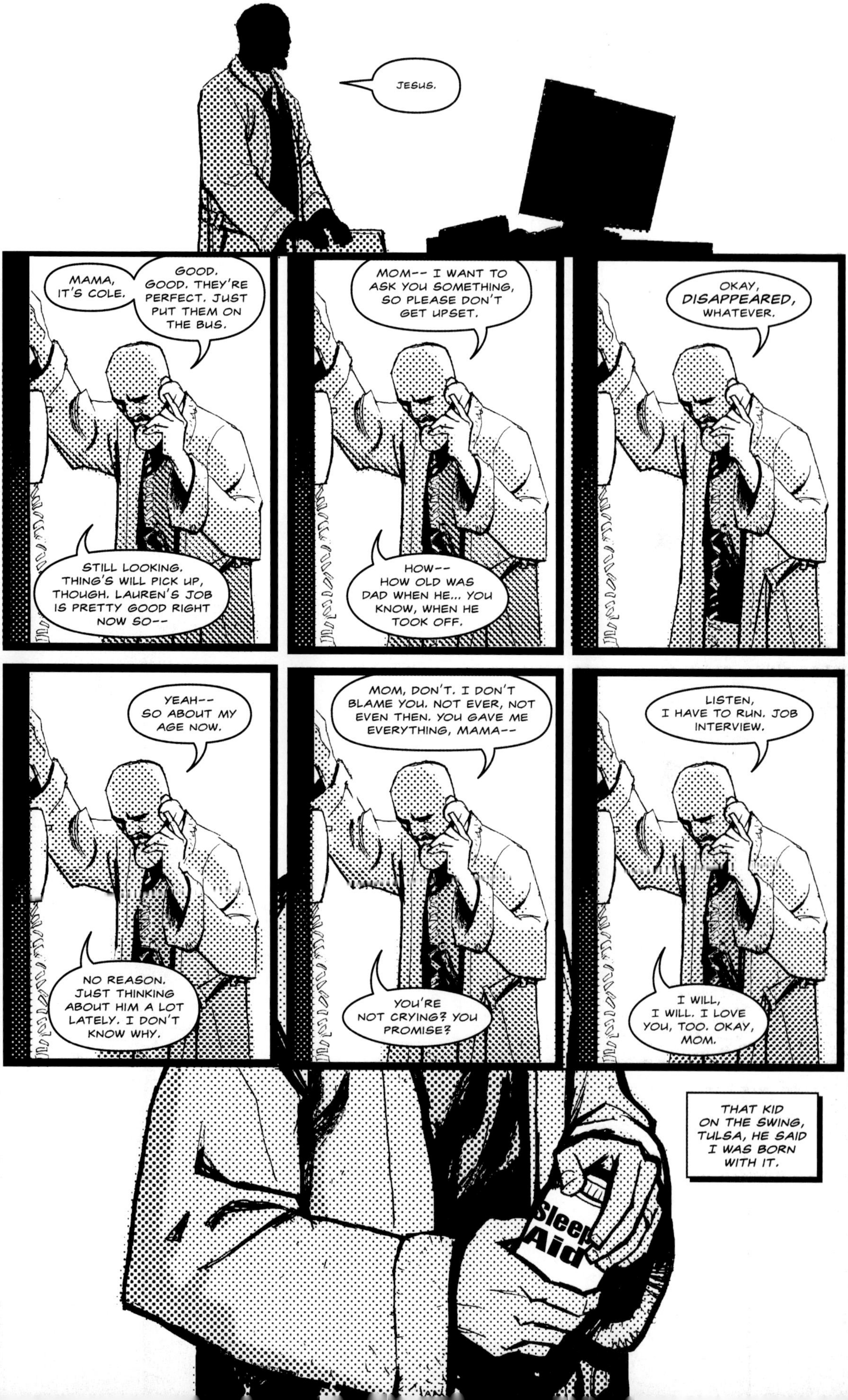
JESUS.
MAMA, IT'S COLE.
GOOD. GOOD. THEY'RE PERFECT. JUST PUT THEM ON THE BUS.
STILL LOOKING. THING'S WILL PICK UP, THOUGH. LAUREN'S JOB IS PRETTY GOOD RIGHT NOW SO--
MOM-- I WANT TO ASK YOU SOMETHING, SO PLEASE DON'T GET UPSET.
HOW-- HOW OLD WAS DAD WHEN HE... YOU KNOW, WHEN HE TOOK OFF.
OKAY, DISAPPEARED, WHATEVER.
YEAH-- SO ABOUT MY AGE NOW.
NO REASON. JUST THINKING ABOUT HIM A LOT LATELY. I DON'T KNOW WHY.
MOM, DON'T. I DON'T BLAME YOU. NOT EVER, NOT EVEN THEN. YOU GAVE ME EVERYTHING, MAMA--
YOU'RE NOT CRYING? YOU PROMISE?
LISTEN, I HAVE TO RUN. JOB INTERVIEW.
I WILL, I WILL. I LOVE YOU, TOO. OKAY, MOM.
THAT KID ON THE SWING, TULSA, HE SAID I WAS BORN WITH IT.
Sleep Aid

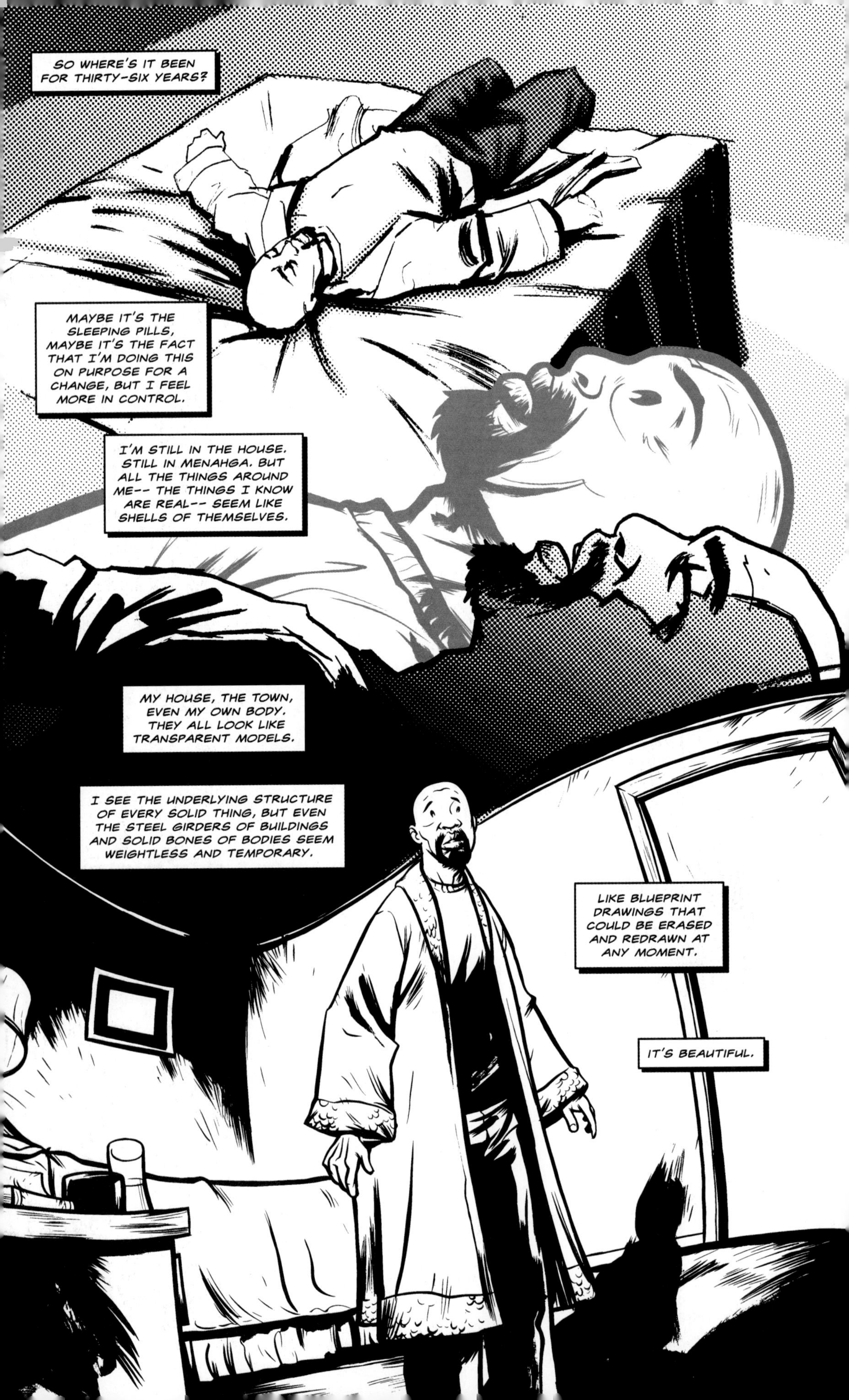
SO WHERE'S IT BEEN FOR THIRTY-SIX YEARS?
MAYBE IT'S THE SLEEPING PILLS, MAYBE IT'S THE FACT THAT I'M DOING THIS ON PURPOSE FOR A CHANGE, BUT I FEEL MORE IN CONTROL.
I'M STILL IN THE HOUSE. STILL IN MENAHGA. BUT ALL THE THINGS AROUND ME-- THE THINGS I KNOW ARE REAL-- SEEM LIKE SHELLS OF THEMSELVES.
MY HOUSE, THE TOWN, EVEN MY OWN BODY. THEY ALL LOOK LIKE TRANSPARENT MODELS.
I SEE THE UNDERLYING STRUCTURE OF EVERY SOLID THING, BUT EVEN THE STEEL GIRDERS OF BUILDINGS AND SOLID BONES OF BODIES SEEM WEIGHTLESS AND TEMPORARY.
LIKE BLUEPRINT DRAWINGS THAT COULD BE ERASED AND REDRAWN AT ANY MOMENT.
IT'S BEAUTIFUL.

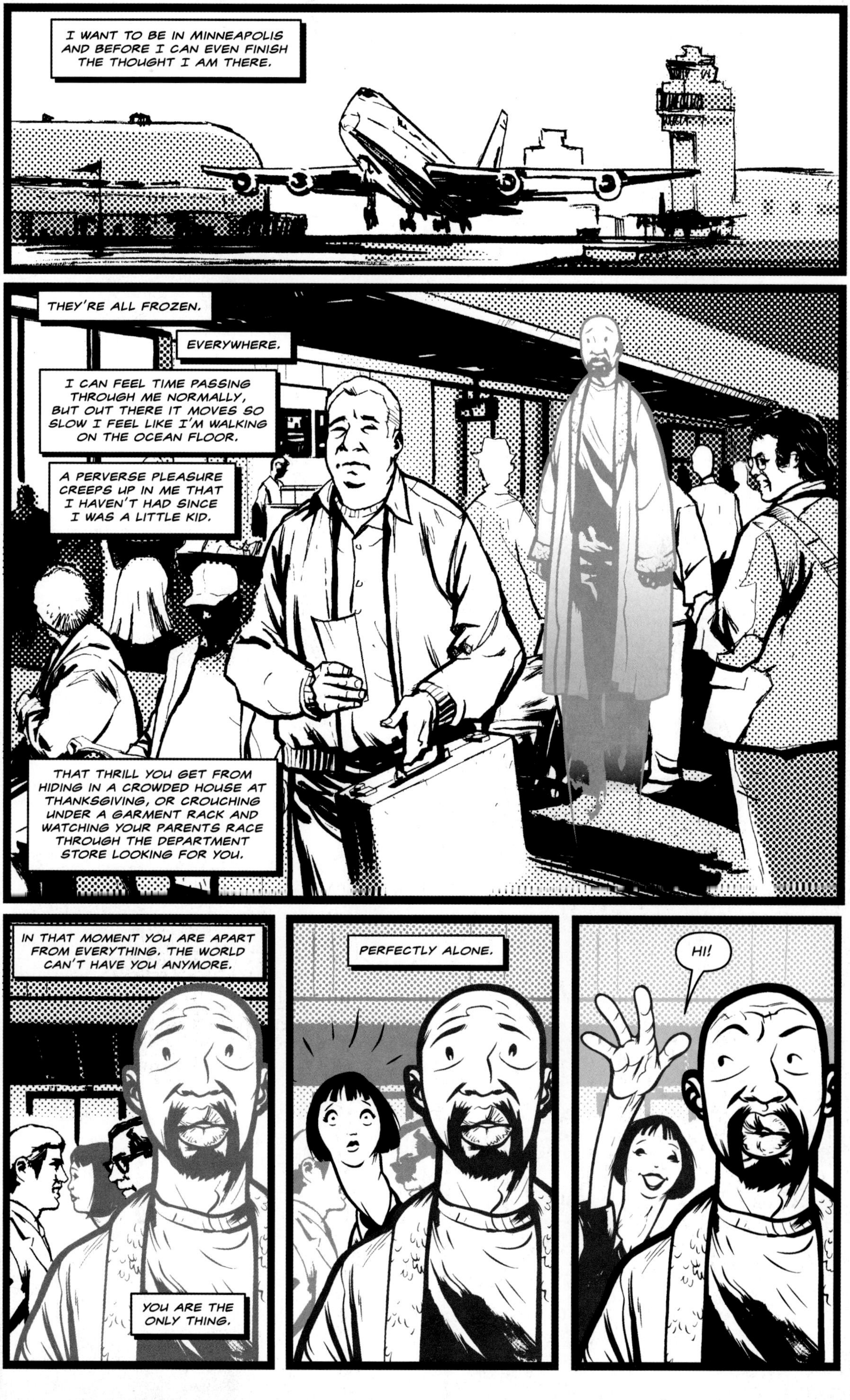
I WANT TO BE IN MINNEAPOLIS AND BEFORE I CAN EVEN FINISH THE THOUGHT I AM THERE.
THEY'RE ALL FROZEN.
EVERYWHERE.
I CAN FEEL TIME PASSING THROUGH ME NORMALLY, BUT OUT THERE IT MOVES SO SLOW I FEEL LIKE I'M WALKING ON THE OCEAN FLOOR.
A PERVERSE PLEASURE CREEPS UP IN ME THAT I HAVEN'T HAD SINCE I WAS A LITTLE KID.
THAT THRILL YOU GET FROM HIDING IN A CROWDED HOUSE AT THANKSGIVING, OR CROUCHING UNDER A GARMENT RACK AND WATCHING YOUR PARENTS RACE THROUGH THE DEPARTMENT STORE LOOKING FOR YOU.
IN THAT MOMENT YOU ARE APART FROM EVERYTHING. THE WORLD CAN'T HAVE YOU ANYMORE.
YOU ARE THE ONLY THING.
PERFECTLY ALONE.
HI!

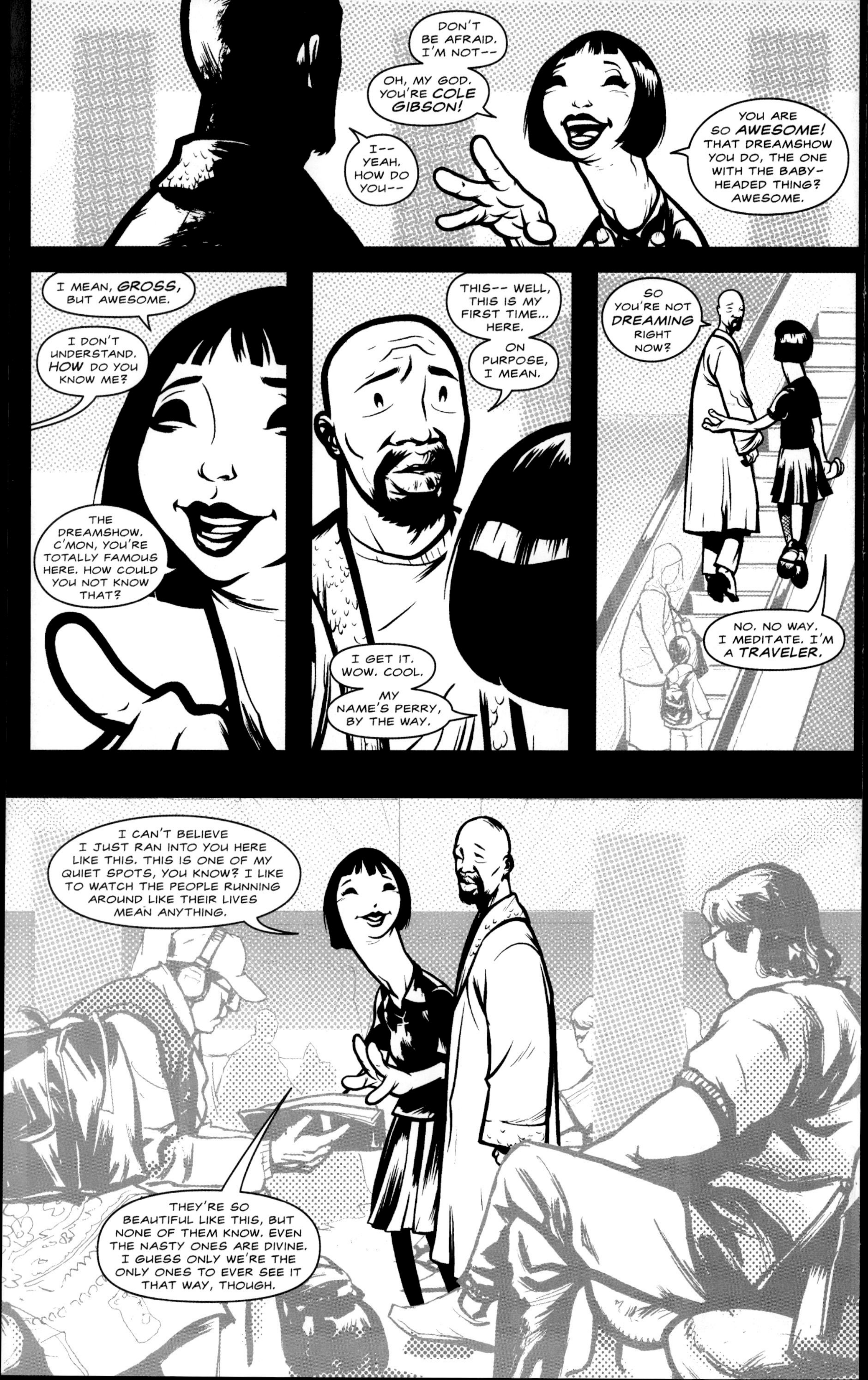
DON'T BE AFRAID. I'M NOT--
OH, MY GOD. YOU'RE COLE GIBSON!
I-- YEAH. HOW DO YOU--
YOU ARE SO AWESOME! THAT DREAMSHOW YOU DO, THE ONE WITH THE BABY-HEADED THING? AWESOME.
I MEAN, GROSS, BUT AWESOME.
I DON'T UNDERSTAND. HOW DO YOU KNOW ME?
THE DREAMSHOW. C'MON, YOU'RE TOTALLY FAMOUS HERE. HOW COULD YOU NOT KNOW THAT?
THIS-- WELL, THIS IS MY FIRST TIME... HERE.
ON PURPOSE, I MEAN.
I GET IT. WOW. COOL.
MY NAME'S PERRY, BY THE WAY.
SO YOU'RE NOT DREAMING RIGHT NOW?
NO. NO WAY. I MEDITATE. I'M A TRAVELER.
I CAN'T BELIEVE I JUST RAN INTO YOU HERE LIKE THIS. THIS IS ONE OF MY QUIET SPOTS, YOU KNOW? I LIKE TO WATCH THE PEOPLE RUNNING AROUND LIKE THEIR LIVES MEAN ANYTHING.
THEY'RE SO BEAUTIFUL LIKE THIS, BUT NONE OF THEM KNOW. EVEN THE NASTY ONES ARE DIVINE. I GUESS ONLY WE'RE THE ONLY ONES TO EVER SEE IT THAT WAY, THOUGH.

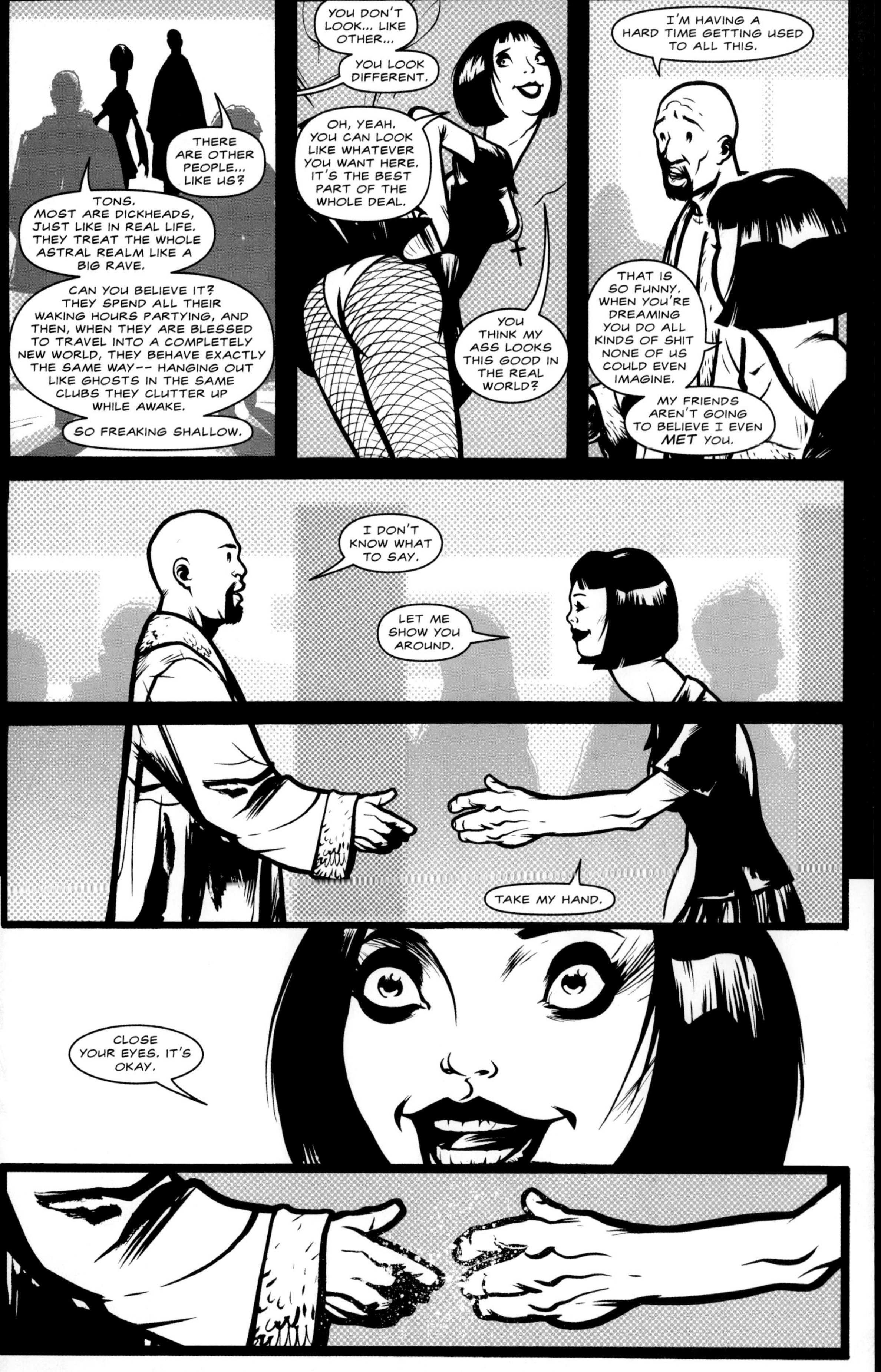
THERE ARE OTHER PEOPLE... LIKE US?
TONS. MOST ARE DICKHEADS, JUST LIKE IN REAL LIFE. THEY TREAT THE WHOLE ASTRAL REALM LIKE A BIG RAVE.
CAN YOU BELIEVE IT? THEY SPEND ALL THEIR WAKING HOURS PARTYING, AND THEN, WHEN THEY ARE BLESSED TO TRAVEL INTO A COMPLETELY NEW WORLD, THEY BEHAVE EXACTLY THE SAME WAY-- HANGING OUT LIKE GHOSTS IN THE SAME CLUBS THEY CLUTTER UP WHILE AWAKE.
SO FREAKING SHALLOW.
YOU DON'T LOOK... LIKE OTHER...
YOU LOOK DIFFERENT.
OH, YEAH. YOU CAN LOOK LIKE WHATEVER YOU WANT HERE. IT'S THE BEST PART OF THE WHOLE DEAL.
YOU THINK MY ASS LOOKS THIS GOOD IN THE REAL WORLD?
I'M HAVING A HARD TIME GETTING USED TO ALL THIS.
THAT IS SO FUNNY. WHEN YOU'RE DREAMING YOU DO ALL KINDS OF SHIT NONE OF US COULD EVEN IMAGINE.
MY FRIENDS AREN'T GOING TO BELIEVE I EVEN MET YOU.
I DON'T KNOW WHAT TO SAY.
LET ME SHOW YOU AROUND.
TAKE MY HAND.
CLOSE YOUR EYES. IT'S OKAY.

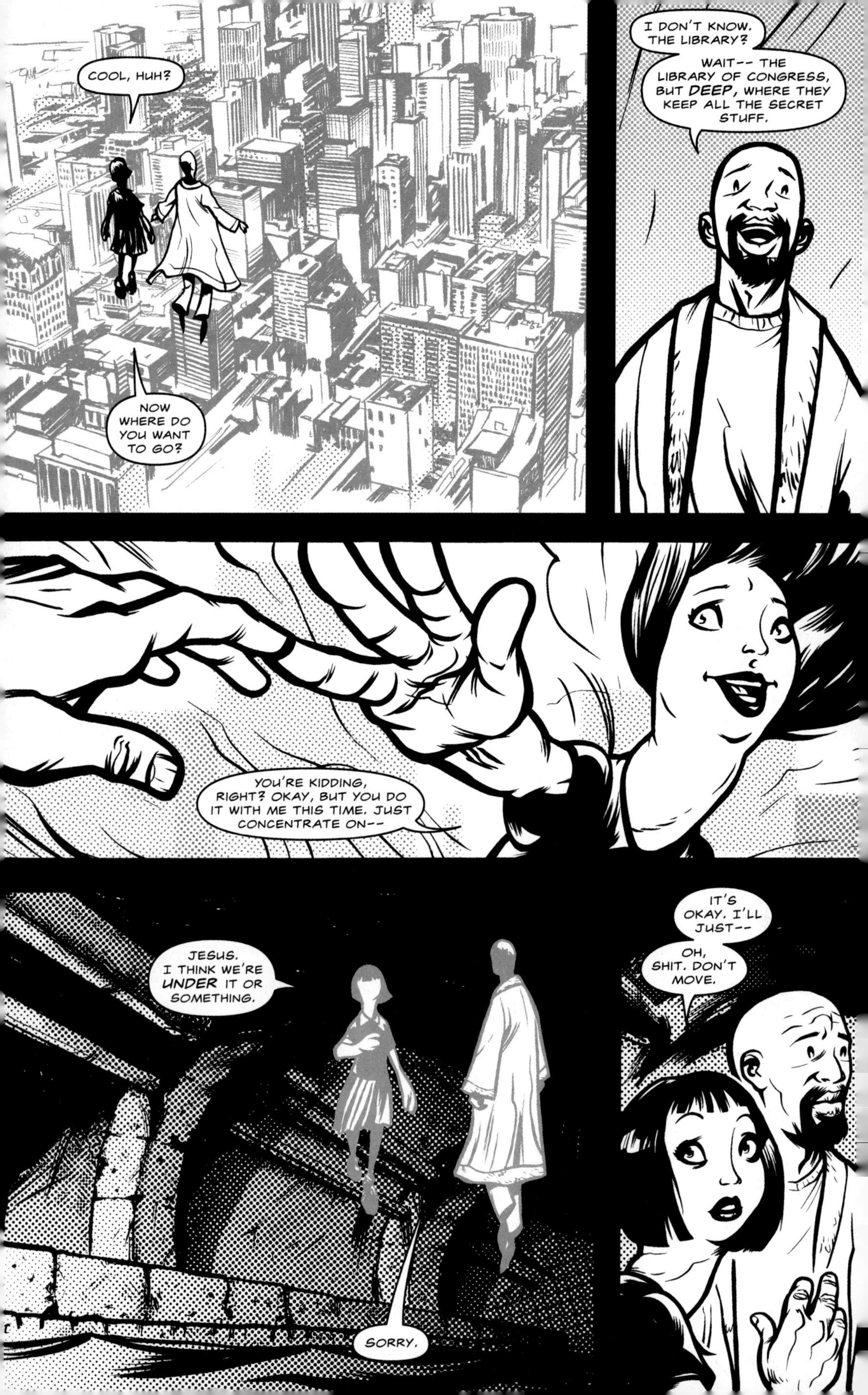
COOL, HUH?
NOW WHERE DO YOU WANT TO GO?
I DON'T KNOW. THE LIBRARY?
WAIT-- THE LIBRARY OF CONGRESS, BUT DEEP, WHERE THEY KEEP ALL THE SECRET STUFF.
YOU'RE KIDDING, RIGHT? OKAY, BUT YOU DO IT WITH ME THIS TIME. JUST CONCENTRATE ON--
JESUS. I THINK WE'RE UNDER IT OR SOMETHING.
SORRY.
IT'S OKAY. I'LL JUST--
OH, SHIT. DON'T MOVE.

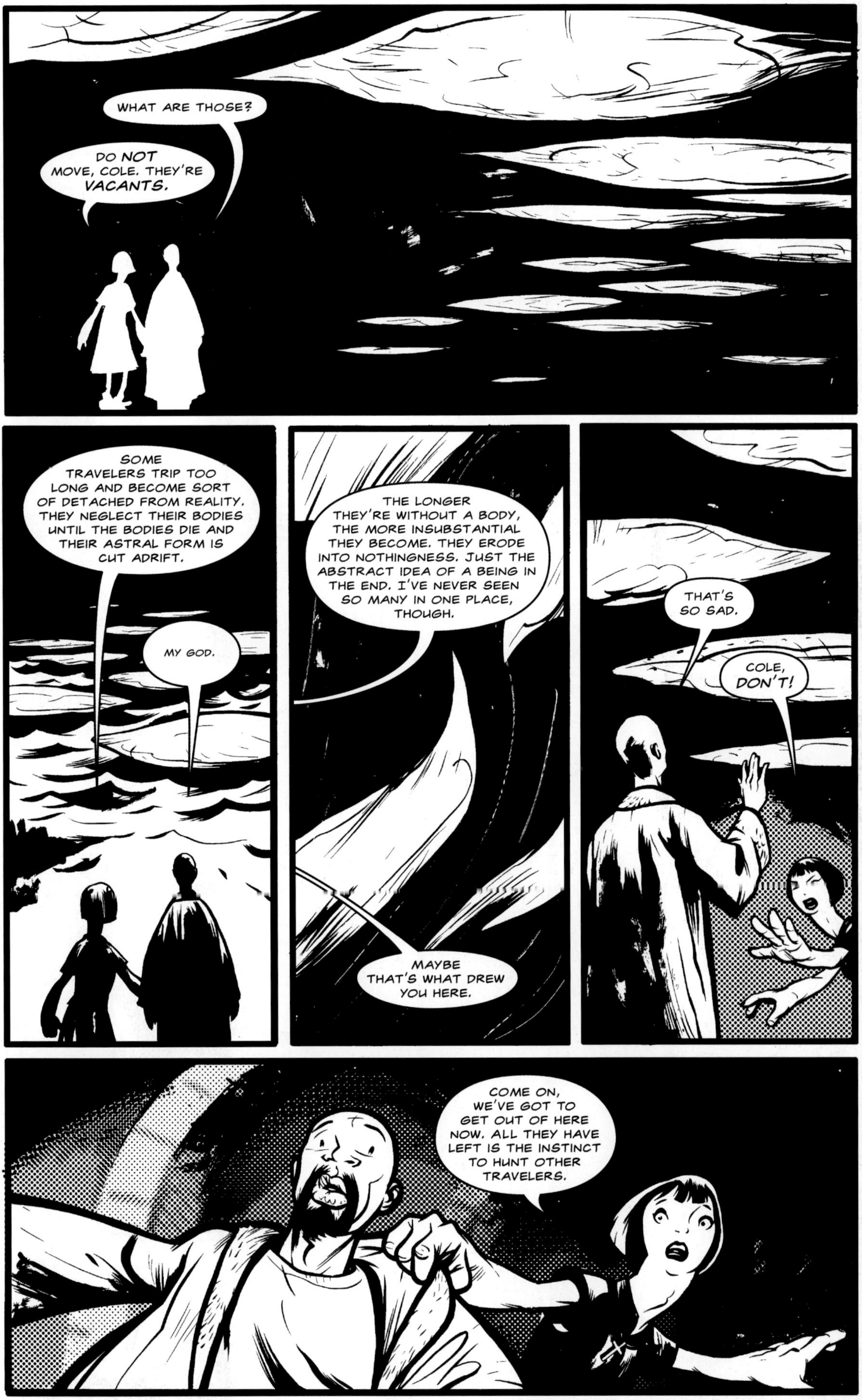
WHAT ARE THOSE?
DO NOT MOVE, COLE. THEY'RE VACANTS.
SOME TRAVELERS TRIP TOO LONG AND BECOME SORT OF DETACHED FROM REALITY. THEY NEGLECT THEIR BODIES UNTIL THE BODIES DIE AND THEIR ASTRAL FORM IS CUT ADRIFT.
MY GOD.
THE LONGER THEY'RE WITHOUT A BODY, THE MORE INSUBSTANTIAL THEY BECOME. THEY ERODE INTO NOTHINGNESS. JUST THE ABSTRACT IDEA OF A BEING IN THE END. I'VE NEVER SEEN SO MANY IN ONE PLACE, THOUGH.
MAYBE THAT'S WHAT DREW YOU HERE.
THAT'S SO SAD.
COLE, DON'T!
COME ON, WE'VE GOT TO GET OUT OF HERE NOW. ALL THEY HAVE LEFT IS THE INSTINCT TO HUNT OTHER TRAVELERS.

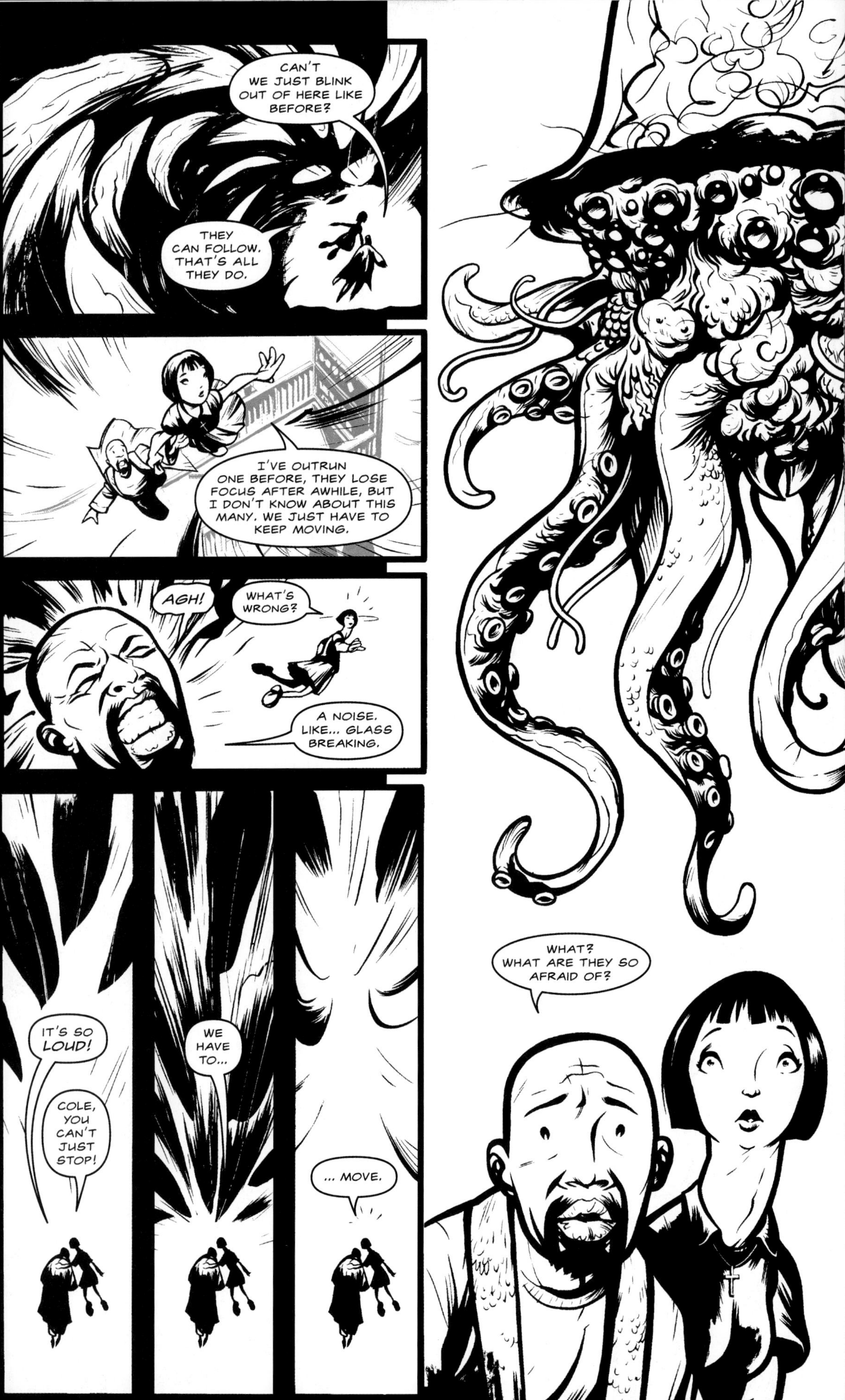
CAN'T WE JUST BLINK OUT OF HERE LIKE BEFORE?
THEY CAN FOLLOW. THAT'S ALL THEY DO.
I'VE OUTRUN ONE BEFORE, THEY LOSE FOCUS AFTER AWHILE, BUT I DON'T KNOW ABOUT THIS MANY. WE JUST HAVE TO KEEP MOVING.
AGH!
WHAT'S WRONG?
A NOISE. LIKE... GLASS BREAKING.
IT'S SO LOUD!
COLE, YOU CAN'T JUST STOP!
WE HAVE TO...
... MOVE.
WHAT? WHAT ARE THEY SO AFRAID OF?

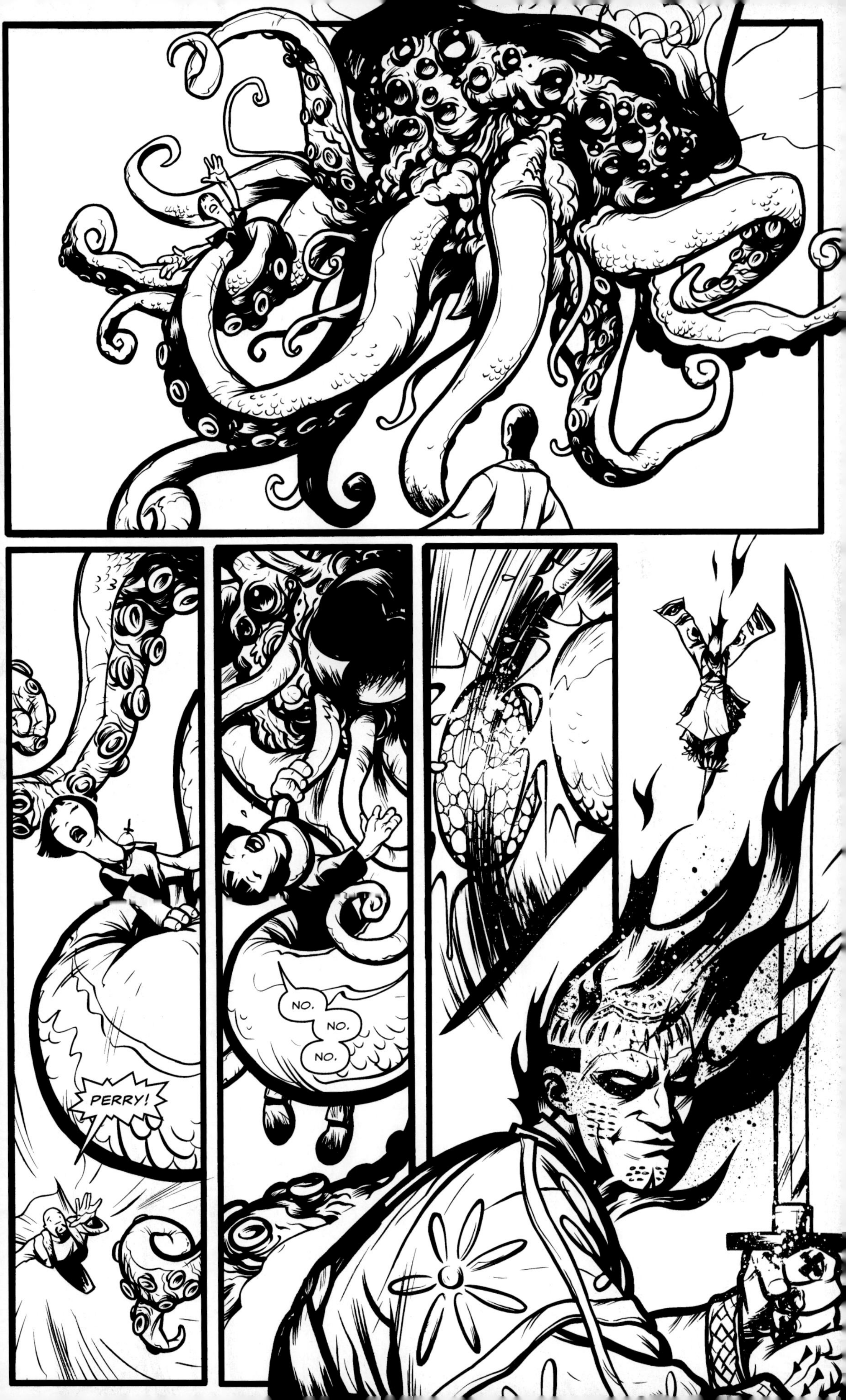
PERRY!
NO.
NO.
NO.

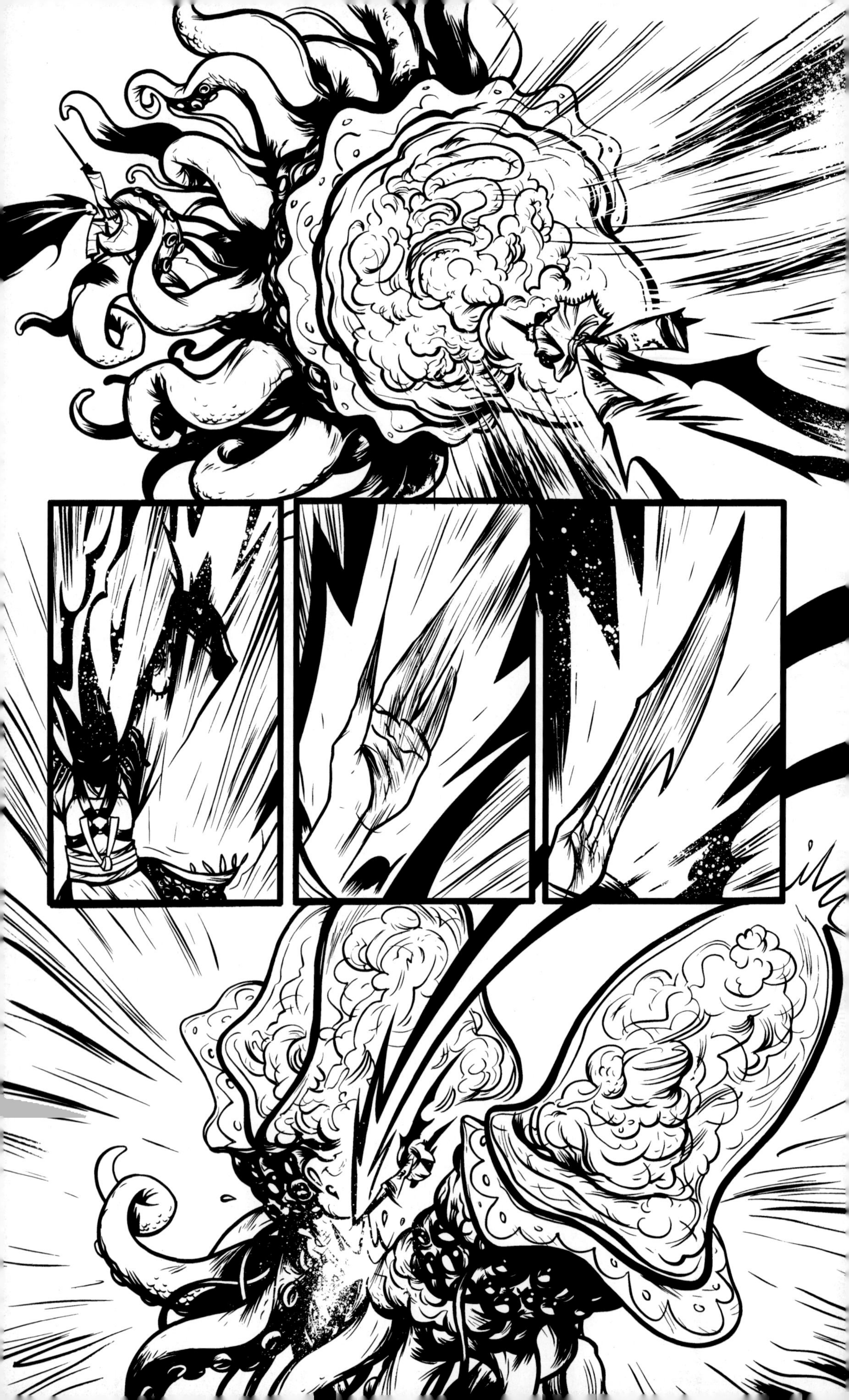

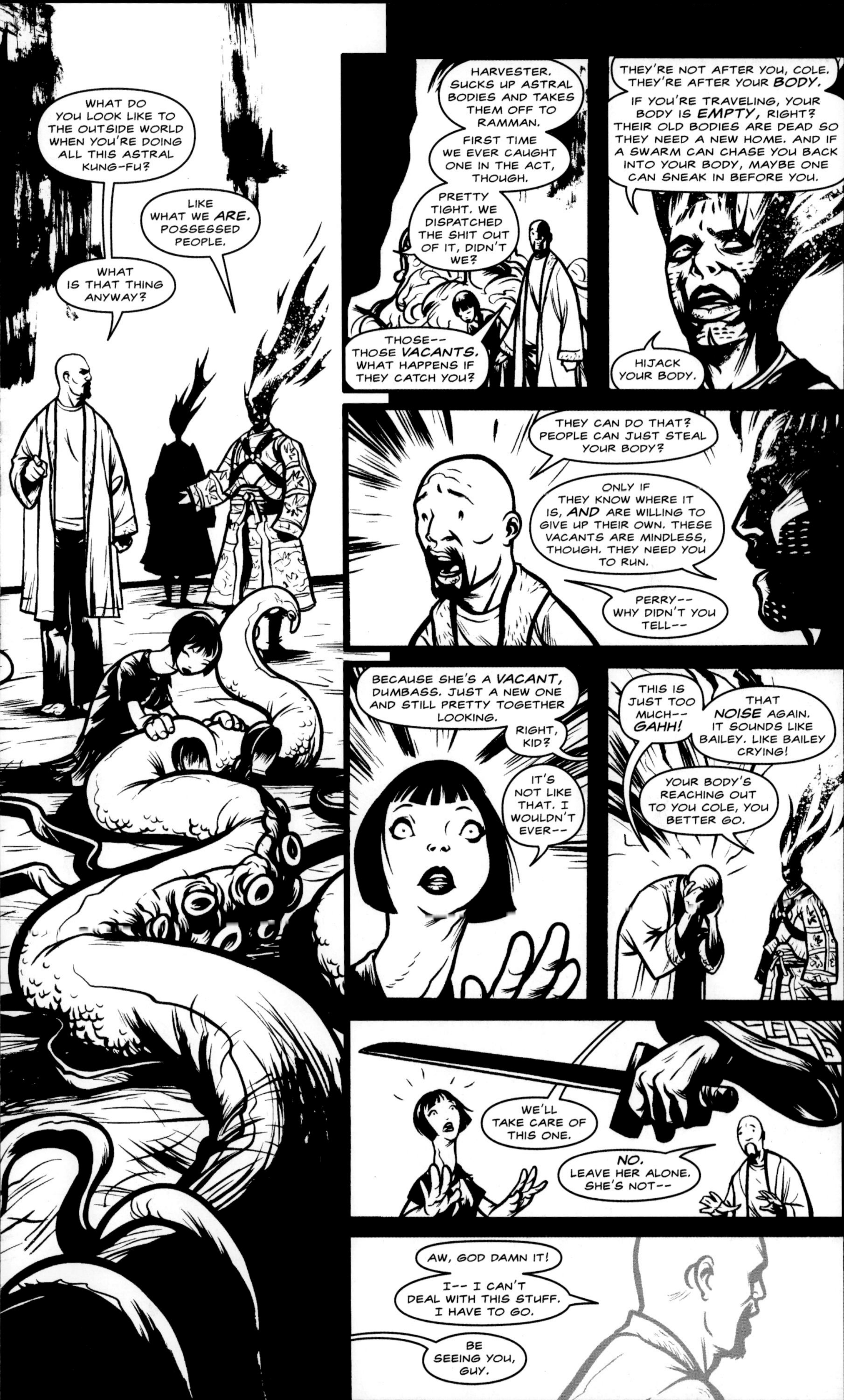
WHAT DO YOU LOOK LIKE TO THE OUTSIDE WORLD WHEN YOU'RE DOING ALL THIS ASTRAL KUNG-FU?
LIKE WHAT WE ARE. POSSESSED PEOPLE.
WHAT IS THAT THING ANYWAY?
HARVESTER. SUCKS UP ASTRAL BODIES AND TAKES THEM OFF TO RAMMAN.
FIRST TIME WE EVER CAUGHT ONE IN THE ACT, THOUGH.
PRETTY TIGHT. WE DISPATCHED THE SHIT OUT OF IT, DIDN'T WE?
THOSE-- THOSE VACANTS. WHAT HAPPENS IF THEY CATCH YOU?
THEY'RE NOT AFTER YOU, COLE. THEY'RE AFTER YOUR BODY.
IF YOU'RE TRAVELING, YOUR BODY IS EMPTY, RIGHT? THEIR OLD BODIES ARE DEAD SO THEY NEED A NEW HOME. AND IF A SWARM CAN CHASE YOU BACK INTO YOUR BODY, MAYBE ONE CAN SNEAK IN BEFORE YOU.
HIJACK YOUR BODY.
THEY CAN DO THAT? PEOPLE CAN JUST STEAL YOUR BODY?
ONLY IF THEY KNOW WHERE IT IS, AND ARE WILLING TO GIVE UP THEIR OWN. THESE VACANTS ARE MINDLESS, THOUGH. THEY NEED YOU TO RUN.
PERRY-- WHY DIDN'T YOU TELL--
BECAUSE SHE'S A VACANT, DUMBASS. JUST A NEW ONE AND STILL PRETTY TOGETHER LOOKING.
RIGHT, KID?
IT'S NOT LIKE THAT. I WOULDN'T EVER--
THIS IS JUST TOO MUCH-- GAHH!
THAT NOISE AGAIN. IT SOUNDS LIKE BAILEY. LIKE BAILEY CRYING!
YOUR BODY'S REACHING OUT TO YOU COLE, YOU BETTER GO.
WE'LL TAKE CARE OF THIS ONE.
NO. LEAVE HER ALONE. SHE'S NOT--
AW, GOD DAMN IT!
I-- I CAN'T DEAL WITH THIS STUFF. I HAVE TO GO.
BE SEEING YOU, GUY.

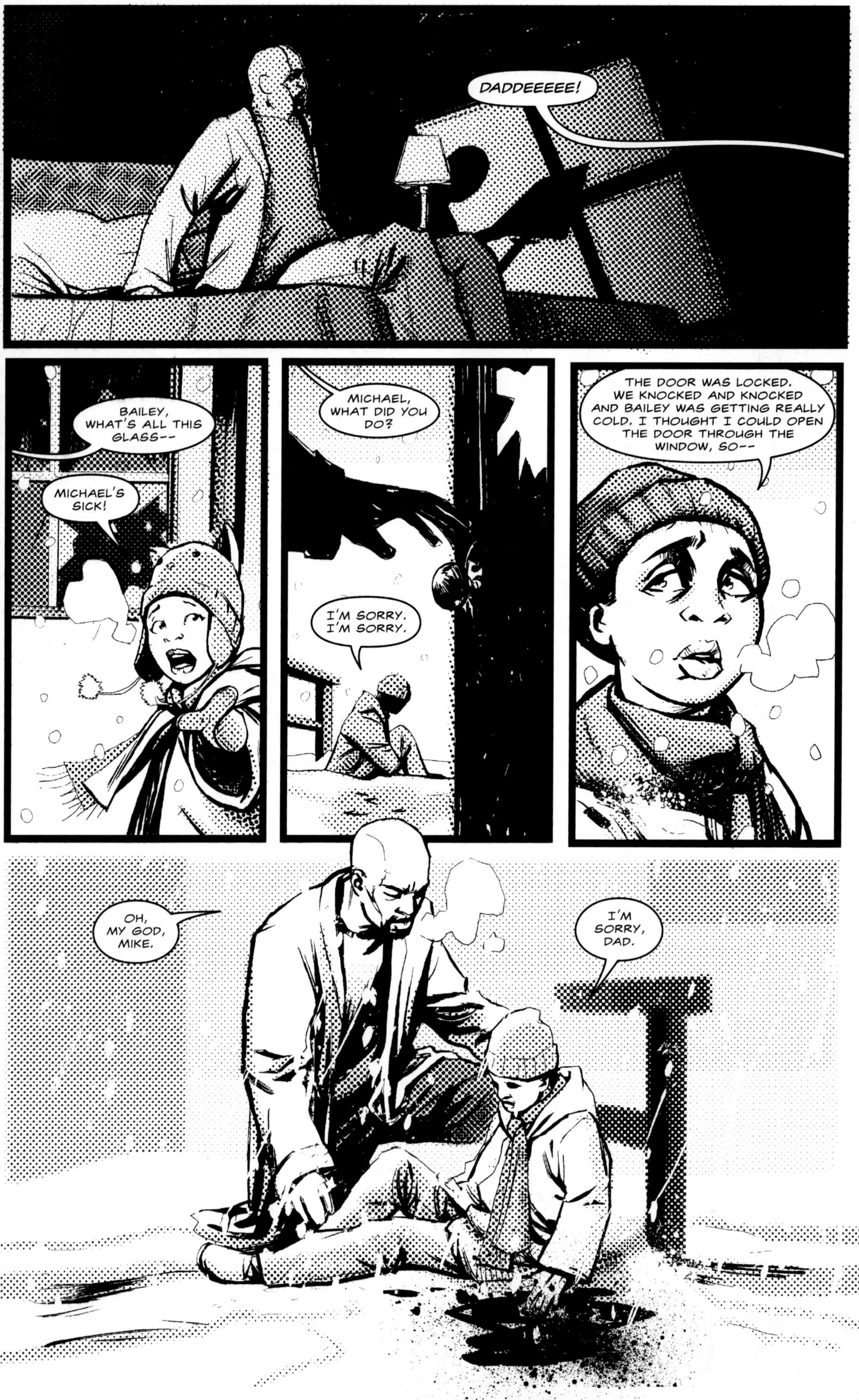
DADDEEEEE!
BAILEY, WHAT'S ALL THIS GLASS--
MICHAEL'S SICK!
MICHAEL, WHAT DID YOU DO?
I'M SORRY. I'M SORRY.
THE DOOR WAS LOCKED. WE KNOCKED AND KNOCKED AND BAILEY WAS GETTING REALLY COLD. I THOUGHT I COULD OPEN THE DOOR THROUGH THE WINDOW, SO--
OH, MY GOD, MIKE.
I'M SORRY, DAD.

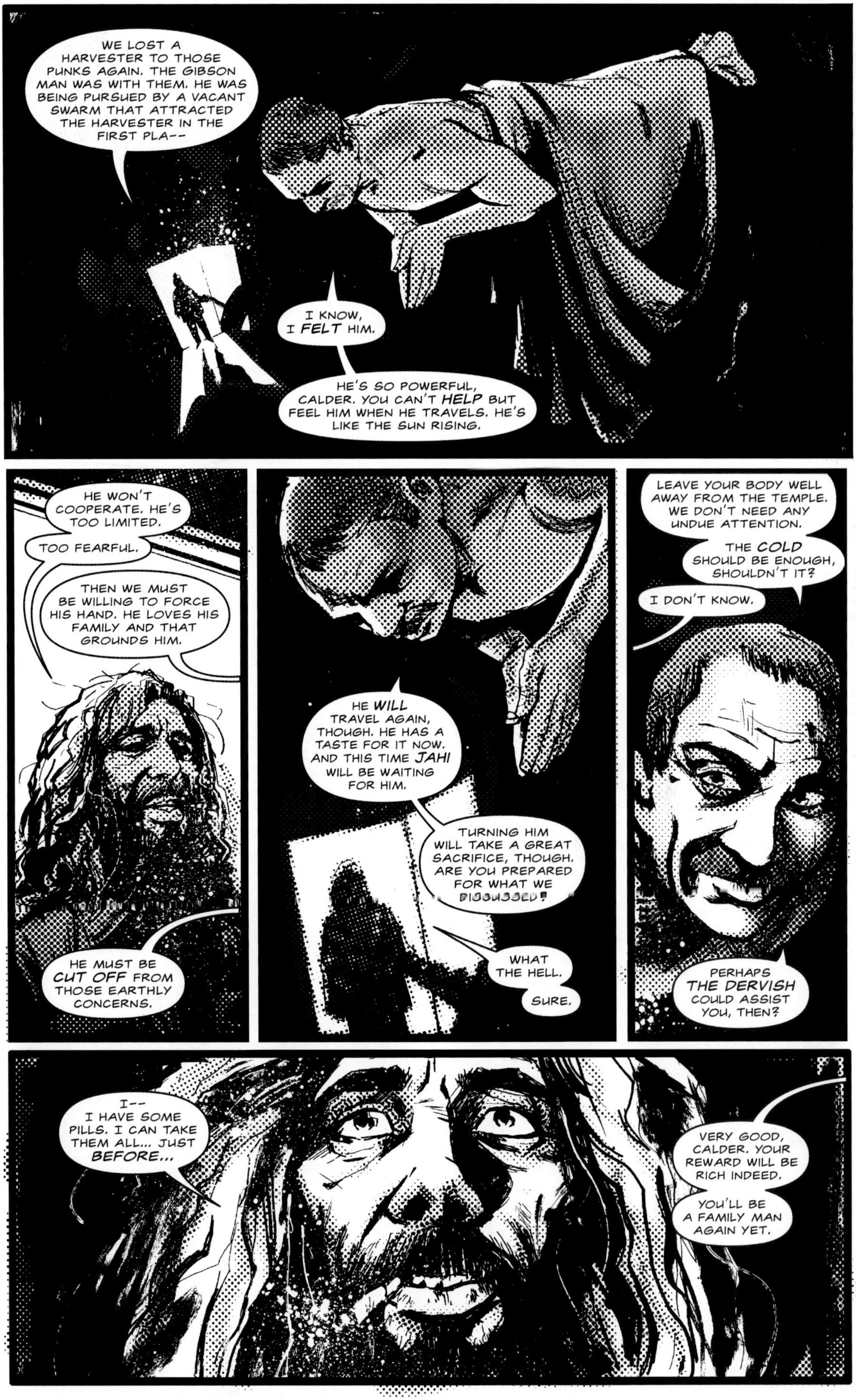
WE LOST A HARVESTER TO THOSE PUNKS AGAIN. THE GIBSON MAN WAS WITH THEM. HE WAS BEING PURSUED BY A VACANT SWARM THAT ATTRACTED THE HARVESTER IN THE FIRST PLA--
I KNOW, I FELT HIM.
HE'S SO POWERFUL, CALDER. YOU CAN'T HELP BUT FEEL HIM WHEN HE TRAVELS. HE'S LIKE THE SUN RISING.
HE WON'T COOPERATE. HE'S TOO LIMITED.
TOO FEARFUL.
THEN WE MUST BE WILLING TO FORCE HIS HAND. HE LOVES HIS FAMILY AND THAT GROUNDS HIM.
HE MUST BE CUT OFF FROM THOSE EARTHLY CONCERNS.
HE WILL TRAVEL AGAIN, THOUGH. HE HAS A TASTE FOR IT NOW. AND THIS TIME JAHI WILL BE WAITING FOR HIM.
TURNING HIM WILL TAKE A GREAT SACRIFICE, THOUGH. ARE YOU PREPARED FOR WHAT WE DISCUSSED?
WHAT THE HELL.
SURE.
LEAVE YOUR BODY WELL AWAY FROM THE TEMPLE. WE DON'T NEED ANY UNDUE ATTENTION.
THE COLD SHOULD BE ENOUGH, SHOULDN'T IT?
I DON'T KNOW.
PERHAPS THE DERVISH COULD ASSIST YOU, THEN?
I-- I HAVE SOME PILLS. I CAN TAKE THEM ALL... JUST BEFORE...
VERY GOOD, CALDER. YOUR REWARD WILL BE RICH INDEED.
YOU'LL BE A FAMILY MAN AGAIN YET.

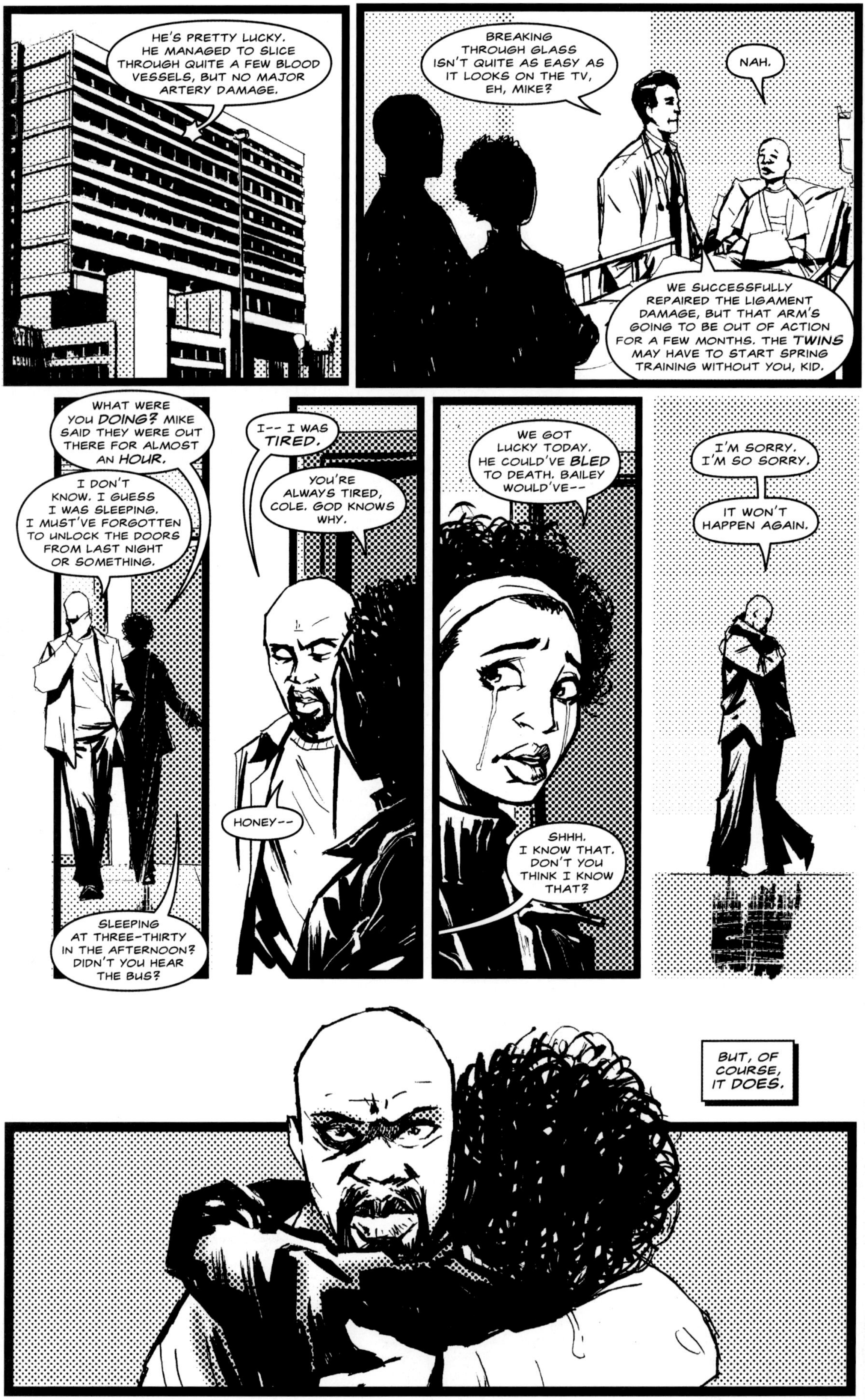
HE'S PRETTY LUCKY. HE MANAGED TO SLICE THROUGH QUITE A FEW BLOOD VESSELS, BUT NO MAJOR ARTERY DAMAGE.
BREAKING THROUGH GLASS ISN'T QUITE AS EASY AS IT LOOKS ON THE TV, EH, MIKE?
NAH.
WE SUCCESSFULLY REPAIRED THE LIGAMENT DAMAGE, BUT THAT ARM'S GOING TO BE OUT OF ACTION FOR A FEW MONTHS. THE TWINS MAY HAVE TO START SPRING TRAINING WITHOUT YOU, KID.
WHAT WERE YOU DOING? MIKE SAID THEY WERE OUT THERE FOR ALMOST AN HOUR.
I DON'T KNOW. I GUESS I WAS SLEEPING. I MUST'VE FORGOTTEN TO UNLOCK THE DOORS FROM LAST NIGHT OR SOMETHING.
SLEEPING AT THREE-THIRTY IN THE AFTERNOON? DIDN'T YOU HEAR THE BUS?
I-- I WAS TIRED.
YOU'RE ALWAYS TIRED, COLE. GOD KNOWS WHY.
HONEY--
WE GOT LUCKY TODAY. HE COULD'VE BLED TO DEATH. BAILEY WOULD'VE--
SHHH. I KNOW THAT. DON'T YOU THINK I KNOW THAT?
I'M SORRY. I'M SO SORRY.
IT WON'T HAPPEN AGAIN.
BUT, OF COURSE, IT DOES.

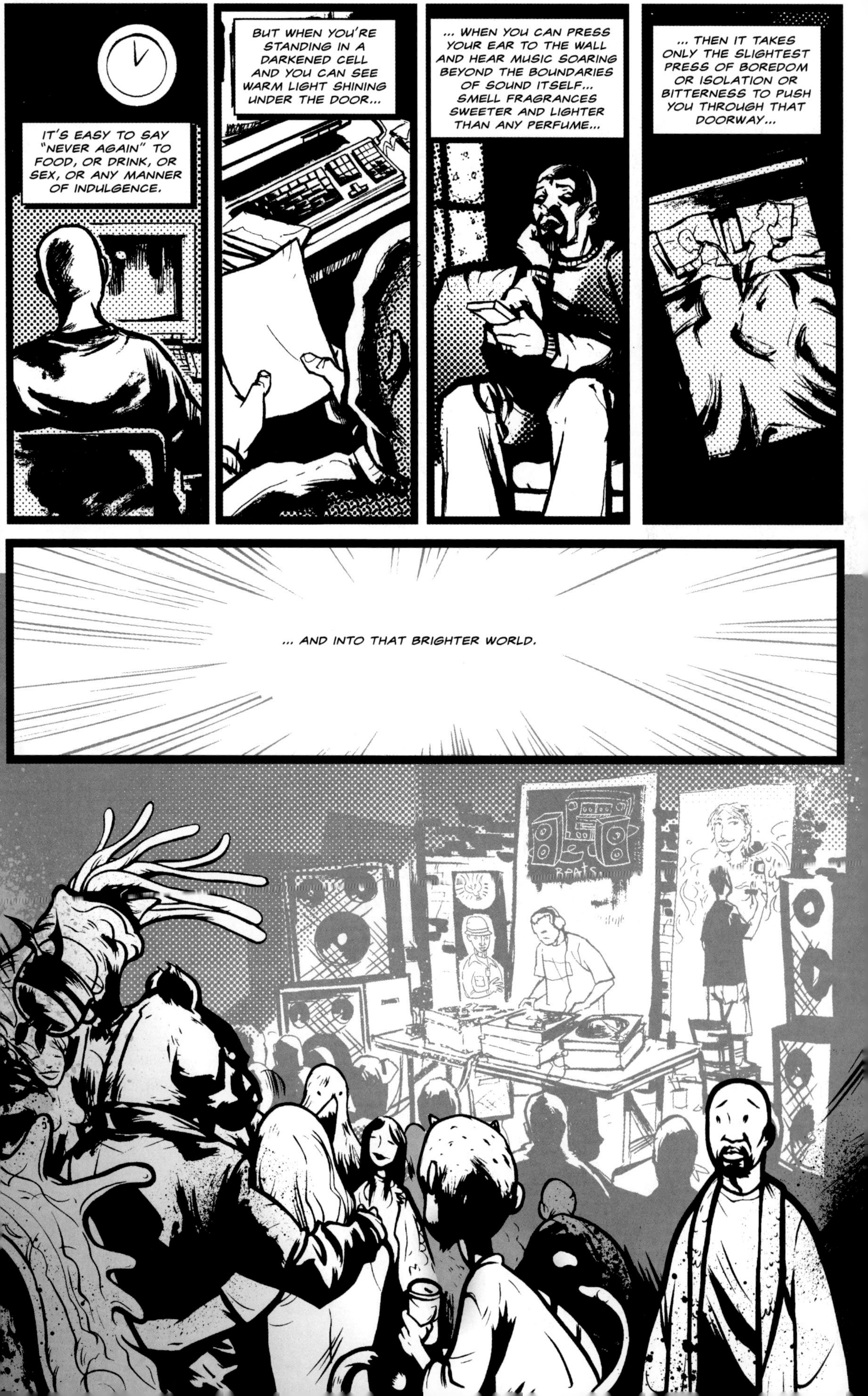
IT'S EASY TO SAY "NEVER AGAIN" TO FOOD, OR DRINK, OR SEX, OR ANY MANNER OF INDULGENCE.
BUT WHEN YOU'RE STANDING IN A DARKENED CELL AND YOU CAN SEE WARM LIGHT SHINING UNDER THE DOOR...
... WHEN YOU CAN PRESS YOUR EAR TO THE WALL AND HEAR MUSIC SOARING BEYOND THE BOUNDARIES OF SOUND ITSELF... SMELL FRAGRANCES SWEETER AND LIGHTER THAN ANY PERFUME...
... THEN IT TAKES ONLY THE SLIGHTEST PRESS OF BOREDOM OR ISOLATION OR BITTERNESS TO PUSH YOU THROUGH THAT DOORWAY...
... AND INTO THAT BRIGHTER WORLD.

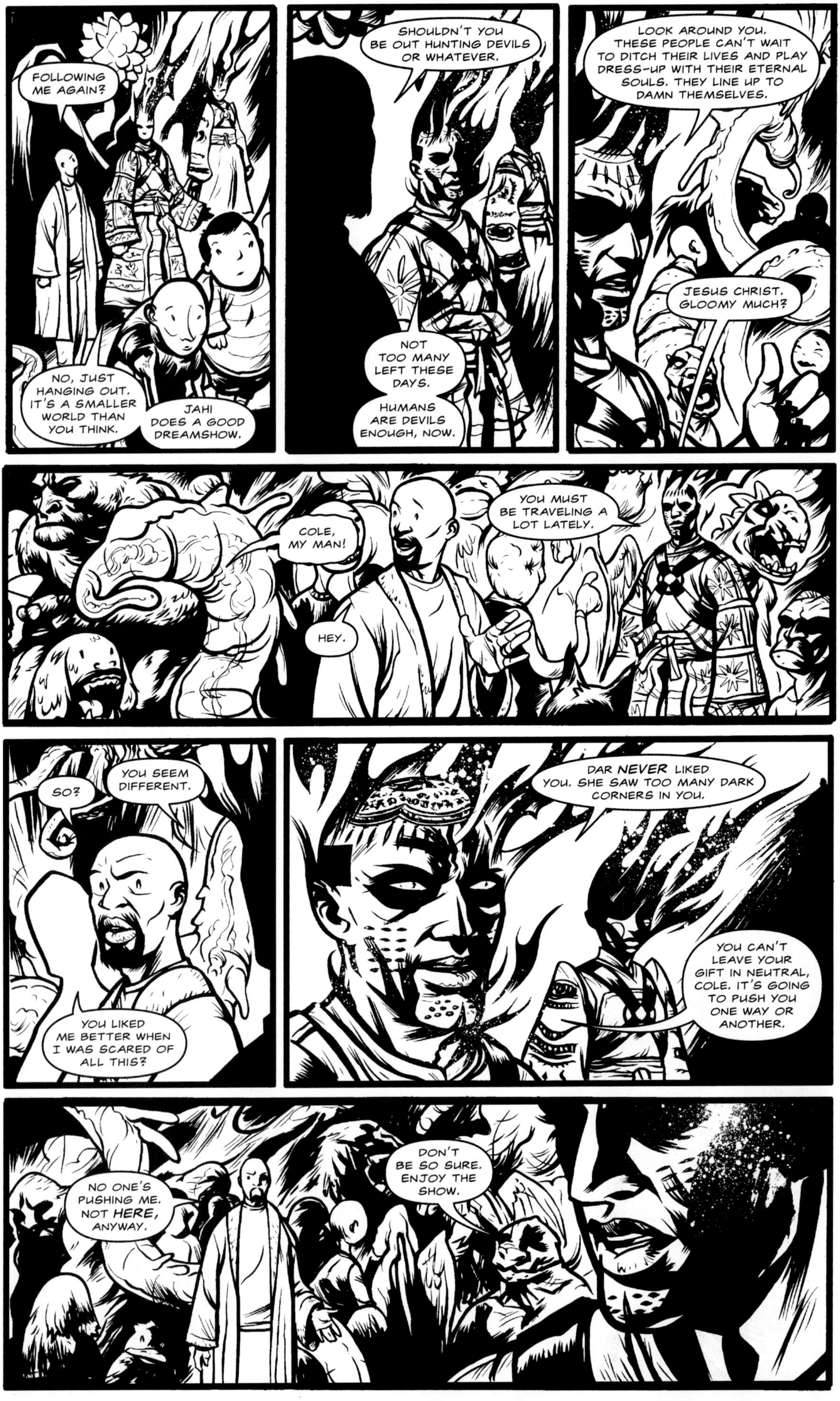
FOLLOWING ME AGAIN?
NO, JUST HANGING OUT. IT'S A SMALLER WORLD THAN YOU THINK.
JAHI DOES A GOOD DREAMSHOW.
SHOULDN'T YOU BE OUT HUNTING DEVILS OR WHATEVER.
NOT TOO MANY LEFT THESE DAYS.
HUMANS ARE DEVILS ENOUGH, NOW.
LOOK AROUND YOU. THESE PEOPLE CAN'T WAIT TO DITCH THEIR LIVES AND PLAY DRESS-UP WITH THEIR ETERNAL SOULS. THEY LINE UP TO DAMN THEMSELVES.
JESUS CHRIST. GLOOMY MUCH?
COLE, MY MAN!
HEY.
YOU MUST BE TRAVELING A LOT LATELY.
SO?
YOU SEEM DIFFERENT.
YOU LIKED ME BETTER WHEN I WAS SCARED OF ALL THIS?
DAR NEVER LIKED YOU. SHE SAW TOO MANY DARK CORNERS IN YOU.
YOU CAN'T LEAVE YOUR GIFT IN NEUTRAL, COLE. IT'S GOING TO PUSH YOU ONE WAY OR ANOTHER.
NO ONE'S PUSHING ME. NOT HERE, ANYWAY.
DON'T BE SO SURE. ENJOY THE SHOW.

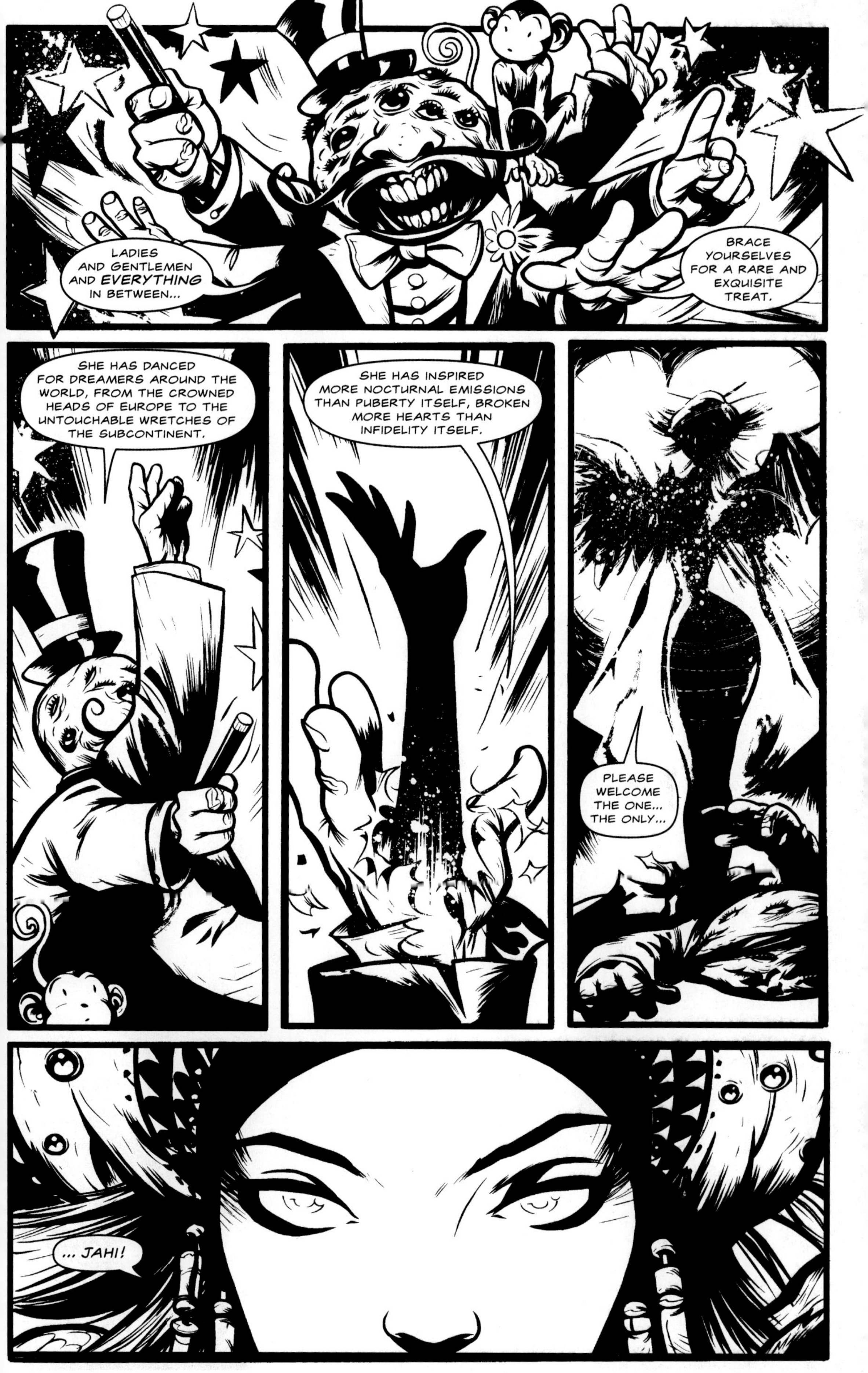

LADIES AND GENTLEMEN AND EVERYTHING IN BETWEEN...
BRACE YOURSELVES FOR A RARE AND EXQUISITE TREAT.
SHE HAS DANCED FOR DREAMERS AROUND THE WORLD, FROM THE CROWNED HEADS OF EUROPE TO THE UNTOUCHABLE WRETCHES OF THE SUBCONTINENT.
SHE HAS INSPIRED MORE NOCTURNAL EMISSIONS THAN PUBERTY ITSELF, BROKEN MORE HEARTS THAN INFIDELITY ITSELF.
PLEASE WELCOME THE ONE... THE ONLY...
... JAHI!

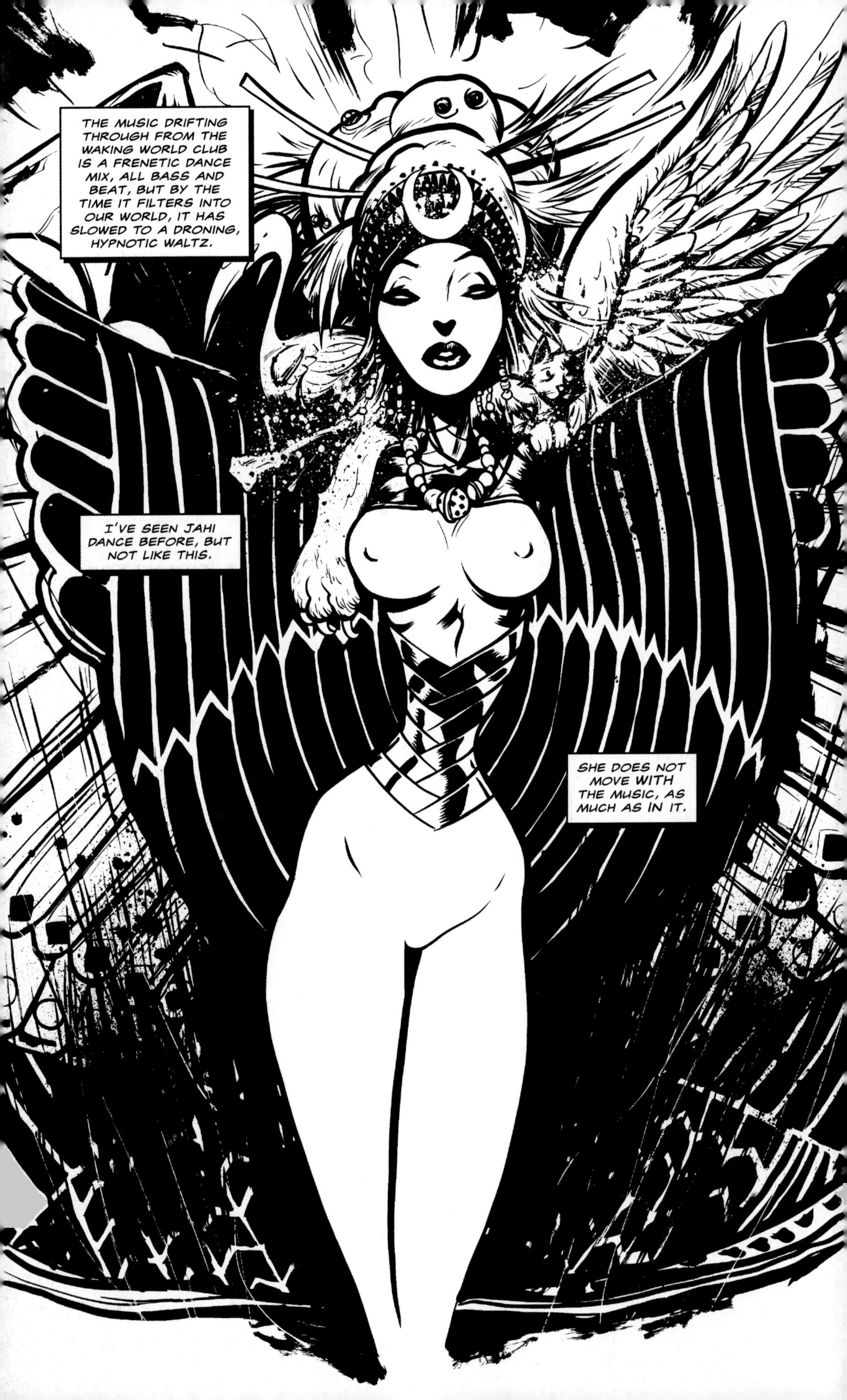
THE MUSIC DRIFTING THROUGH FROM THE WAKING WORLD CLUB IS A FRENETIC DANCE MIX, ALL BASS AND BEAT, BUT BY THE TIME IT FILTERS INTO OUR WORLD, IT HAS SLOWED TO A DRONING, HYPNOTIC WALTZ.
I'VE SEEN JAHI DANCE BEFORE, BUT NOT LIKE THIS.
SHE DOES NOT MOVE WITH THE MUSIC, AS MUCH AS IN IT.

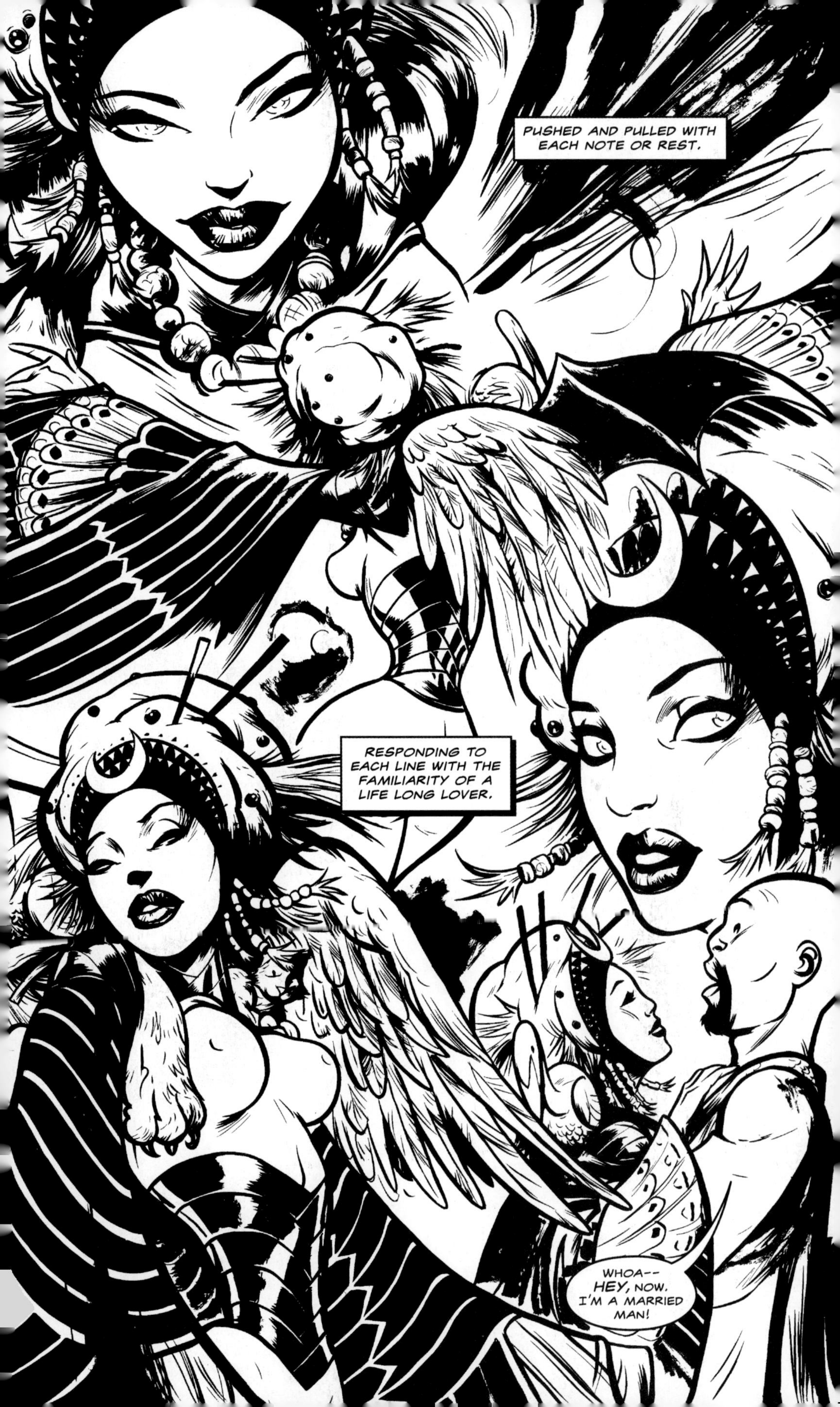
PUSHED AND PULLED WITH EACH NOTE OR REST.
RESPONDING TO EACH LINE WITH THE FAMILIARITY OF A LIFE LONG LOVER.
WHOA-- HEY, NOW. I'M A MARRIED MAN!

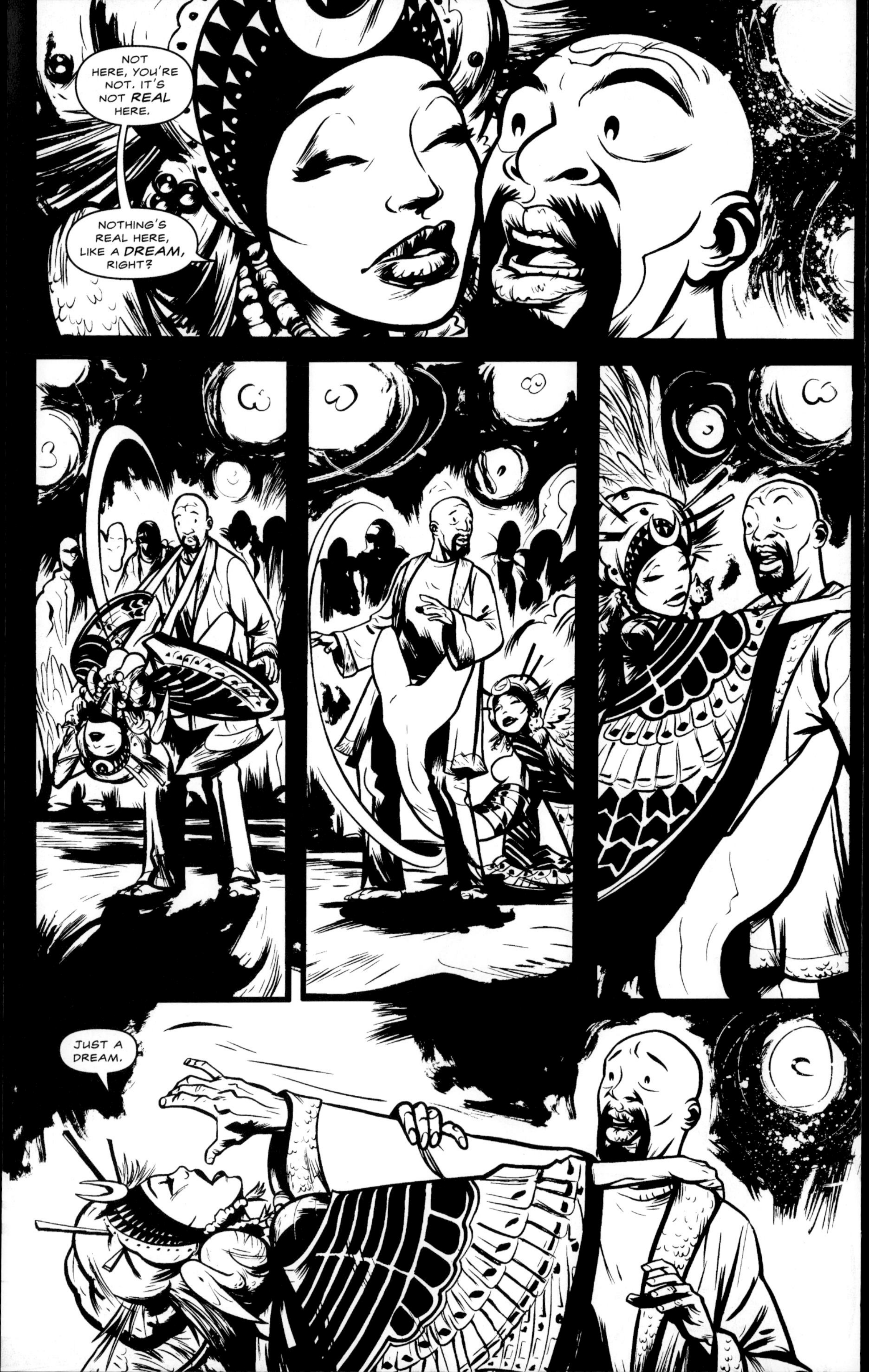
NOT HERE, YOU'RE NOT. IT'S NOT REAL HERE.
NOTHING'S REAL HERE, LIKE A DREAM, RIGHT?
JUST A DREAM.

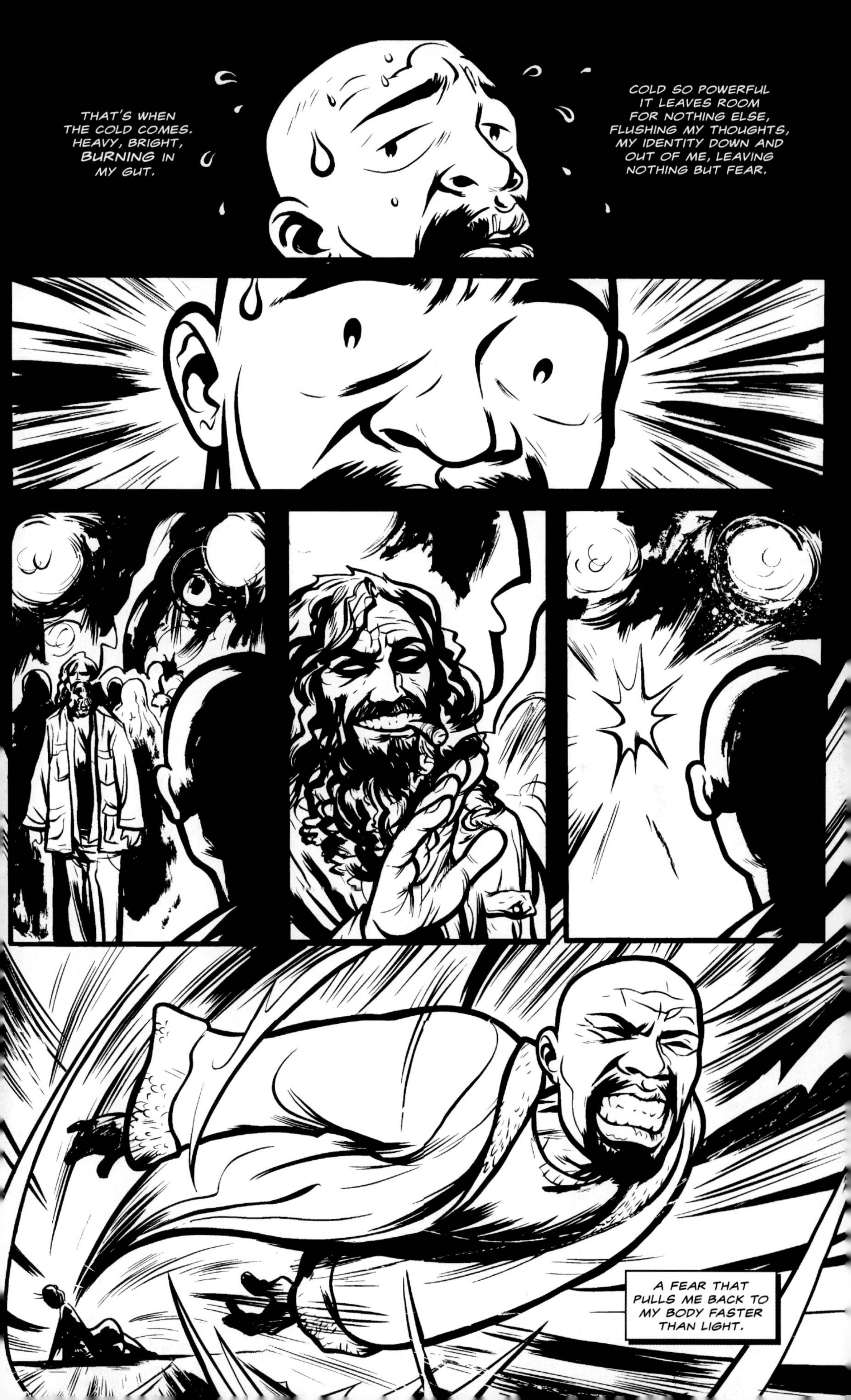
THAT'S WHEN THE COLD COMES. HEAVY, BRIGHT, BURNING IN MY GUT.
COLD SO POWERFUL IT LEAVES ROOM FOR NOTHING ELSE, FLUSHING MY THOUGHTS, MY IDENTITY DOWN AND OUT OF ME, LEAVING NOTHING BUT FEAR.
A FEAR THAT PULLS ME BACK TO MY BODY FASTER THAN LIGHT.

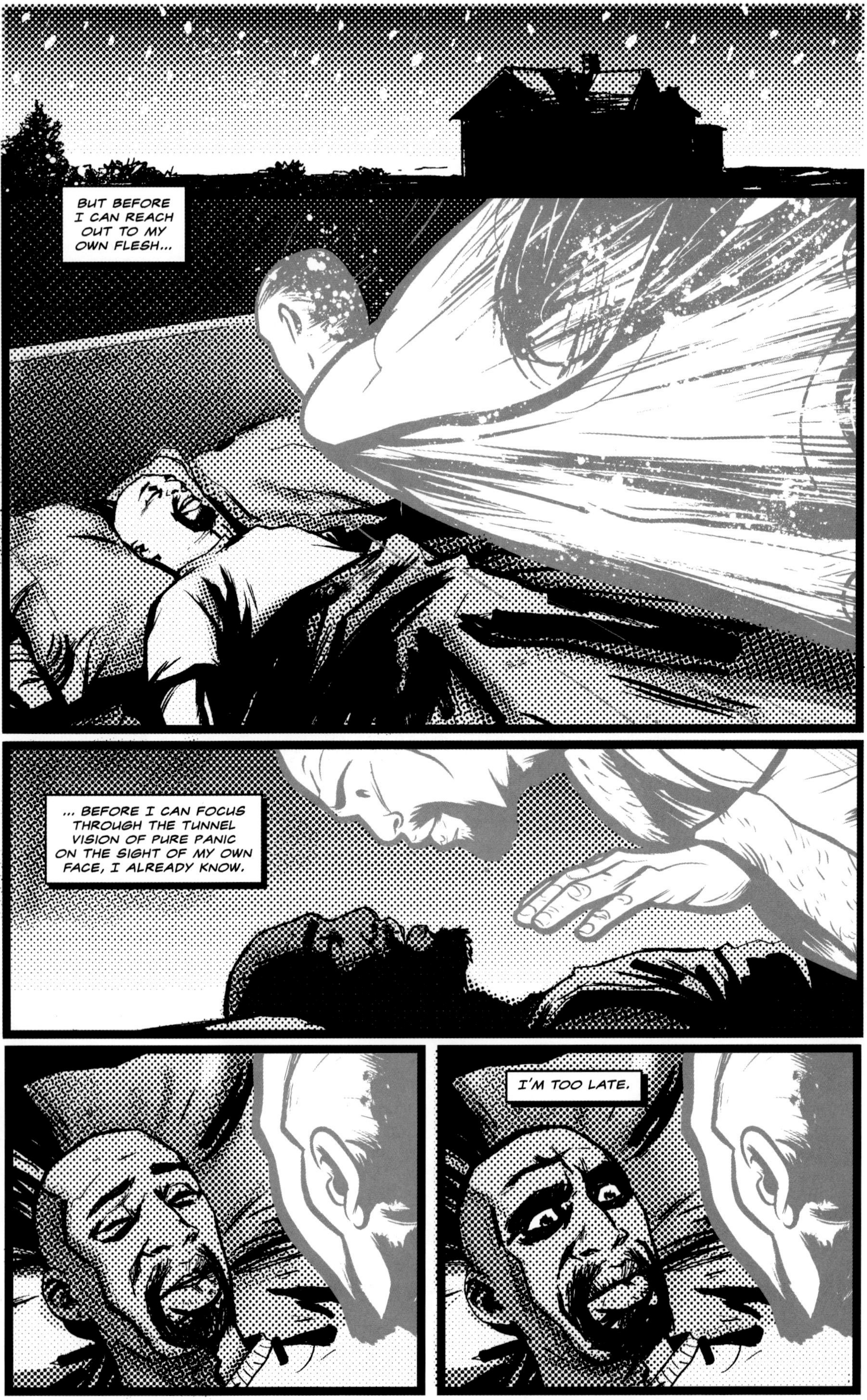
BUT BEFORE I CAN REACH OUT TO MY OWN FLESH...
... BEFORE I CAN FOCUS THROUGH THE TUNNEL VISION OF PURE PANIC ON THE SIGHT OF MY OWN FACE, I ALREADY KNOW.
I'M TOO LATE.

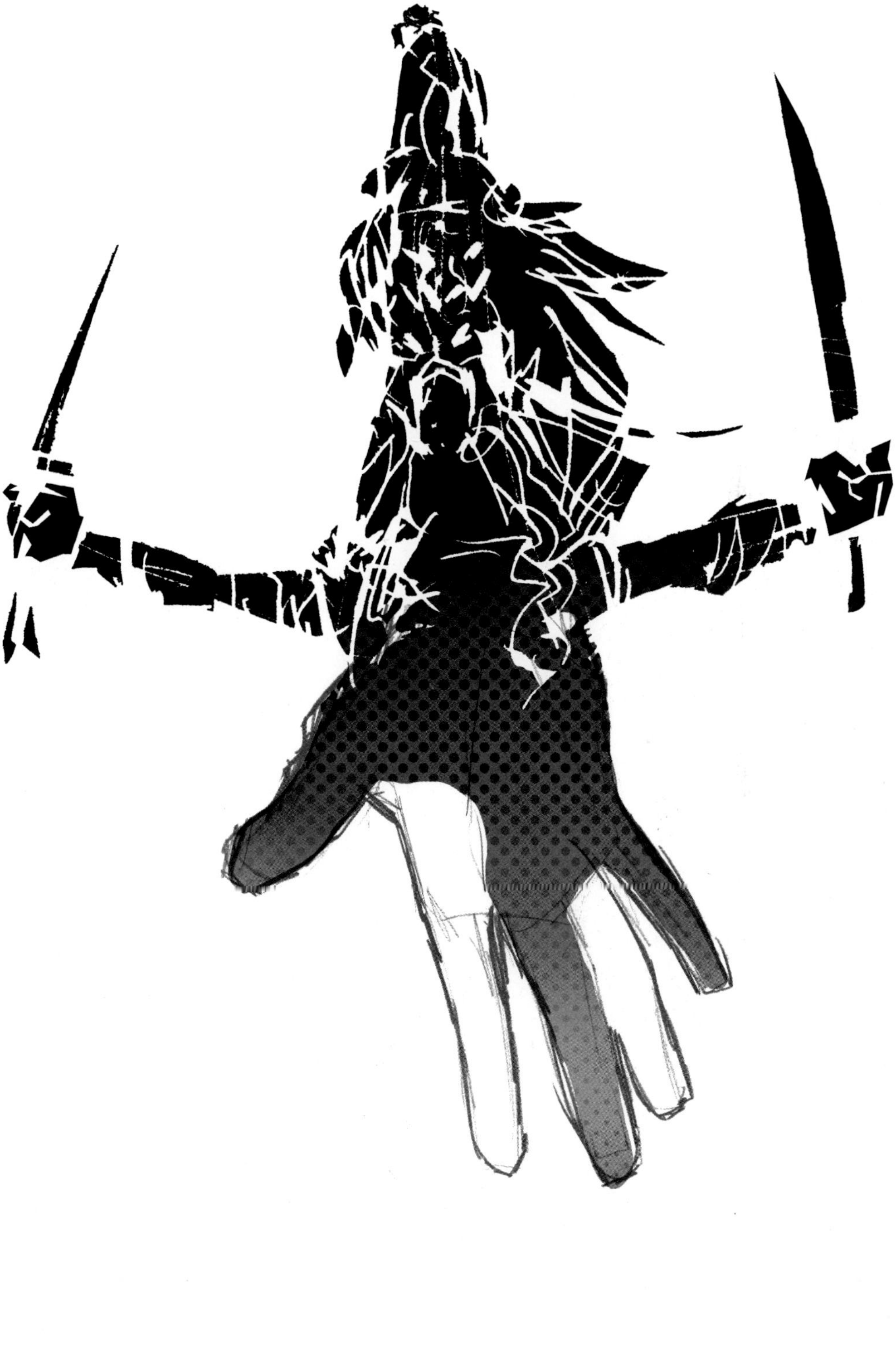

THE VACANT

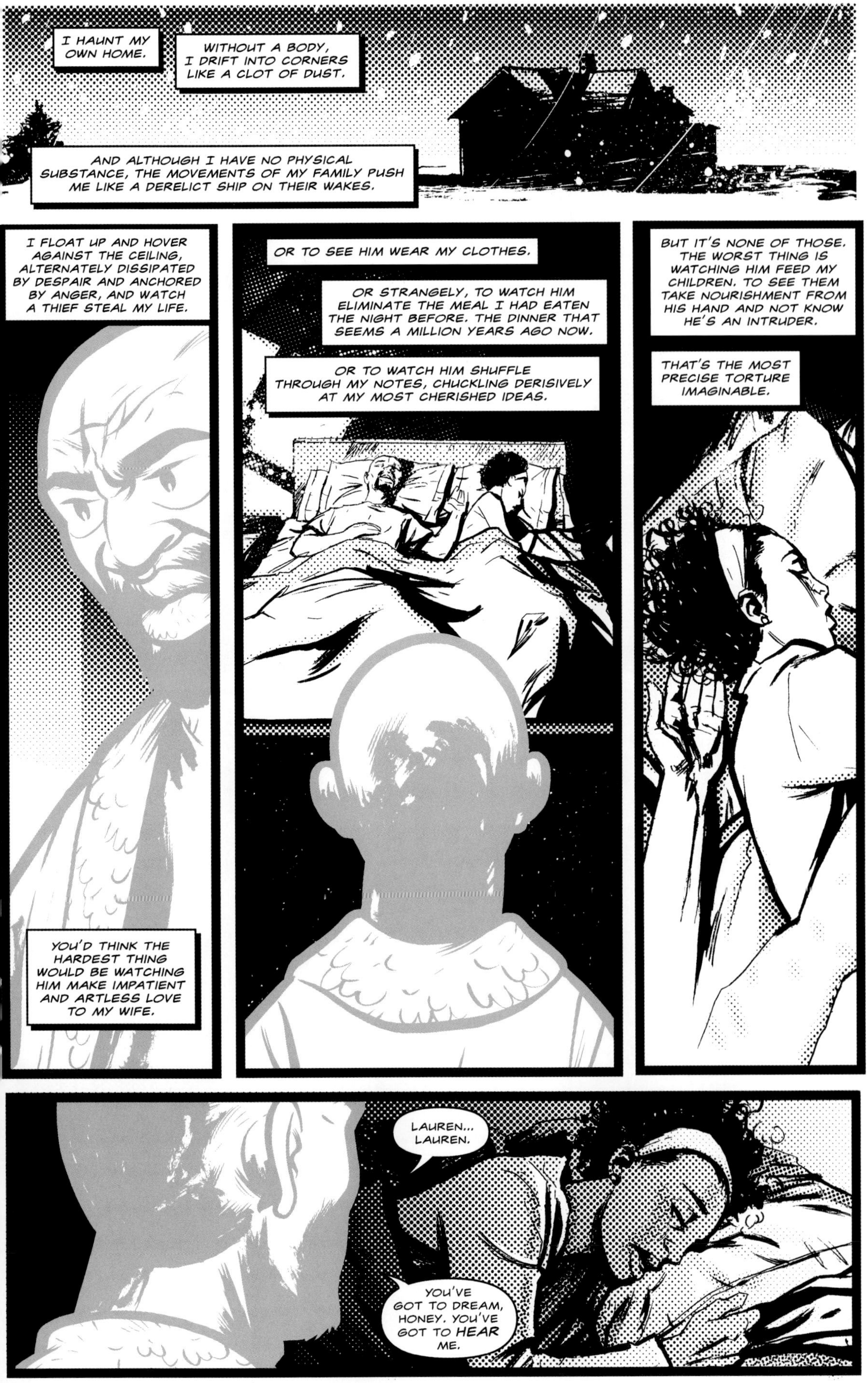

I HAUNT MY OWN HOME.
WITHOUT A BODY, I DRIFT INTO CORNERS LIKE A CLOT OF DUST.
AND ALTHOUGH I HAVE NO PHYSICAL SUBSTANCE, THE MOVEMENTS OF MY FAMILY PUSH ME LIKE A DERELICT SHIP ON THEIR WAKES.
I FLOAT UP AND HOVER AGAINST THE CEILING, ALTERNATELY DISSIPATED BY DESPAIR AND ANCHORED BY ANGER, AND WATCH A THIEF STEAL MY LIFE.
YOU'D THINK THE HARDEST THING WOULD BE WATCHING HIM MAKE IMPATIENT AND ARTLESS LOVE TO MY WIFE.
OR TO SEE HIM WEAR MY CLOTHES.
OR STRANGELY, TO WATCH HIM ELIMINATE THE MEAL I HAD EATEN THE NIGHT BEFORE. THE DINNER THAT SEEMS A MILLION YEARS AGO NOW.
OR TO WATCH HIM SHUFFLE THROUGH MY NOTES, CHUCKLING DERISIVELY AT MY MOST CHERISHED IDEAS.
BUT IT'S NONE OF THOSE. THE WORST THING IS WATCHING HIM FEED MY CHILDREN. TO SEE THEM TAKE NOURISHMENT FROM HIS HAND AND NOT KNOW HE'S AN INTRUDER.
THAT'S THE MOST PRECISE TORTURE IMAGINABLE.
LAUREN... LAUREN.
YOU'VE GOT TO DREAM, HONEY. YOU'VE GOT TO HEAR ME.

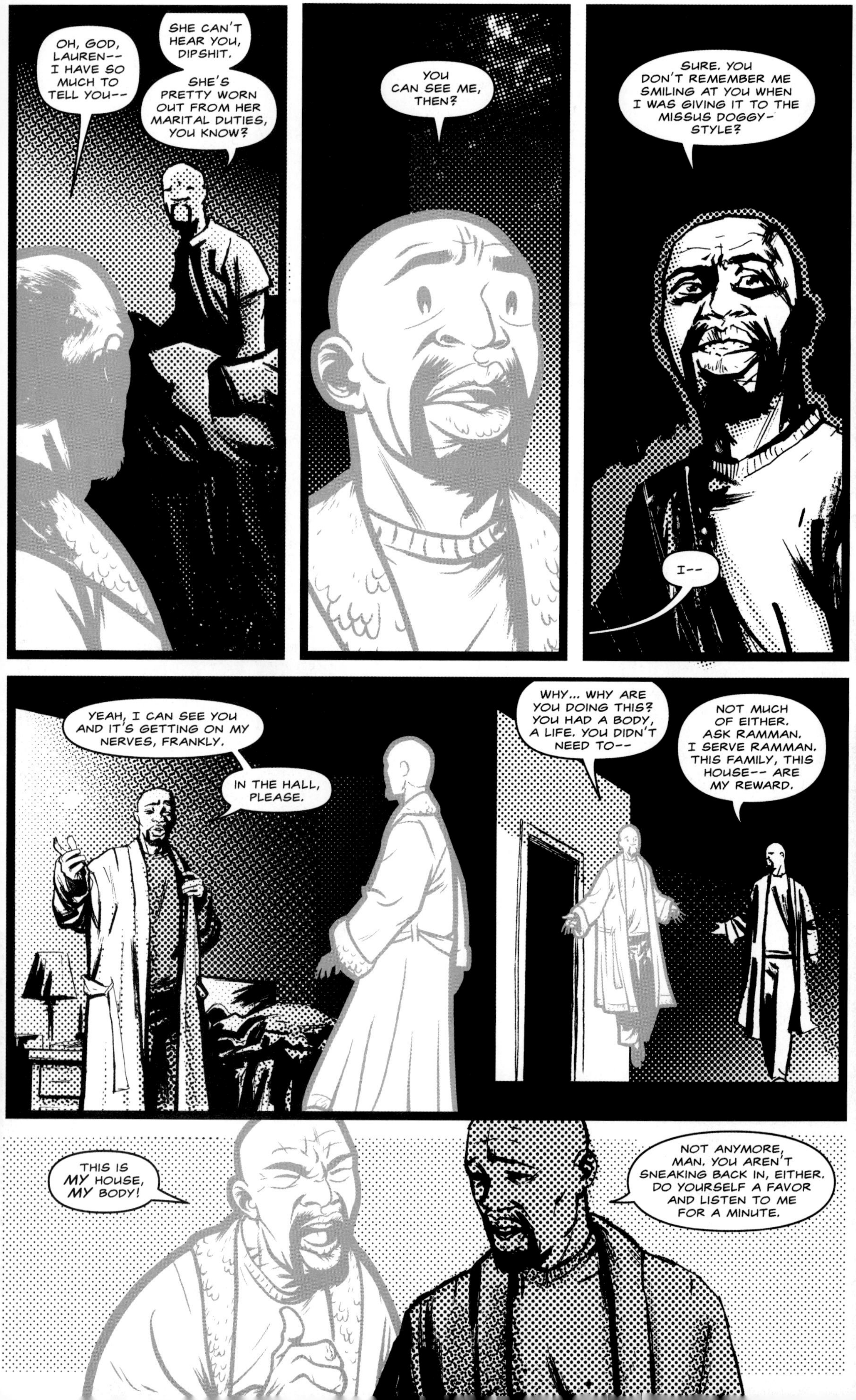
OH, GOD, LAUREN-- I HAVE SO MUCH TO TELL YOU--
SHE CAN'T HEAR YOU, DIPSHIT.
SHE'S PRETTY WORN OUT FROM HER MARITAL DUTIES, YOU KNOW?
YOU CAN SEE ME, THEN?
SURE. YOU DON'T REMEMBER ME SMILING AT YOU WHEN I WAS GIVING IT TO THE MISSUS DOGGY-STYLE?
I--
YEAH, I CAN SEE YOU AND IT'S GETTING ON MY NERVES, FRANKLY.
IN THE HALL, PLEASE.
WHY... WHY ARE YOU DOING THIS? YOU HAD A BODY, A LIFE. YOU DIDN'T NEED TO--
NOT MUCH OF EITHER. ASK RAMMAN. I SERVE RAMMAN. THIS FAMILY, THIS HOUSE-- ARE MY REWARD.
THIS IS *MY* HOUSE, *MY* BODY!
NOT ANYMORE, MAN. YOU AREN'T SNEAKING BACK IN, EITHER. DO YOURSELF A FAVOR AND LISTEN TO ME FOR A MINUTE.

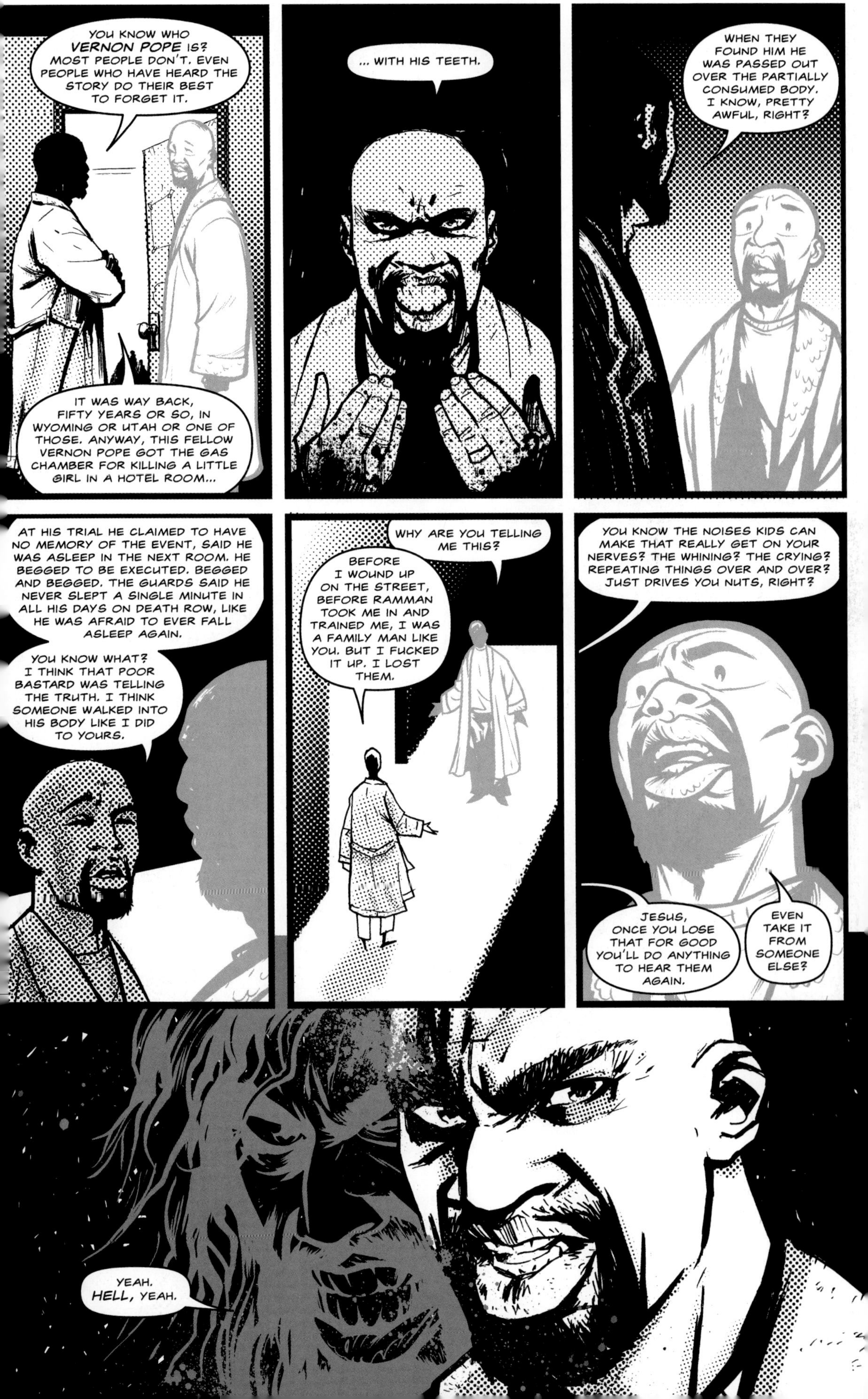
YOU KNOW WHO VERNON POPE IS? MOST PEOPLE DON'T. EVEN PEOPLE WHO HAVE HEARD THE STORY DO THEIR BEST TO FORGET IT.
IT WAS WAY BACK, FIFTY YEARS OR SO, IN WYOMING OR UTAH OR ONE OF THOSE. ANYWAY, THIS FELLOW VERNON POPE GOT THE GAS CHAMBER FOR KILLING A LITTLE GIRL IN A HOTEL ROOM...
... WITH HIS TEETH.
WHEN THEY FOUND HIM HE WAS PASSED OUT OVER THE PARTIALLY CONSUMED BODY. I KNOW, PRETTY AWFUL, RIGHT?
AT HIS TRIAL HE CLAIMED TO HAVE NO MEMORY OF THE EVENT, SAID HE WAS ASLEEP IN THE NEXT ROOM. HE BEGGED TO BE EXECUTED. BEGGED AND BEGGED. THE GUARDS SAID HE NEVER SLEPT A SINGLE MINUTE IN ALL HIS DAYS ON DEATH ROW, LIKE HE WAS AFRAID TO EVER FALL ASLEEP AGAIN.
YOU KNOW WHAT? I THINK THAT POOR BASTARD WAS TELLING THE TRUTH. I THINK SOMEONE WALKED INTO HIS BODY LIKE I DID TO YOURS.
WHY ARE YOU TELLING ME THIS?
BEFORE I WOUND UP ON THE STREET, BEFORE RAMMAN TOOK ME IN AND TRAINED ME, I WAS A FAMILY MAN LIKE YOU. BUT I FUCKED IT UP. I LOST THEM.
YOU KNOW THE NOISES KIDS CAN MAKE THAT REALLY GET ON YOUR NERVES? THE WHINING? THE CRYING? REPEATING THINGS OVER AND OVER? JUST DRIVES YOU NUTS, RIGHT?
JESUS, ONCE YOU LOSE THAT FOR GOOD YOU'LL DO ANYTHING TO HEAR THEM AGAIN.
EVEN TAKE IT FROM SOMEONE ELSE?
YEAH. HELL, YEAH.

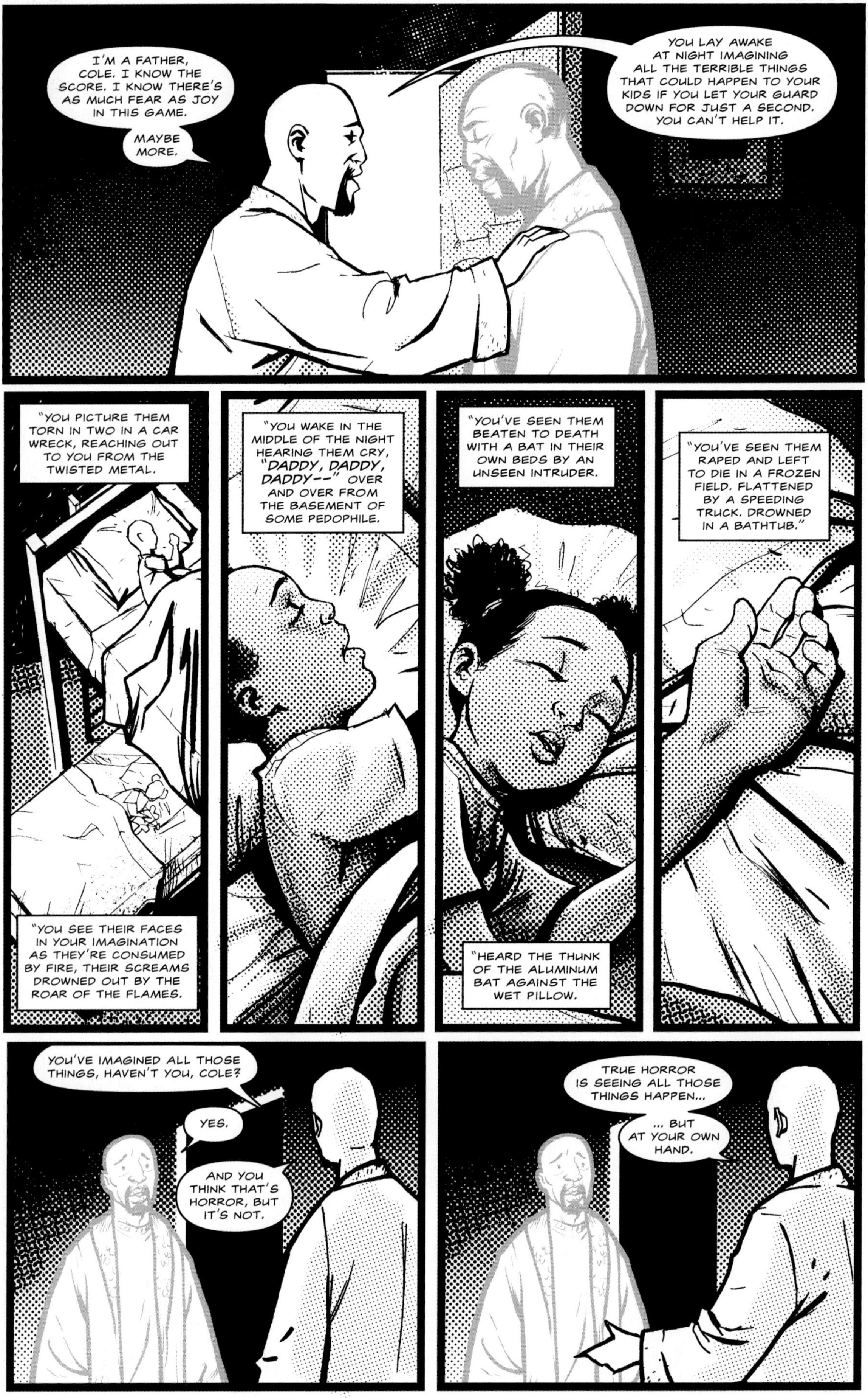
I'M A FATHER, COLE. I KNOW THE SCORE. I KNOW THERE'S AS MUCH FEAR AS JOY IN THIS GAME.
MAYBE MORE.
YOU LAY AWAKE AT NIGHT IMAGINING ALL THE TERRIBLE THINGS THAT COULD HAPPEN TO YOUR KIDS IF YOU LET YOUR GUARD DOWN FOR JUST A SECOND. YOU CAN'T HELP IT.
"YOU PICTURE THEM TORN IN TWO IN A CAR WRECK, REACHING OUT TO YOU FROM THE TWISTED METAL.
"YOU SEE THEIR FACES IN YOUR IMAGINATION AS THEY'RE CONSUMED BY FIRE, THEIR SCREAMS DROWNED OUT BY THE ROAR OF THE FLAMES.
"YOU WAKE IN THE MIDDLE OF THE NIGHT HEARING THEM CRY, "DADDY, DADDY, DADDY--" OVER AND OVER FROM THE BASEMENT OF SOME PEDOPHILE.
"YOU'VE SEEN THEM BEATEN TO DEATH WITH A BAT IN THEIR OWN BEDS BY AN UNSEEN INTRUDER.
"HEARD THE THUNK OF THE ALUMINUM BAT AGAINST THE WET PILLOW.
"YOU'VE SEEN THEM RAPED AND LEFT TO DIE IN A FROZEN FIELD. FLATTENED BY A SPEEDING TRUCK. DROWNED IN A BATHTUB."
YOU'VE IMAGINED ALL THOSE THINGS, HAVEN'T YOU, COLE?
YES.
AND YOU THINK THAT'S HORROR, BUT IT'S NOT.
TRUE HORROR IS SEEING ALL THOSE THINGS HAPPEN...
... BUT AT YOUR OWN HAND.

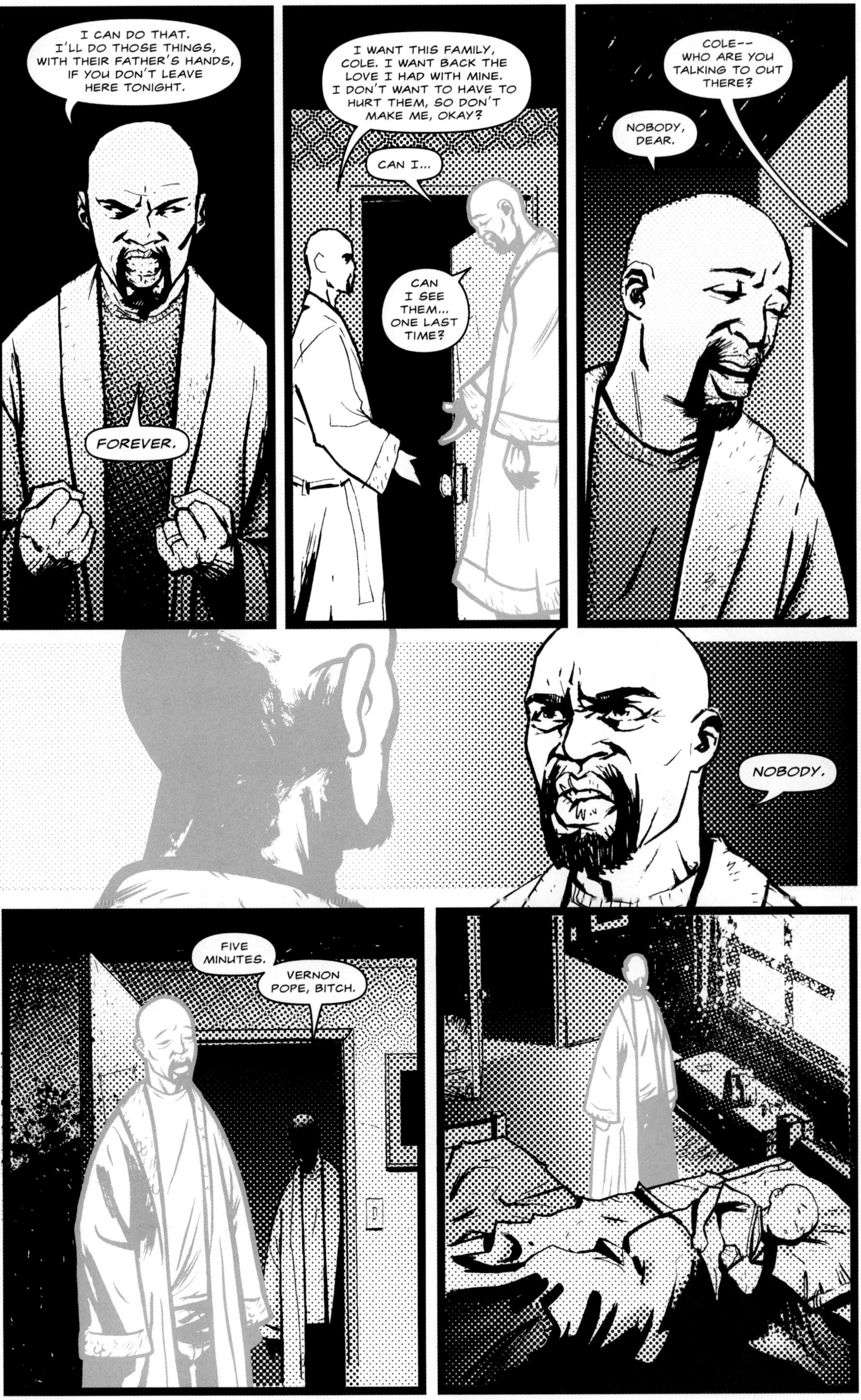
I CAN DO THAT. I'LL DO THOSE THINGS, WITH THEIR FATHER'S HANDS, IF YOU DON'T LEAVE HERE TONIGHT.
FOREVER.
I WANT THIS FAMILY, COLE. I WANT BACK THE LOVE I HAD WITH MINE. I DON'T WANT TO HAVE TO HURT THEM, SO DON'T MAKE ME, OKAY?
CAN I...
CAN I SEE THEM... ONE LAST TIME?
COLE-- WHO ARE YOU TALKING TO OUT THERE?
NOBODY, DEAR.
NOBODY.
FIVE MINUTES.
VERNON POPE, BITCH.

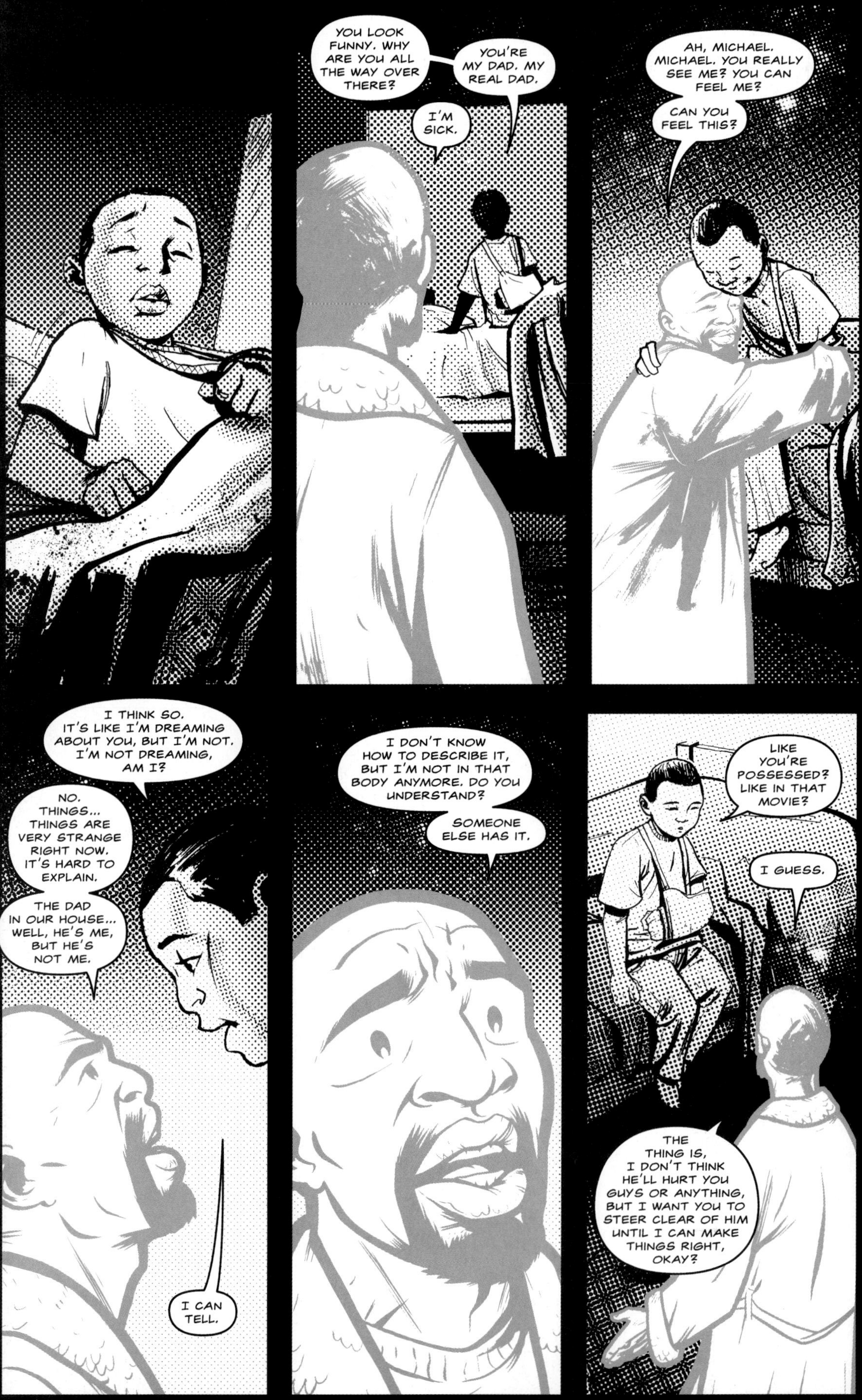
YOU LOOK FUNNY. WHY ARE YOU ALL THE WAY OVER THERE?
YOU'RE MY DAD. MY REAL DAD.
I'M SICK.
AH, MICHAEL. MICHAEL. YOU REALLY SEE ME? YOU CAN FEEL ME?
CAN YOU FEEL THIS?
I THINK SO. IT'S LIKE I'M DREAMING ABOUT YOU, BUT I'M NOT. I'M NOT DREAMING, AM I?
NO. THINGS... THINGS ARE VERY STRANGE RIGHT NOW. IT'S HARD TO EXPLAIN.
THE DAD IN OUR HOUSE... WELL, HE'S ME, BUT HE'S NOT ME.
I CAN TELL.
I DON'T KNOW HOW TO DESCRIBE IT, BUT I'M NOT IN THAT BODY ANYMORE. DO YOU UNDERSTAND?
SOMEONE ELSE HAS IT.
LIKE YOU'RE POSSESSED? LIKE IN THAT MOVIE?
I GUESS.
THE THING IS, I DON'T THINK HE'LL HURT YOU GUYS OR ANYTHING, BUT I WANT YOU TO STEER CLEAR OF HIM UNTIL I CAN MAKE THINGS RIGHT, OKAY?

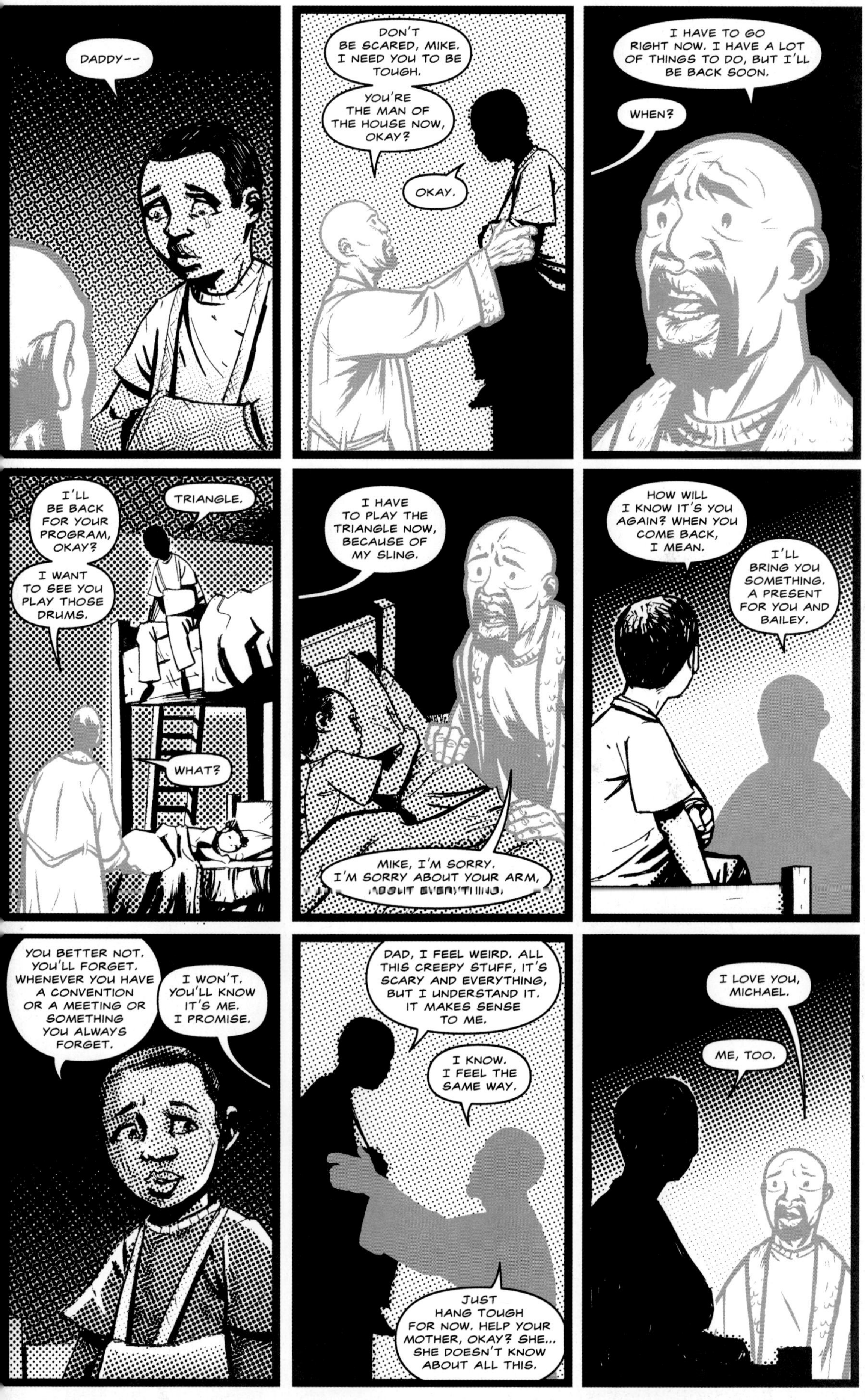
DADDY--
DON'T BE SCARED, MIKE. I NEED YOU TO BE TOUGH.
YOU'RE THE MAN OF THE HOUSE NOW, OKAY?
OKAY.
I HAVE TO GO RIGHT NOW. I HAVE A LOT OF THINGS TO DO, BUT I'LL BE BACK SOON.
WHEN?
I'LL BE BACK FOR YOUR PROGRAM, OKAY?
I WANT TO SEE YOU PLAY THOSE DRUMS.
TRIANGLE.
WHAT?
I HAVE TO PLAY THE TRIANGLE NOW, BECAUSE OF MY SLING.
MIKE, I'M SORRY. I'M SORRY ABOUT YOUR ARM, ABOUT EVERYTHING.
HOW WILL I KNOW IT'S YOU AGAIN? WHEN YOU COME BACK, I MEAN.
I'LL BRING YOU SOMETHING. A PRESENT FOR YOU AND BAILEY.
YOU BETTER NOT. YOU'LL FORGET. WHENEVER YOU HAVE A CONVENTION OR A MEETING OR SOMETHING YOU ALWAYS FORGET.
I WON'T. YOU'LL KNOW IT'S ME. I PROMISE.
DAD, I FEEL WEIRD. ALL THIS CREEPY STUFF, IT'S SCARY AND EVERYTHING, BUT I UNDERSTAND IT. IT MAKES SENSE TO ME.
I KNOW. I FEEL THE SAME WAY.
JUST HANG TOUGH FOR NOW. HELP YOUR MOTHER, OKAY? SHE... SHE DOESN'T KNOW ABOUT ALL THIS.
I LOVE YOU, MICHAEL.
ME, TOO.

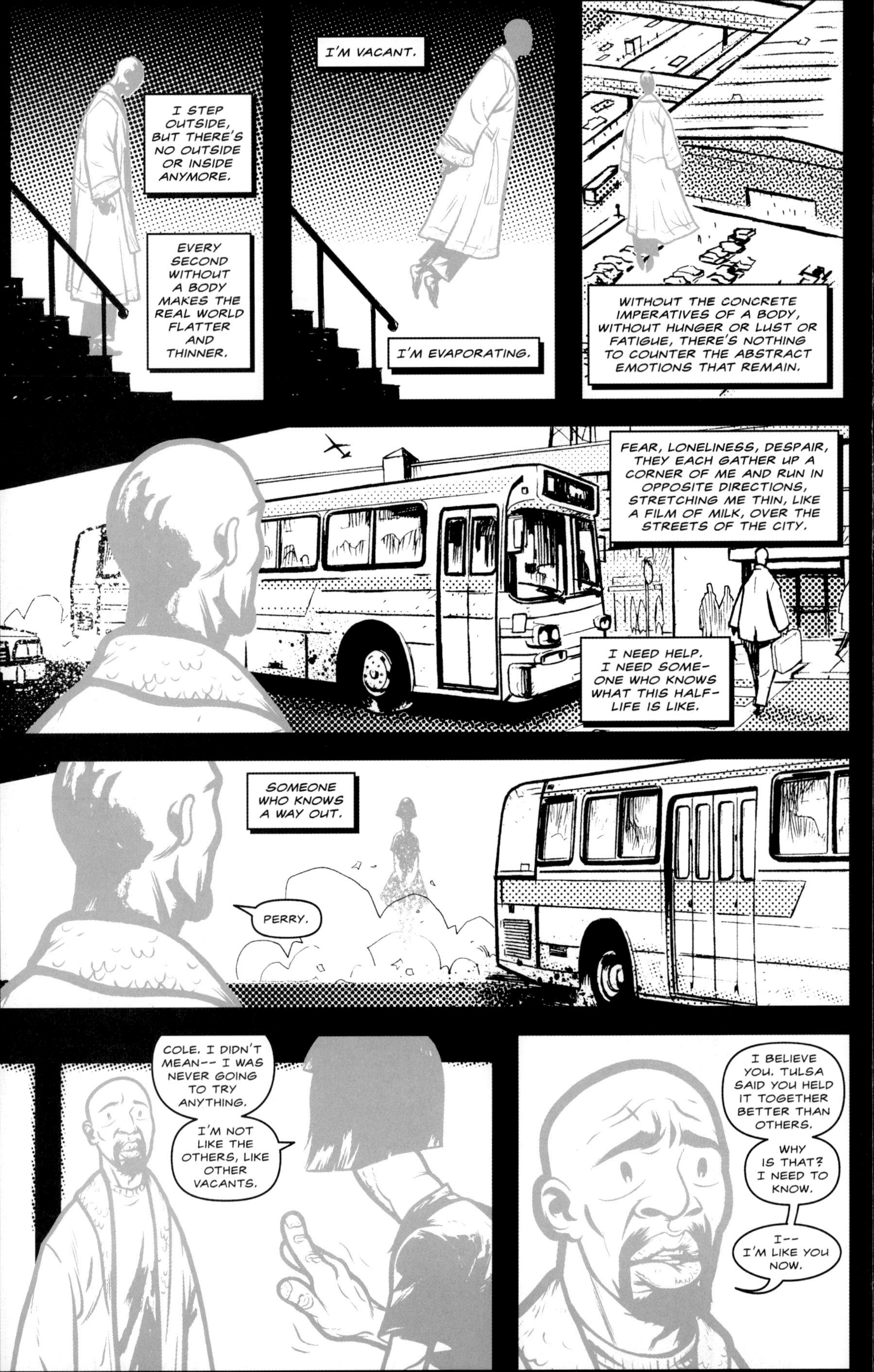
I STEP OUTSIDE, BUT THERE'S NO OUTSIDE OR INSIDE ANYMORE.
EVERY SECOND WITHOUT A BODY MAKES THE REAL WORLD FLATTER AND THINNER.
I'M VACANT.
I'M EVAPORATING.
WITHOUT THE CONCRETE IMPERATIVES OF A BODY, WITHOUT HUNGER OR LUST OR FATIGUE, THERE'S NOTHING TO COUNTER THE ABSTRACT EMOTIONS THAT REMAIN.
FEAR, LONELINESS, DESPAIR, THEY EACH GATHER UP A CORNER OF ME AND RUN IN OPPOSITE DIRECTIONS, STRETCHING ME THIN, LIKE A FILM OF MILK, OVER THE STREETS OF THE CITY.
I NEED HELP. I NEED SOME-ONE WHO KNOWS WHAT THIS HALF-LIFE IS LIKE.
SOMEONE WHO KNOWS A WAY OUT.
PERRY.
COLE. I DIDN'T MEAN-- I WAS NEVER GOING TO TRY ANYTHING.
I'M NOT LIKE THE OTHERS, LIKE OTHER VACANTS.
I BELIEVE YOU. TULSA SAID YOU HELD IT TOGETHER BETTER THAN OTHERS.
WHY IS THAT? I NEED TO KNOW.
I-- I'M LIKE YOU NOW.

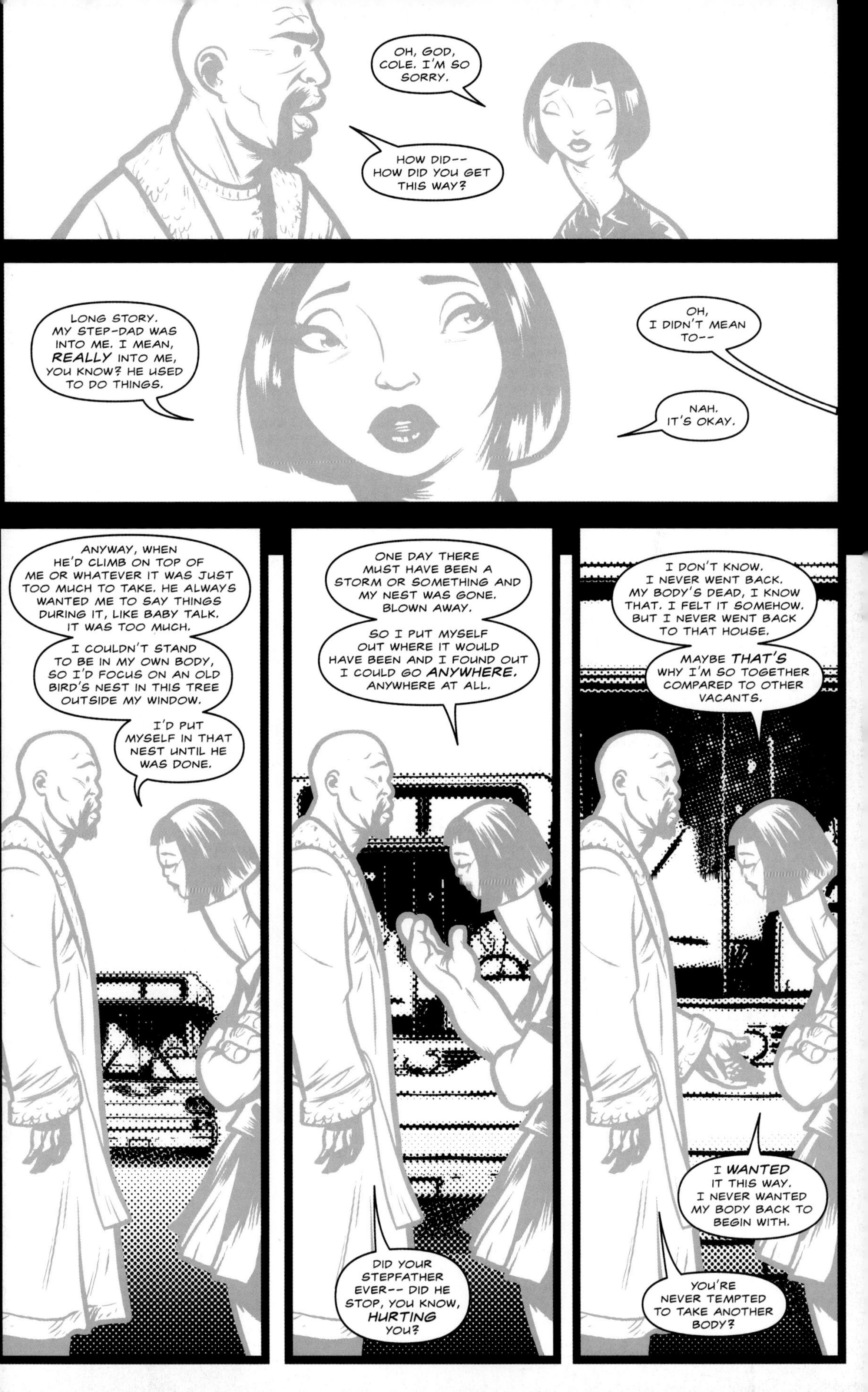

OH, GOD, COLE. I'M SO SORRY.
HOW DID-- HOW DID YOU GET THIS WAY?
LONG STORY. MY STEP-DAD WAS INTO ME. I MEAN, REALLY INTO ME, YOU KNOW? HE USED TO DO THINGS.
OH, I DIDN'T MEAN TO--
NAH. IT'S OKAY.
ANYWAY, WHEN HE'D CLIMB ON TOP OF ME OR WHATEVER IT WAS JUST TOO MUCH TO TAKE. HE ALWAYS WANTED ME TO SAY THINGS DURING IT, LIKE BABY TALK. IT WAS TOO MUCH.
I COULDN'T STAND TO BE IN MY OWN BODY, SO I'D FOCUS ON AN OLD BIRD'S NEST IN THIS TREE OUTSIDE MY WINDOW.
I'D PUT MYSELF IN THAT NEST UNTIL HE WAS DONE.
ONE DAY THERE MUST HAVE BEEN A STORM OR SOMETHING AND MY NEST WAS GONE. BLOWN AWAY.
SO I PUT MYSELF OUT WHERE IT WOULD HAVE BEEN AND I FOUND OUT I COULD GO ANYWHERE. ANYWHERE AT ALL.
DID YOUR STEPFATHER EVER-- DID HE STOP, YOU KNOW, HURTING YOU?
I DON'T KNOW. I NEVER WENT BACK. MY BODY'S DEAD, I KNOW THAT. I FELT IT SOMEHOW. BUT I NEVER WENT BACK TO THAT HOUSE.
MAYBE THAT'S WHY I'M SO TOGETHER COMPARED TO OTHER VACANTS.
I WANTED IT THIS WAY. I NEVER WANTED MY BODY BACK TO BEGIN WITH.
YOU'RE NEVER TEMPTED TO TAKE ANOTHER BODY?

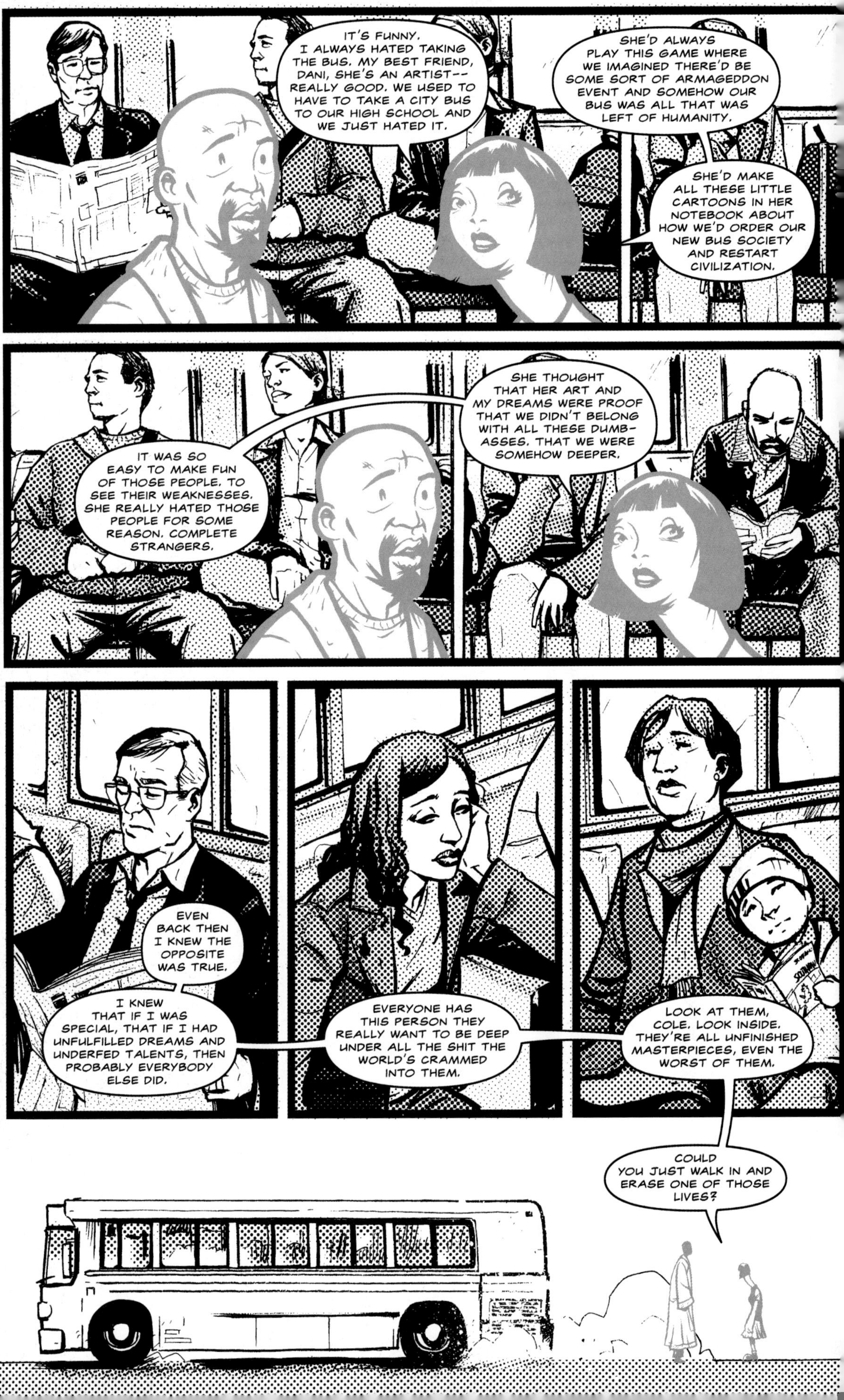
IT'S FUNNY. I ALWAYS HATED TAKING THE BUS. MY BEST FRIEND, DANI, SHE'S AN ARTIST-- REALLY GOOD. WE USED TO HAVE TO TAKE A CITY BUS TO OUR HIGH SCHOOL AND WE JUST HATED IT.
SHE'D ALWAYS PLAY THIS GAME WHERE WE IMAGINED THERE'D BE SOME SORT OF ARMAGEDDON EVENT AND SOMEHOW OUR BUS WAS ALL THAT WAS LEFT OF HUMANITY.
SHE'D MAKE ALL THESE LITTLE CARTOONS IN HER NOTEBOOK ABOUT HOW WE'D ORDER OUR NEW BUS SOCIETY AND RESTART CIVILIZATION.
IT WAS SO EASY TO MAKE FUN OF THOSE PEOPLE. TO SEE THEIR WEAKNESSES. SHE REALLY HATED THOSE PEOPLE FOR SOME REASON. COMPLETE STRANGERS.
SHE THOUGHT THAT HER ART AND MY DREAMS WERE PROOF THAT WE DIDN'T BELONG WITH ALL THESE DUMB-ASSES. THAT WE WERE SOMEHOW DEEPER.
EVEN BACK THEN I KNEW THE OPPOSITE WAS TRUE.
I KNEW THAT IF I WAS SPECIAL, THAT IF I HAD UNFULFILLED DREAMS AND UNDERFED TALENTS, THEN PROBABLY EVERYBODY ELSE DID.
EVERYONE HAS THIS PERSON THEY REALLY WANT TO BE DEEP UNDER ALL THE SHIT THE WORLD'S CRAMMED INTO THEM.
LOOK AT THEM, COLE. LOOK INSIDE. THEY'RE ALL UNFINISHED MASTERPIECES, EVEN THE WORST OF THEM.
COULD YOU JUST WALK IN AND ERASE ONE OF THOSE LIVES?

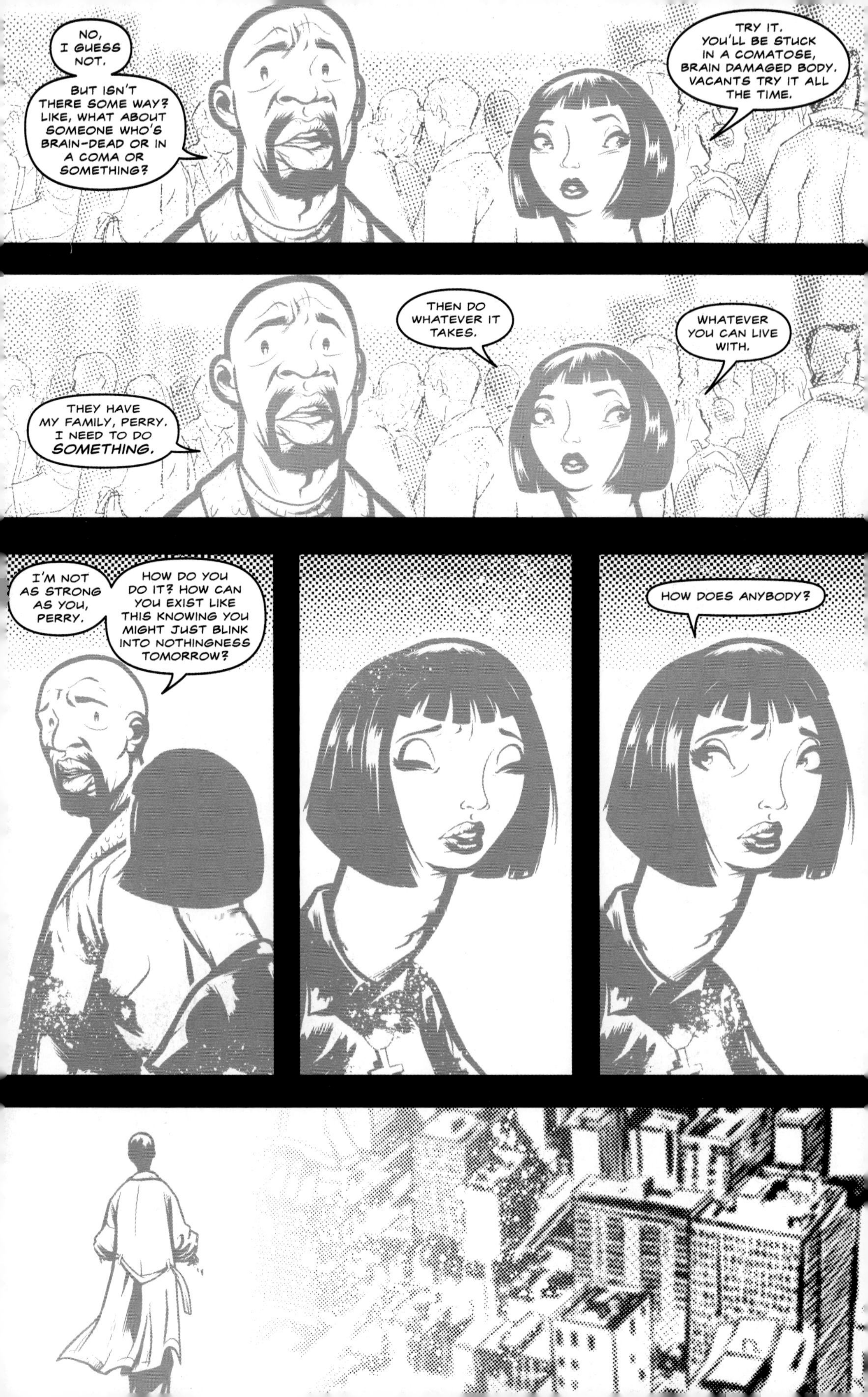
NO, I GUESS NOT.
BUT ISN'T THERE SOME WAY? LIKE, WHAT ABOUT SOMEONE WHO'S BRAIN-DEAD OR IN A COMA OR SOMETHING?
TRY IT. YOU'LL BE STUCK IN A COMATOSE, BRAIN DAMAGED BODY. VACANTS TRY IT ALL THE TIME.
THEY HAVE MY FAMILY, PERRY. I NEED TO DO SOMETHING.
THEN DO WHATEVER IT TAKES.
WHATEVER YOU CAN LIVE WITH.
I'M NOT AS STRONG AS YOU, PERRY.
HOW DO YOU DO IT? HOW CAN YOU EXIST LIKE THIS KNOWING YOU MIGHT JUST BLINK INTO NOTHINGNESS TOMORROW?
HOW DOES ANYBODY?

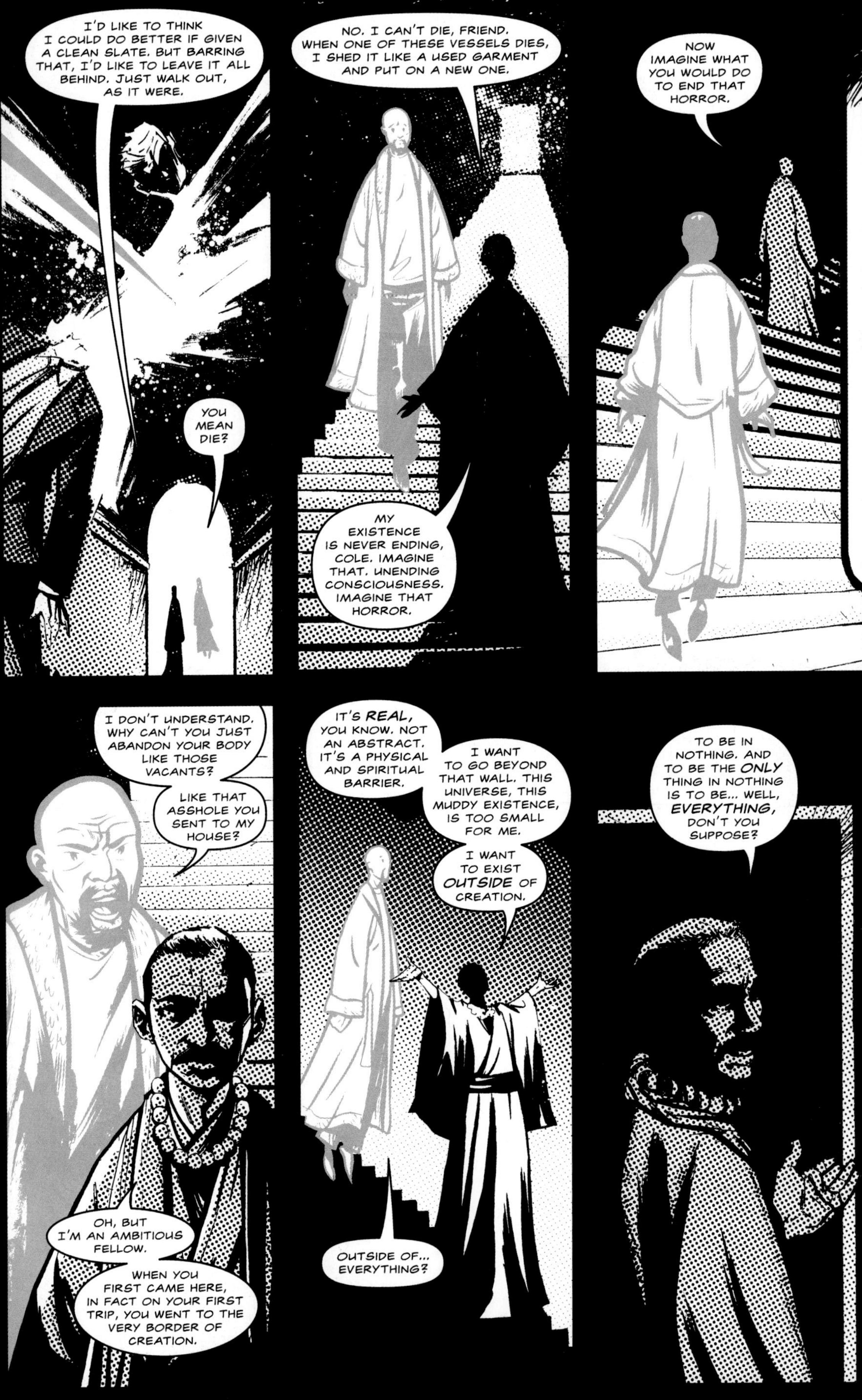
I'D LIKE TO THINK I COULD DO BETTER IF GIVEN A CLEAN SLATE. BUT BARRING THAT, I'D LIKE TO LEAVE IT ALL BEHIND. JUST WALK OUT, AS IT WERE.
YOU MEAN DIE?
NO. I CAN'T DIE, FRIEND. WHEN ONE OF THESE VESSELS DIES, I SHED IT LIKE A USED GARMENT AND PUT ON A NEW ONE.
MY EXISTENCE IS NEVER ENDING, COLE. IMAGINE THAT. UNENDING CONSCIOUSNESS. IMAGINE THAT HORROR.
NOW IMAGINE WHAT YOU WOULD DO TO END THAT HORROR.
I DON'T UNDERSTAND. WHY CAN'T YOU JUST ABANDON YOUR BODY LIKE THOSE VACANTS?
LIKE THAT ASSHOLE YOU SENT TO MY HOUSE?
OH, BUT I'M AN AMBITIOUS FELLOW.
WHEN YOU FIRST CAME HERE, IN FACT ON YOUR FIRST TRIP, YOU WENT TO THE VERY BORDER OF CREATION.
IT'S REAL, YOU KNOW. NOT AN ABSTRACT. IT'S A PHYSICAL AND SPIRITUAL BARRIER.
I WANT TO GO BEYOND THAT WALL. THIS UNIVERSE, THIS MUDDY EXISTENCE, IS TOO SMALL FOR ME.
I WANT TO EXIST OUTSIDE OF CREATION.
OUTSIDE OF... EVERYTHING?
TO BE IN NOTHING. AND TO BE THE ONLY THING IN NOTHING IS TO BE... WELL, EVERYTHING, DON'T YOU SUPPOSE?

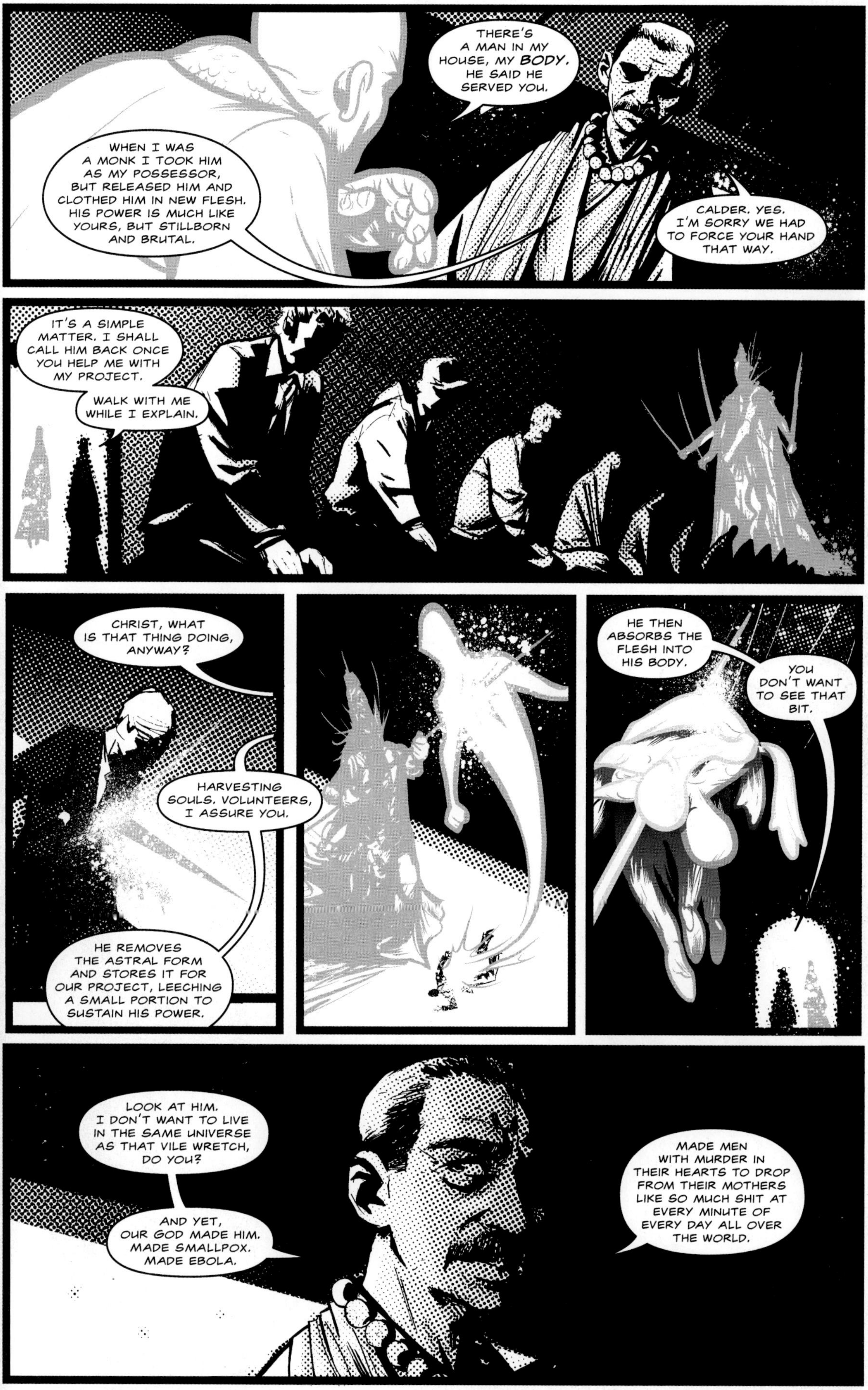
THERE'S A MAN IN MY HOUSE, MY BODY. HE SAID HE SERVED YOU.
WHEN I WAS A MONK I TOOK HIM AS MY POSSESSOR, BUT RELEASED HIM AND CLOTHED HIM IN NEW FLESH. HIS POWER IS MUCH LIKE YOURS, BUT STILLBORN AND BRUTAL.
CALDER. YES. I'M SORRY WE HAD TO FORCE YOUR HAND THAT WAY.
IT'S A SIMPLE MATTER. I SHALL CALL HIM BACK ONCE YOU HELP ME WITH MY PROJECT.
WALK WITH ME WHILE I EXPLAIN.
CHRIST, WHAT IS THAT THING DOING, ANYWAY?
HARVESTING SOULS. VOLUNTEERS, I ASSURE YOU.
HE REMOVES THE ASTRAL FORM AND STORES IT FOR OUR PROJECT, LEECHING A SMALL PORTION TO SUSTAIN HIS POWER.
HE THEN ABSORBS THE FLESH INTO HIS BODY.
YOU DON'T WANT TO SEE THAT BIT.
LOOK AT HIM. I DON'T WANT TO LIVE IN THE SAME UNIVERSE AS THAT VILE WRETCH, DO YOU?
AND YET, OUR GOD MADE HIM. MADE SMALLPOX. MADE EBOLA.
MADE MEN WITH MURDER IN THEIR HEARTS TO DROP FROM THEIR MOTHERS LIKE SO MUCH SHIT AT EVERY MINUTE OF EVERY DAY ALL OVER THE WORLD.

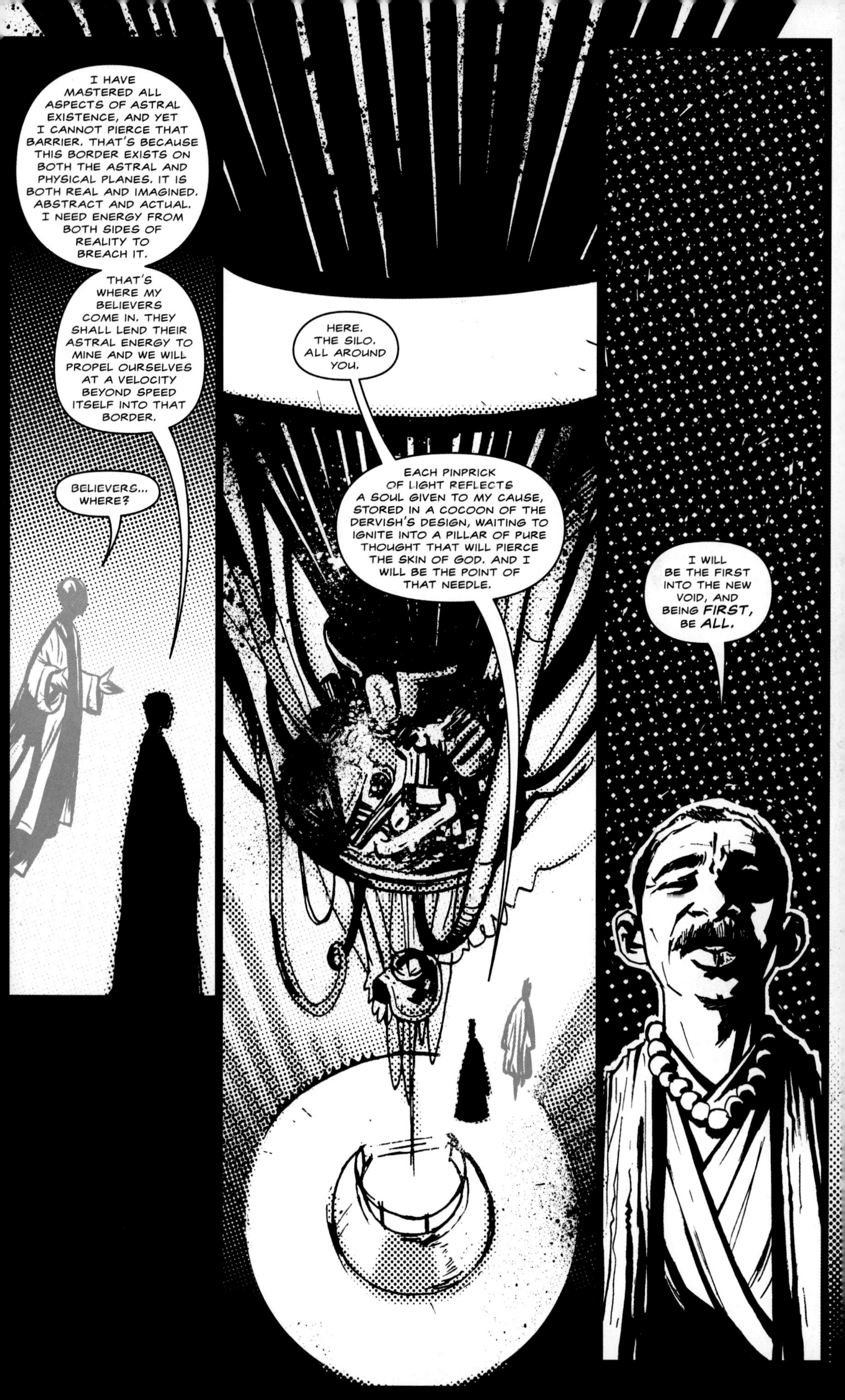
I HAVE MASTERED ALL ASPECTS OF ASTRAL EXISTENCE, AND YET I CANNOT PIERCE THAT BARRIER. THAT'S BECAUSE THIS BORDER EXISTS ON BOTH THE ASTRAL AND PHYSICAL PLANES. IT IS BOTH REAL AND IMAGINED. ABSTRACT AND ACTUAL. I NEED ENERGY FROM BOTH SIDES OF REALITY TO BREACH IT.
THAT'S WHERE MY BELIEVERS COME IN. THEY SHALL LEND THEIR ASTRAL ENERGY TO MINE AND WE WILL PROPEL OURSELVES AT A VELOCITY BEYOND SPEED ITSELF INTO THAT BORDER.
BELIEVERS... WHERE?
HERE. THE SILO. ALL AROUND YOU.
EACH PINPRICK OF LIGHT REFLECTS A SOUL GIVEN TO MY CAUSE, STORED IN A COCOON OF THE DERVISH'S DESIGN, WAITING TO IGNITE INTO A PILLAR OF PURE THOUGHT THAT WILL PIERCE THE SKIN OF GOD. AND I WILL BE THE POINT OF THAT NEEDLE.
I WILL BE THE FIRST INTO THE NEW VOID, AND BEING *FIRST*, BE *ALL*.

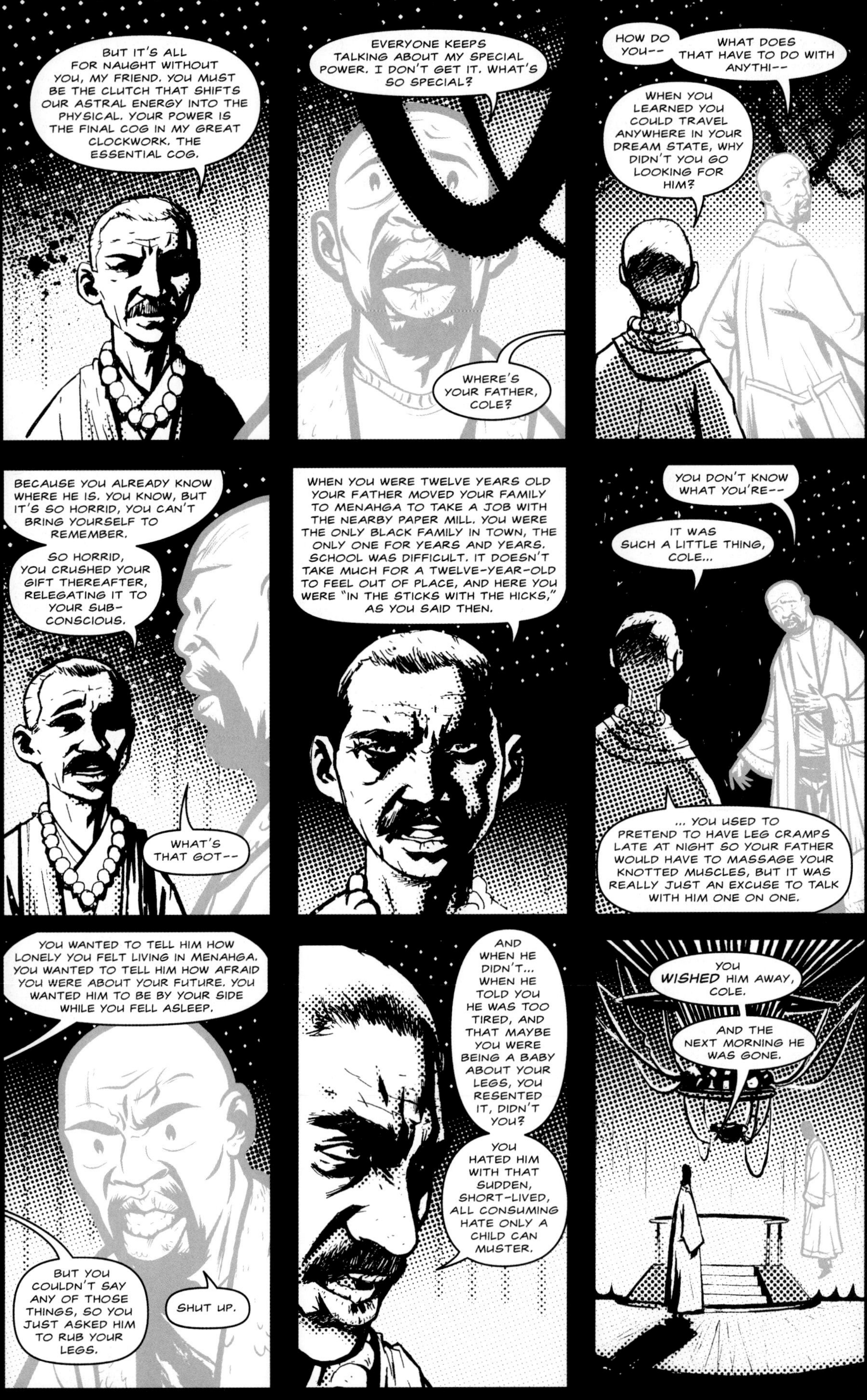
BUT IT'S ALL FOR NAUGHT WITHOUT YOU, MY FRIEND. YOU MUST BE THE CLUTCH THAT SHIFTS OUR ASTRAL ENERGY INTO THE PHYSICAL. YOUR POWER IS THE FINAL COG IN MY GREAT CLOCKWORK. THE ESSENTIAL COG.
EVERYONE KEEPS TALKING ABOUT MY SPECIAL POWER. I DON'T GET IT. WHAT'S SO SPECIAL?
WHERE'S YOUR FATHER, COLE?
HOW DO YOU--
WHAT DOES THAT HAVE TO DO WITH ANYTHI--
WHEN YOU LEARNED YOU COULD TRAVEL ANYWHERE IN YOUR DREAM STATE, WHY DIDN'T YOU GO LOOKING FOR HIM?
BECAUSE YOU ALREADY KNOW WHERE HE IS. YOU KNOW, BUT IT'S SO HORRID, YOU CAN'T BRING YOURSELF TO REMEMBER.
SO HORRID, YOU CRUSHED YOUR GIFT THEREAFTER, RELEGATING IT TO YOUR SUB-CONSCIOUS.
WHAT'S THAT GOT--
WHEN YOU WERE TWELVE YEARS OLD YOUR FATHER MOVED YOUR FAMILY TO MENAHGA TO TAKE A JOB WITH THE NEARBY PAPER MILL. YOU WERE THE ONLY BLACK FAMILY IN TOWN, THE ONLY ONE FOR YEARS AND YEARS. SCHOOL WAS DIFFICULT. IT DOESN'T TAKE MUCH FOR A TWELVE-YEAR-OLD TO FEEL OUT OF PLACE, AND HERE YOU WERE "IN THE STICKS WITH THE HICKS," AS YOU SAID THEN.
YOU DON'T KNOW WHAT YOU'RE--
IT WAS SUCH A LITTLE THING, COLE...
... YOU USED TO PRETEND TO HAVE LEG CRAMPS LATE AT NIGHT SO YOUR FATHER WOULD HAVE TO MASSAGE YOUR KNOTTED MUSCLES, BUT IT WAS REALLY JUST AN EXCUSE TO TALK WITH HIM ONE ON ONE.
YOU WANTED TO TELL HIM HOW LONELY YOU FELT LIVING IN MENAHGA. YOU WANTED TO TELL HIM HOW AFRAID YOU WERE ABOUT YOUR FUTURE. YOU WANTED HIM TO BE BY YOUR SIDE WHILE YOU FELL ASLEEP.
BUT YOU COULDN'T SAY ANY OF THOSE THINGS, SO YOU JUST ASKED HIM TO RUB YOUR LEGS.
SHUT UP.
AND WHEN HE DIDN'T... WHEN HE TOLD YOU HE WAS TOO TIRED, AND THAT MAYBE YOU WERE BEING A BABY ABOUT YOUR LEGS, YOU RESENTED IT, DIDN'T YOU?
YOU HATED HIM WITH THAT SUDDEN, SHORT-LIVED, ALL CONSUMING HATE ONLY A CHILD CAN MUSTER.
YOU *WISHED* HIM AWAY, COLE.
AND THE NEXT MORNING HE WAS GONE.

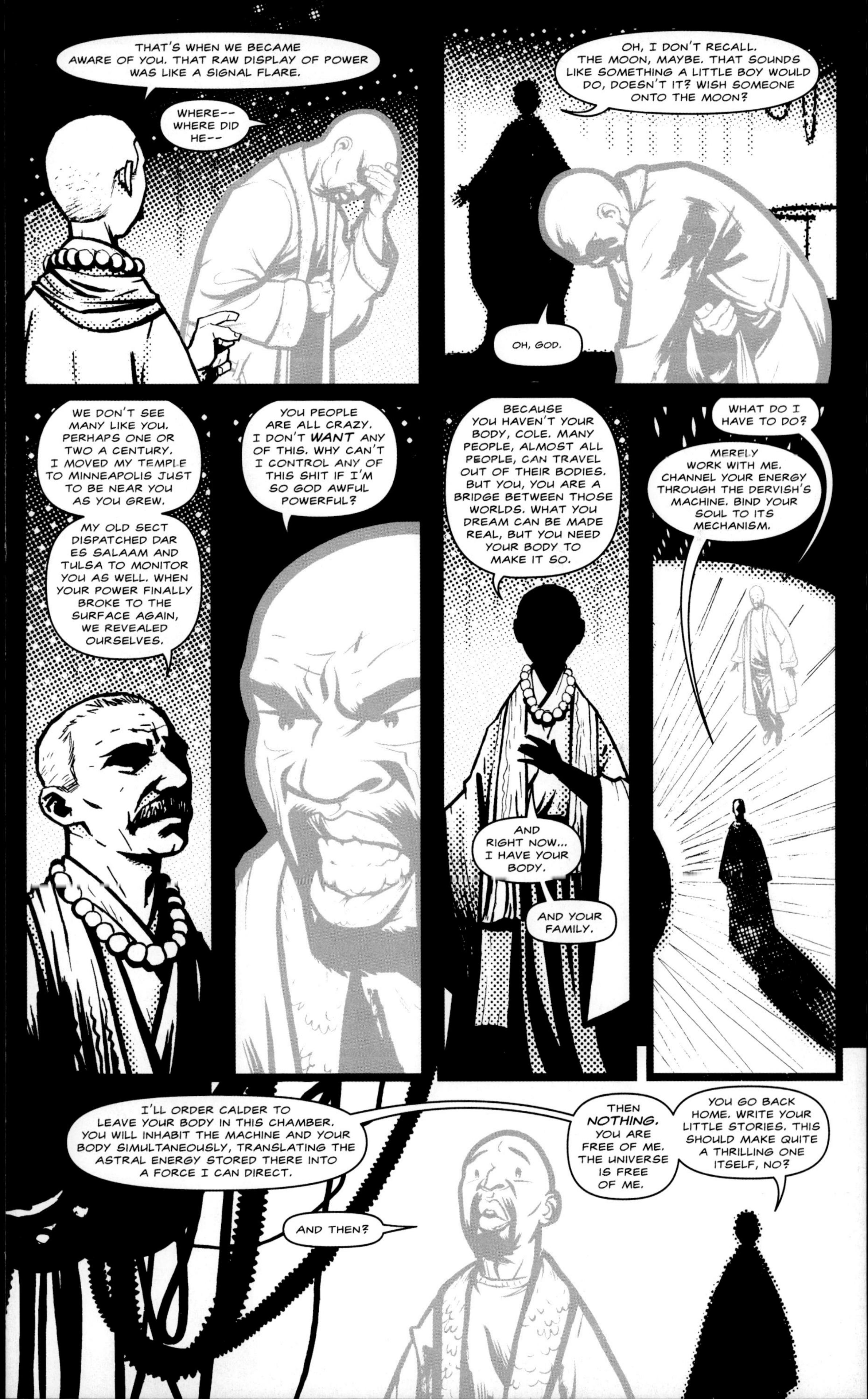
THAT'S WHEN WE BECAME AWARE OF YOU. THAT RAW DISPLAY OF POWER WAS LIKE A SIGNAL FLARE.
WHERE-- WHERE DID HE--
OH, I DON'T RECALL. THE MOON, MAYBE. THAT SOUNDS LIKE SOMETHING A LITTLE BOY WOULD DO, DOESN'T IT? WISH SOMEONE ONTO THE MOON?
OH, GOD.
WE DON'T SEE MANY LIKE YOU. PERHAPS ONE OR TWO A CENTURY. I MOVED MY TEMPLE TO MINNEAPOLIS JUST TO BE NEAR YOU AS YOU GREW.
MY OLD SECT DISPATCHED DAR ES SALAAM AND TULSA TO MONITOR YOU AS WELL. WHEN YOUR POWER FINALLY BROKE TO THE SURFACE AGAIN, WE REVEALED OURSELVES.
YOU PEOPLE ARE ALL CRAZY. I DON'T WANT ANY OF THIS. WHY CAN'T I CONTROL ANY OF THIS SHIT IF I'M SO GOD AWFUL POWERFUL?
BECAUSE YOU HAVEN'T YOUR BODY, COLE. MANY PEOPLE, ALMOST ALL PEOPLE, CAN TRAVEL OUT OF THEIR BODIES. BUT YOU, YOU ARE A BRIDGE BETWEEN THOSE WORLDS. WHAT YOU DREAM CAN BE MADE REAL, BUT YOU NEED YOUR BODY TO MAKE IT SO.
AND RIGHT NOW... I HAVE YOUR BODY.
AND YOUR FAMILY.
WHAT DO I HAVE TO DO?
MERELY WORK WITH ME. CHANNEL YOUR ENERGY THROUGH THE DERVISH'S MACHINE. BIND YOUR SOUL TO ITS MECHANISM.
I'LL ORDER CALDER TO LEAVE YOUR BODY IN THIS CHAMBER. YOU WILL INHABIT THE MACHINE AND YOUR BODY SIMULTANEOUSLY, TRANSLATING THE ASTRAL ENERGY STORED THERE INTO A FORCE I CAN DIRECT.
AND THEN?
THEN NOTHING. YOU ARE FREE OF ME. THE UNIVERSE IS FREE OF ME.
YOU GO BACK HOME. WRITE YOUR LITTLE STORIES. THIS SHOULD MAKE QUITE A THRILLING ONE ITSELF, NO?

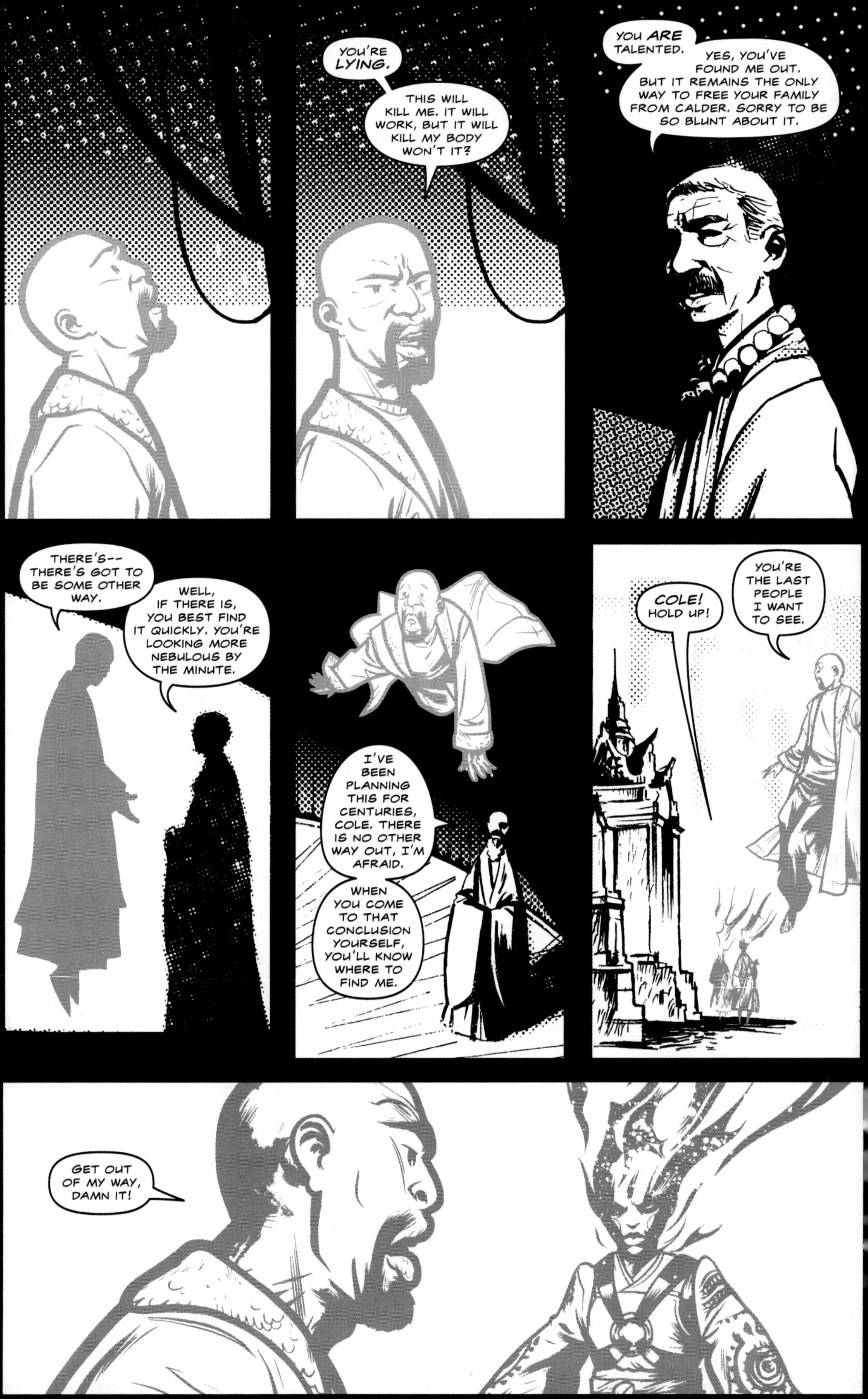
YOU'RE LYING.
THIS WILL KILL ME. IT WILL WORK, BUT IT WILL KILL MY BODY WON'T IT?
YOU ARE TALENTED.
YES, YOU'VE FOUND ME OUT. BUT IT REMAINS THE ONLY WAY TO FREE YOUR FAMILY FROM CALDER. SORRY TO BE SO BLUNT ABOUT IT.
THERE'S-- THERE'S GOT TO BE SOME OTHER WAY.
WELL, IF THERE IS, YOU BEST FIND IT QUICKLY. YOU'RE LOOKING MORE NEBULOUS BY THE MINUTE.
I'VE BEEN PLANNING THIS FOR CENTURIES, COLE. THERE IS NO OTHER WAY OUT, I'M AFRAID.
WHEN YOU COME TO THAT CONCLUSION YOURSELF, YOU'LL KNOW WHERE TO FIND ME.
COLE! HOLD UP!
YOU'RE THE LAST PEOPLE I WANT TO SEE.
GET OUT OF MY WAY, DAMN IT!

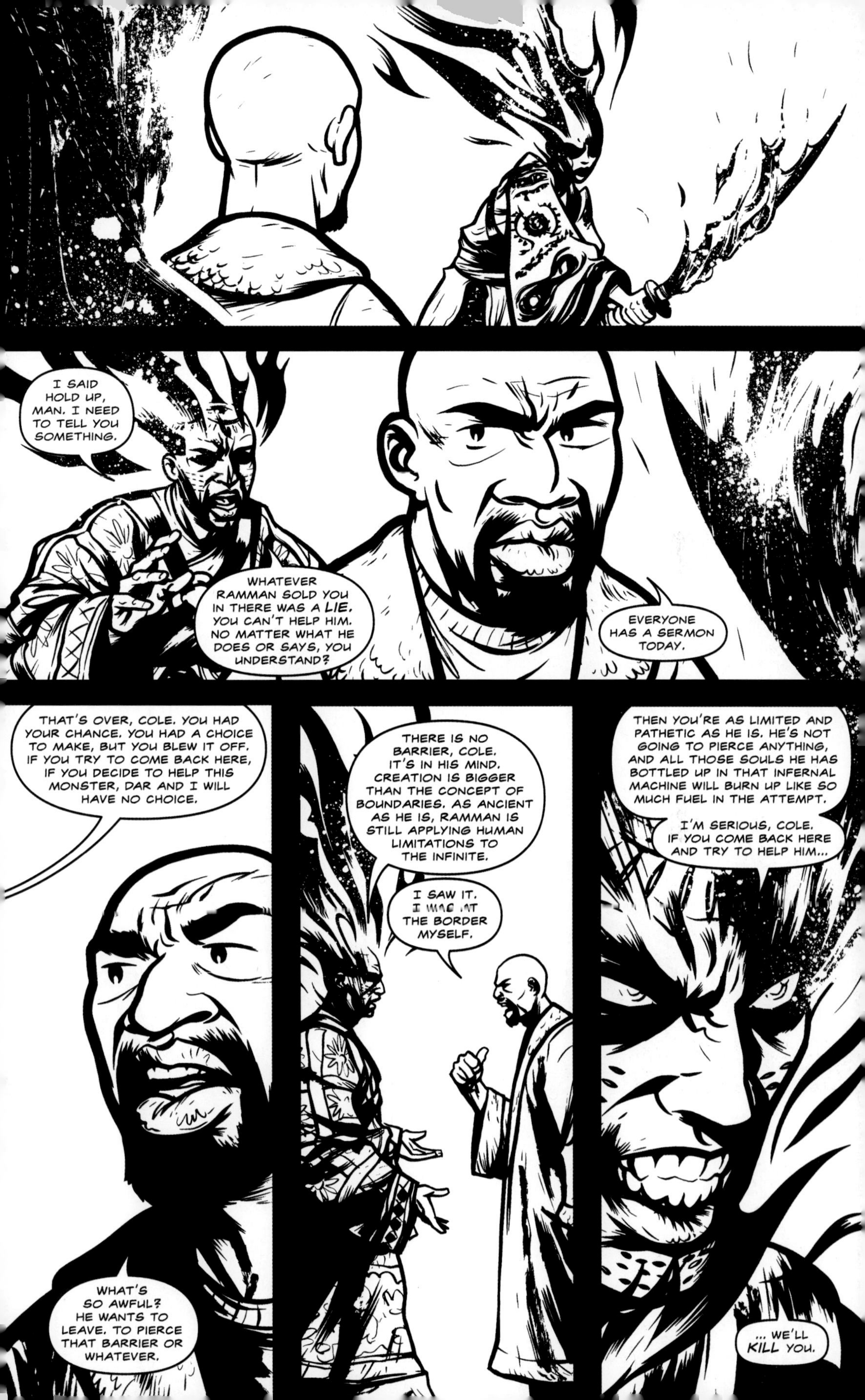
I SAID HOLD UP, MAN. I NEED TO TELL YOU SOMETHING.
WHATEVER RAMMAN SOLD YOU IN THERE WAS A **LIE.** YOU CAN'T HELP HIM. NO MATTER WHAT HE DOES OR SAYS, YOU UNDERSTAND?
EVERYONE HAS A SERMON TODAY.
THAT'S OVER, COLE. YOU HAD YOUR CHANCE. YOU HAD A CHOICE TO MAKE, BUT YOU BLEW IT OFF. IF YOU TRY TO COME BACK HERE, IF YOU DECIDE TO HELP THIS MONSTER, DAR AND I WILL HAVE NO CHOICE.
WHAT'S SO AWFUL? HE WANTS TO LEAVE. TO PIERCE THAT BARRIER OR WHATEVER.
THERE IS NO BARRIER, COLE. IT'S IN HIS MIND. CREATION IS BIGGER THAN THE CONCEPT OF BOUNDARIES. AS ANCIENT AS HE IS, RAMMAN IS STILL APPLYING HUMAN LIMITATIONS TO THE INFINITE.
I SAW IT. I WAS AT THE BORDER MYSELF.
THEN YOU'RE AS LIMITED AND PATHETIC AS HE IS. HE'S NOT GOING TO PIERCE ANYTHING, AND ALL THOSE SOULS HE HAS BOTTLED UP IN THAT INFERNAL MACHINE WILL BURN UP LIKE SO MUCH FUEL IN THE ATTEMPT.
I'M SERIOUS, COLE. IF YOU COME BACK HERE AND TRY TO HELP HIM...
... WE'LL **KILL** YOU.

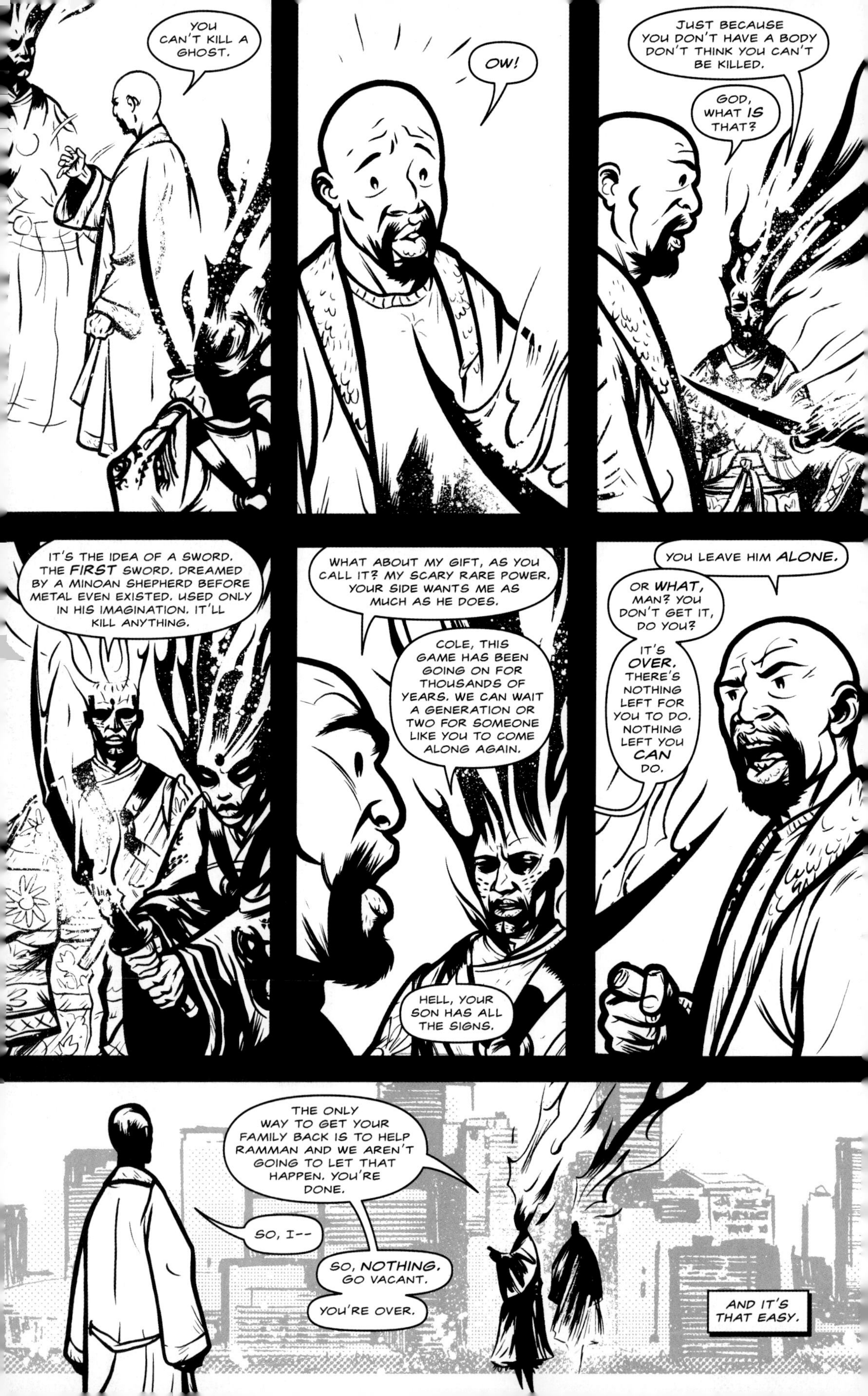
YOU CAN'T KILL A GHOST.
OW!
JUST BECAUSE YOU DON'T HAVE A BODY DON'T THINK YOU CAN'T BE KILLED.
GOD, WHAT IS THAT?
IT'S THE IDEA OF A SWORD. THE FIRST SWORD. DREAMED BY A MINOAN SHEPHERD BEFORE METAL EVEN EXISTED. USED ONLY IN HIS IMAGINATION. IT'LL KILL ANYTHING.
WHAT ABOUT MY GIFT, AS YOU CALL IT? MY SCARY RARE POWER. YOUR SIDE WANTS ME AS MUCH AS HE DOES.
COLE, THIS GAME HAS BEEN GOING ON FOR THOUSANDS OF YEARS. WE CAN WAIT A GENERATION OR TWO FOR SOMEONE LIKE YOU TO COME ALONG AGAIN.
HELL, YOUR SON HAS ALL THE SIGNS.
YOU LEAVE HIM ALONE.
OR WHAT, MAN? YOU DON'T GET IT, DO YOU?
IT'S OVER. THERE'S NOTHING LEFT FOR YOU TO DO. NOTHING LEFT YOU CAN DO.
THE ONLY WAY TO GET YOUR FAMILY BACK IS TO HELP RAMMAN AND WE AREN'T GOING TO LET THAT HAPPEN. YOU'RE DONE.
SO, I--
SO, NOTHING. GO VACANT.
YOU'RE OVER.
AND IT'S THAT EASY.

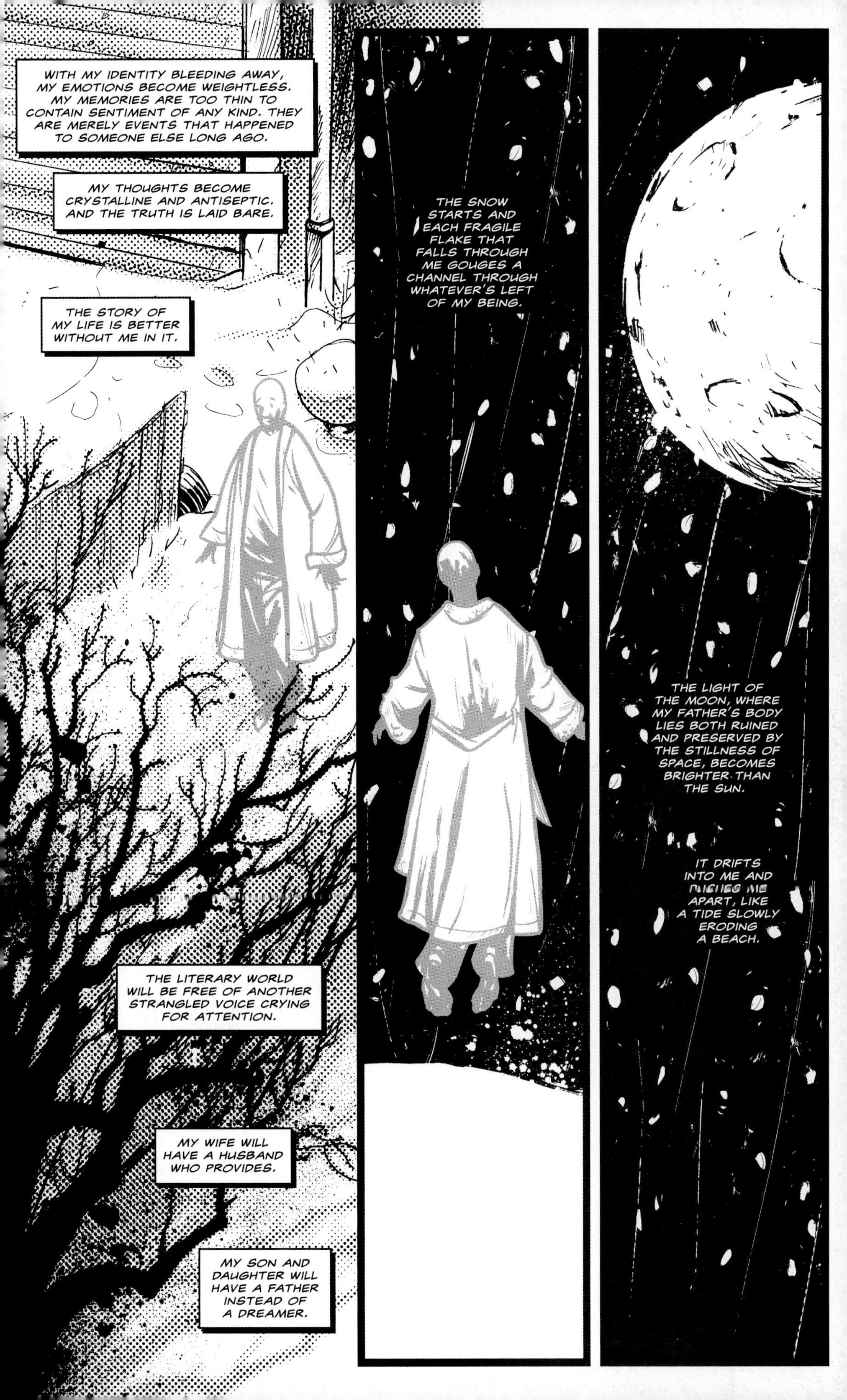
WITH MY IDENTITY BLEEDING AWAY, MY EMOTIONS BECOME WEIGHTLESS. MY MEMORIES ARE TOO THIN TO CONTAIN SENTIMENT OF ANY KIND. THEY ARE MERELY EVENTS THAT HAPPENED TO SOMEONE ELSE LONG AGO.
MY THOUGHTS BECOME CRYSTALLINE AND ANTISEPTIC. AND THE TRUTH IS LAID BARE.
THE STORY OF MY LIFE IS BETTER WITHOUT ME IN IT.
THE LITERARY WORLD WILL BE FREE OF ANOTHER STRANGLED VOICE CRYING FOR ATTENTION.
MY WIFE WILL HAVE A HUSBAND WHO PROVIDES.
MY SON AND DAUGHTER WILL HAVE A FATHER INSTEAD OF A DREAMER.
THE SNOW STARTS AND EACH FRAGILE FLAKE THAT FALLS THROUGH ME GOUGES A CHANNEL THROUGH WHATEVER'S LEFT OF MY BEING.
THE LIGHT OF THE MOON, WHERE MY FATHER'S BODY LIES BOTH RUINED AND PRESERVED BY THE STILLNESS OF SPACE, BECOMES BRIGHTER THAN THE SUN.
IT DRIFTS INTO ME AND
APART, LIKE A TIDE SLOWLY ERODING A BEACH.

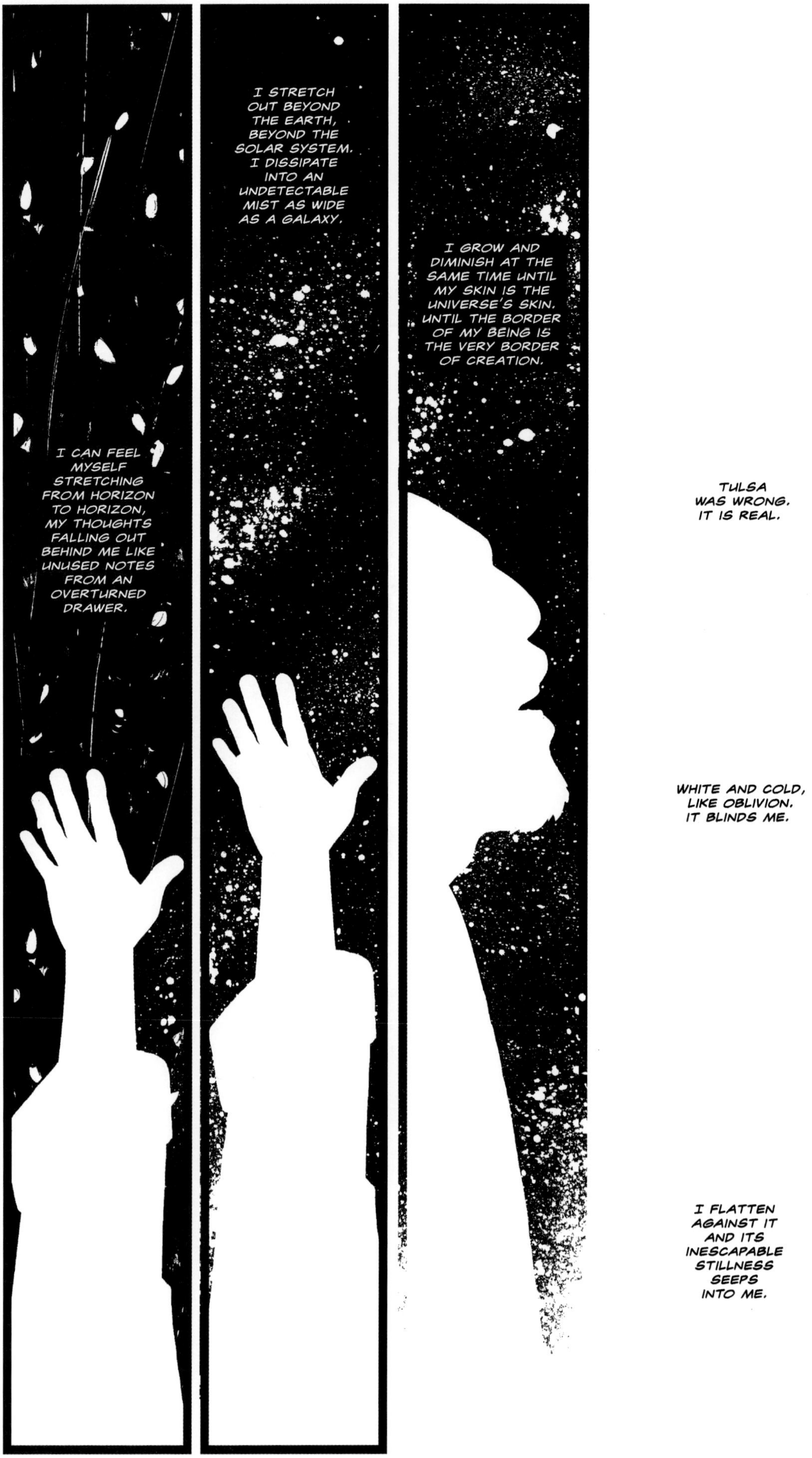
I CAN FEEL MYSELF STRETCHING FROM HORIZON TO HORIZON, MY THOUGHTS FALLING OUT BEHIND ME LIKE UNUSED NOTES FROM AN OVERTURNED DRAWER.
I STRETCH OUT BEYOND THE EARTH, BEYOND THE SOLAR SYSTEM. I DISSIPATE INTO AN UNDETECTABLE MIST AS WIDE AS A GALAXY.
I GROW AND DIMINISH AT THE SAME TIME UNTIL MY SKIN IS THE UNIVERSE'S SKIN. UNTIL THE BORDER OF MY BEING IS THE VERY BORDER OF CREATION.
TULSA WAS WRONG. IT IS REAL.
WHITE AND COLD, LIKE OBLIVION. IT BLINDS ME.
I FLATTEN AGAINST IT AND ITS INESCAPABLE STILLNESS SEEPS INTO ME.

I BECOME NOTHING.

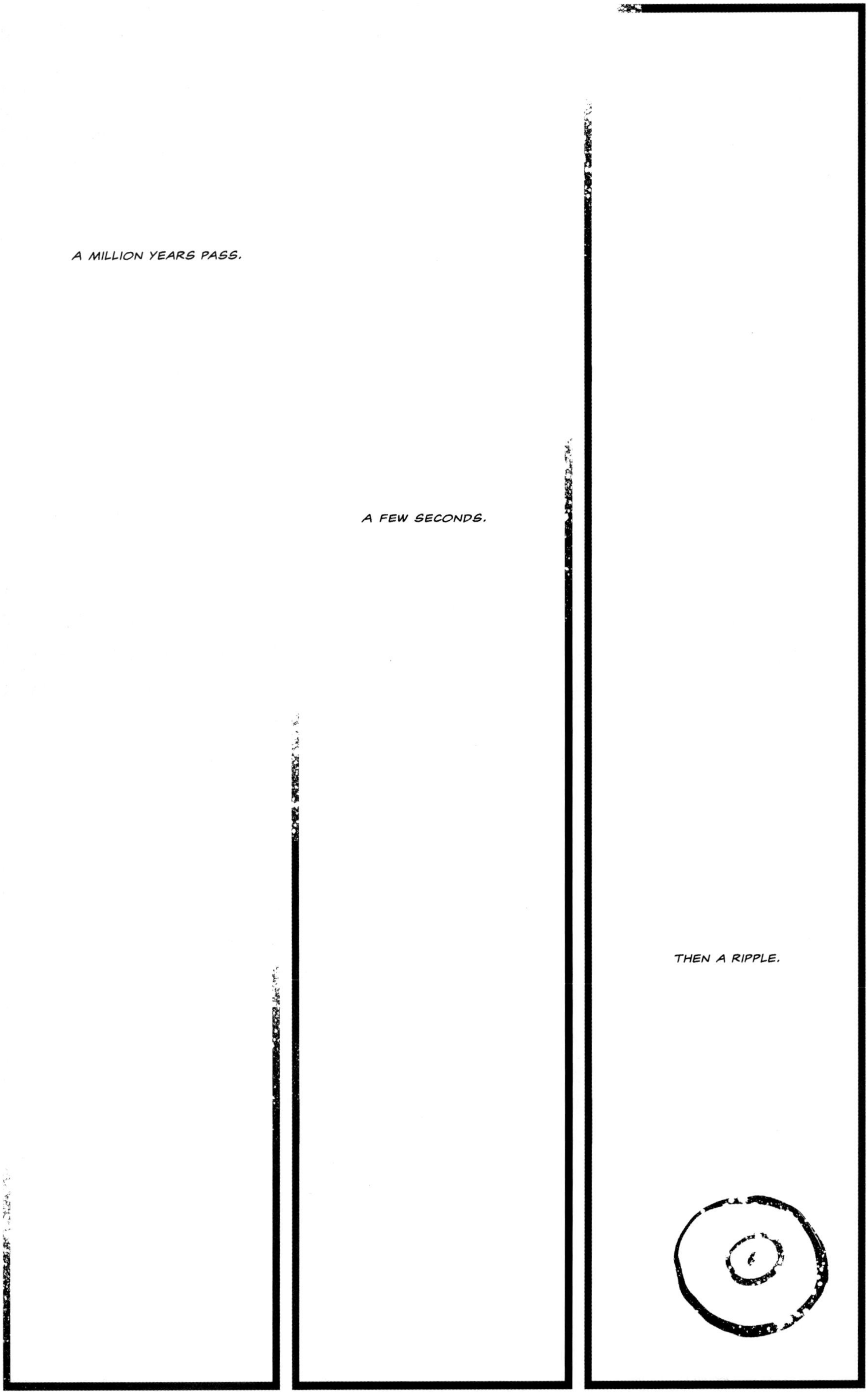
A MILLION YEARS PASS.
A FEW SECONDS.
THEN A RIPPLE.

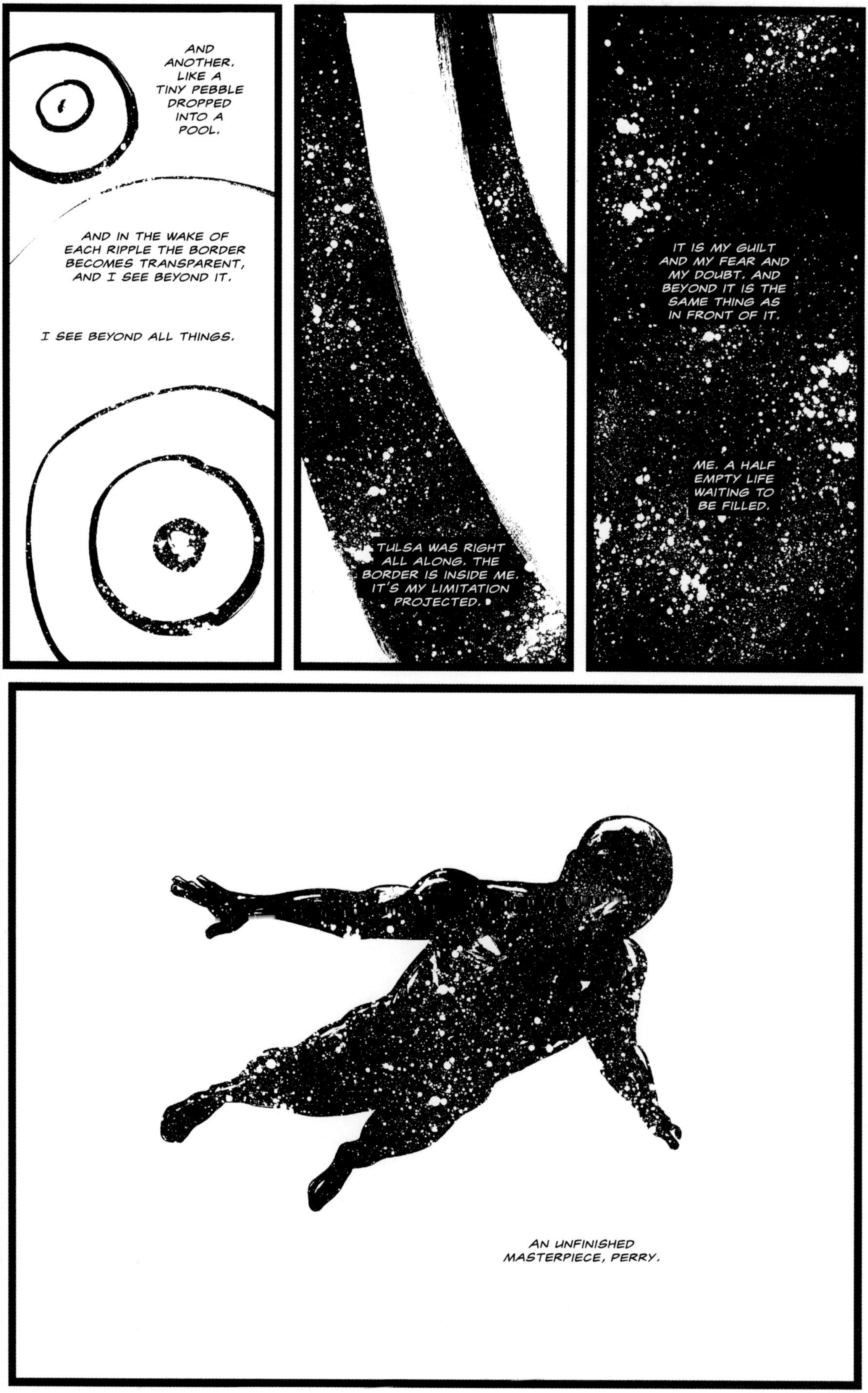
AND ANOTHER. LIKE A TINY PEBBLE DROPPED INTO A POOL.
AND IN THE WAKE OF EACH RIPPLE THE BORDER BECOMES TRANSPARENT, AND I SEE BEYOND IT.
I SEE BEYOND ALL THINGS.
TULSA WAS RIGHT ALL ALONG. THE BORDER IS INSIDE ME. IT'S MY LIMITATION PROJECTED.
IT IS MY GUILT AND MY FEAR AND MY DOUBT. AND BEYOND IT IS THE SAME THING AS IN FRONT OF IT.
ME. A HALF EMPTY LIFE WAITING TO BE FILLED.
AN UNFINISHED MASTERPIECE, PERRY.

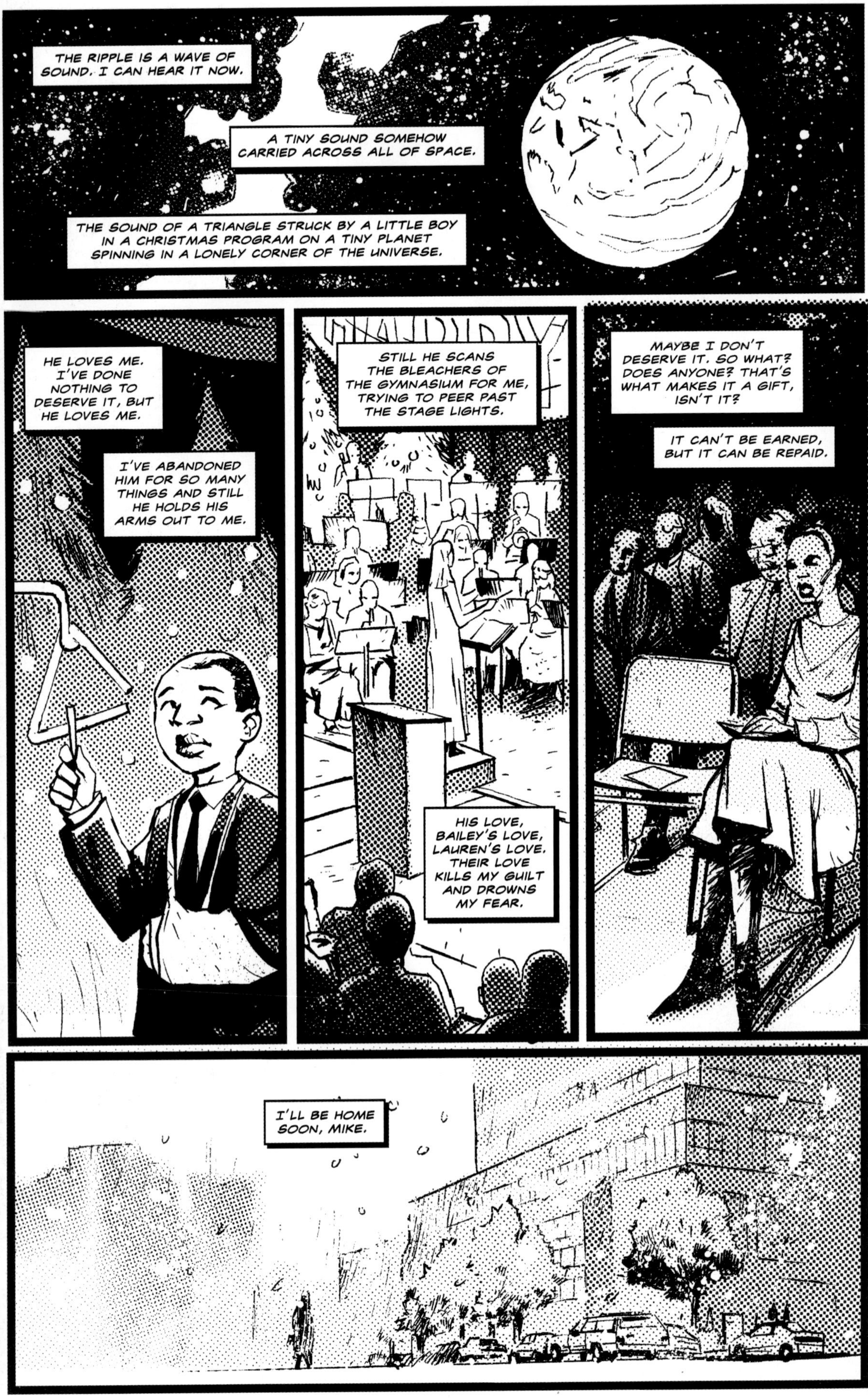
THE RIPPLE IS A WAVE OF SOUND. I CAN HEAR IT NOW.
A TINY SOUND SOMEHOW CARRIED ACROSS ALL OF SPACE.
THE SOUND OF A TRIANGLE STRUCK BY A LITTLE BOY IN A CHRISTMAS PROGRAM ON A TINY PLANET SPINNING IN A LONELY CORNER OF THE UNIVERSE.
HE LOVES ME. I'VE DONE NOTHING TO DESERVE IT, BUT HE LOVES ME.
I'VE ABANDONED HIM FOR SO MANY THINGS AND STILL HE HOLDS HIS ARMS OUT TO ME.
STILL HE SCANS THE BLEACHERS OF THE GYMNASIUM FOR ME, TRYING TO PEER PAST THE STAGE LIGHTS.
HIS LOVE, BAILEY'S LOVE, LAUREN'S LOVE. THEIR LOVE KILLS MY GUILT AND DROWNS MY FEAR.
MAYBE I DON'T DESERVE IT. SO WHAT? DOES ANYONE? THAT'S WHAT MAKES IT A GIFT, ISN'T IT?
IT CAN'T BE EARNED, BUT IT CAN BE REPAID.
I'LL BE HOME SOON, MIKE.

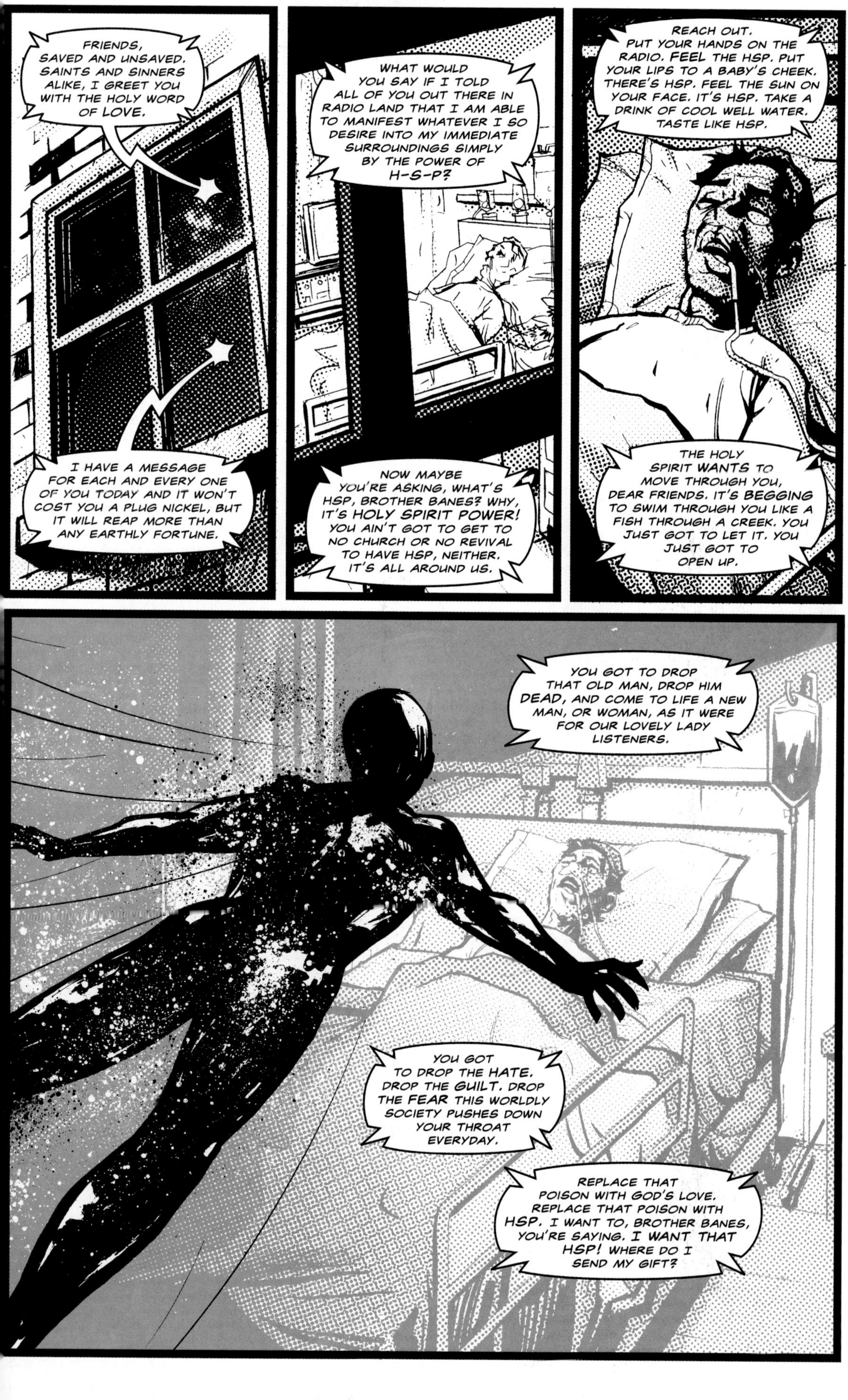
FRIENDS, SAVED AND UNSAVED, SAINTS AND SINNERS ALIKE, I GREET YOU WITH THE HOLY WORD OF LOVE.
I HAVE A MESSAGE FOR EACH AND EVERY ONE OF YOU TODAY AND IT WON'T COST YOU A PLUG NICKEL, BUT IT WILL REAP MORE THAN ANY EARTHLY FORTUNE.
WHAT WOULD YOU SAY IF I TOLD ALL OF YOU OUT THERE IN RADIO LAND THAT I AM ABLE TO MANIFEST WHATEVER I SO DESIRE INTO MY IMMEDIATE SURROUNDINGS SIMPLY BY THE POWER OF H-S-P?
NOW MAYBE YOU'RE ASKING, WHAT'S HSP, BROTHER BANES? WHY, IT'S HOLY SPIRIT POWER! YOU AIN'T GOT TO GET TO NO CHURCH OR NO REVIVAL TO HAVE HSP, NEITHER. IT'S ALL AROUND US.
REACH OUT. PUT YOUR HANDS ON THE RADIO. FEEL THE HSP. PUT YOUR LIPS TO A BABY'S CHEEK. THERE'S HSP. FEEL THE SUN ON YOUR FACE. IT'S HSP. TAKE A DRINK OF COOL WELL WATER. TASTE LIKE HSP.
THE HOLY SPIRIT WANTS TO MOVE THROUGH YOU, DEAR FRIENDS. IT'S BEGGING TO SWIM THROUGH YOU LIKE A FISH THROUGH A CREEK. YOU JUST GOT TO LET IT. YOU JUST GOT TO OPEN UP.
YOU GOT TO DROP THAT OLD MAN, DROP HIM DEAD, AND COME TO LIFE A NEW MAN, OR WOMAN, AS IT WERE FOR OUR LOVELY LADY LISTENERS.
YOU GOT TO DROP THE HATE. DROP THE GUILT. DROP THE FEAR THIS WORLDLY SOCIETY PUSHES DOWN YOUR THROAT EVERYDAY.
REPLACE THAT POISON WITH GOD'S LOVE. REPLACE THAT POISON WITH HSP. I WANT TO, BROTHER BANES, YOU'RE SAYING. I WANT THAT HSP! WHERE DO I SEND MY GIFT?

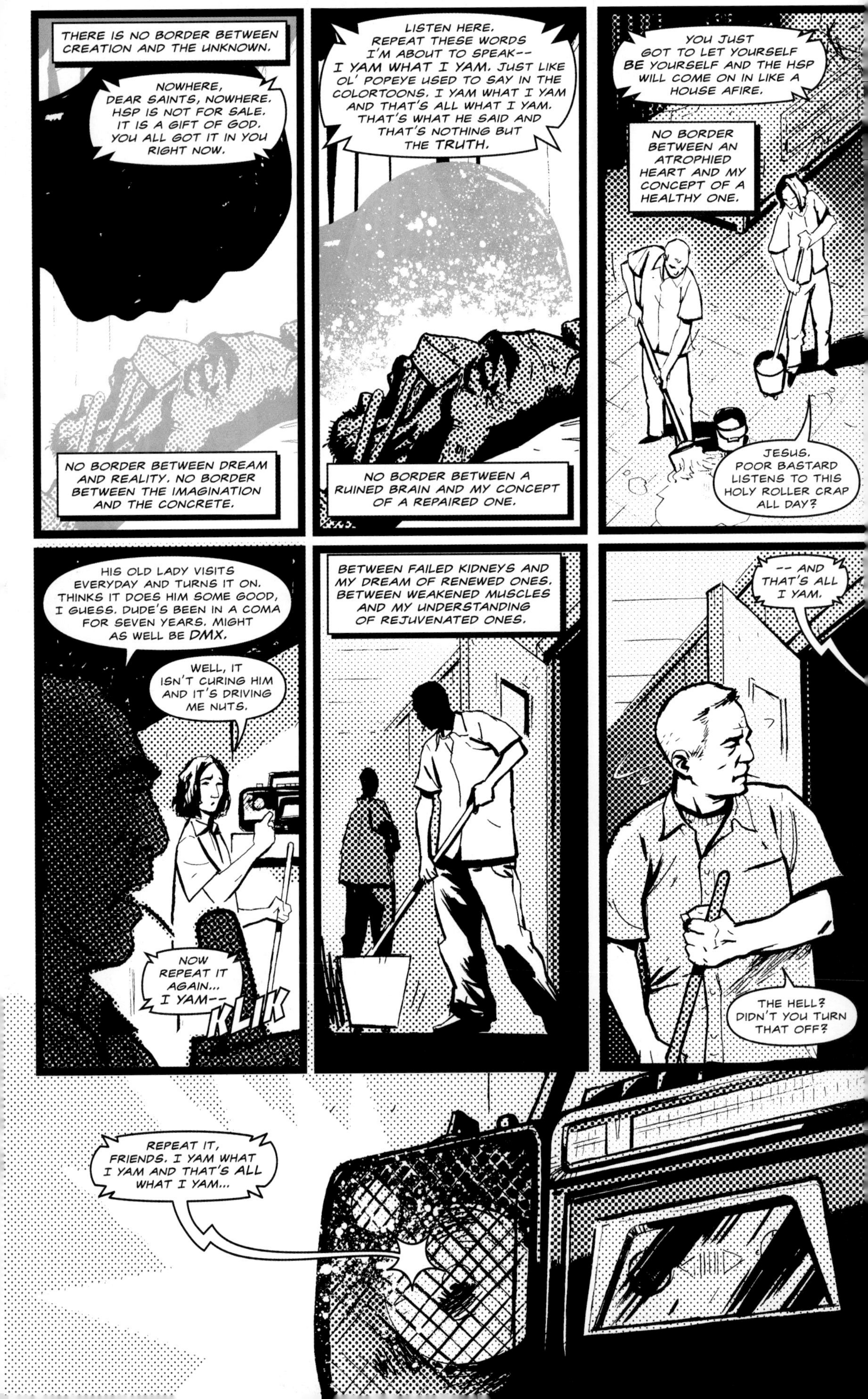
THERE IS NO BORDER BETWEEN CREATION AND THE UNKNOWN.
NOWHERE, DEAR SAINTS, NOWHERE. HSP IS NOT FOR SALE. IT IS A GIFT OF GOD. YOU ALL GOT IT IN YOU RIGHT NOW.
NO BORDER BETWEEN DREAM AND REALITY. NO BORDER BETWEEN THE IMAGINATION AND THE CONCRETE.
LISTEN HERE. REPEAT THESE WORDS I'M ABOUT TO SPEAK-- I YAM WHAT I YAM. JUST LIKE OL' POPEYE USED TO SAY IN THE COLORTOONS. I YAM WHAT I YAM AND THAT'S ALL WHAT I YAM. THAT'S WHAT HE SAID AND THAT'S NOTHING BUT THE TRUTH.
NO BORDER BETWEEN A RUINED BRAIN AND MY CONCEPT OF A REPAIRED ONE.
YOU JUST GOT TO LET YOURSELF BE YOURSELF AND THE HSP WILL COME ON IN LIKE A HOUSE AFIRE.
NO BORDER BETWEEN AN ATROPHIED HEART AND MY CONCEPT OF A HEALTHY ONE.
JESUS. POOR BASTARD LISTENS TO THIS HOLY ROLLER CRAP ALL DAY?
HIS OLD LADY VISITS EVERYDAY AND TURNS IT ON. THINKS IT DOES HIM SOME GOOD, I GUESS. DUDE'S BEEN IN A COMA FOR SEVEN YEARS. MIGHT AS WELL BE DMX.
WELL, IT ISN'T CURING HIM AND IT'S DRIVING ME NUTS.
NOW REPEAT IT AGAIN... I YAM--
KLIK
BETWEEN FAILED KIDNEYS AND MY DREAM OF RENEWED ONES. BETWEEN WEAKENED MUSCLES AND MY UNDERSTANDING OF REJUVENATED ONES.
-- AND THAT'S ALL I YAM.
THE HELL? DIDN'T YOU TURN THAT OFF?
REPEAT IT, FRIENDS. I YAM WHAT I YAM AND THAT'S ALL WHAT I YAM...

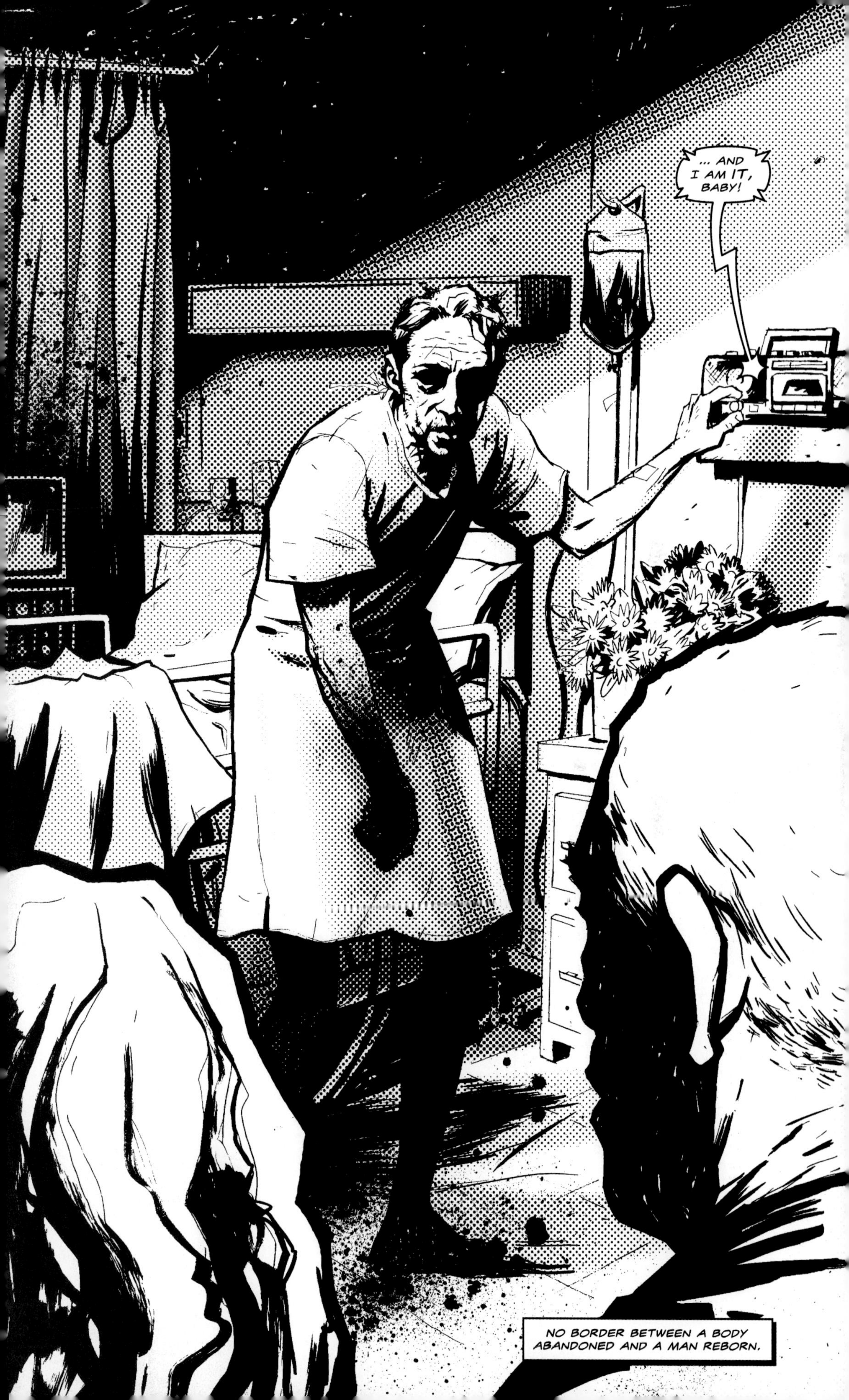
... AND I AM IT, BABY!
NO BORDER BETWEEN A BODY ABANDONED AND A MAN REBORN.

DEEP SLEEPER

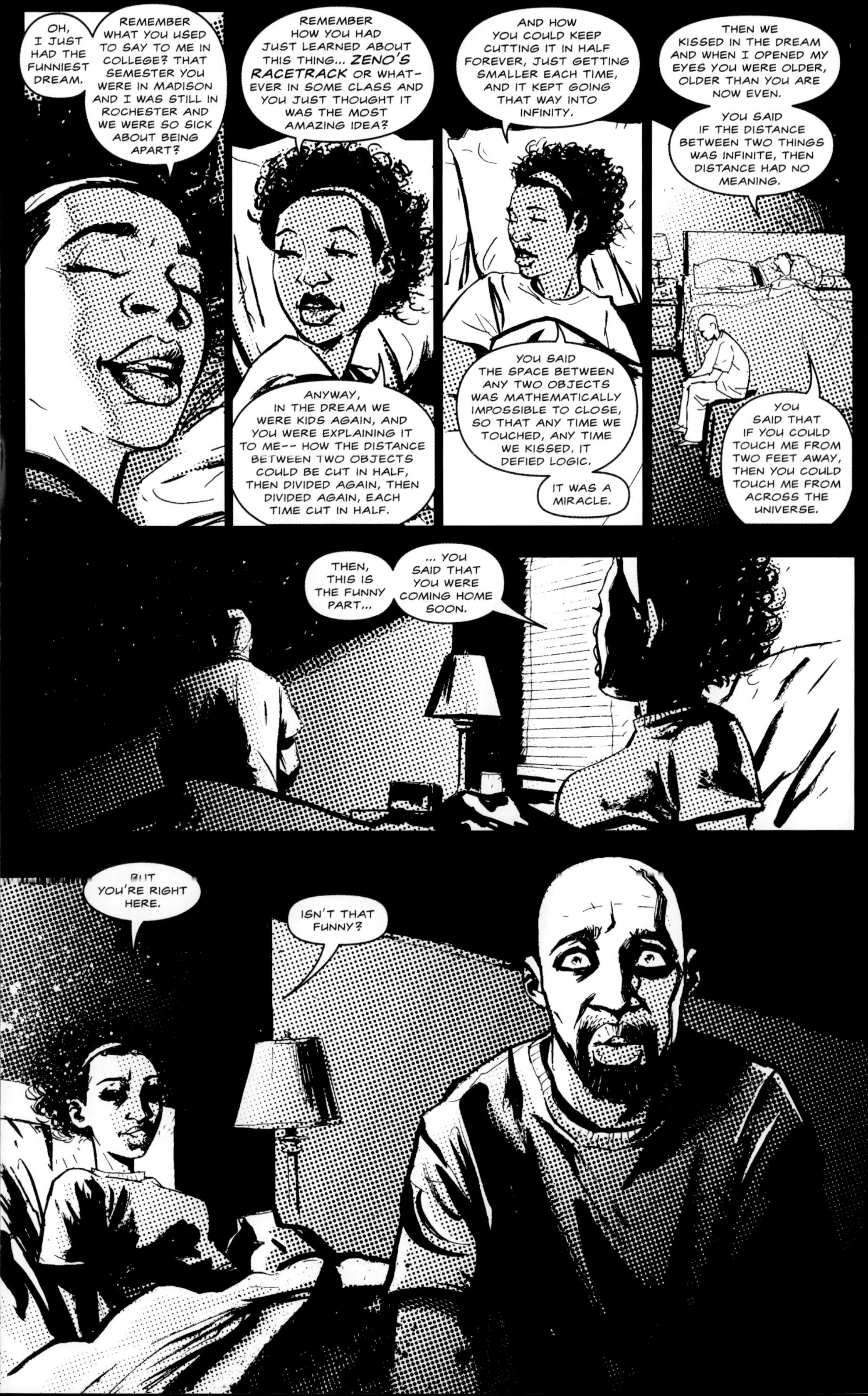
OH, I JUST HAD THE FUNNIEST DREAM.
REMEMBER WHAT YOU USED TO SAY TO ME IN COLLEGE? THAT SEMESTER YOU WERE IN MADISON AND I WAS STILL IN ROCHESTER AND WE WERE SO SICK ABOUT BEING APART?
REMEMBER HOW YOU HAD JUST LEARNED ABOUT THIS THING... ZENO'S RACETRACK OR WHATEVER IN SOME CLASS AND YOU JUST THOUGHT IT WAS THE MOST AMAZING IDEA?
ANYWAY, IN THE DREAM WE WERE KIDS AGAIN, AND YOU WERE EXPLAINING IT TO ME-- HOW THE DISTANCE BETWEEN TWO OBJECTS COULD BE CUT IN HALF, THEN DIVIDED AGAIN, THEN DIVIDED AGAIN, EACH TIME CUT IN HALF.
AND HOW YOU COULD KEEP CUTTING IT IN HALF FOREVER, JUST GETTING SMALLER EACH TIME, AND IT KEPT GOING THAT WAY INTO INFINITY.
YOU SAID THE SPACE BETWEEN ANY TWO OBJECTS WAS MATHEMATICALLY IMPOSSIBLE TO CLOSE, SO THAT ANY TIME WE TOUCHED, ANY TIME WE KISSED, IT DEFIED LOGIC.
IT WAS A MIRACLE.
THEN WE KISSED IN THE DREAM AND WHEN I OPENED MY EYES YOU WERE OLDER, OLDER THAN YOU ARE NOW EVEN.
YOU SAID IF THE DISTANCE BETWEEN TWO THINGS WAS INFINITE, THEN DISTANCE HAD NO MEANING.
YOU SAID THAT IF YOU COULD TOUCH ME FROM TWO FEET AWAY, THEN YOU COULD TOUCH ME FROM ACROSS THE UNIVERSE.
THEN, THIS IS THE FUNNY PART...
... YOU SAID THAT YOU WERE COMING HOME SOON.
BUT YOU'RE RIGHT HERE.
ISN'T THAT FUNNY?

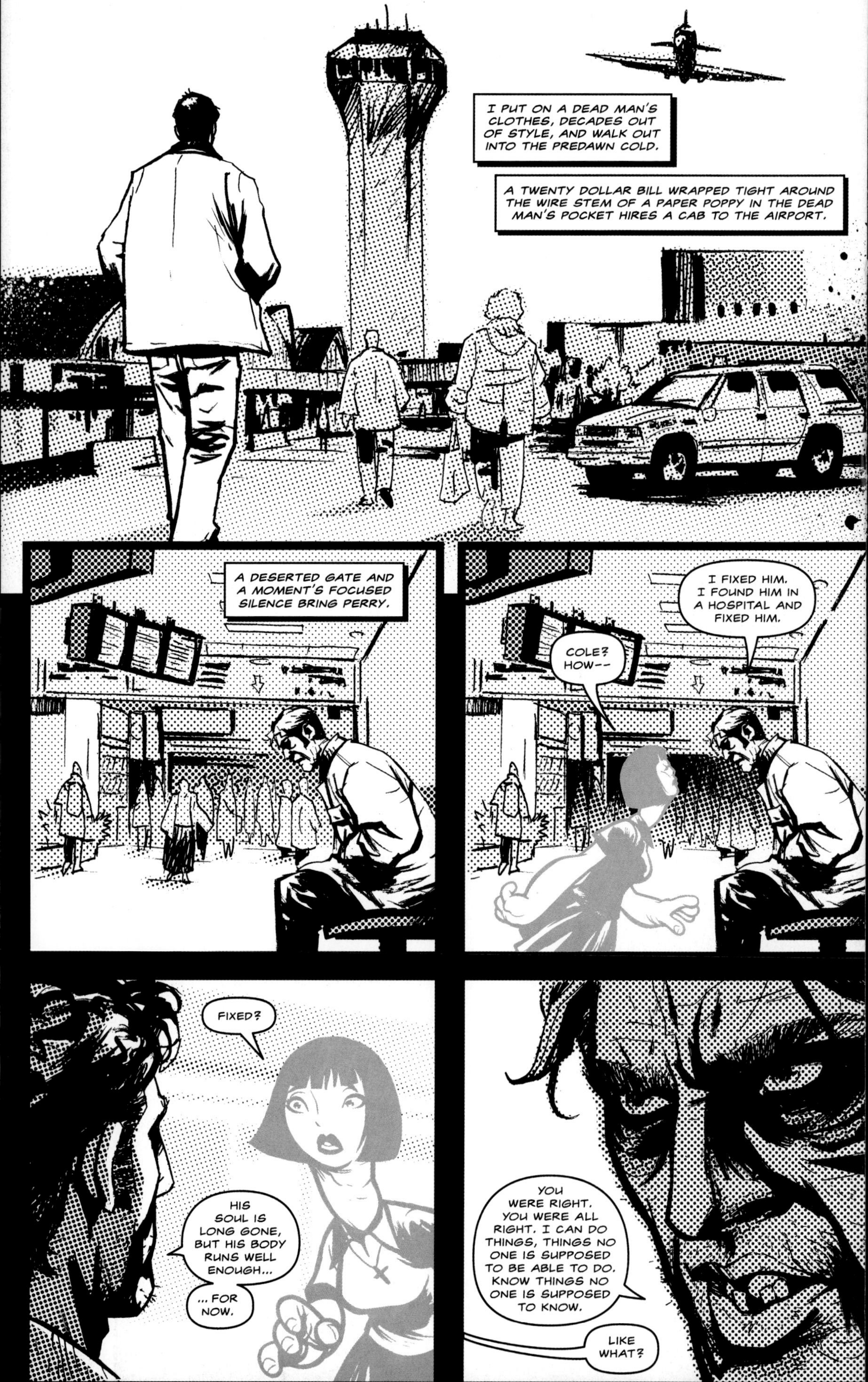
I PUT ON A DEAD MAN'S CLOTHES, DECADES OUT OF STYLE, AND WALK OUT INTO THE PREDAWN COLD.
A TWENTY DOLLAR BILL WRAPPED TIGHT AROUND THE WIRE STEM OF A PAPER POPPY IN THE DEAD MAN'S POCKET HIRES A CAB TO THE AIRPORT.
A DESERTED GATE AND A MOMENT'S FOCUSED SILENCE BRING PERRY.
COLE? HOW--
I FIXED HIM. I FOUND HIM IN A HOSPITAL AND FIXED HIM.
FIXED?
HIS SOUL IS LONG GONE, BUT HIS BODY RUNS WELL ENOUGH...
... FOR NOW.
YOU WERE RIGHT. YOU WERE ALL RIGHT. I CAN DO THINGS, THINGS NO ONE IS SUPPOSED TO BE ABLE TO DO. KNOW THINGS NO ONE IS SUPPOSED TO KNOW.
LIKE WHAT?

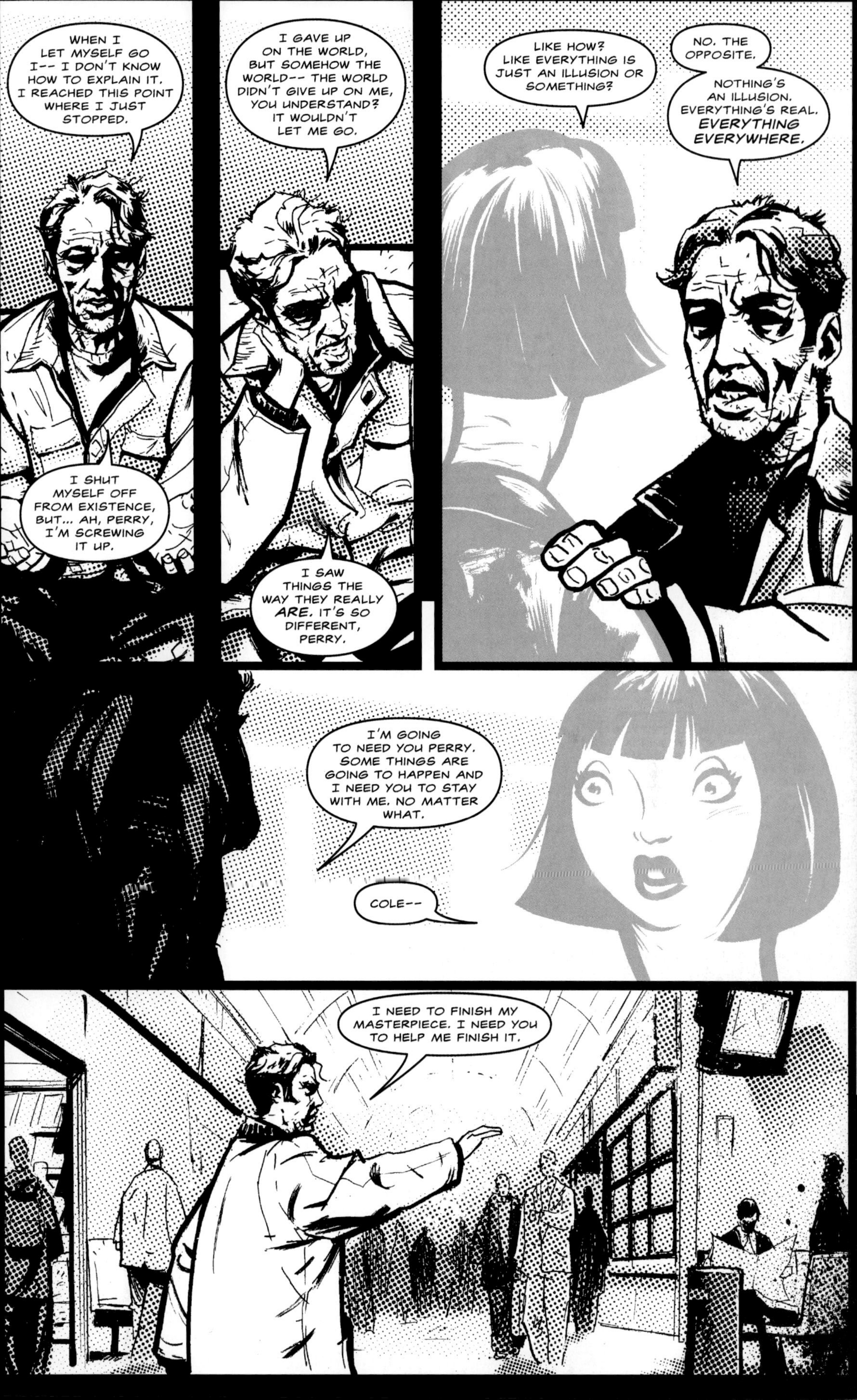
WHEN I LET MYSELF GO I-- I DON'T KNOW HOW TO EXPLAIN IT. I REACHED THIS POINT WHERE I JUST STOPPED.
I SHUT MYSELF OFF FROM EXISTENCE, BUT... AH, PERRY, I'M SCREWING IT UP.
I GAVE UP ON THE WORLD, BUT SOMEHOW THE WORLD-- THE WORLD DIDN'T GIVE UP ON ME, YOU UNDERSTAND? IT WOULDN'T LET ME GO.
I SAW THINGS THE WAY THEY REALLY ARE. IT'S SO DIFFERENT, PERRY.
LIKE HOW? LIKE EVERYTHING IS JUST AN ILLUSION OR SOMETHING?
NO. THE OPPOSITE.
NOTHING'S AN ILLUSION. EVERYTHING'S REAL. EVERYTHING EVERYWHERE.
I'M GOING TO NEED YOU PERRY. SOME THINGS ARE GOING TO HAPPEN AND I NEED YOU TO STAY WITH ME. NO MATTER WHAT.
COLE--
I NEED TO FINISH MY MASTERPIECE. I NEED YOU TO HELP ME FINISH IT.

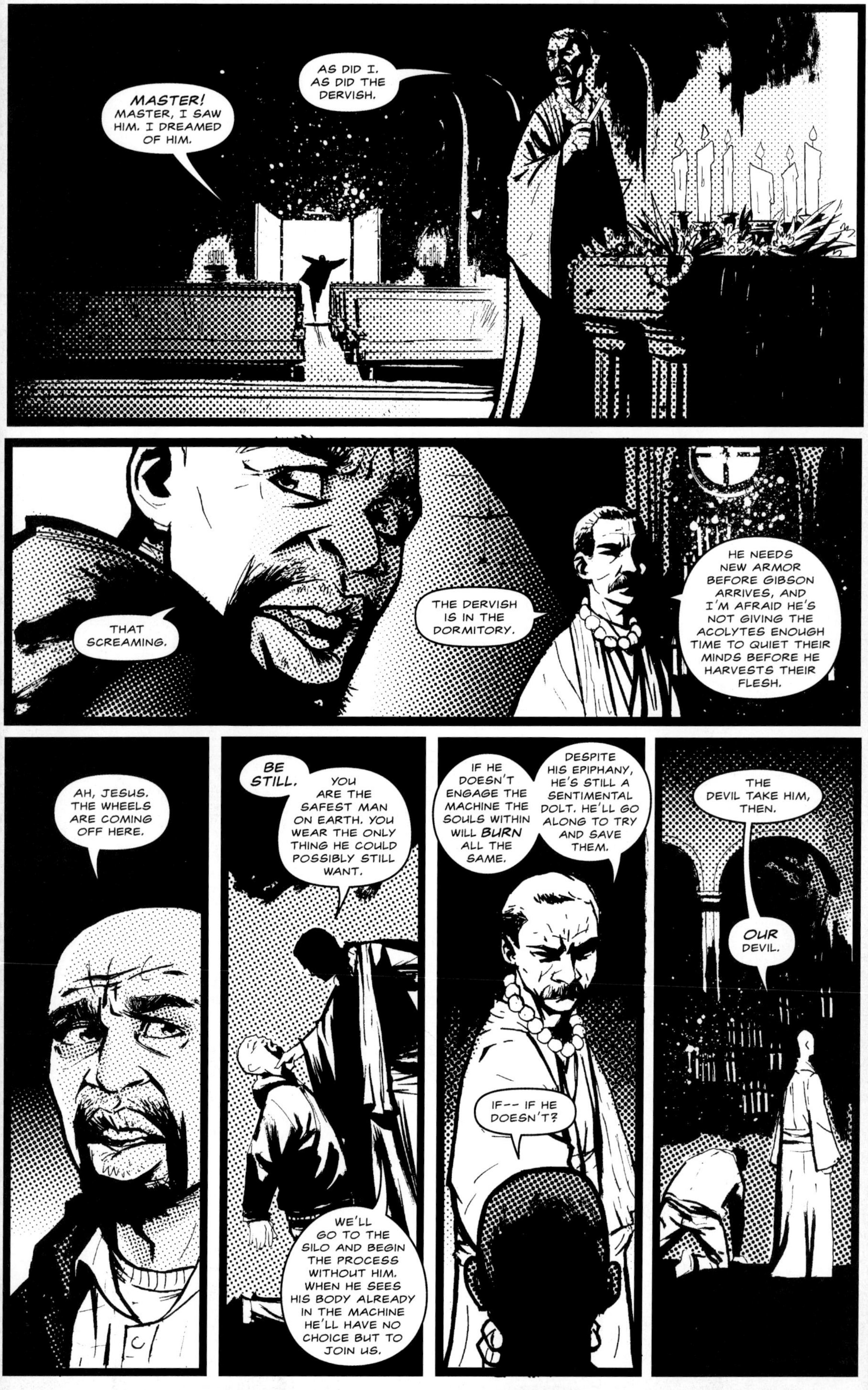
MASTER! MASTER, I SAW HIM. I DREAMED OF HIM.
AS DID I. AS DID THE DERVISH.
THAT SCREAMING.
THE DERVISH IS IN THE DORMITORY.
HE NEEDS NEW ARMOR BEFORE GIBSON ARRIVES, AND I'M AFRAID HE'S NOT GIVING THE ACOLYTES ENOUGH TIME TO QUIET THEIR MINDS BEFORE HE HARVESTS THEIR FLESH.
AH, JESUS. THE WHEELS ARE COMING OFF HERE.
BE STILL.
YOU ARE THE SAFEST MAN ON EARTH. YOU WEAR THE ONLY THING HE COULD POSSIBLY STILL WANT.
WE'LL GO TO THE SILO AND BEGIN THE PROCESS WITHOUT HIM. WHEN HE SEES HIS BODY ALREADY IN THE MACHINE HE'LL HAVE NO CHOICE BUT TO JOIN US.
IF HE DOESN'T ENGAGE THE MACHINE THE SOULS WITHIN WILL BURN ALL THE SAME.
DESPITE HIS EPIPHANY, HE'S STILL A SENTIMENTAL DOLT. HE'LL GO ALONG TO TRY AND SAVE THEM.
IF-- IF HE DOESN'T?
THE DEVIL TAKE HIM, THEN.
OUR DEVIL.

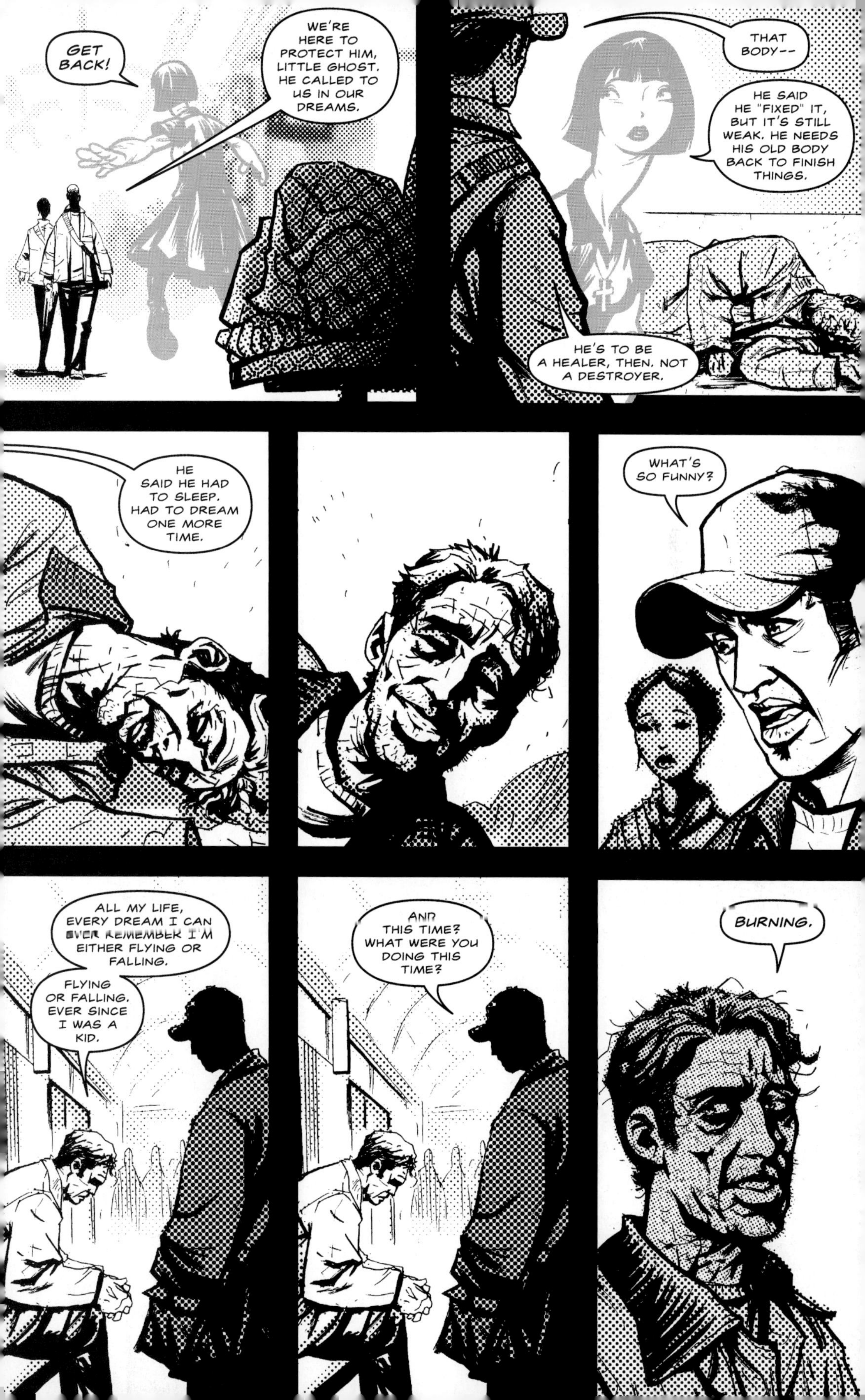
GET BACK!
WE'RE HERE TO PROTECT HIM, LITTLE GHOST. HE CALLED TO US IN OUR DREAMS.
THAT BODY--
HE SAID HE "FIXED" IT, BUT IT'S STILL WEAK. HE NEEDS HIS OLD BODY BACK TO FINISH THINGS.
HE'S TO BE A HEALER, THEN. NOT A DESTROYER.
HE SAID HE HAD TO SLEEP. HAD TO DREAM ONE MORE TIME.
WHAT'S SO FUNNY?
ALL MY LIFE, EVERY DREAM I CAN EVER REMEMBER I'M EITHER FLYING OR FALLING.
FLYING OR FALLING. EVER SINCE I WAS A KID.
AND THIS TIME? WHAT WERE YOU DOING THIS TIME?
BURNING.

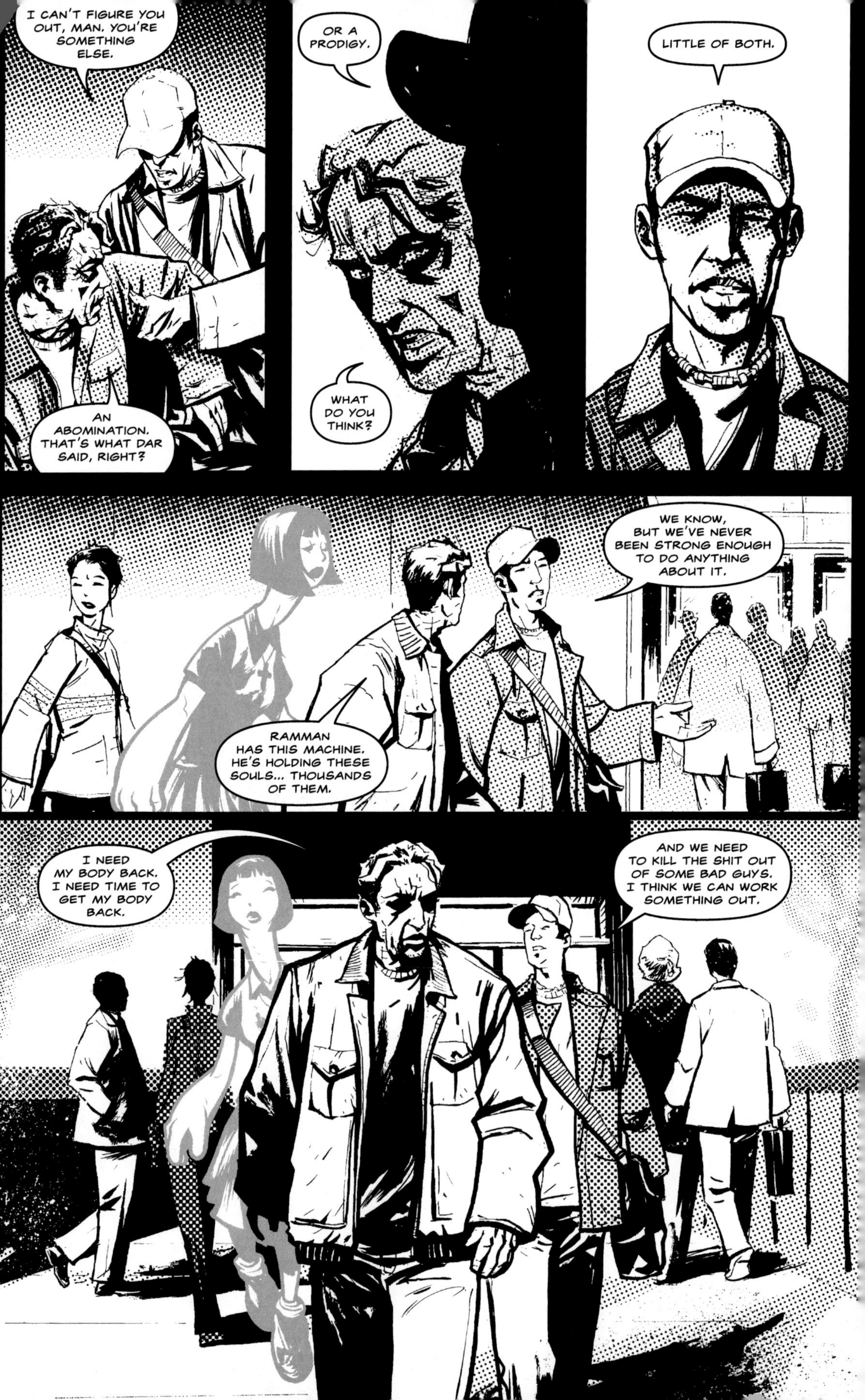
I CAN'T FIGURE YOU OUT, MAN. YOU'RE SOMETHING ELSE.
AN ABOMINATION. THAT'S WHAT DAR SAID, RIGHT?
OR A PRODIGY.
WHAT DO YOU THINK?
LITTLE OF BOTH.
WE KNOW, BUT WE'VE NEVER BEEN STRONG ENOUGH TO DO ANYTHING ABOUT IT.
RAMMAN HAS THIS MACHINE. HE'S HOLDING THESE SOULS... THOUSANDS OF THEM.
I NEED MY BODY BACK. I NEED TIME TO GET MY BODY BACK.
AND WE NEED TO KILL THE SHIT OUT OF SOME BAD GUYS. I THINK WE CAN WORK SOMETHING OUT.

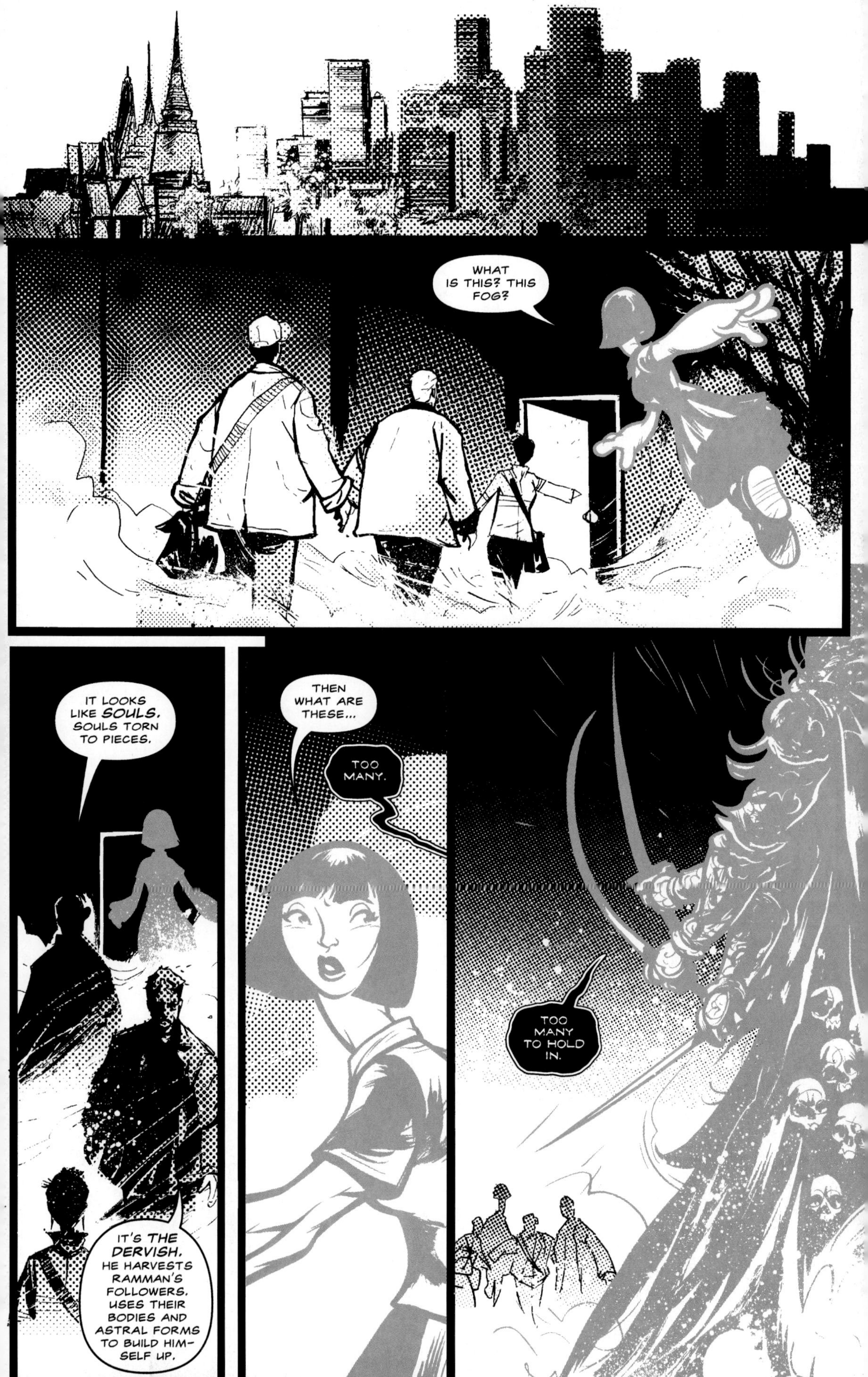
WHAT IS THIS? THIS FOG?
IT LOOKS LIKE SOULS. SOULS TORN TO PIECES.
IT'S THE DERVISH. HE HARVESTS RAMMAN'S FOLLOWERS. USES THEIR BODIES AND ASTRAL FORMS TO BUILD HIM-SELF UP.
THEN WHAT ARE THESE...
TOO MANY.
TOO MANY TO HOLD IN.

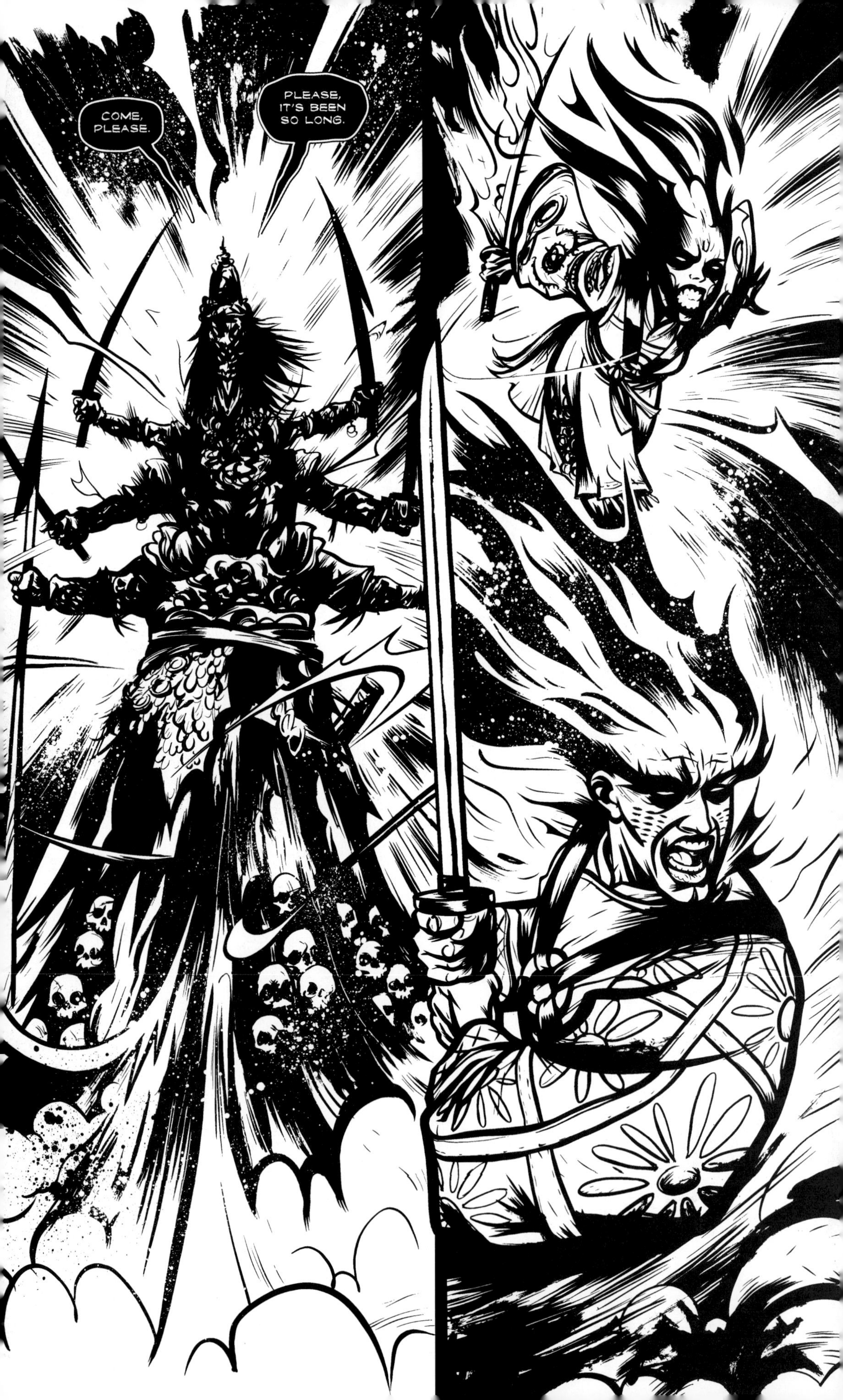
COME, PLEASE.
PLEASE, IT'S BEEN SO LONG.

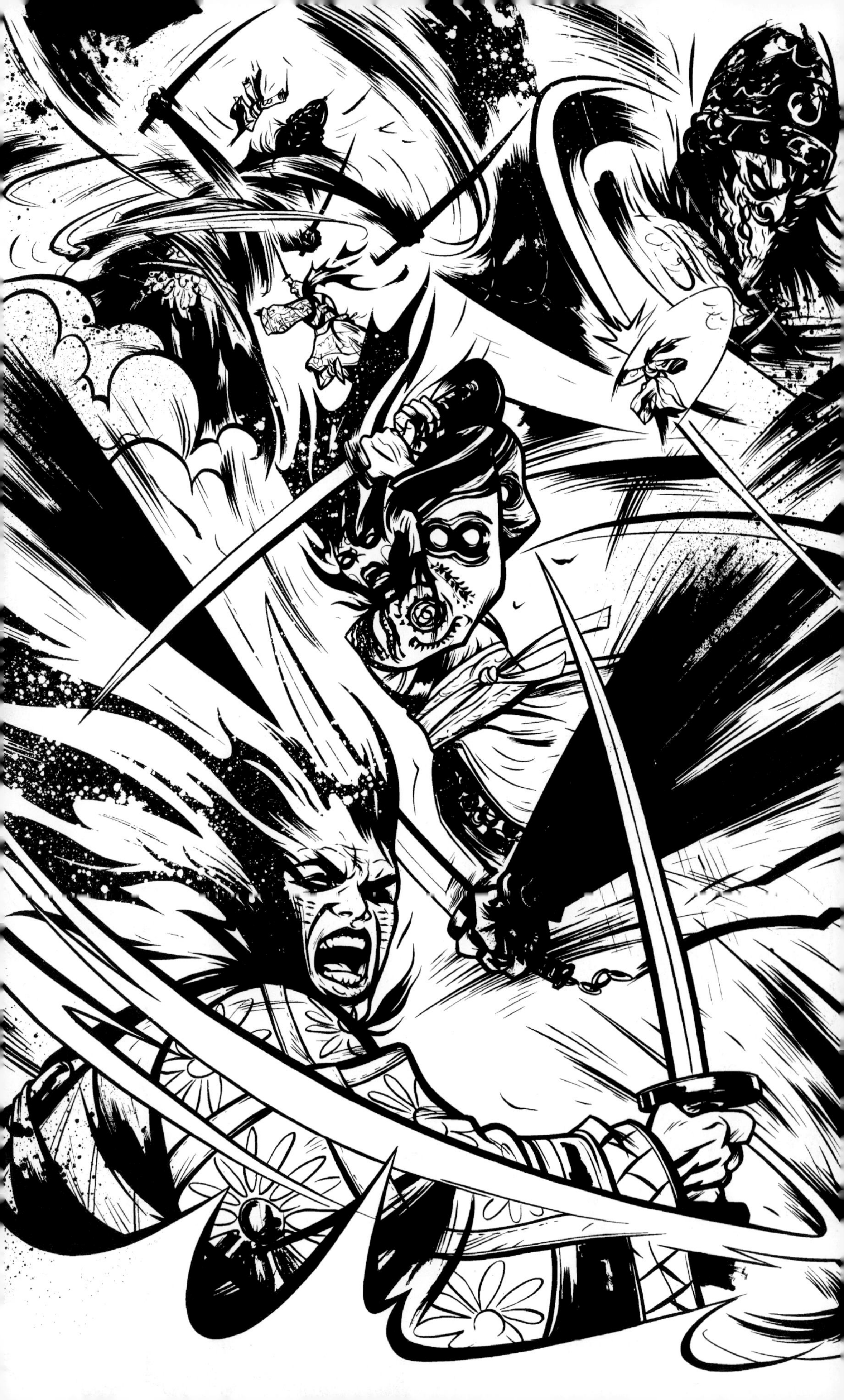

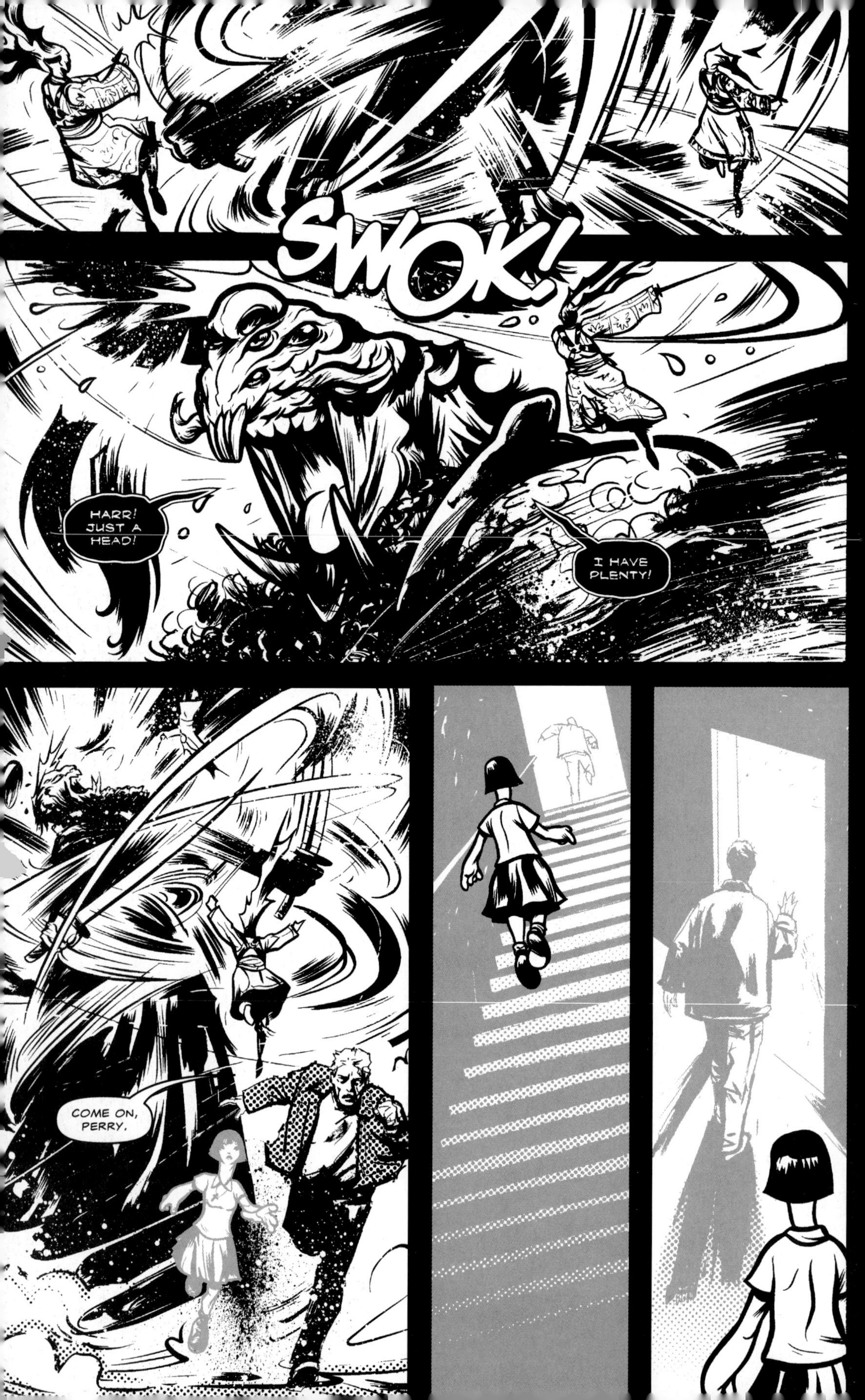
SWOK!
HARR! JUST A HEAD!
I HAVE PLENTY!
COME ON, PERRY.

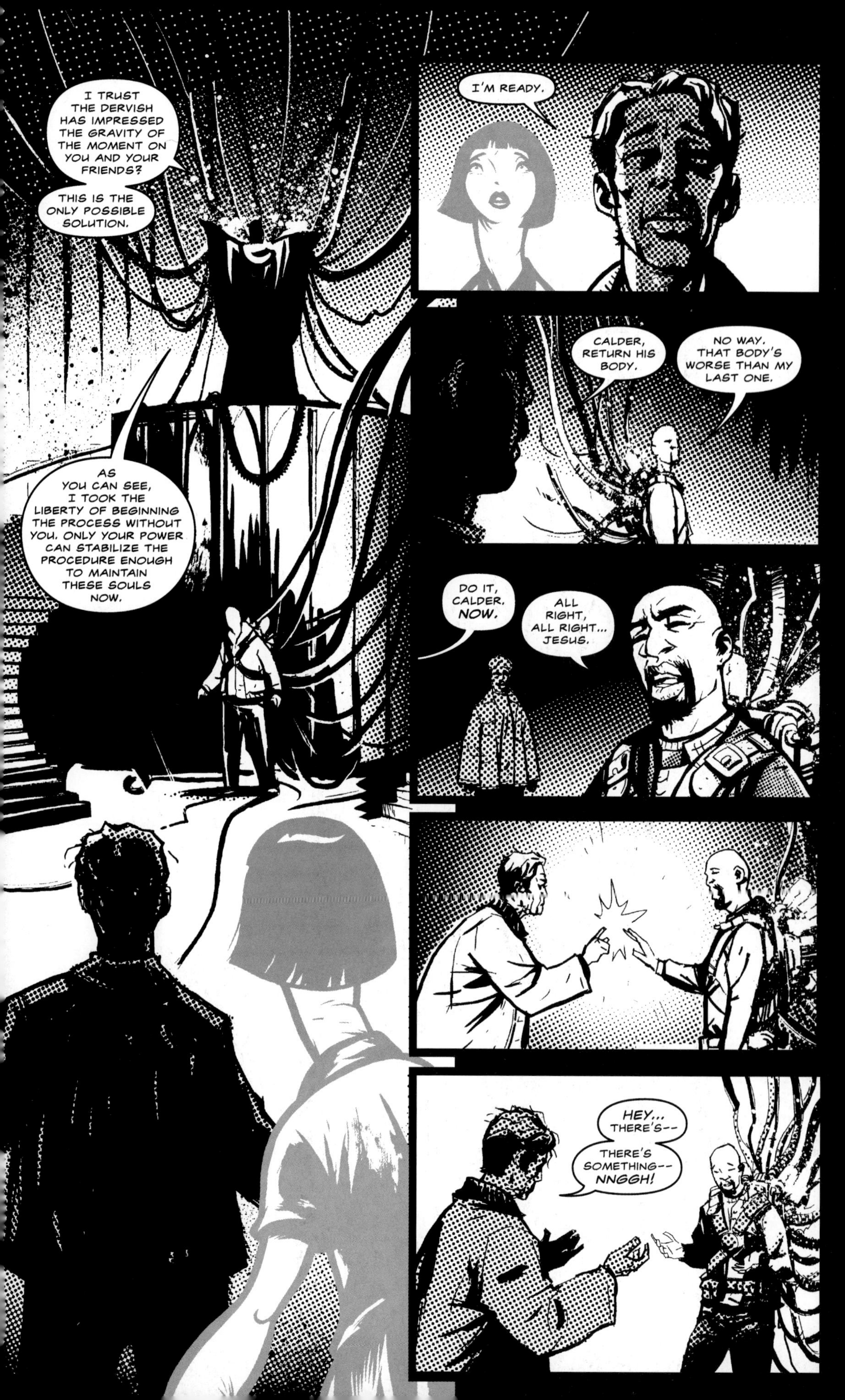
I TRUST THE DERVISH HAS IMPRESSED THE GRAVITY OF THE MOMENT ON YOU AND YOUR FRIENDS?
THIS IS THE ONLY POSSIBLE SOLUTION.
AS YOU CAN SEE, I TOOK THE LIBERTY OF BEGINNING THE PROCESS WITHOUT YOU. ONLY YOUR POWER CAN STABILIZE THE PROCEDURE ENOUGH TO MAINTAIN THESE SOULS NOW.
I'M READY.
CALDER, RETURN HIS BODY.
NO WAY. THAT BODY'S WORSE THAN MY LAST ONE.
DO IT, CALDER. NOW.
ALL RIGHT, ALL RIGHT... JESUS.
HEY... THERE'S--
THERE'S SOMETHING-- NNGGH!

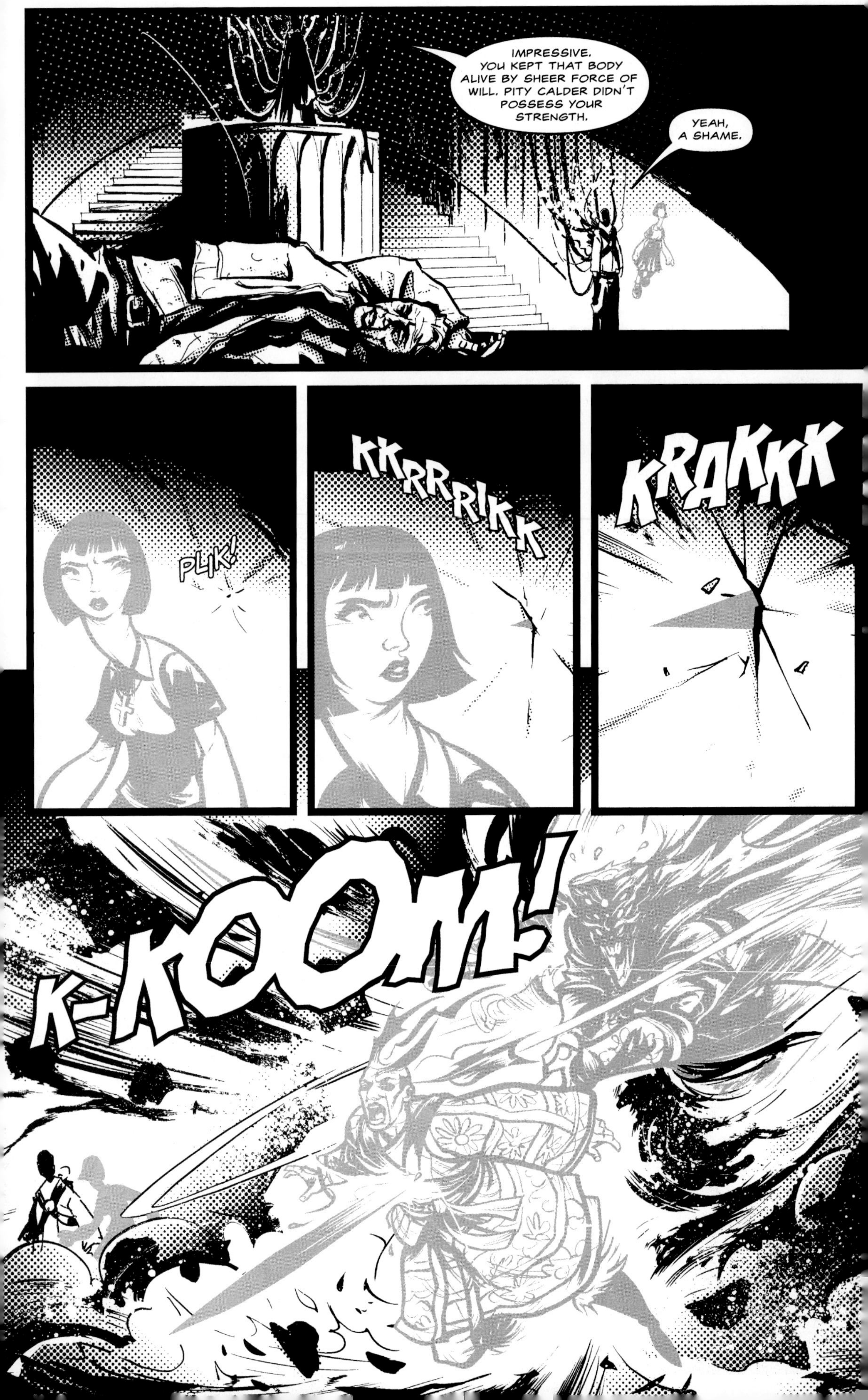
IMPRESSIVE. YOU KEPT THAT BODY ALIVE BY SHEER FORCE OF WILL. PITY CALDER DIDN'T POSSESS YOUR STRENGTH.
YEAH, A SHAME.
PLIK!
KKRRRRIKK
KRAKKK
K-KOOM!

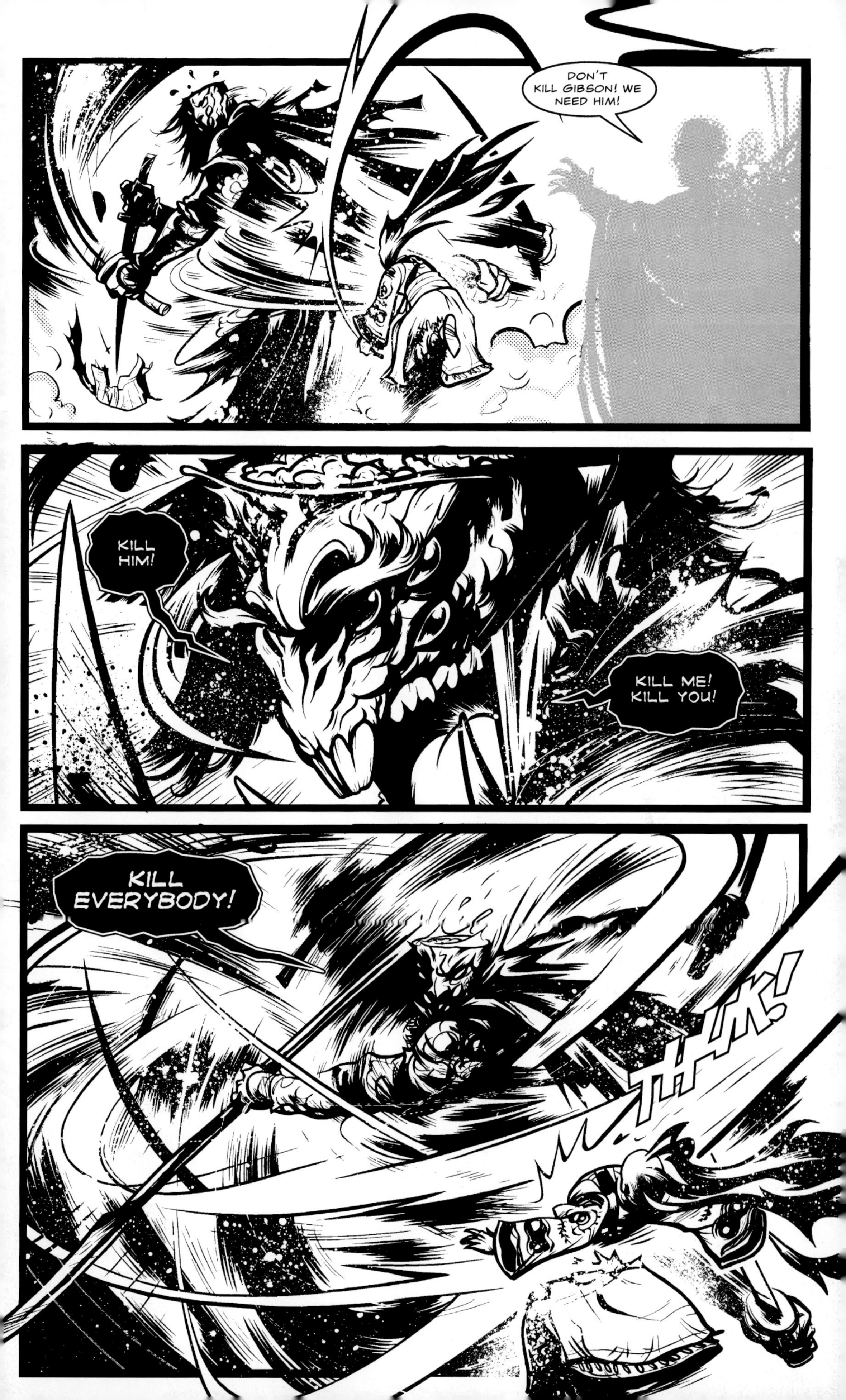
DON'T KILL GIBSON! WE NEED HIM!
KILL HIM!
KILL ME! KILL YOU!
KILL EVERYBODY!
THUNK!

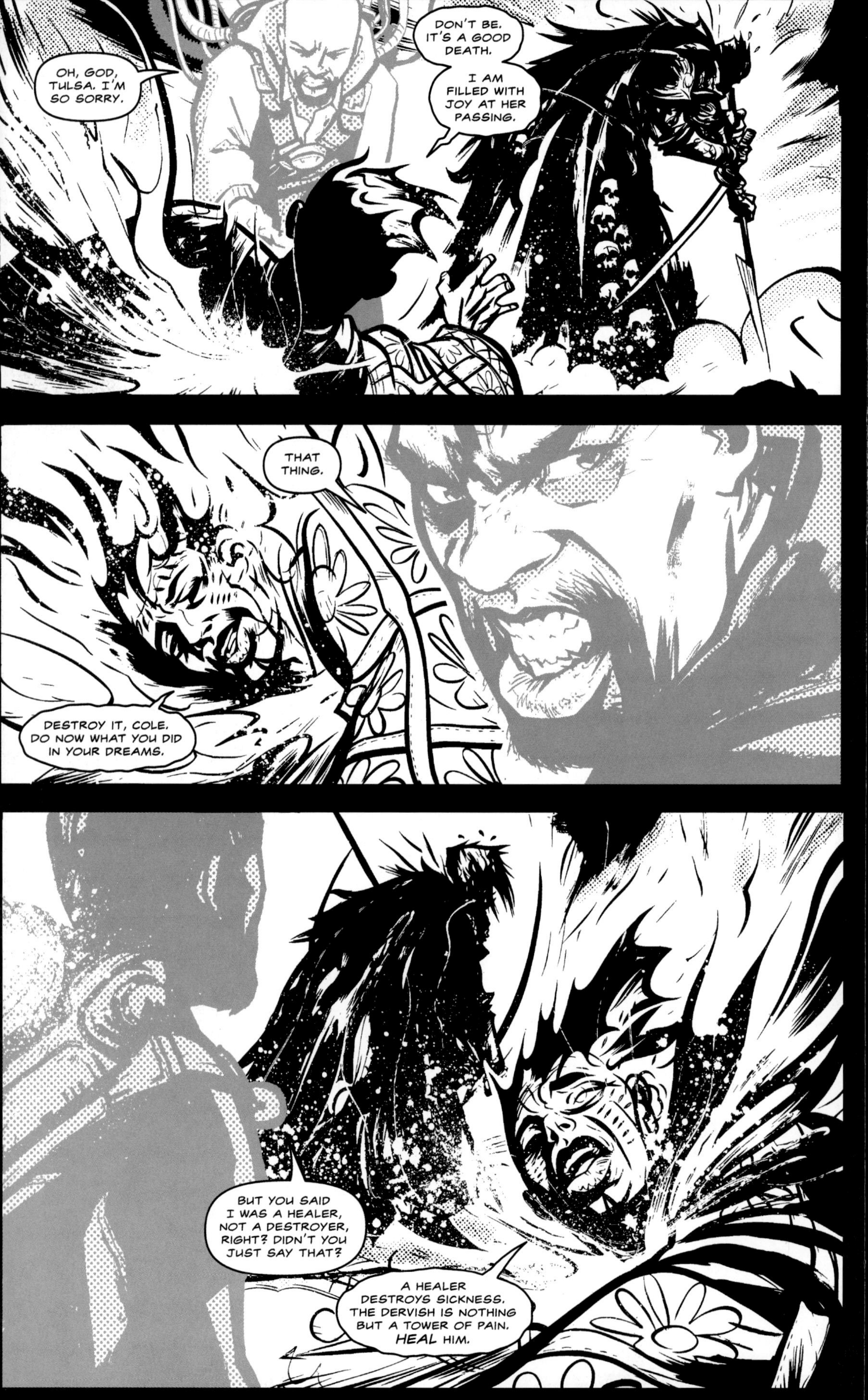
OH, GOD, TULSA. I'M SO SORRY.
DON'T BE. IT'S A GOOD DEATH.
I AM FILLED WITH JOY AT HER PASSING.
THAT THING.
DESTROY IT, COLE. DO NOW WHAT YOU DID IN YOUR DREAMS.
BUT YOU SAID I WAS A HEALER, NOT A DESTROYER, RIGHT? DIDN'T YOU JUST SAY THAT?
A HEALER DESTROYS SICKNESS. THE DERVISH IS NOTHING BUT A TOWER OF PAIN. *HEAL* HIM.

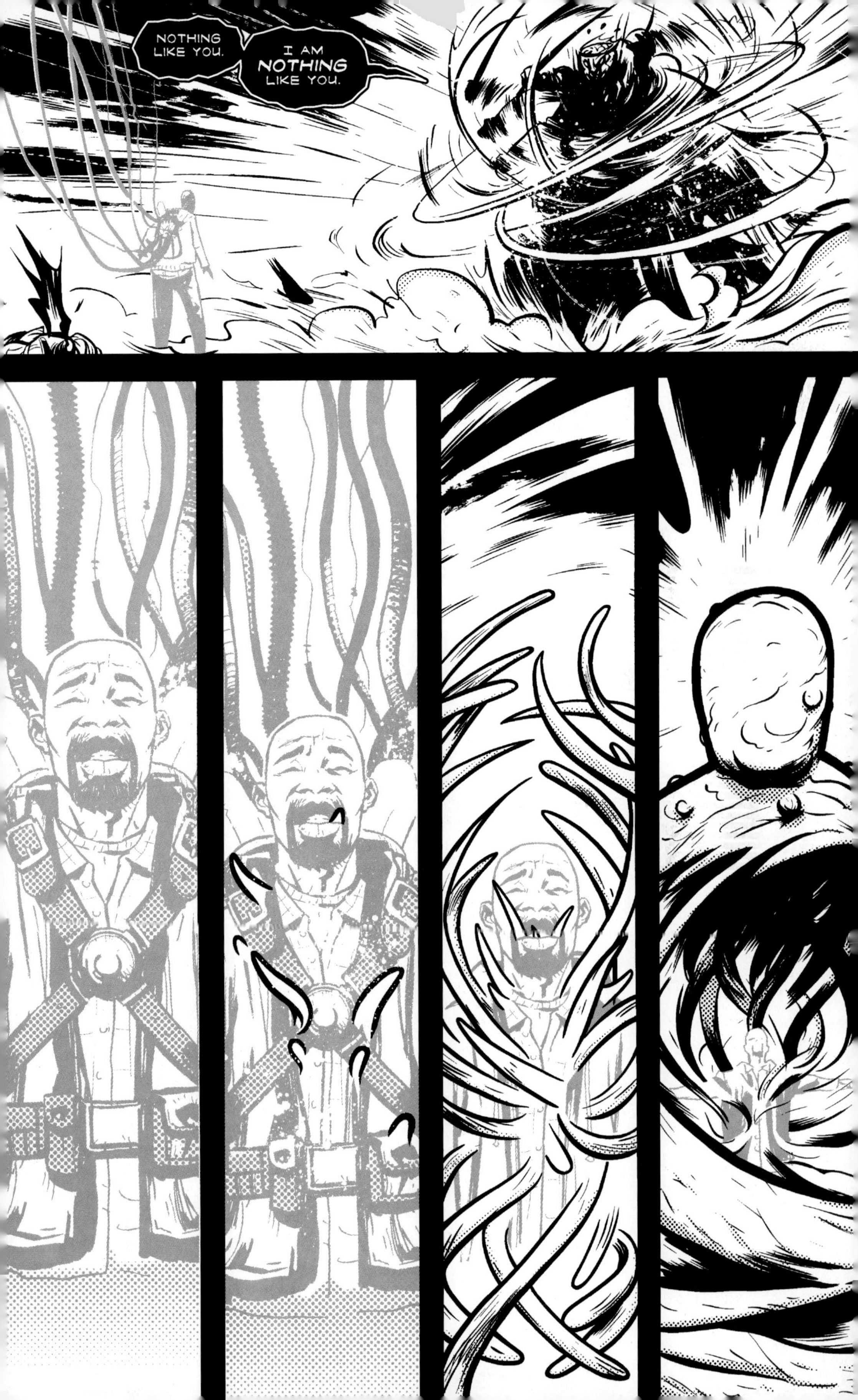
NOTHING LIKE YOU.
I AM NOTHING LIKE YOU.

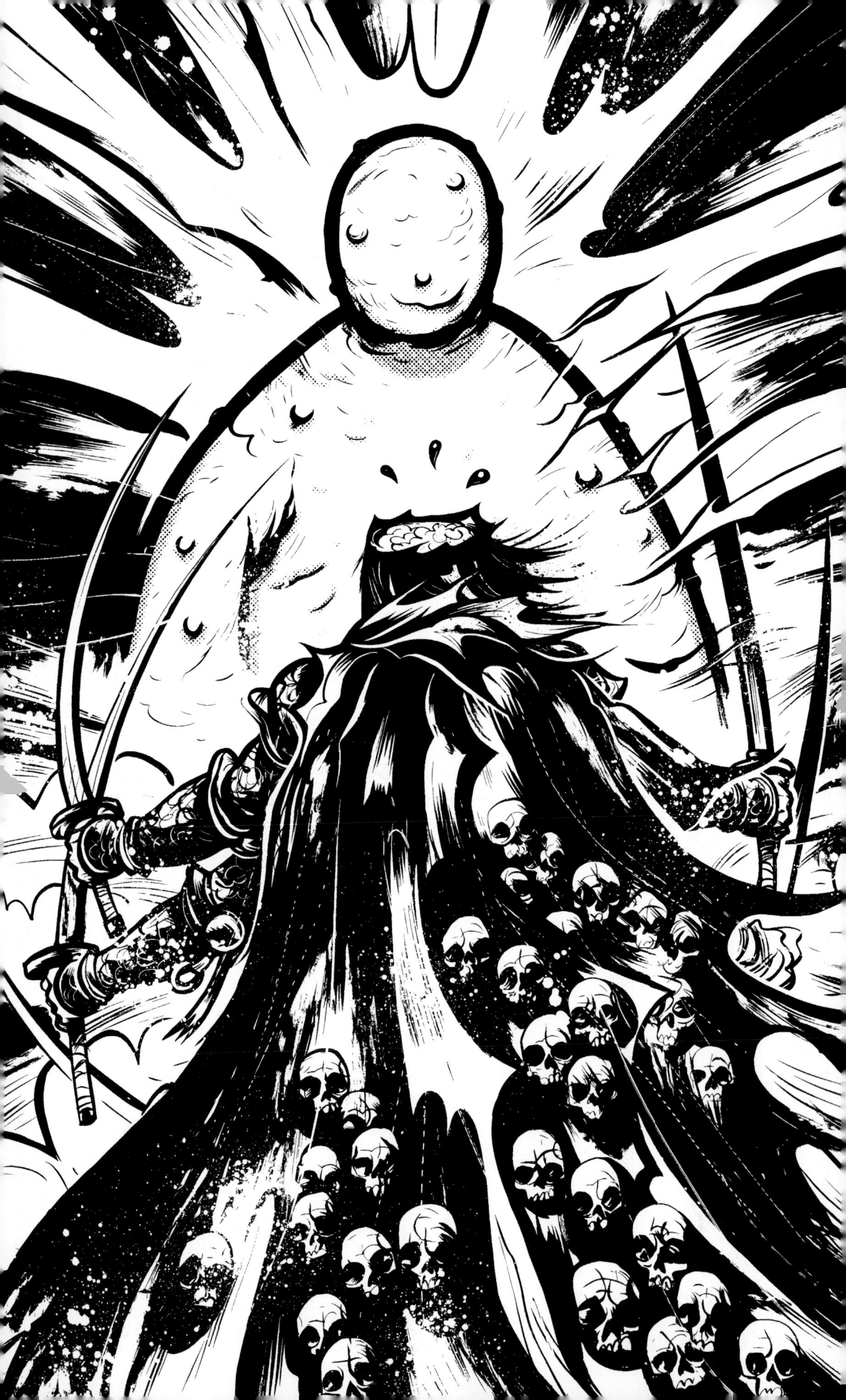

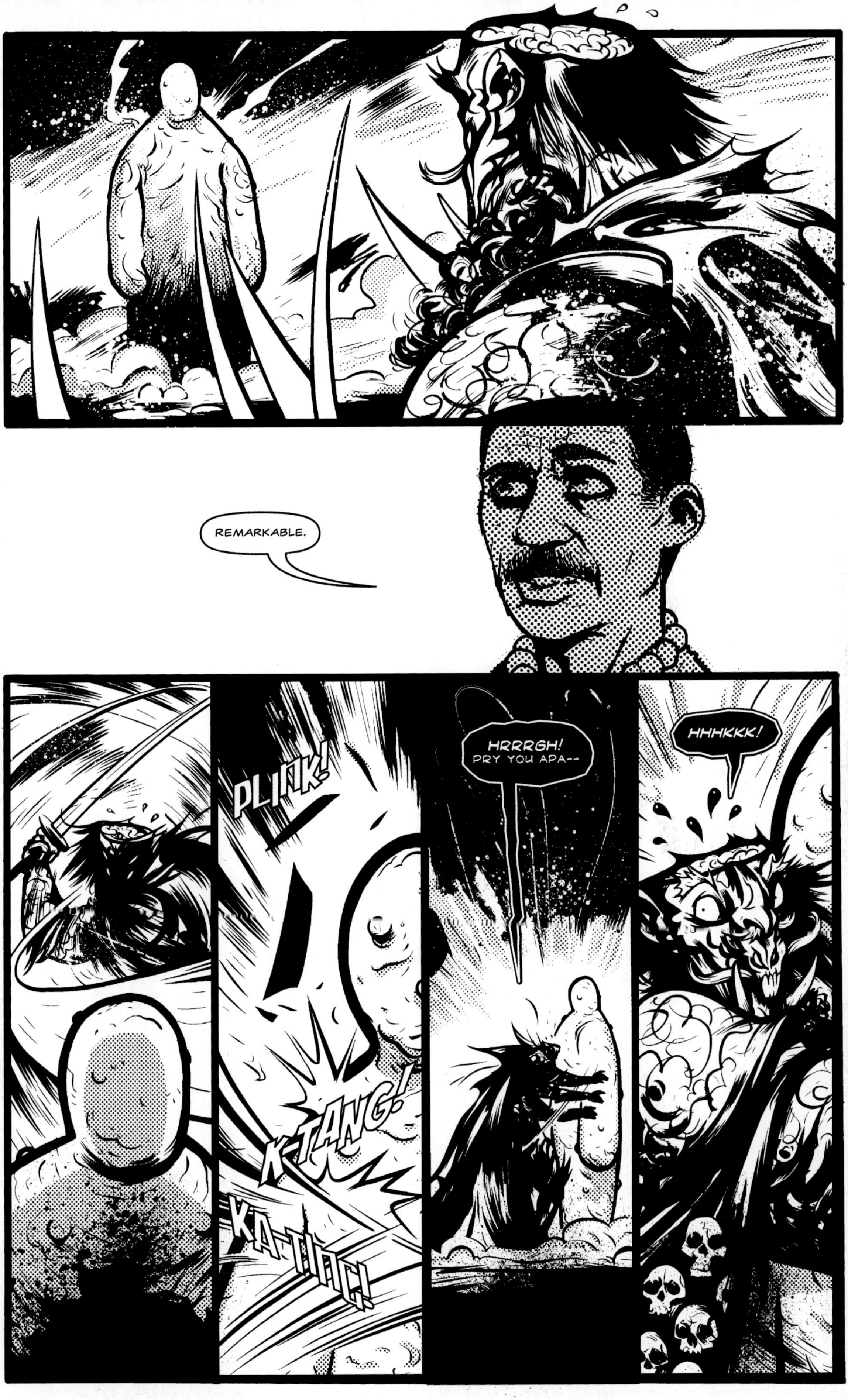
REMARKABLE.
PLINK!
K-TANG!
KA-TING!
HRRRGH!
PRY YOU APA--
HHHKKK!

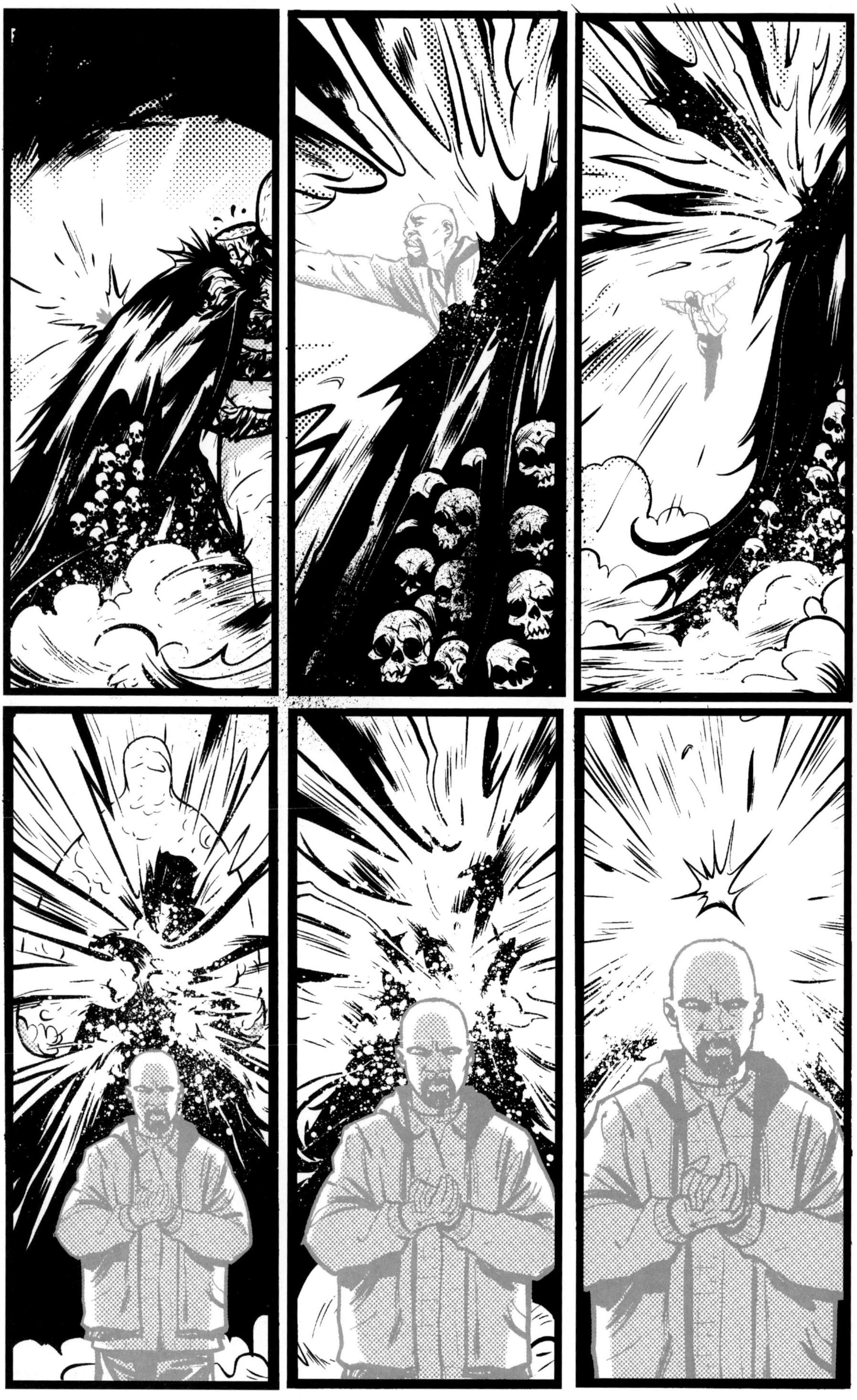

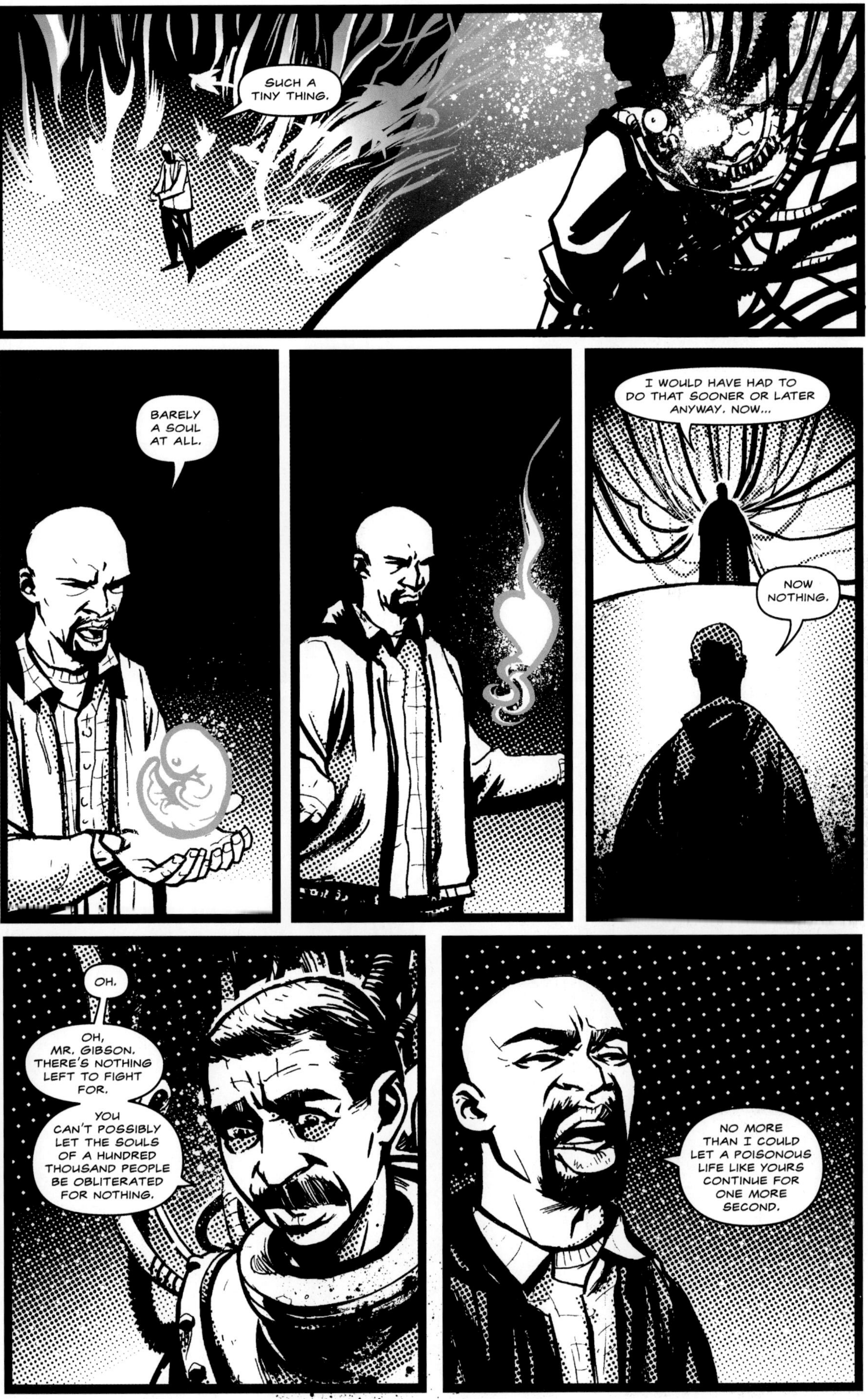
SUCH A TINY THING.
BARELY A SOUL AT ALL.
I WOULD HAVE HAD TO DO THAT SOONER OR LATER ANYWAY. NOW...
NOW NOTHING.
OH.
OH, MR. GIBSON. THERE'S NOTHING LEFT TO FIGHT FOR.
YOU CAN'T POSSIBLY LET THE SOULS OF A HUNDRED THOUSAND PEOPLE BE OBLITERATED FOR NOTHING.
NO MORE THAN I COULD LET A POISONOUS LIFE LIKE YOURS CONTINUE FOR ONE MORE SECOND.

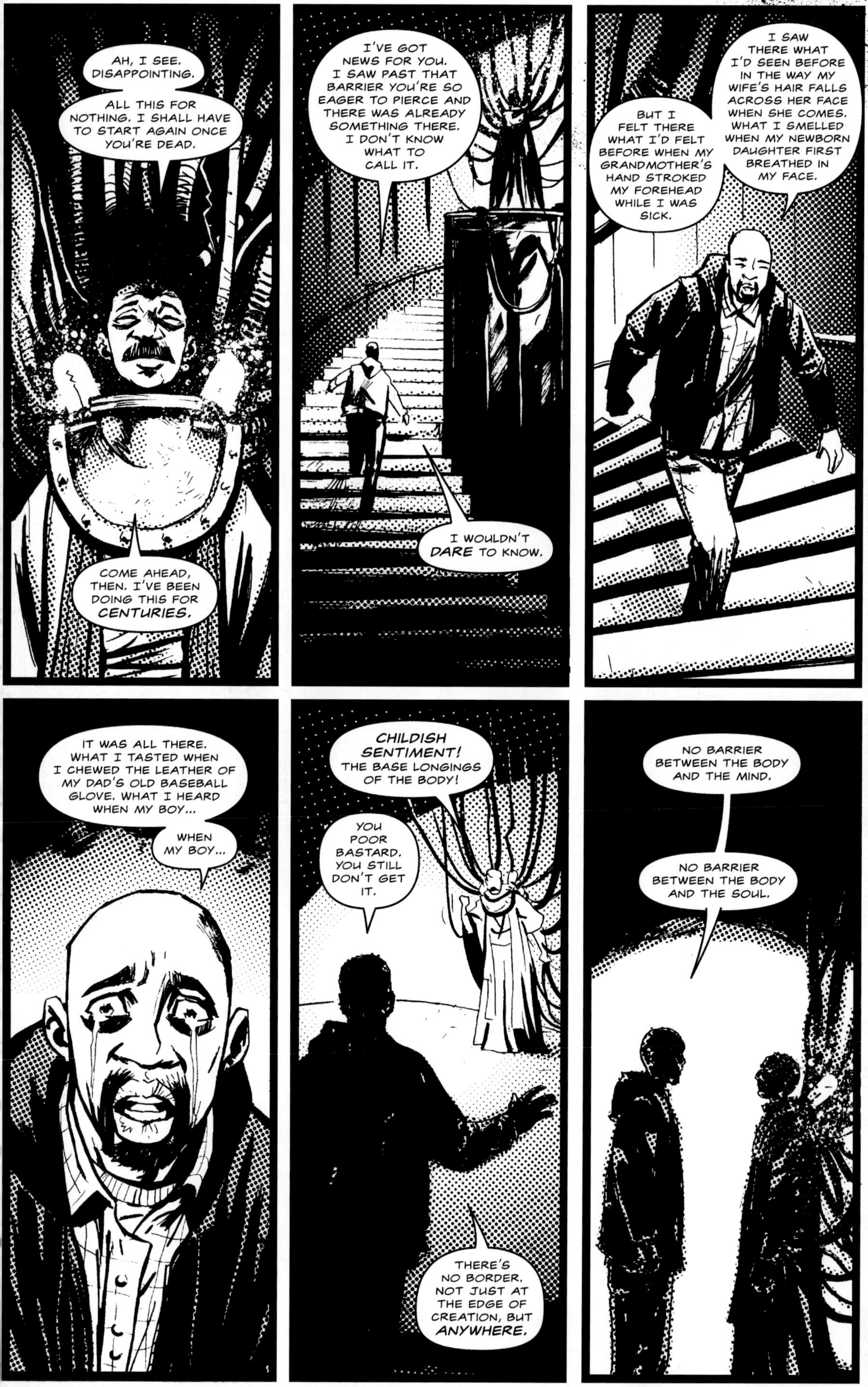
AH, I SEE. DISAPPOINTING.
ALL THIS FOR NOTHING. I SHALL HAVE TO START AGAIN ONCE YOU'RE DEAD.
COME AHEAD, THEN. I'VE BEEN DOING THIS FOR CENTURIES.
I'VE GOT NEWS FOR YOU. I SAW PAST THAT BARRIER YOU'RE SO EAGER TO PIERCE AND THERE WAS ALREADY SOMETHING THERE. I DON'T KNOW WHAT TO CALL IT.
I WOULDN'T DARE TO KNOW.
BUT I FELT THERE WHAT I'D FELT BEFORE WHEN MY GRANDMOTHER'S HAND STROKED MY FOREHEAD WHILE I WAS SICK.
I SAW THERE WHAT I'D SEEN BEFORE IN THE WAY MY WIFE'S HAIR FALLS ACROSS HER FACE WHEN SHE COMES. WHAT I SMELLED WHEN MY NEWBORN DAUGHTER FIRST BREATHED IN MY FACE.
IT WAS ALL THERE. WHAT I TASTED WHEN I CHEWED THE LEATHER OF MY DAD'S OLD BASEBALL GLOVE. WHAT I HEARD WHEN MY BOY...
WHEN MY BOY...
CHILDISH SENTIMENT! THE BASE LONGINGS OF THE BODY!
YOU POOR BASTARD. YOU STILL DON'T GET IT.
THERE'S NO BORDER. NOT JUST AT THE EDGE OF CREATION, BUT ANYWHERE.
NO BARRIER BETWEEN THE BODY AND THE MIND.
NO BARRIER BETWEEN THE BODY AND THE SOUL.

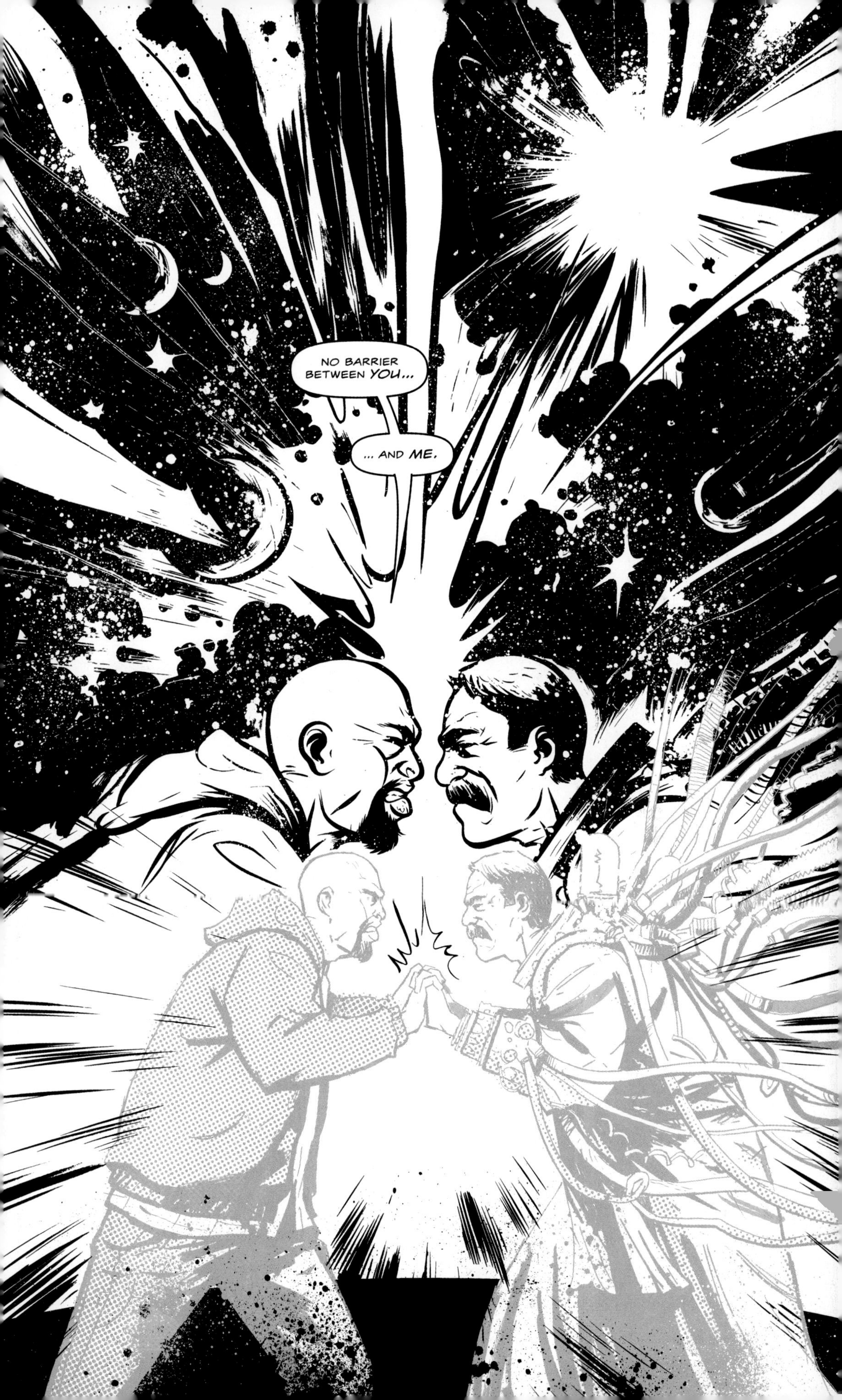

NO BARRIER BETWEEN YOU...
... AND ME.

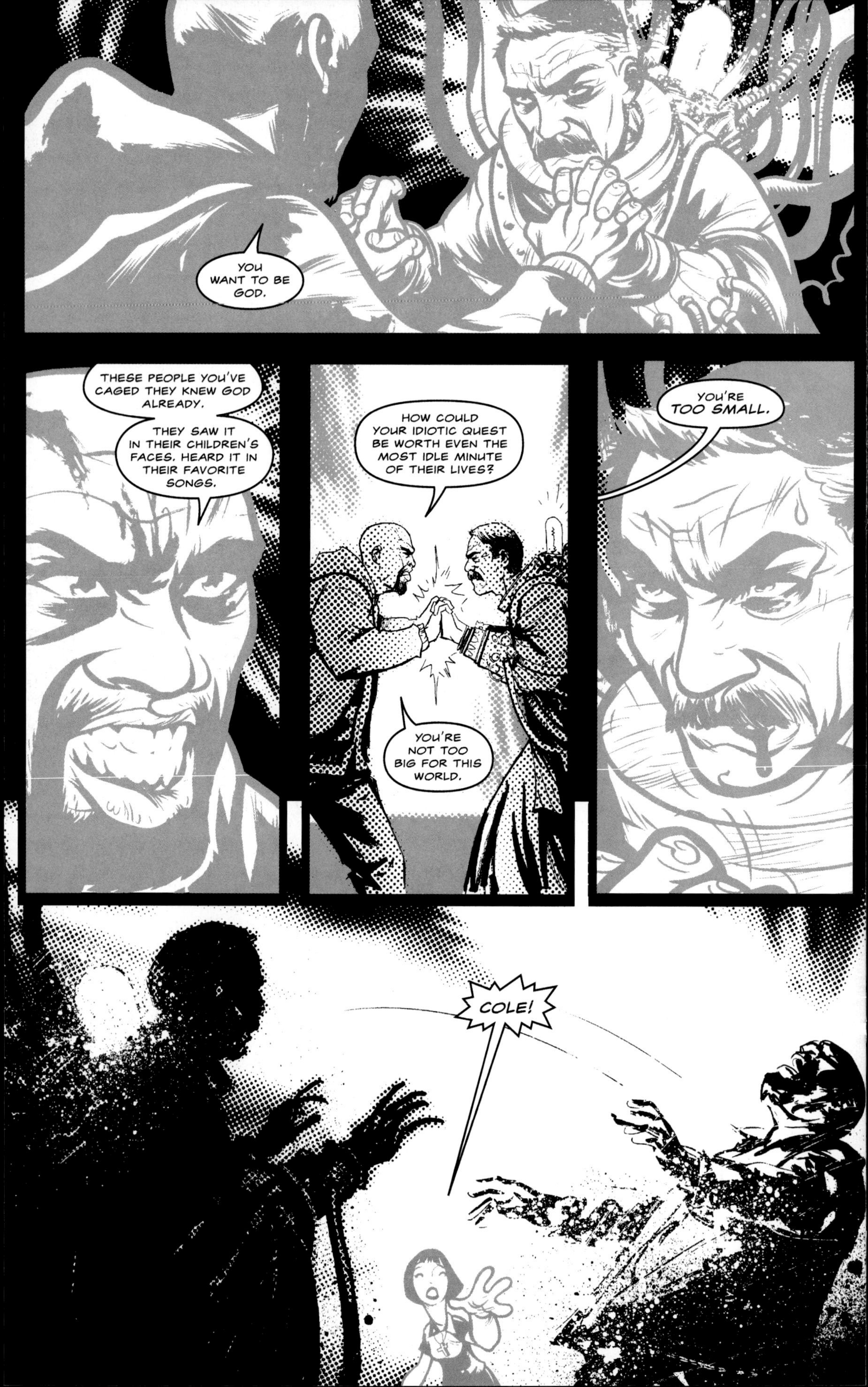
YOU WANT TO BE GOD.
THESE PEOPLE YOU'VE CAGED THEY KNEW GOD ALREADY.
THEY SAW IT IN THEIR CHILDREN'S FACES. HEARD IT IN THEIR FAVORITE SONGS.
HOW COULD YOUR IDIOTIC QUEST BE WORTH EVEN THE MOST IDLE MINUTE OF THEIR LIVES?
YOU'RE NOT TOO BIG FOR THIS WORLD.
YOU'RE TOO SMALL.
COLE!

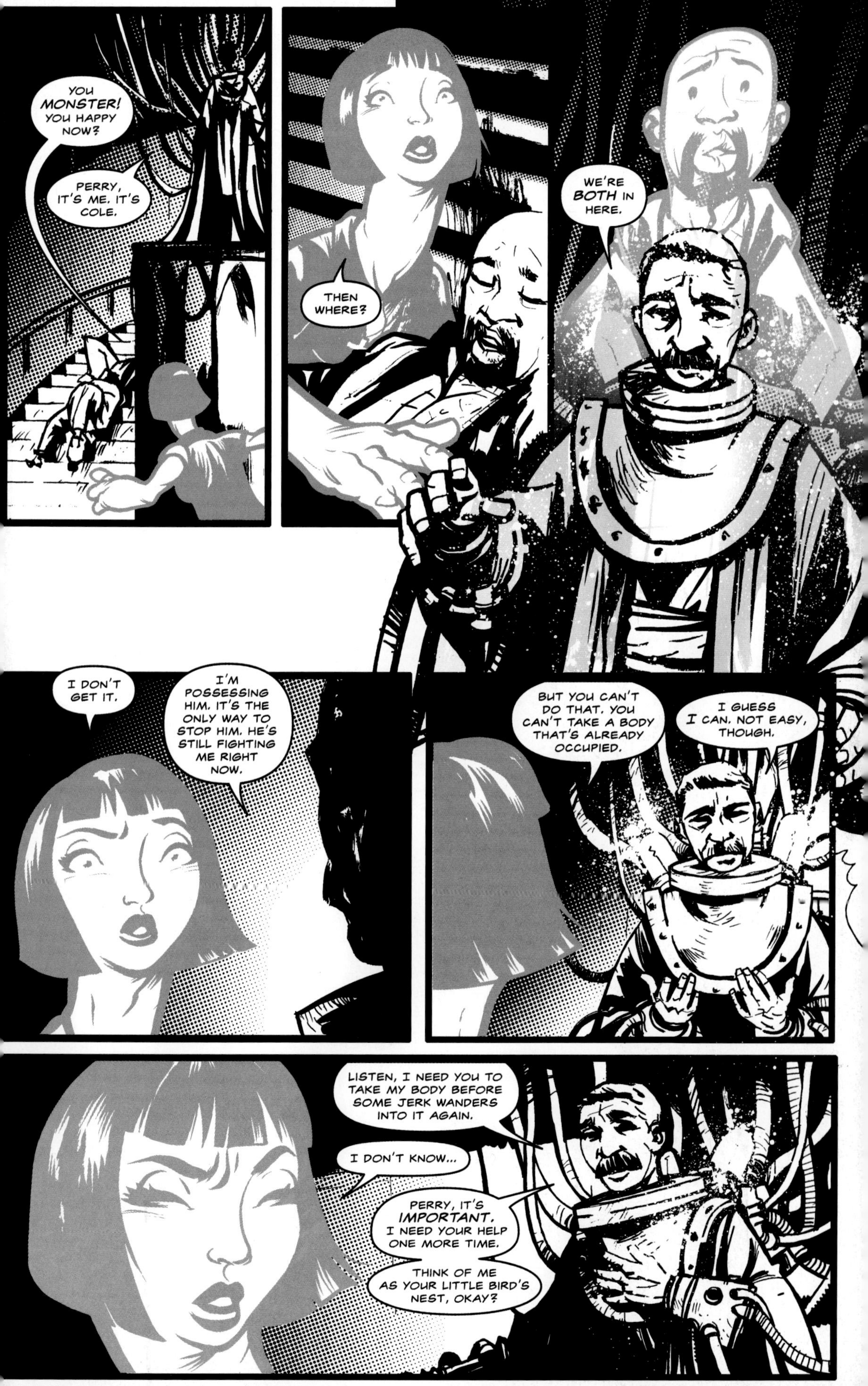
YOU MONSTER! YOU HAPPY NOW?
PERRY, IT'S ME. IT'S COLE.
THEN WHERE?
WE'RE BOTH IN HERE.
I DON'T GET IT.
I'M POSSESSING HIM. IT'S THE ONLY WAY TO STOP HIM. HE'S STILL FIGHTING ME RIGHT NOW.
BUT YOU CAN'T DO THAT. YOU CAN'T TAKE A BODY THAT'S ALREADY OCCUPIED.
I GUESS I CAN. NOT EASY, THOUGH.
LISTEN, I NEED YOU TO TAKE MY BODY BEFORE SOME JERK WANDERS INTO IT AGAIN.
I DON'T KNOW...
PERRY, IT'S IMPORTANT. I NEED YOUR HELP ONE MORE TIME.
THINK OF ME AS YOUR LITTLE BIRD'S NEST, OKAY?

OKAY, OKAY.

WHAT IS IT? WHAT'S WRONG?

NOTHING, I JUST--

IT FEELS *GOOD*.

GOOD, BECAUSE YOU'RE GOING TO HAVE TO STAY THERE AWHILE.

RAMMAN WASN'T LYING. UNLESS THE ENERGY FROM THIS THING IS PROPERLY DIRECTED ALL THESE SOULS WILL BE CUT ADRIFT. THOUSANDS OF VACANTS SCATTERED TO OBLIVION UNLESS I SHOW THEM THE WAY.

THE WAY? THE WAY WHERE?

I DON'T KNOW WHAT TO CALL IT.

HOME?

WHOSE HOME?

EVERYONE'S, PERRY. GET IT?

OH, MAN.

I CAN'T KEEP RAMMAN CONTAINED FOREVER. HE HAS TO DIE HERE AND *NOW*. YOU UNDERSTAND? FOR THE SAKE OF ALL THESE SOULS. ALL THESE MASTERPIECES.

COLE, I DON'T LIKE THIS. IF HIS BODY DIES WHILE YOU'RE STILL IN HIM--

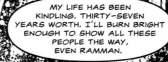

MY LIFE HAS BEEN KINDLING. THIRTY-SEVEN YEARS WORTH. I'LL BURN BRIGHT ENOUGH TO SHOW ALL THESE PEOPLE THE WAY, EVEN RAMMAN.

BRIGHT ENOUGH FOR EVERY VACANT EVERYWHERE.

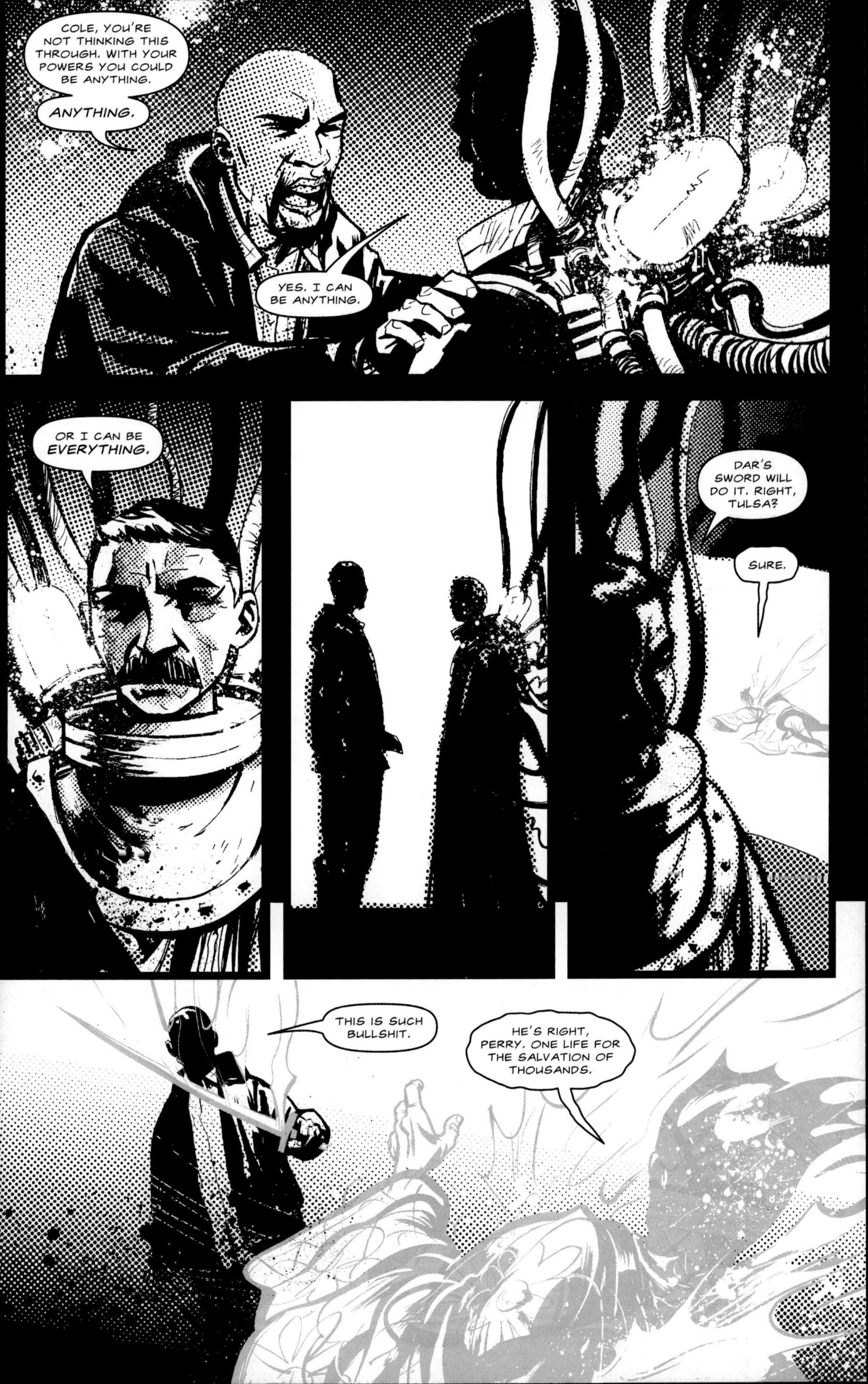
COLE, YOU'RE NOT THINKING THIS THROUGH. WITH YOUR POWERS YOU COULD BE ANYTHING.
ANYTHING.
YES. I CAN BE ANYTHING.
OR I CAN BE EVERYTHING.
DAR'S SWORD WILL DO IT. RIGHT, TULSA?
SURE.
THIS IS SUCH BULLSHIT.
HE'S RIGHT, PERRY. ONE LIFE FOR THE SALVATION OF THOUSANDS.

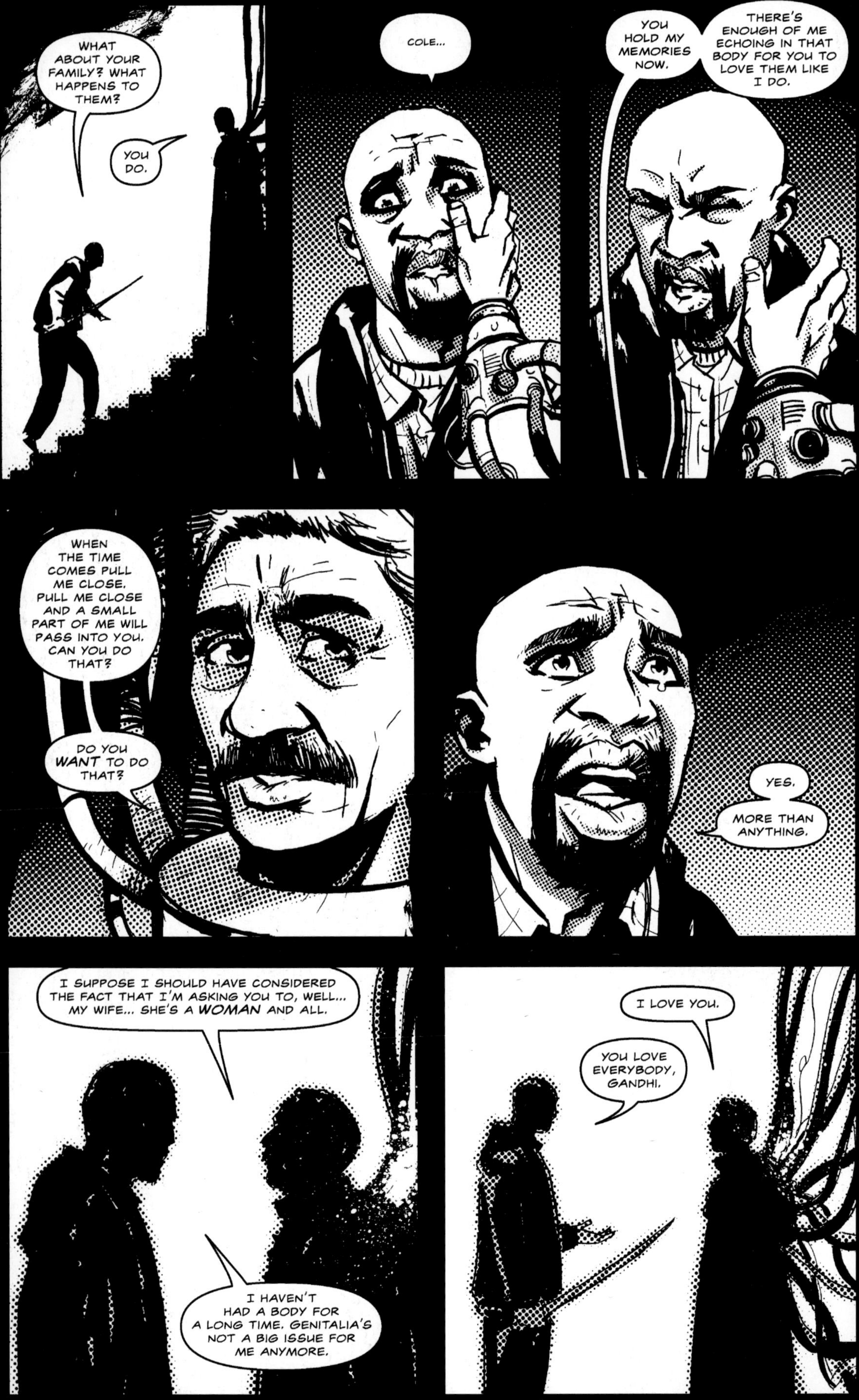
WHAT ABOUT YOUR FAMILY? WHAT HAPPENS TO THEM?
YOU DO.
COLE...
YOU HOLD MY MEMORIES NOW.
THERE'S ENOUGH OF ME ECHOING IN THAT BODY FOR YOU TO LOVE THEM LIKE I DO.
WHEN THE TIME COMES PULL ME CLOSE. PULL ME CLOSE AND A SMALL PART OF ME WILL PASS INTO YOU. CAN YOU DO THAT?
DO YOU WANT TO DO THAT?
YES.
MORE THAN ANYTHING.
I SUPPOSE I SHOULD HAVE CONSIDERED THE FACT THAT I'M ASKING YOU TO, WELL... MY WIFE... SHE'S A WOMAN AND ALL.
I HAVEN'T HAD A BODY FOR A LONG TIME. GENITALIA'S NOT A BIG ISSUE FOR ME ANYMORE.
I LOVE YOU.
YOU LOVE EVERYBODY, GANDHI.

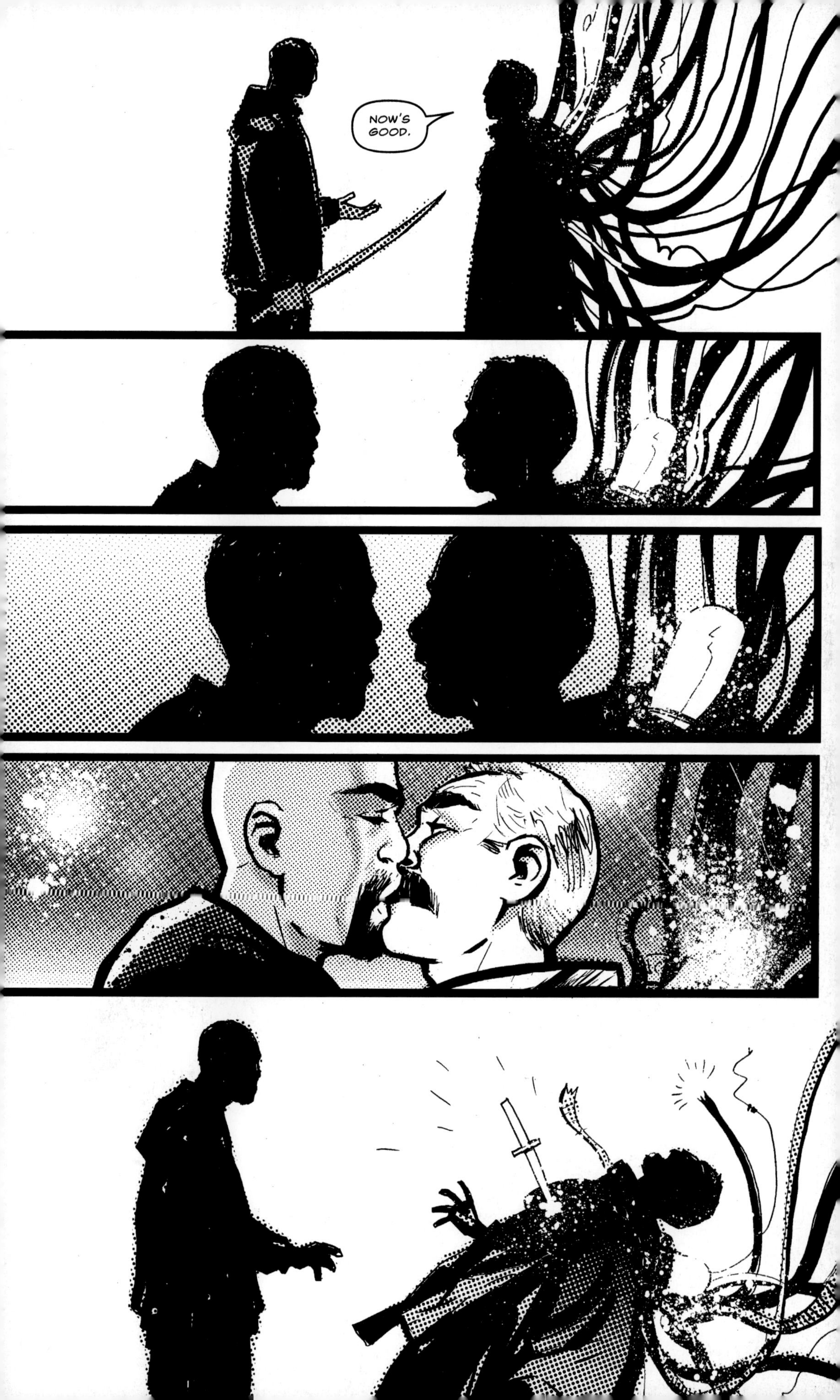
NOW'S GOOD.

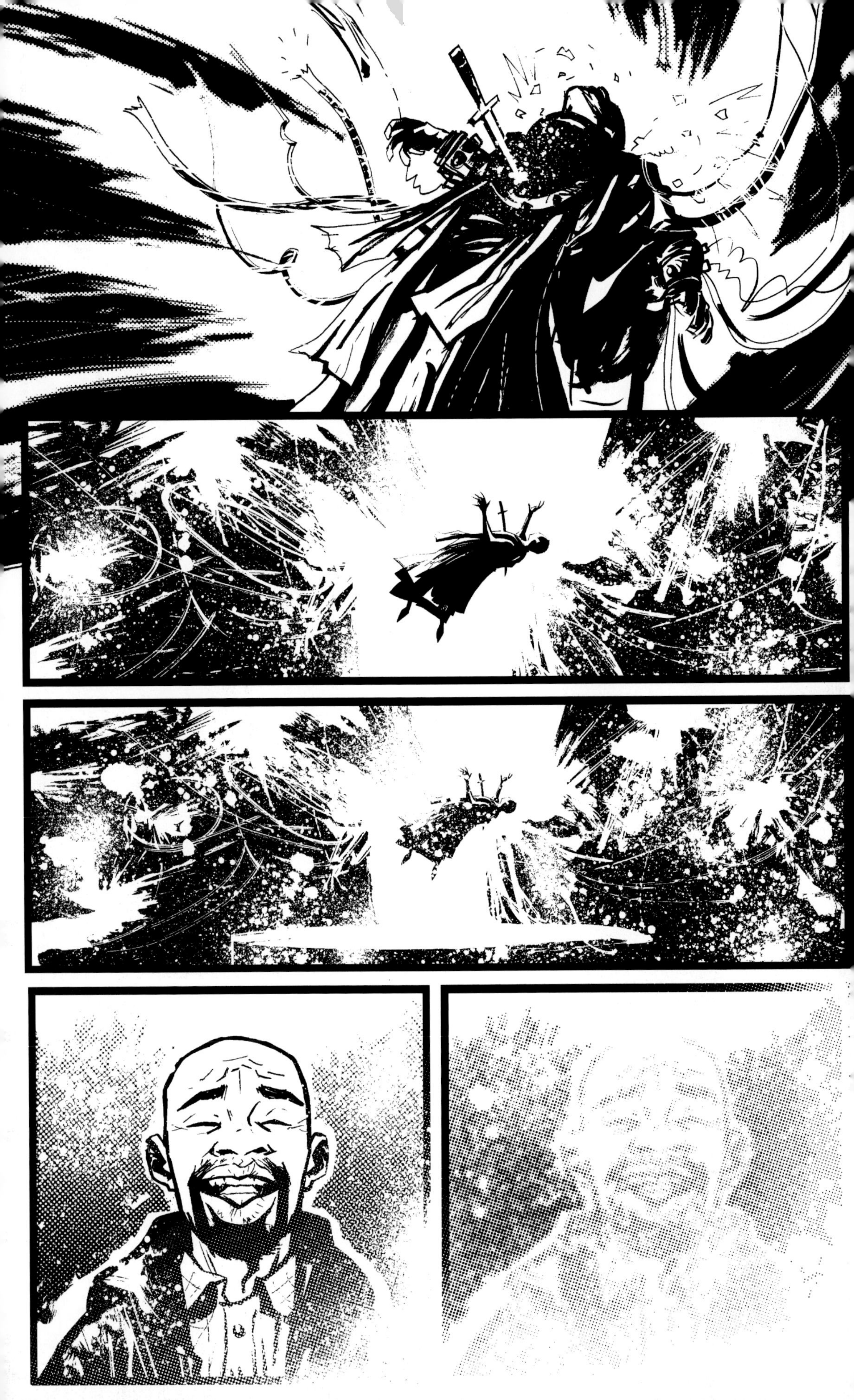

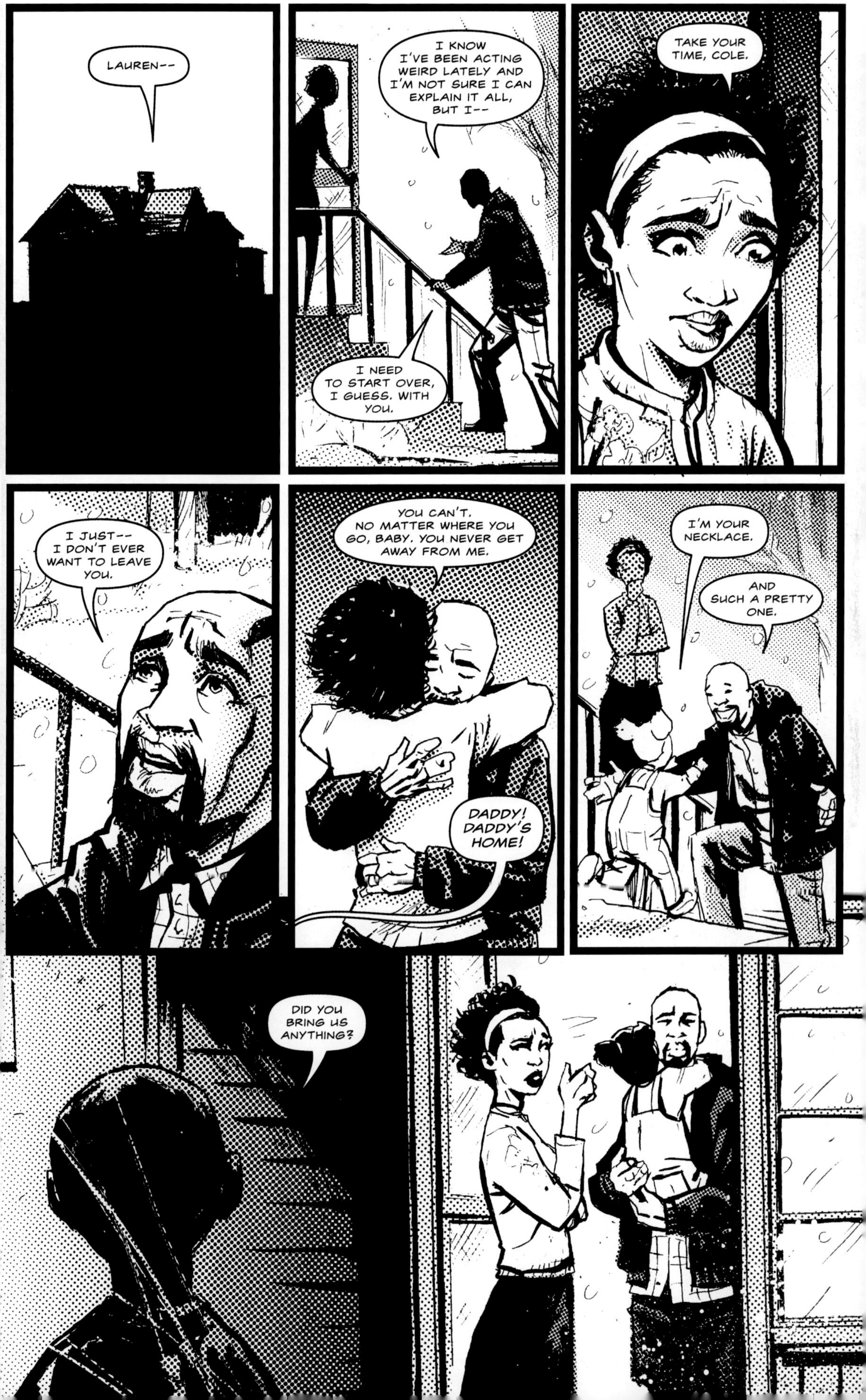

LAUREN--
I KNOW I'VE BEEN ACTING WEIRD LATELY AND I'M NOT SURE I CAN EXPLAIN IT ALL, BUT I--
I NEED TO START OVER, I GUESS. WITH YOU.
TAKE YOUR TIME, COLE.
I JUST-- I DON'T EVER WANT TO LEAVE YOU.
YOU CAN'T. NO MATTER WHERE YOU GO, BABY. YOU NEVER GET AWAY FROM ME.
DADDY! DADDY'S HOME!
I'M YOUR NECKLACE.
AND SUCH A PRETTY ONE.
DID YOU BRING US ANYTHING?

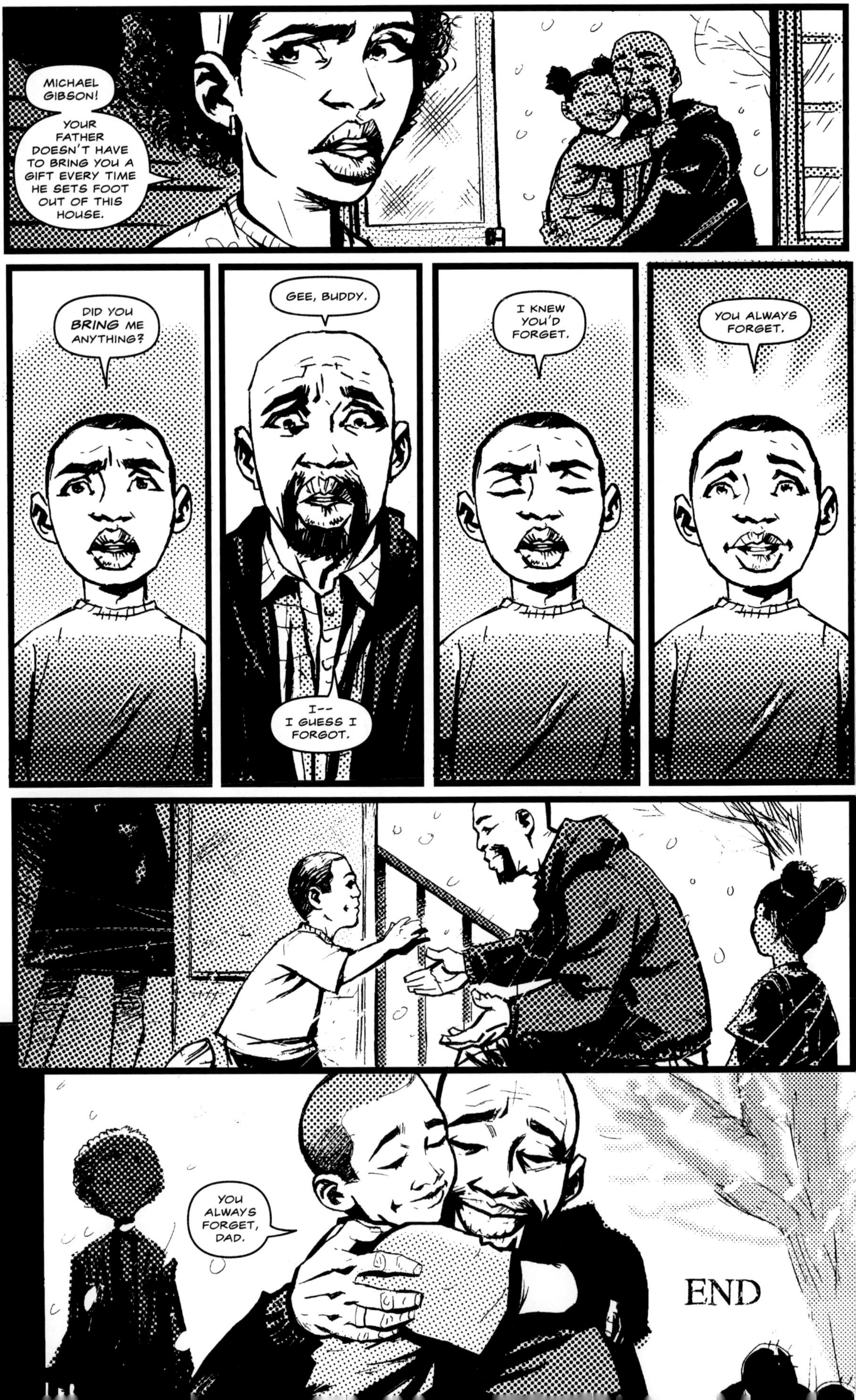
MICHAEL GIBSON!
YOUR FATHER DOESN'T HAVE TO BRING YOU A GIFT EVERY TIME HE SETS FOOT OUT OF THIS HOUSE.
DID YOU BRING ME ANYTHING?
GEE, BUDDY.
I-- I GUESS I FORGOT.
I KNEW YOU'D FORGET.
YOU ALWAYS FORGET.
YOU ALWAYS FORGET, DAD.
END

GALLERY

Dave Crosland

Nathan Fox

Jim Mahfood

Scott Morse

Steve Willaredt

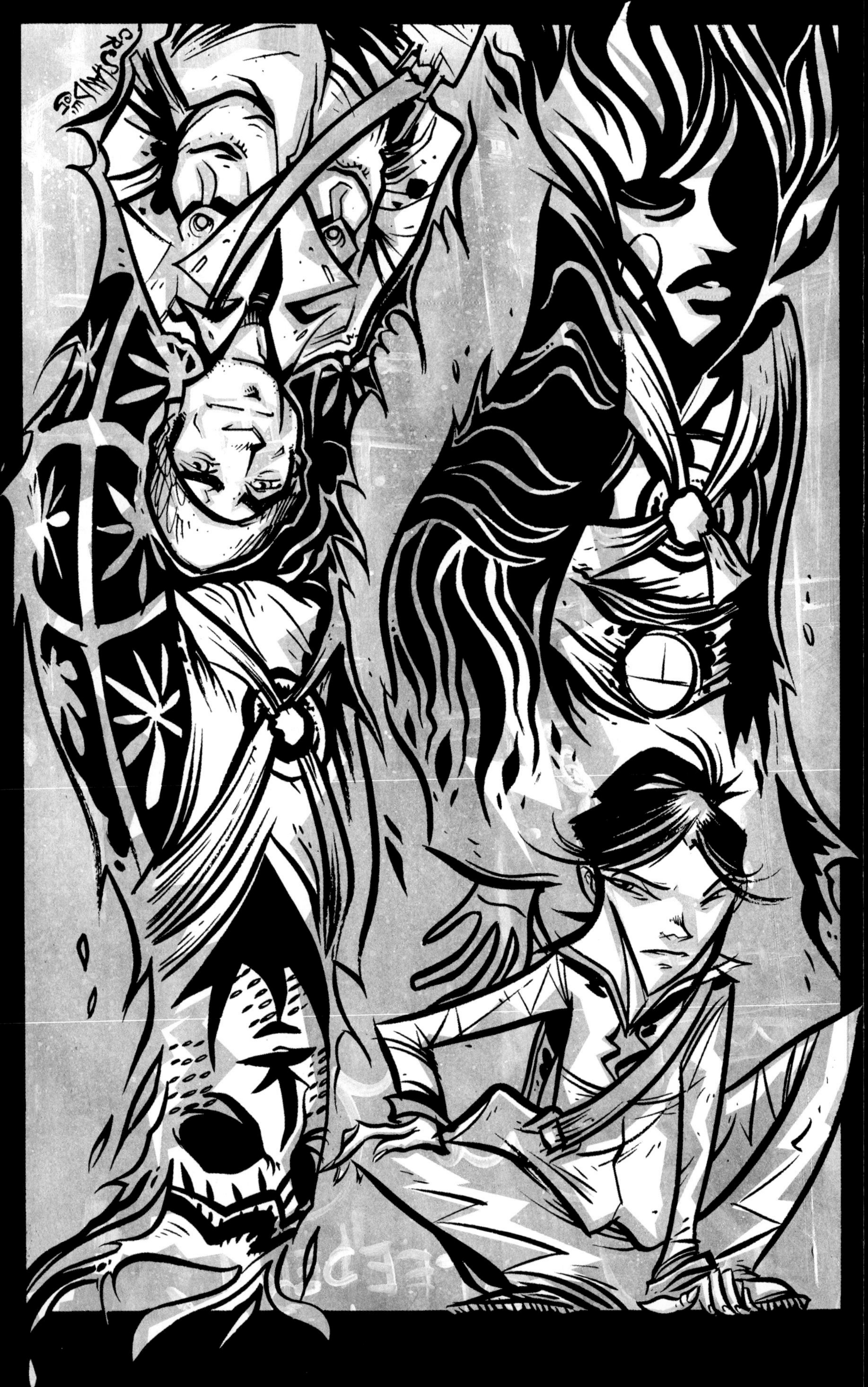

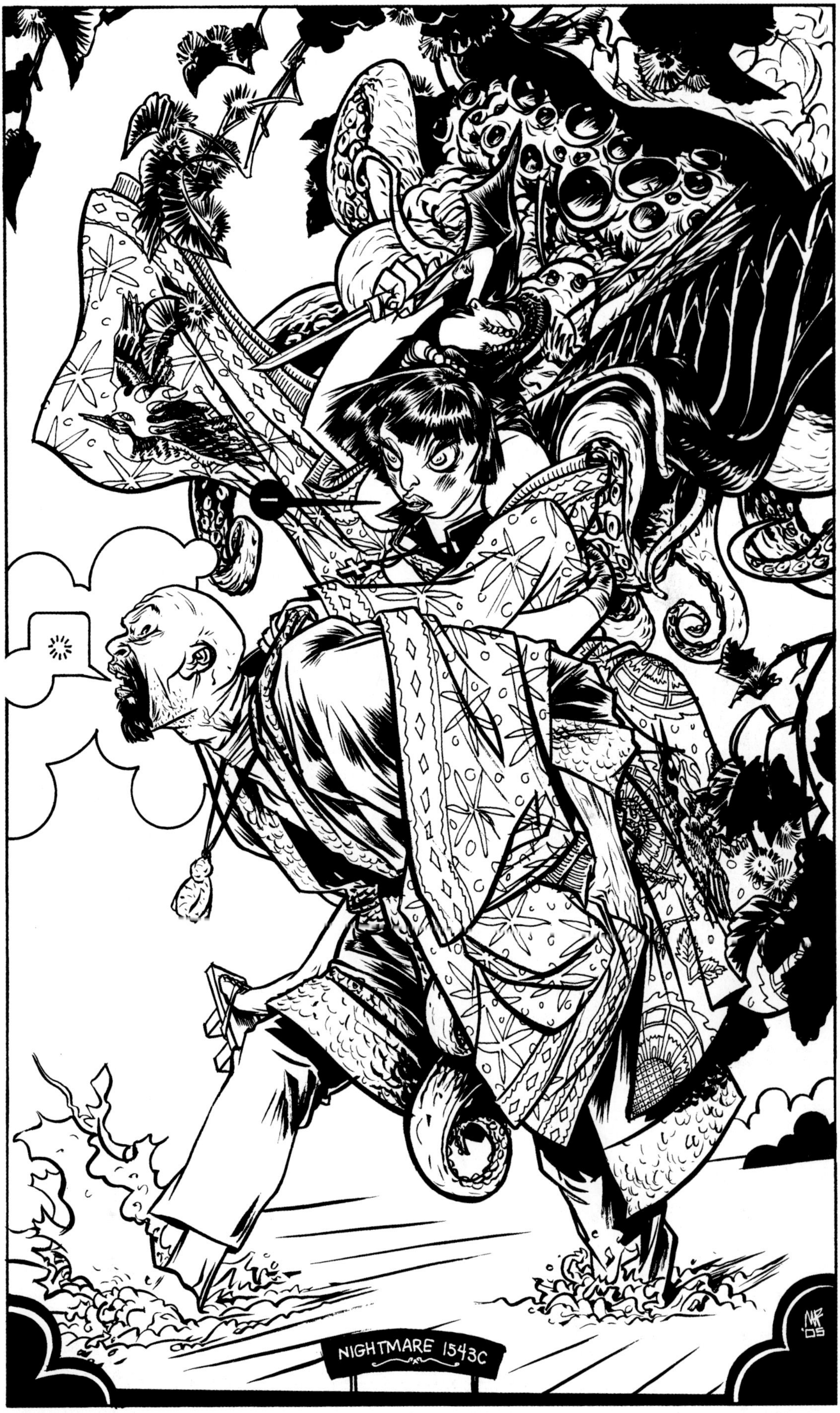
NIGHTMARE 1543C

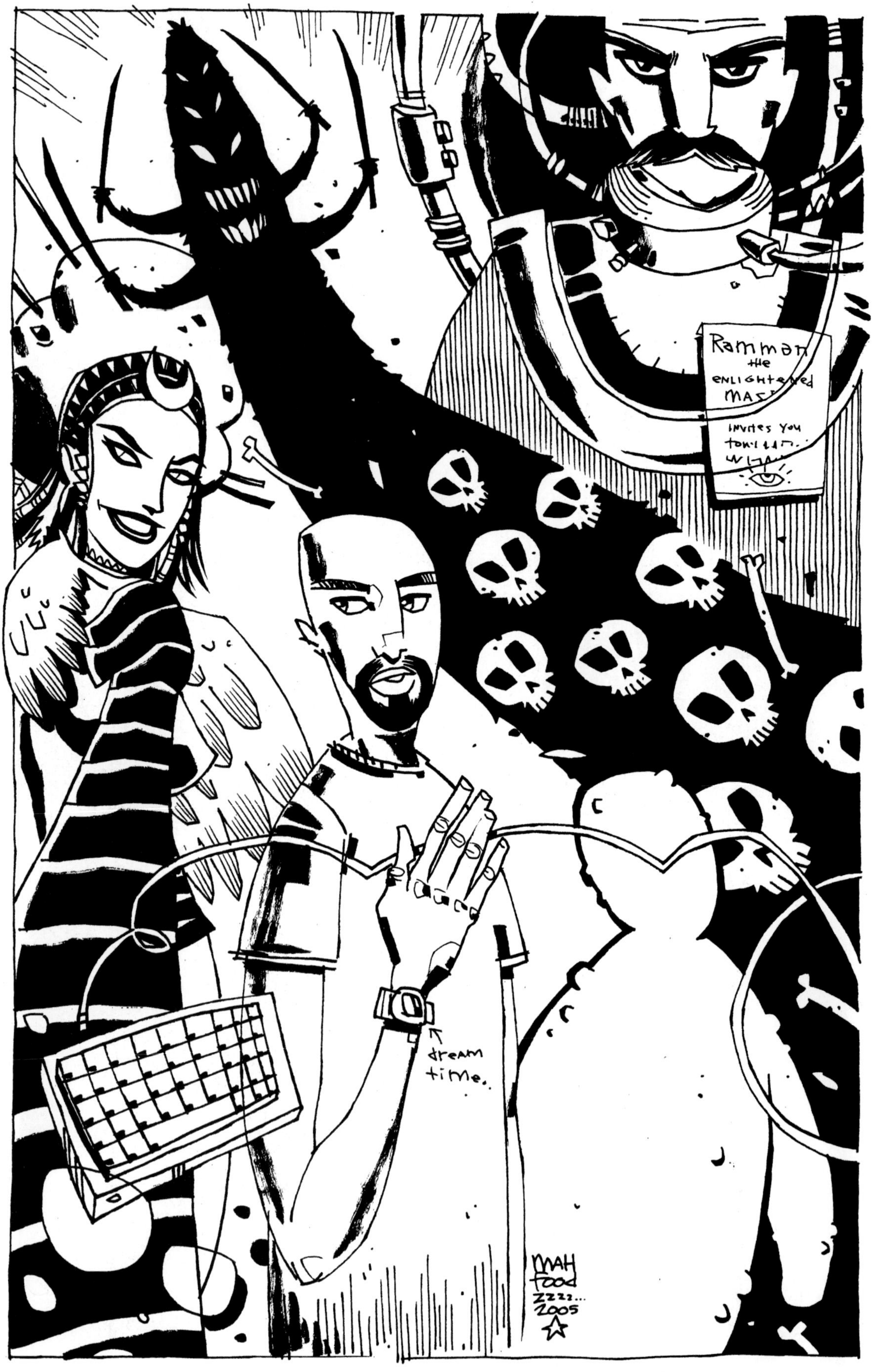
Ramman
the
enlightened
invites you
dream time..
MAH
food
zzzz...
2005

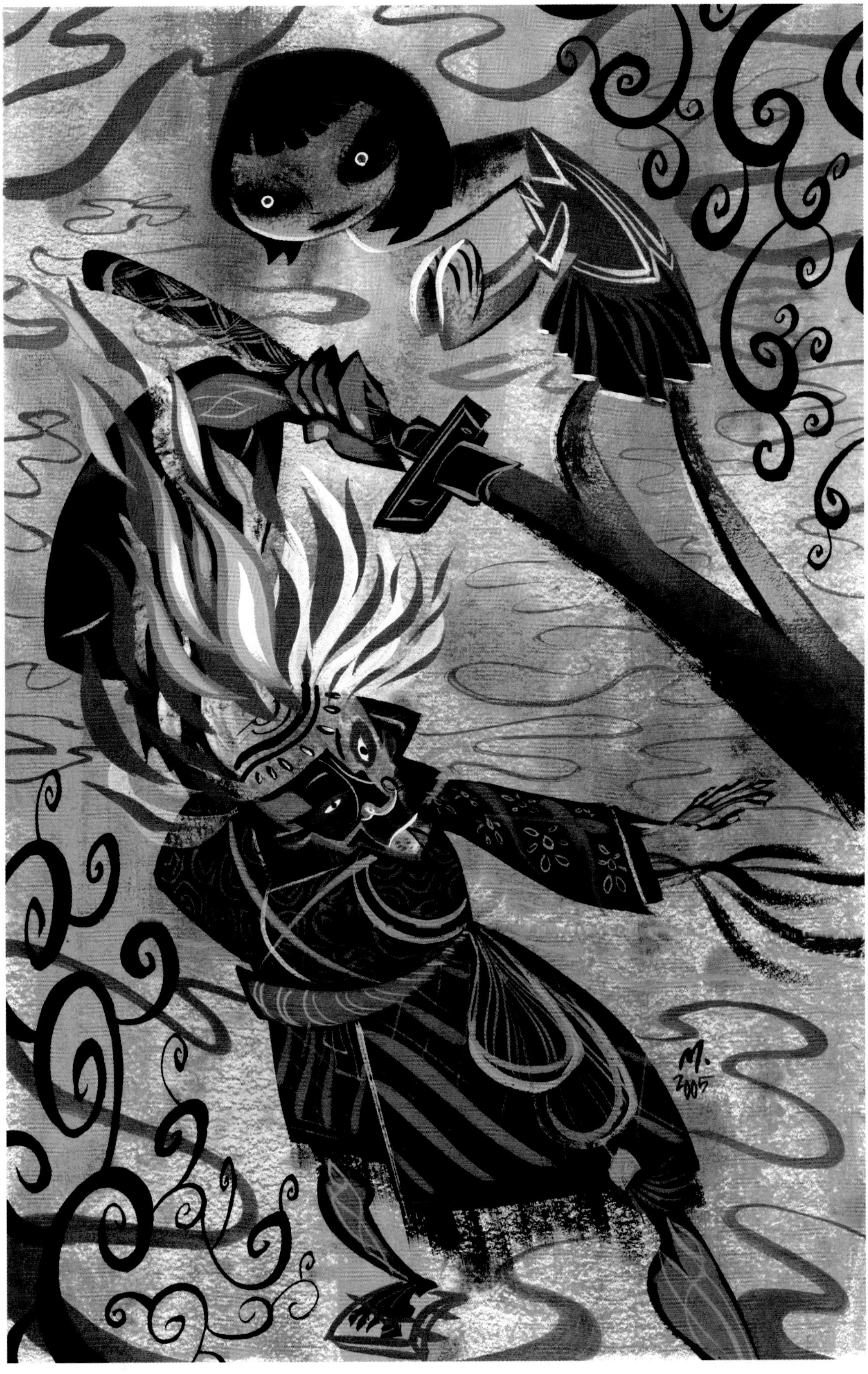
M.
2005

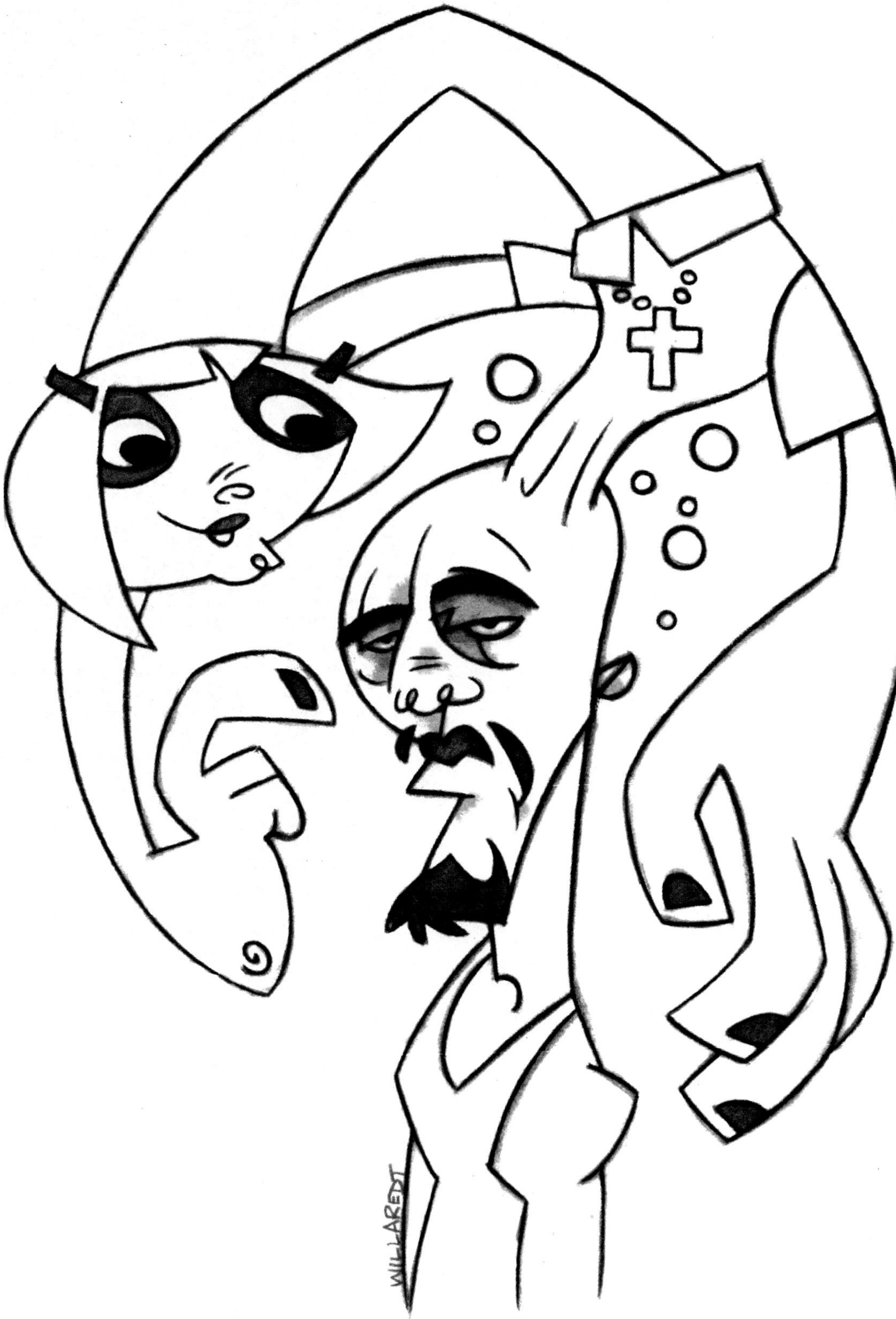
WILLARDT

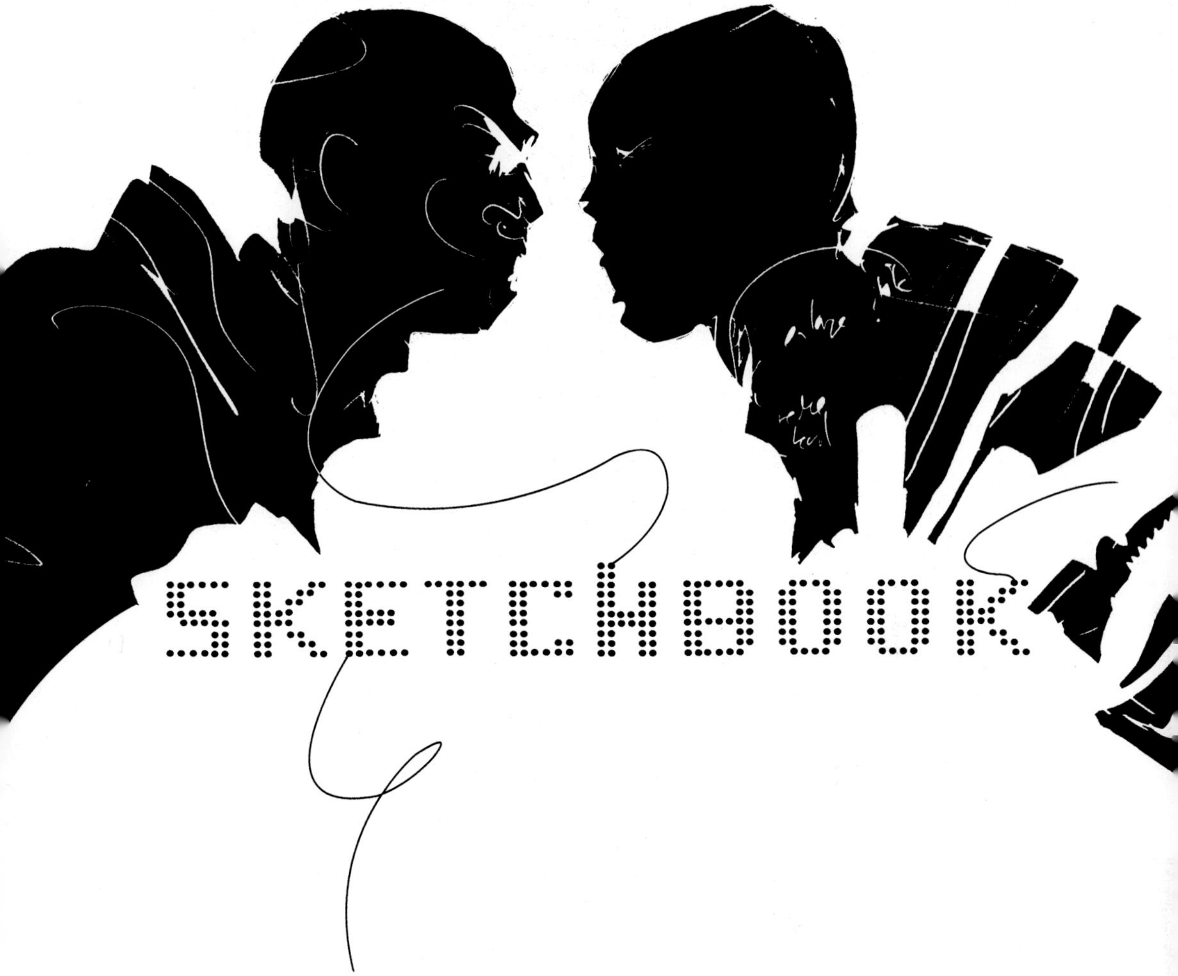
SKETCHBOOK

no horns.

- crown of horns

- get
  hair
  chin

- regular state
- characters can
  for battle.

- design a bat...

STEEL Slave

- photos/painti...
Fire
- cole Drawing w/ style

- cole sketpis
  k-style

DEEP
SLEEPING

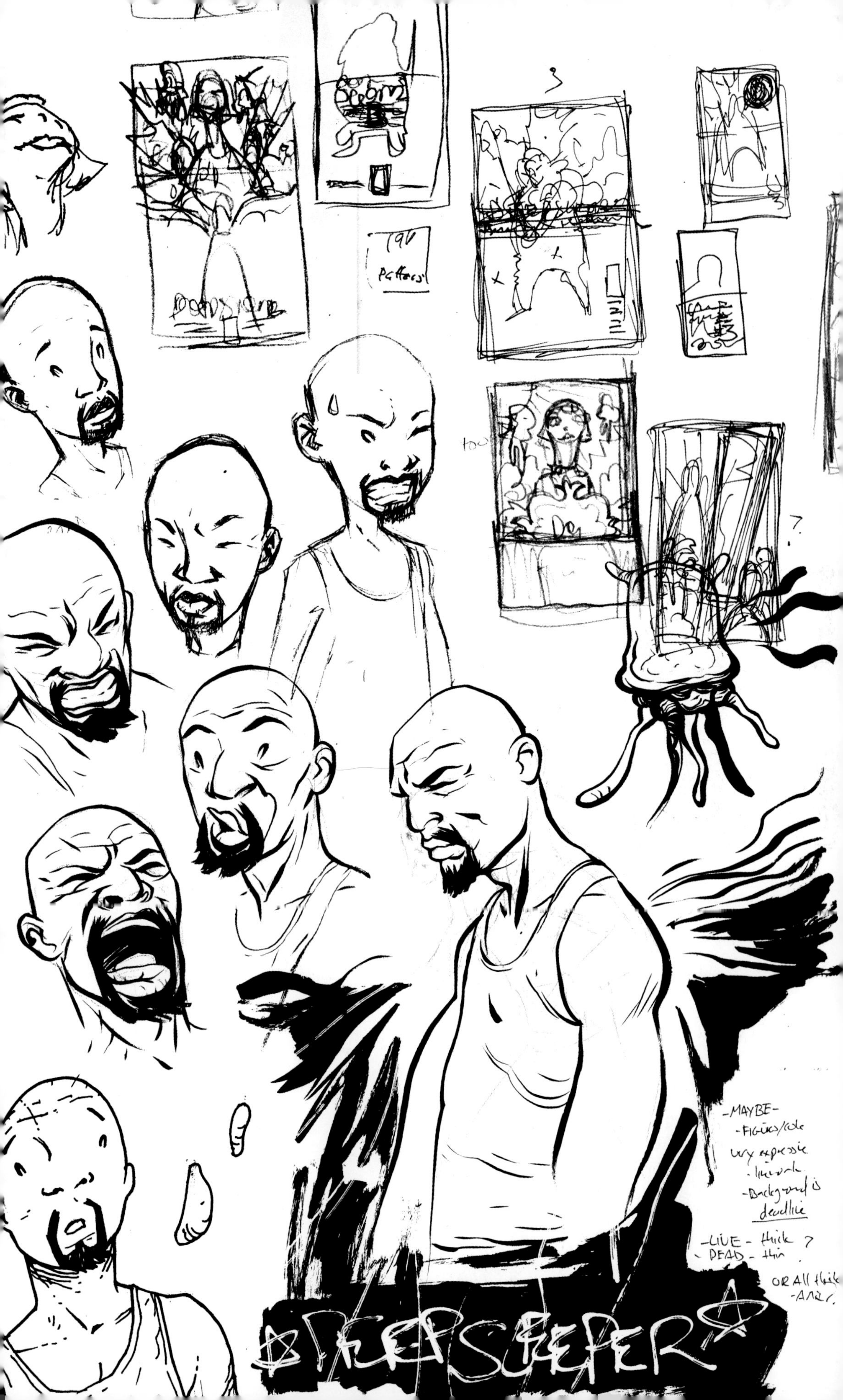
-MAYBE-
-LIVE - thick ?
-DEAD - thin.
OR All thick
DEEPSLEEPER

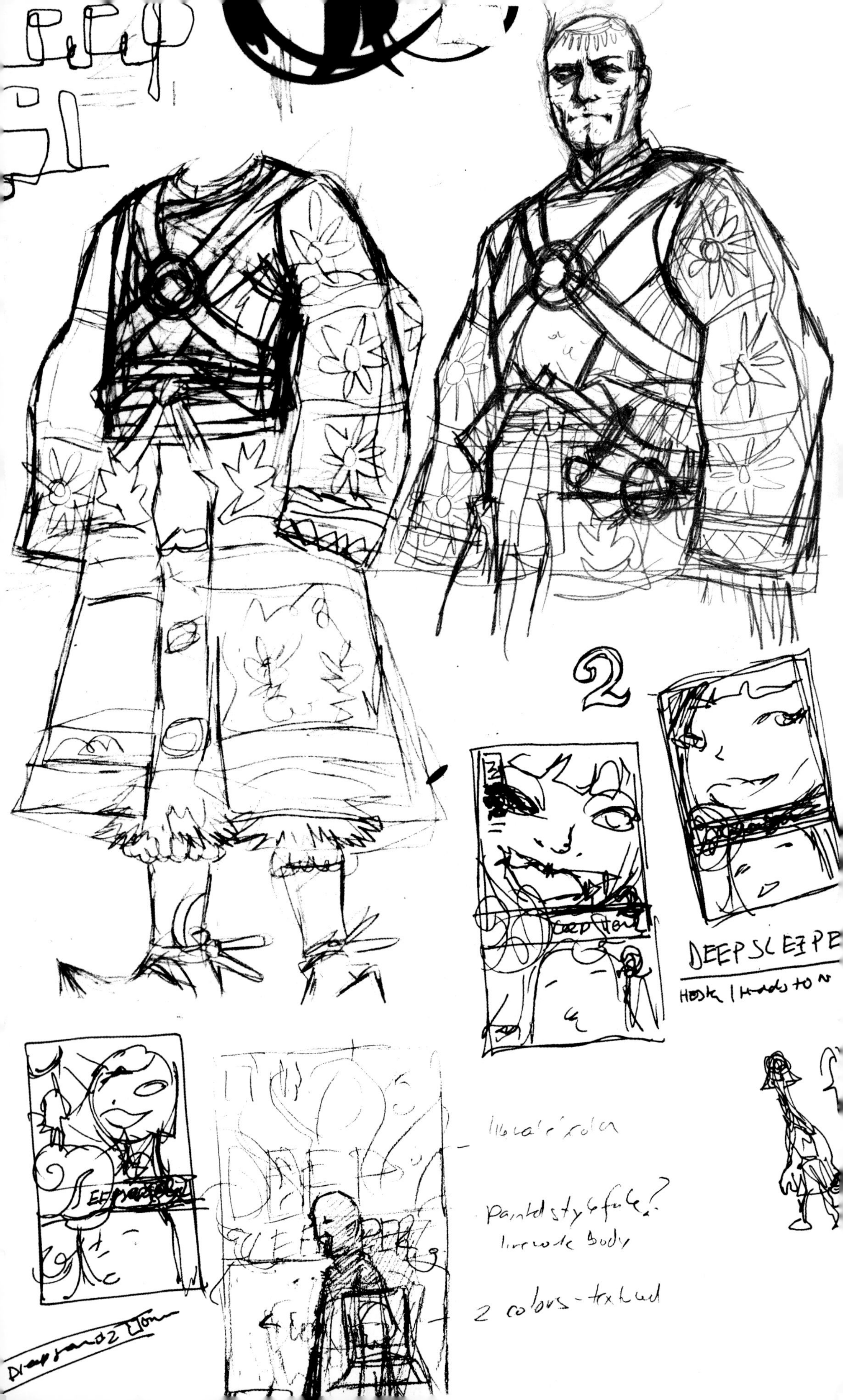
2
DEEPSLEEPE
painted style face?
linework body
2 colors - textured

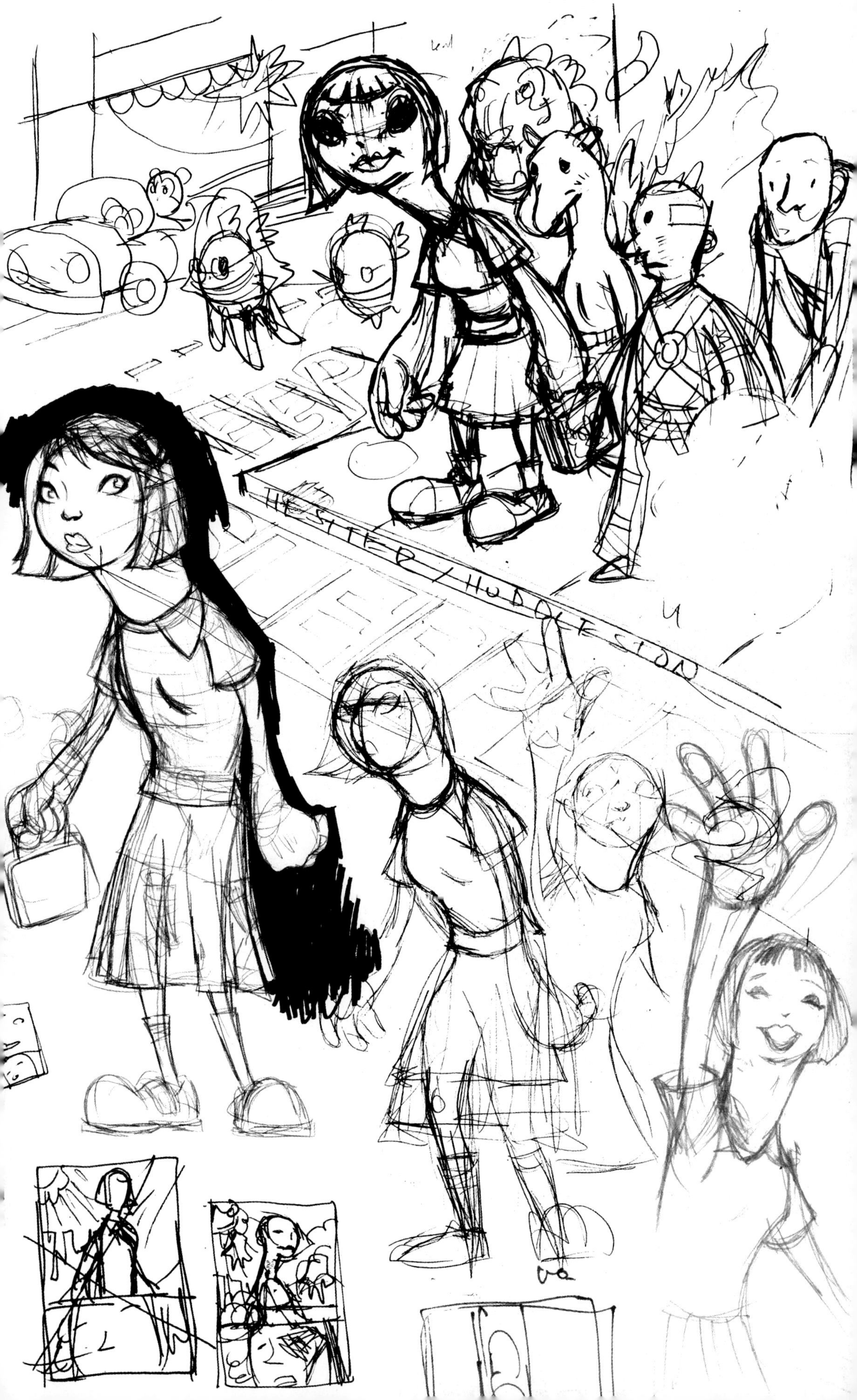
HESTER / HUDDLESTON

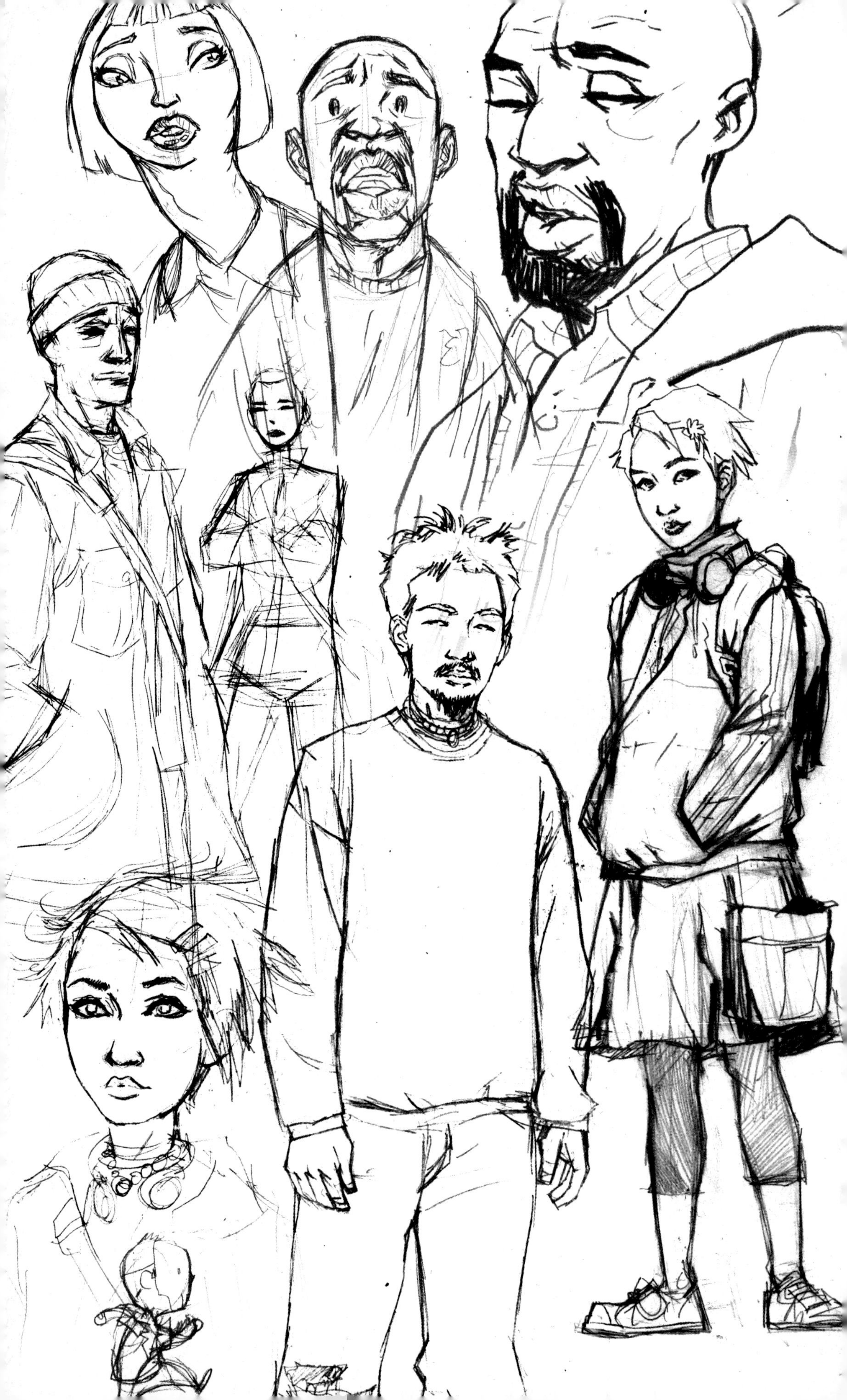

All looms
eyes, hair
'tentacles

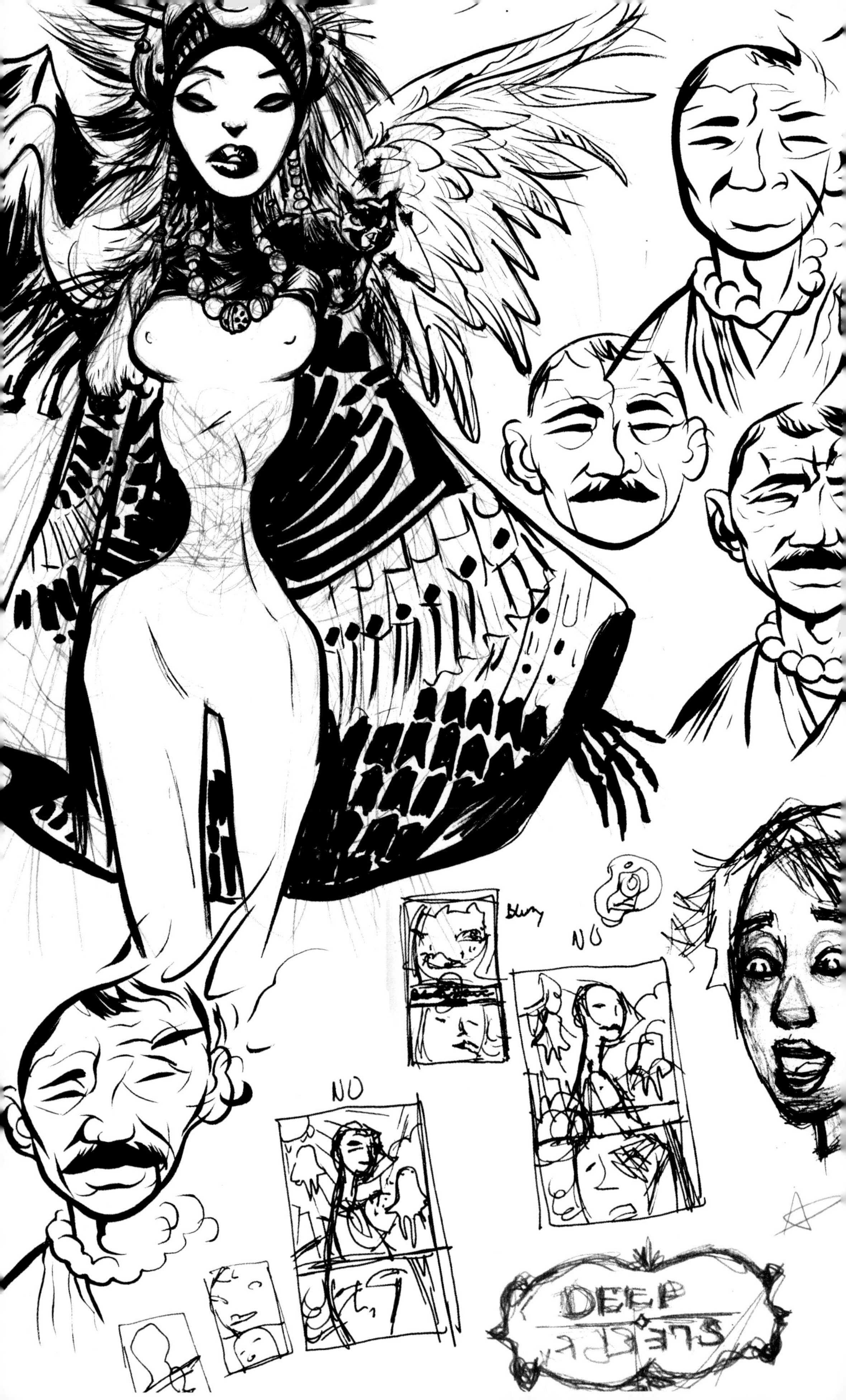
NO
NO
DEEP

Vacant

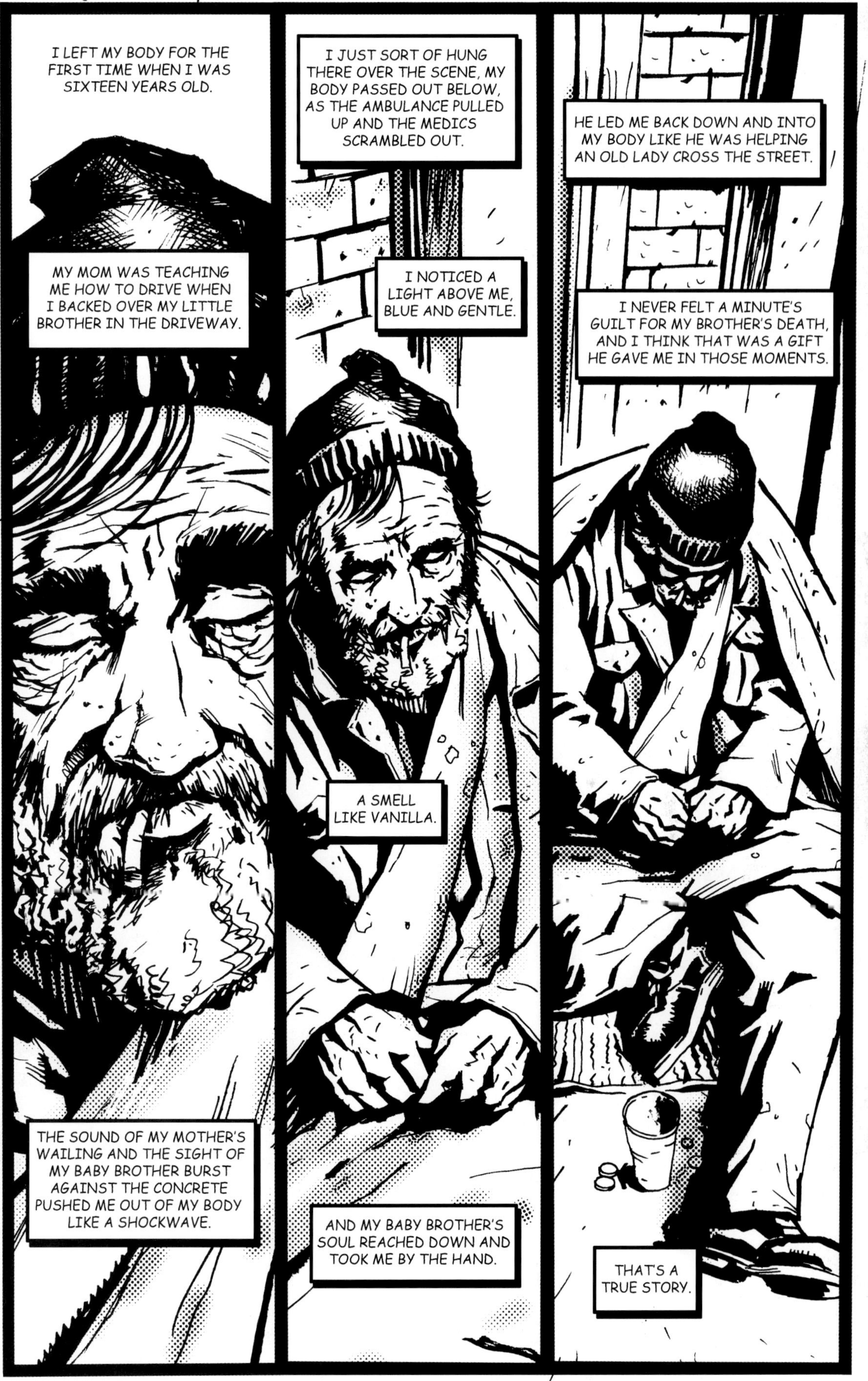
I LEFT MY BODY FOR THE FIRST TIME WHEN I WAS SIXTEEN YEARS OLD.
MY MOM WAS TEACHING ME HOW TO DRIVE WHEN I BACKED OVER MY LITTLE BROTHER IN THE DRIVEWAY.
THE SOUND OF MY MOTHER'S WAILING AND THE SIGHT OF MY BABY BROTHER BURST AGAINST THE CONCRETE PUSHED ME OUT OF MY BODY LIKE A SHOCKWAVE.
I JUST SORT OF HUNG THERE OVER THE SCENE, MY BODY PASSED OUT BELOW, AS THE AMBULANCE PULLED UP AND THE MEDICS SCRAMBLED OUT.
I NOTICED A LIGHT ABOVE ME, BLUE AND GENTLE.
A SMELL LIKE VANILLA.
AND MY BABY BROTHER'S SOUL REACHED DOWN AND TOOK ME BY THE HAND.
HE LED ME BACK DOWN AND INTO MY BODY LIKE HE WAS HELPING AN OLD LADY CROSS THE STREET.
I NEVER FELT A MINUTE'S GUILT FOR MY BROTHER'S DEATH, AND I THINK THAT WAS A GIFT HE GAVE ME IN THOSE MOMENTS.
THAT'S A TRUE STORY.

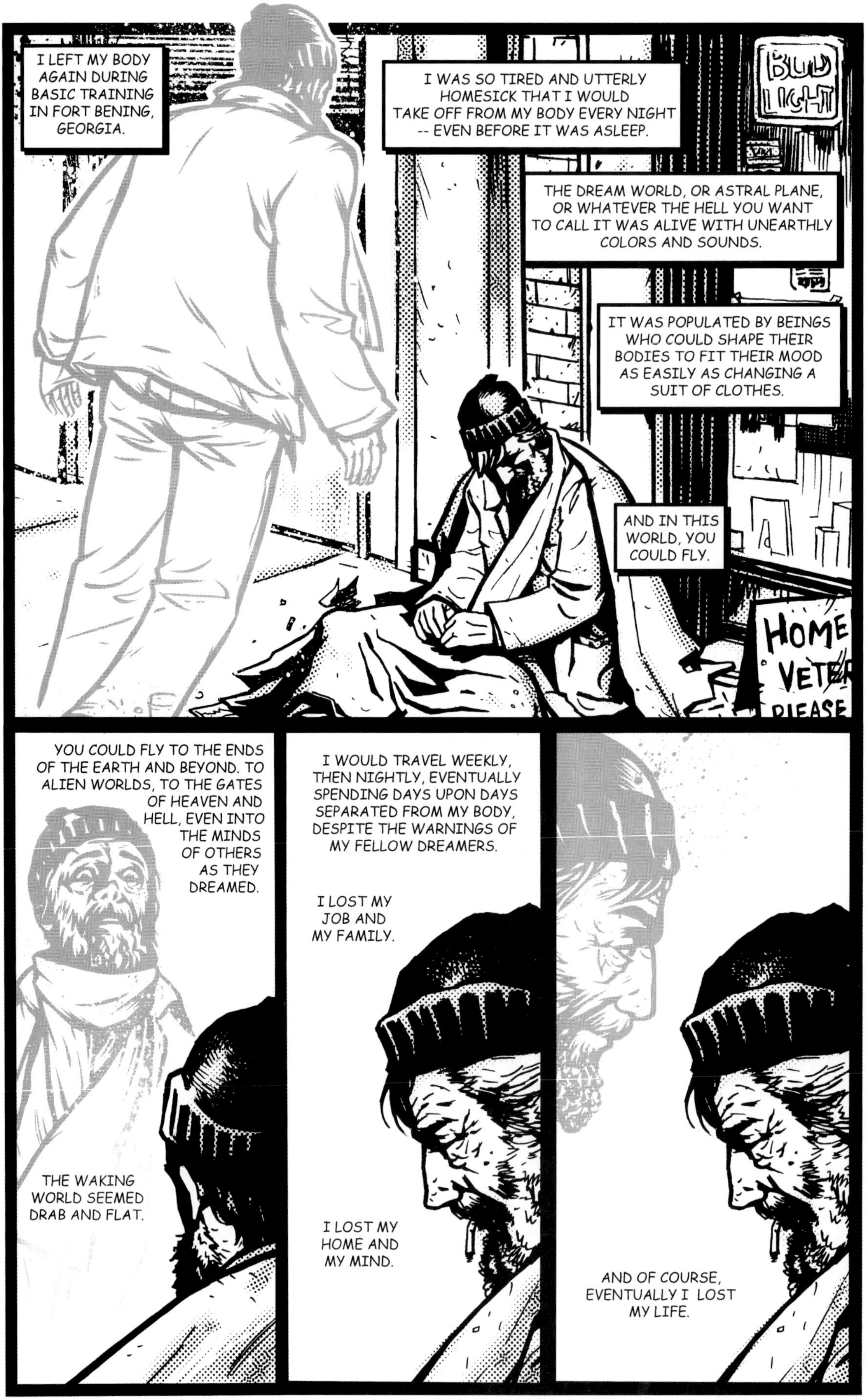
I LEFT MY BODY AGAIN DURING BASIC TRAINING IN FORT BENING, GEORGIA.
I WAS SO TIRED AND UTTERLY HOMESICK THAT I WOULD TAKE OFF FROM MY BODY EVERY NIGHT -- EVEN BEFORE IT WAS ASLEEP.
BUD LIGHT
THE DREAM WORLD, OR ASTRAL PLANE, OR WHATEVER THE HELL YOU WANT TO CALL IT WAS ALIVE WITH UNEARTHLY COLORS AND SOUNDS.
IT WAS POPULATED BY BEINGS WHO COULD SHAPE THEIR BODIES TO FIT THEIR MOOD AS EASILY AS CHANGING A SUIT OF CLOTHES.
AND IN THIS WORLD, YOU COULD FLY.
HOME VETER
YOU COULD FLY TO THE ENDS OF THE EARTH AND BEYOND. TO ALIEN WORLDS, TO THE GATES OF HEAVEN AND HELL, EVEN INTO THE MINDS OF OTHERS AS THEY DREAMED.
THE WAKING WORLD SEEMED DRAB AND FLAT.
I WOULD TRAVEL WEEKLY, THEN NIGHTLY, EVENTUALLY SPENDING DAYS UPON DAYS SEPARATED FROM MY BODY, DESPITE THE WARNINGS OF MY FELLOW DREAMERS.
I LOST MY JOB AND MY FAMILY.
I LOST MY HOME AND MY MIND.
AND OF COURSE, EVENTUALLY I LOST MY LIFE.

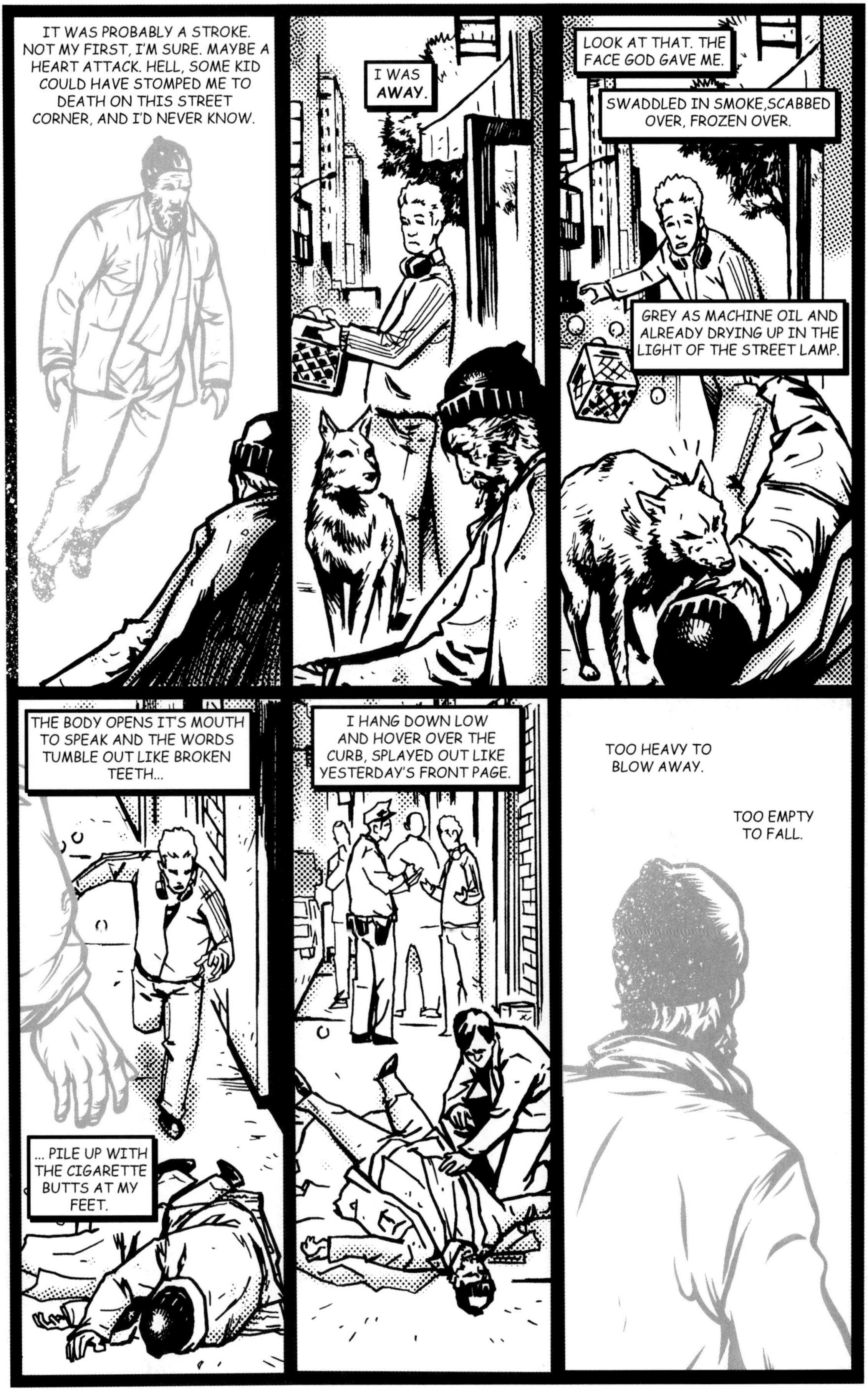
IT WAS PROBABLY A STROKE. NOT MY FIRST, I'M SURE. MAYBE A HEART ATTACK. HELL, SOME KID COULD HAVE STOMPED ME TO DEATH ON THIS STREET CORNER, AND I'D NEVER KNOW.
I WAS **AWAY.**
LOOK AT THAT. THE FACE GOD GAVE ME.
SWADDLED IN SMOKE,SCABBED OVER, FROZEN OVER.
GREY AS MACHINE OIL AND ALREADY DRYING UP IN THE LIGHT OF THE STREET LAMP.
THE BODY OPENS IT'S MOUTH TO SPEAK AND THE WORDS TUMBLE OUT LIKE BROKEN TEETH...
... PILE UP WITH THE CIGARETTE BUTTS AT MY FEET.
I HANG DOWN LOW AND HOVER OVER THE CURB, SPLAYED OUT LIKE YESTERDAY'S FRONT PAGE.
TOO HEAVY TO BLOW AWAY.
TOO EMPTY TO FALL.

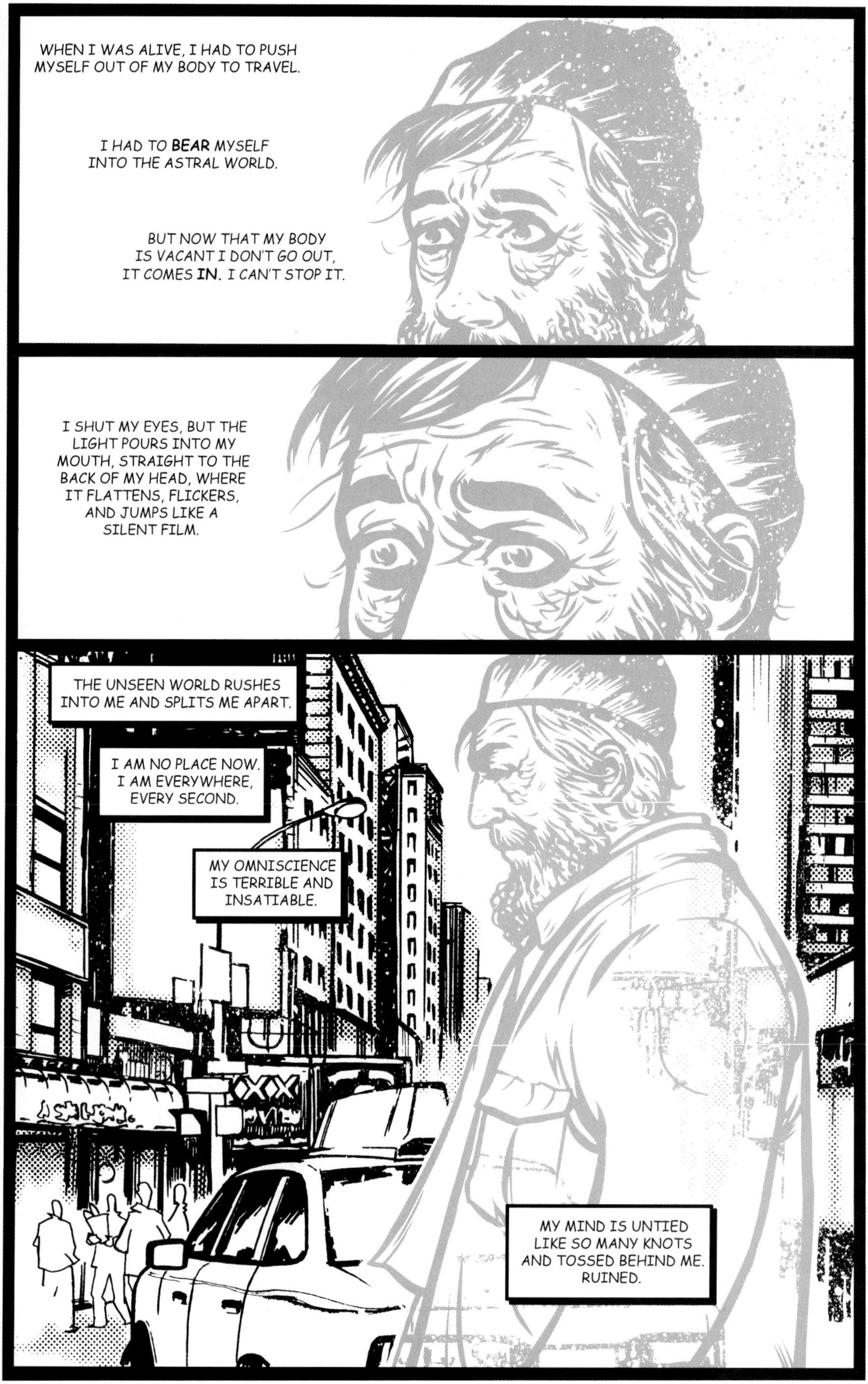
WHEN I WAS ALIVE, I HAD TO PUSH MYSELF OUT OF MY BODY TO TRAVEL.
I HAD TO **BEAR** MYSELF INTO THE ASTRAL WORLD.
BUT NOW THAT MY BODY IS VACANT I DON'T GO OUT, IT COMES **IN.** I CAN'T STOP IT.
I SHUT MY EYES, BUT THE LIGHT POURS INTO MY MOUTH, STRAIGHT TO THE BACK OF MY HEAD, WHERE IT FLATTENS, FLICKERS, AND JUMPS LIKE A SILENT FILM.
THE UNSEEN WORLD RUSHES INTO ME AND SPLITS ME APART.
I AM NO PLACE NOW. I AM EVERYWHERE, EVERY SECOND.
MY OMNISCIENCE IS TERRIBLE AND INSATIABLE.
MY MIND IS UNTIED LIKE SO MANY KNOTS AND TOSSED BEHIND ME. RUINED.

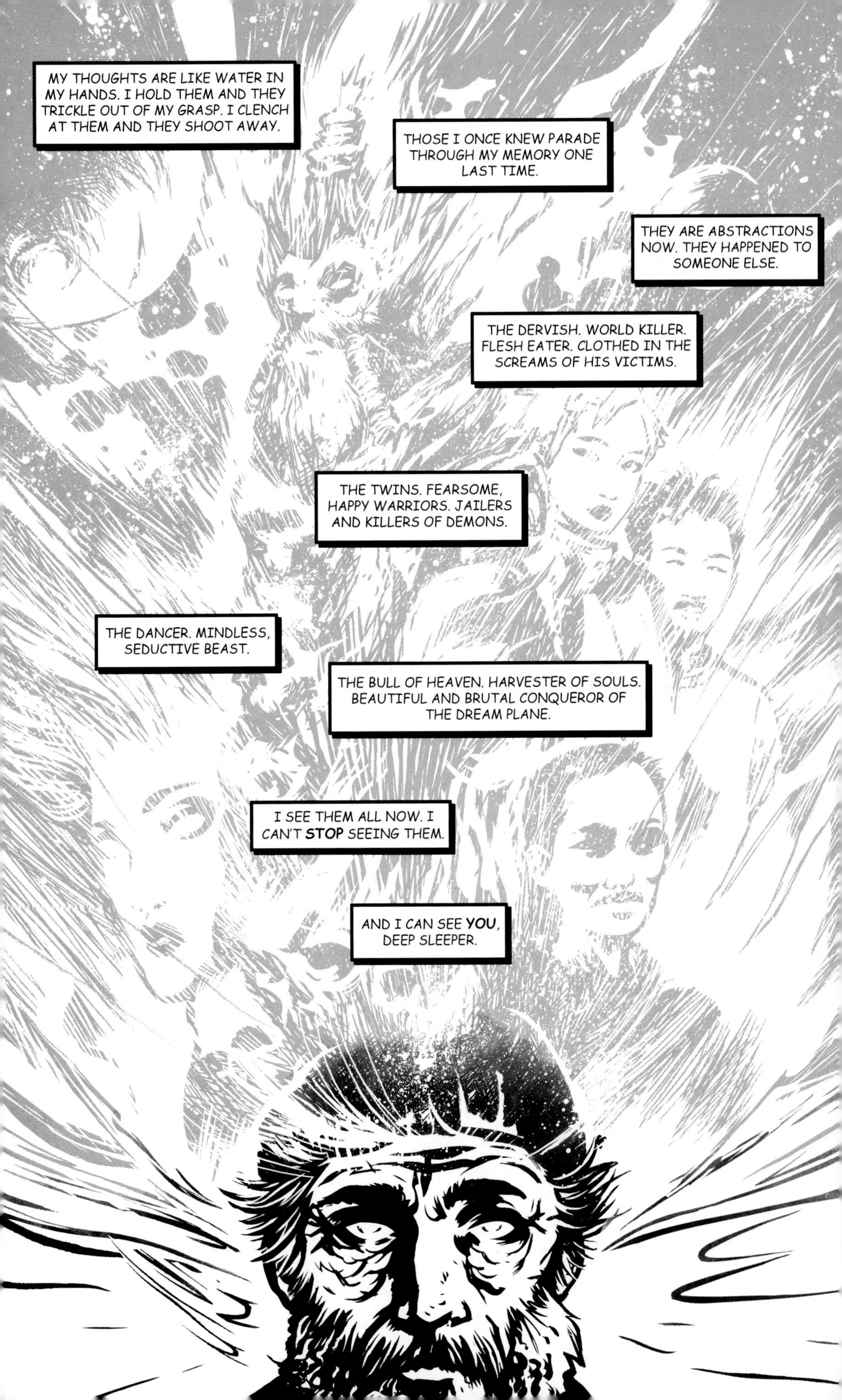

MY THOUGHTS ARE LIKE WATER IN MY HANDS. I HOLD THEM AND THEY TRICKLE OUT OF MY GRASP. I CLENCH AT THEM AND THEY SHOOT AWAY.
THOSE I ONCE KNEW PARADE THROUGH MY MEMORY ONE LAST TIME.
THEY ARE ABSTRACTIONS NOW. THEY HAPPENED TO SOMEONE ELSE.
THE DERVISH. WORLD KILLER. FLESH EATER. CLOTHED IN THE SCREAMS OF HIS VICTIMS.
THE TWINS. FEARSOME, HAPPY WARRIORS. JAILERS AND KILLERS OF DEMONS.
THE DANCER. MINDLESS, SEDUCTIVE BEAST.
THE BULL OF HEAVEN. HARVESTER OF SOULS. BEAUTIFUL AND BRUTAL CONQUEROR OF THE DREAM PLANE.
I SEE THEM ALL NOW. I CAN'T **STOP** SEEING THEM.
AND I CAN SEE **YOU**, DEEP SLEEPER.

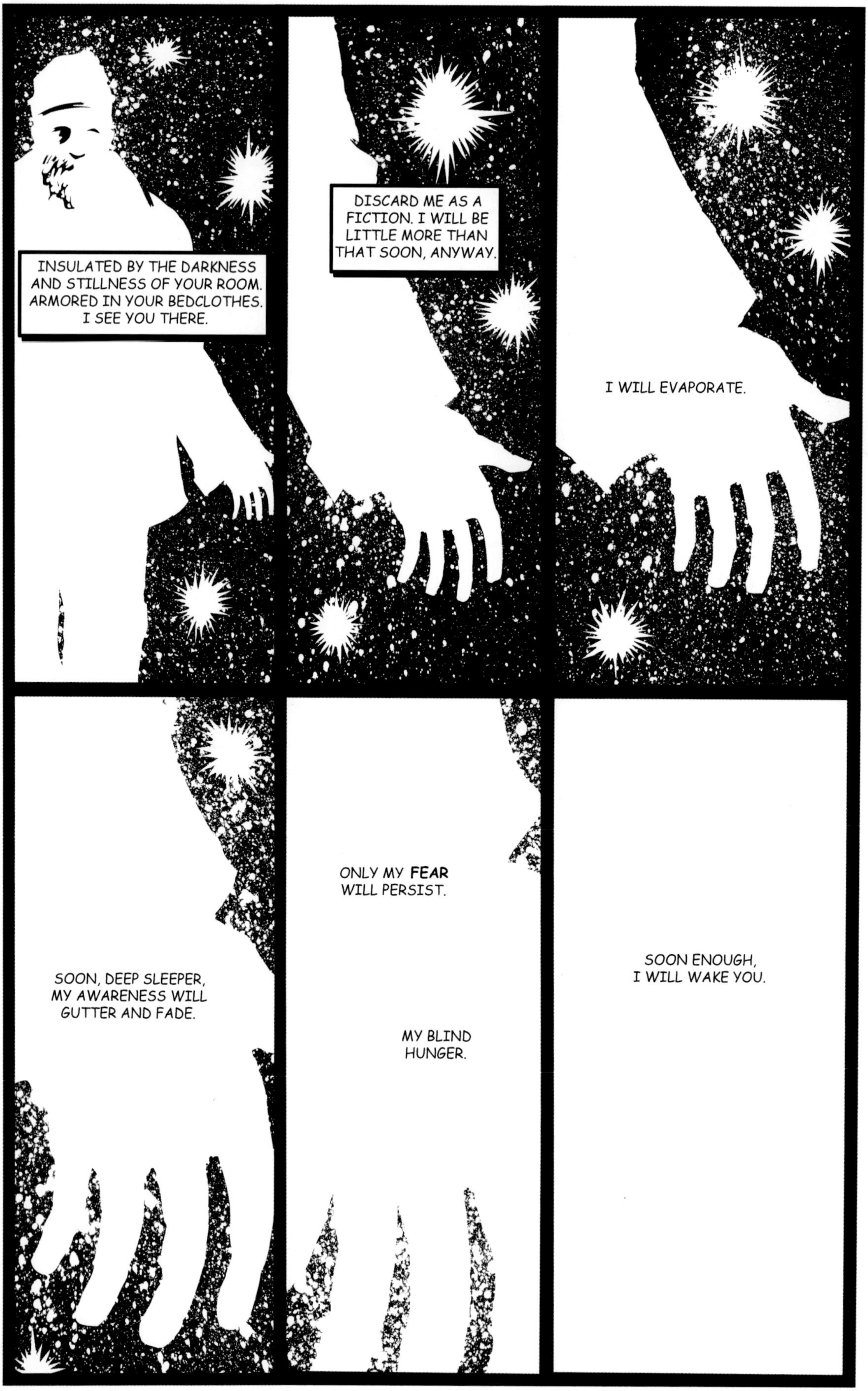
INSULATED BY THE DARKNESS AND STILLNESS OF YOUR ROOM. ARMORED IN YOUR BEDCLOTHES. I SEE YOU THERE.
DISCARD ME AS A FICTION. I WILL BE LITTLE MORE THAN THAT SOON, ANYWAY.
I WILL EVAPORATE.
SOON, DEEP SLEEPER, MY AWARENESS WILL GUTTER AND FADE.
ONLY MY **FEAR** WILL PERSIST.
MY BLIND HUNGER.
SOON ENOUGH, I WILL WAKE YOU.

Words: Phil Hester Art and Letters: Mike Huddleston

COVERS

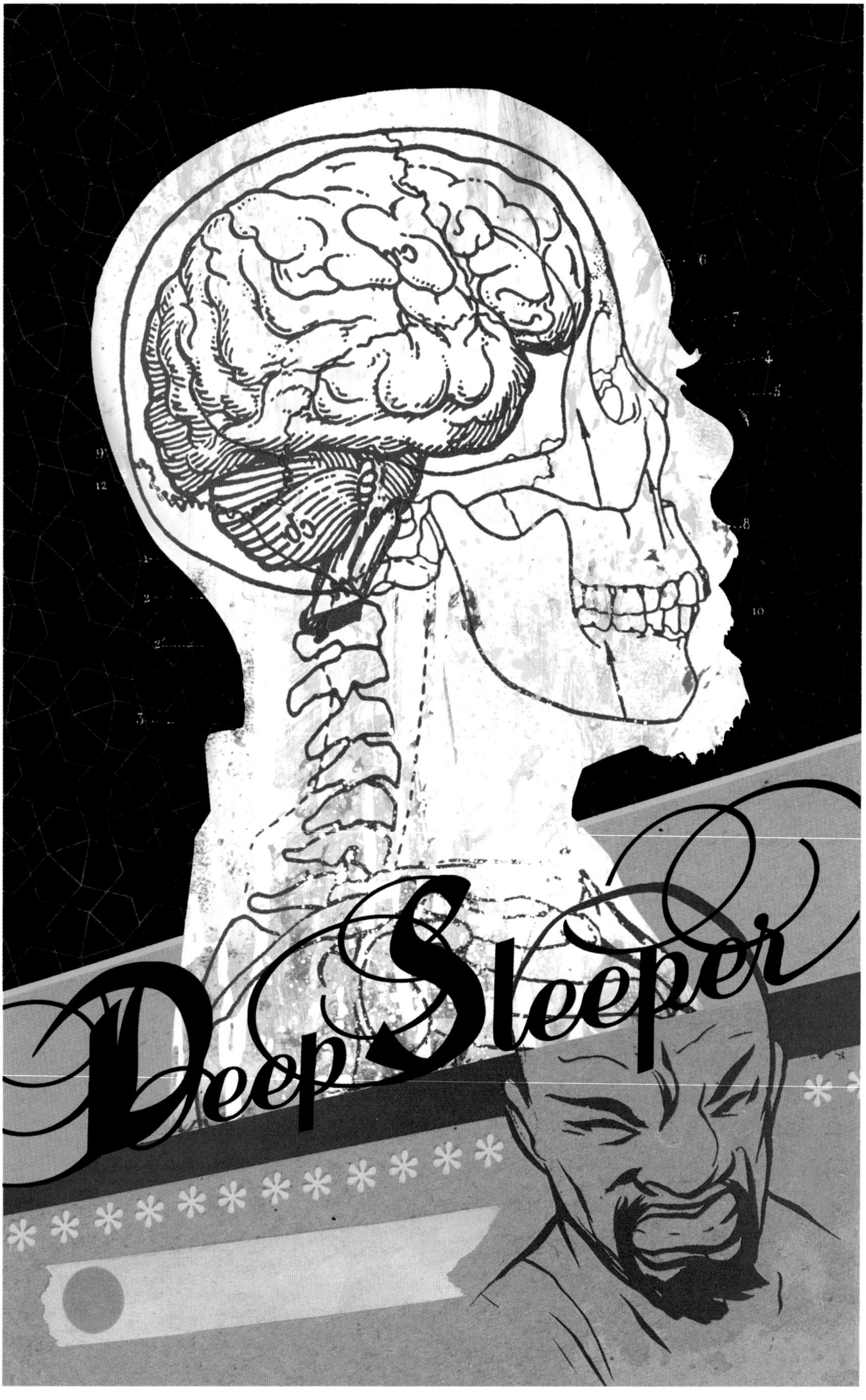
Deep Sleeper

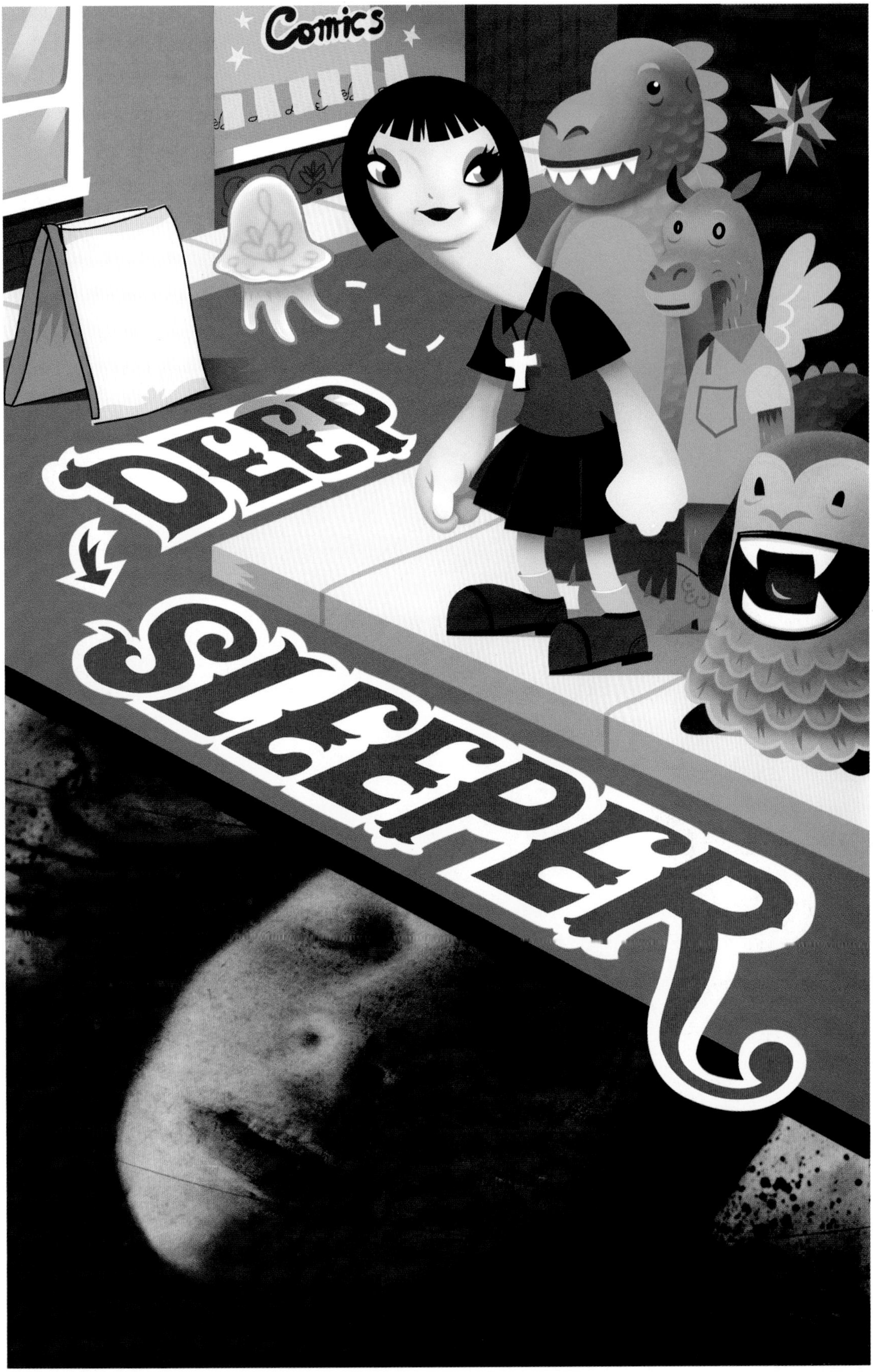

Comics
DEEP
SLEEPER

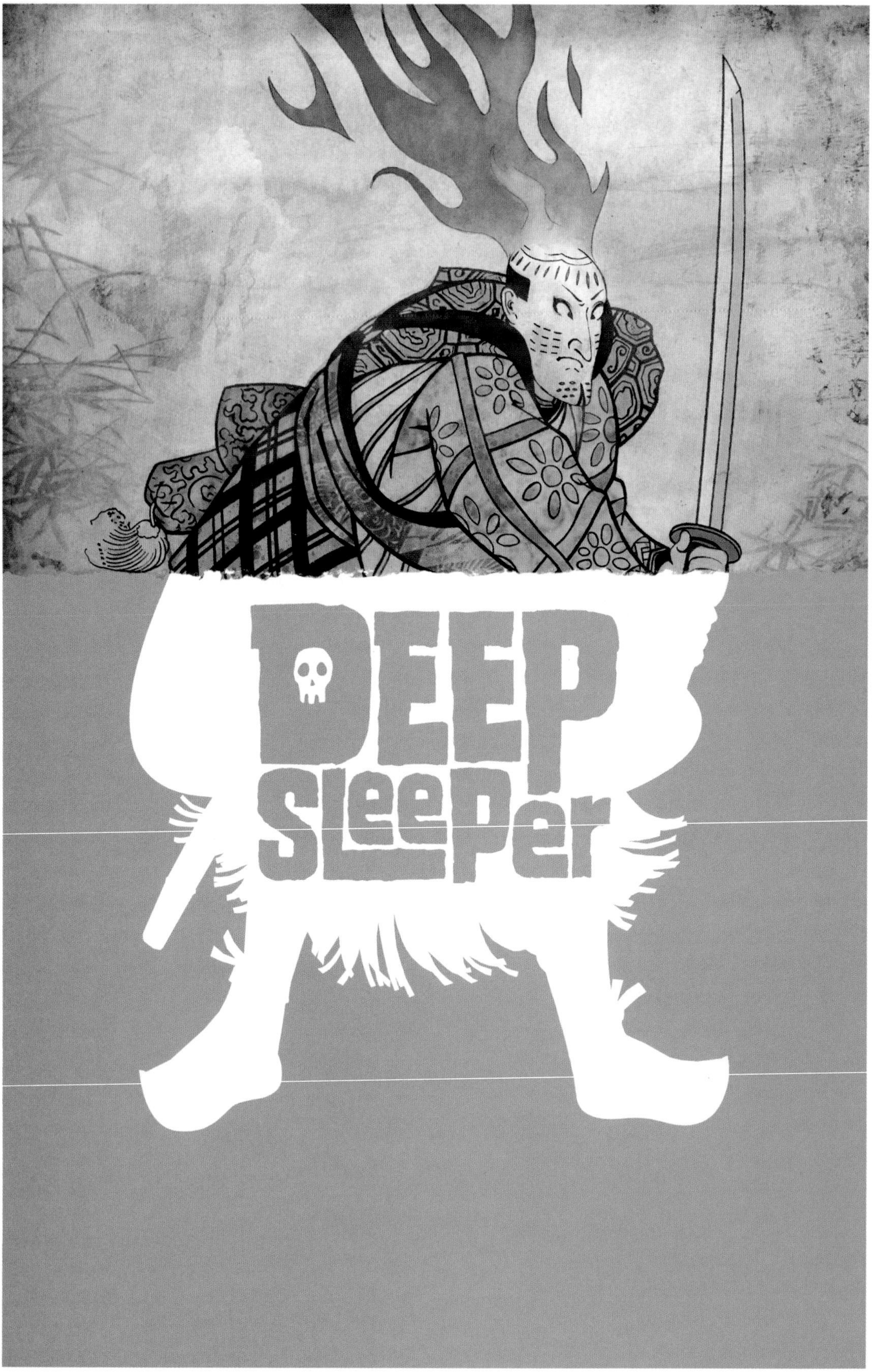
DEEP
SLEEPER

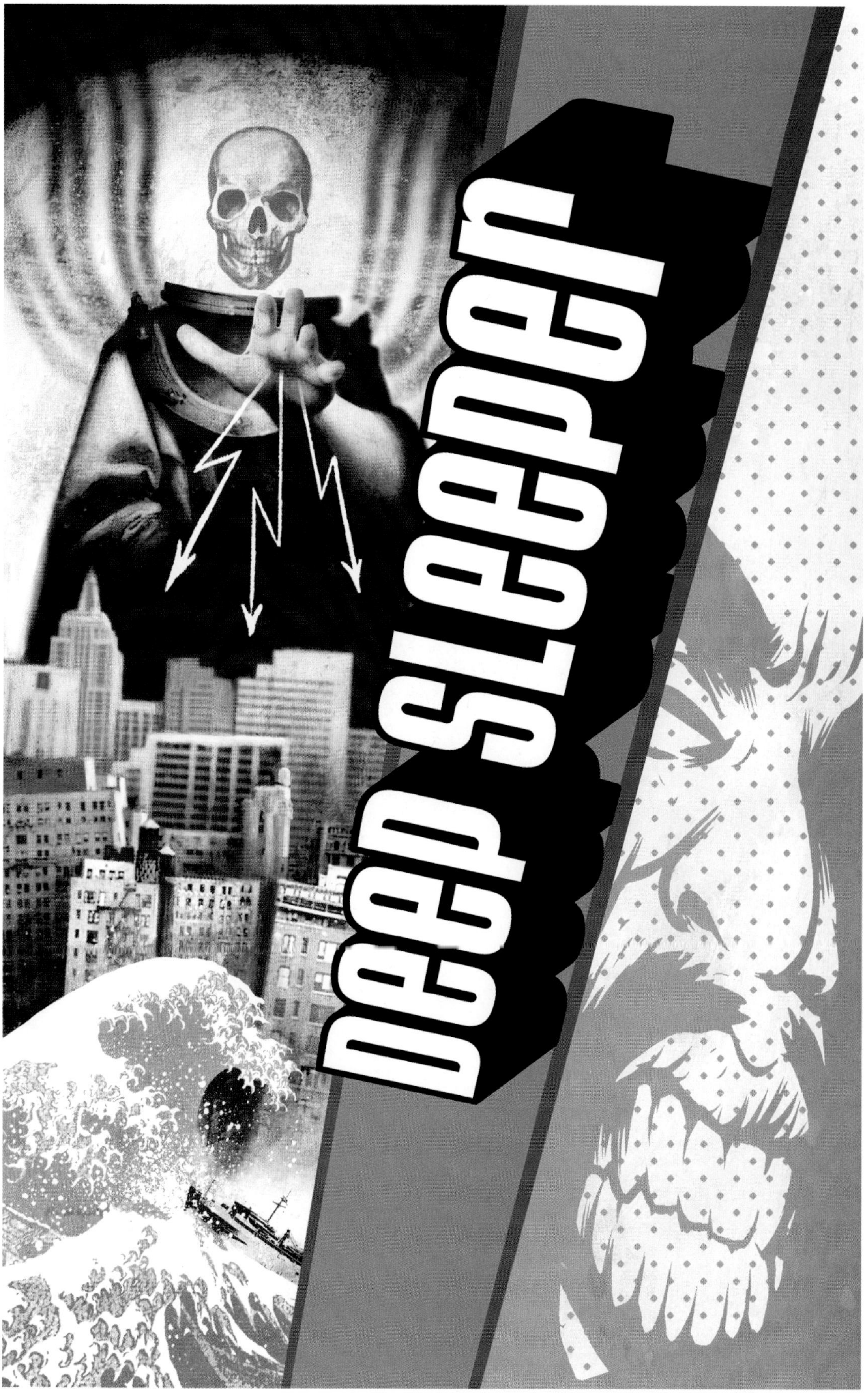
DEEP SLEEPER

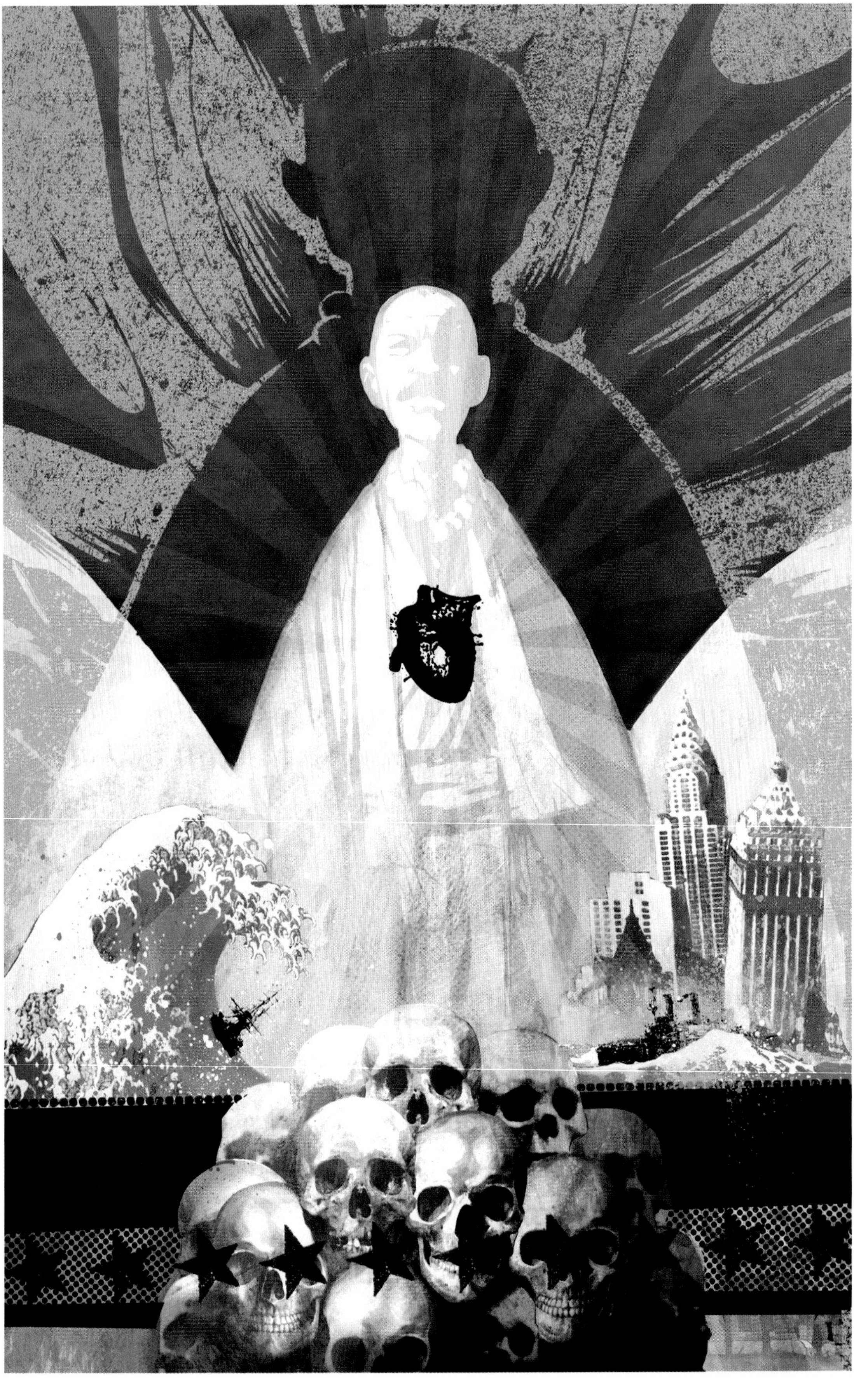

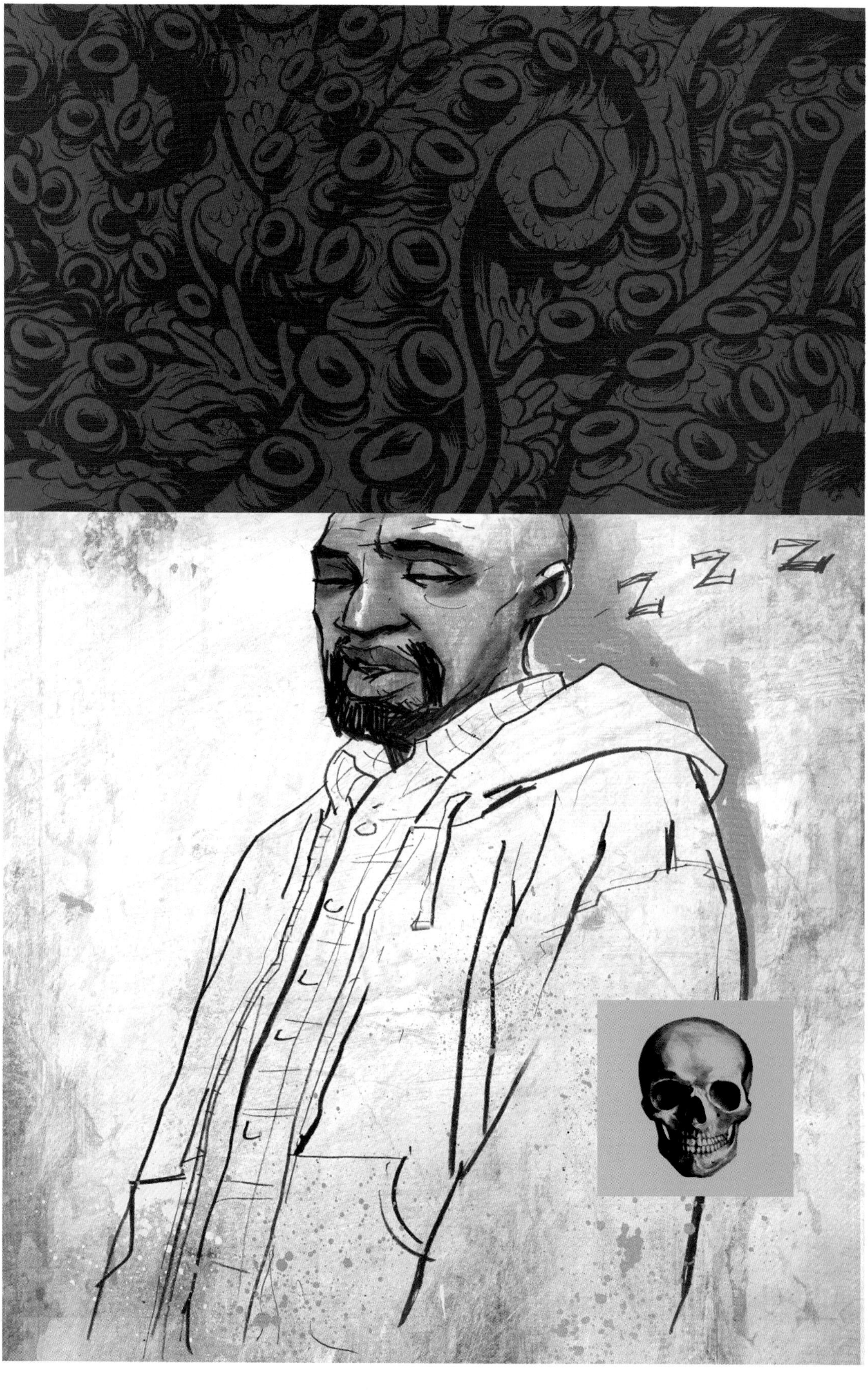
Z Z Z

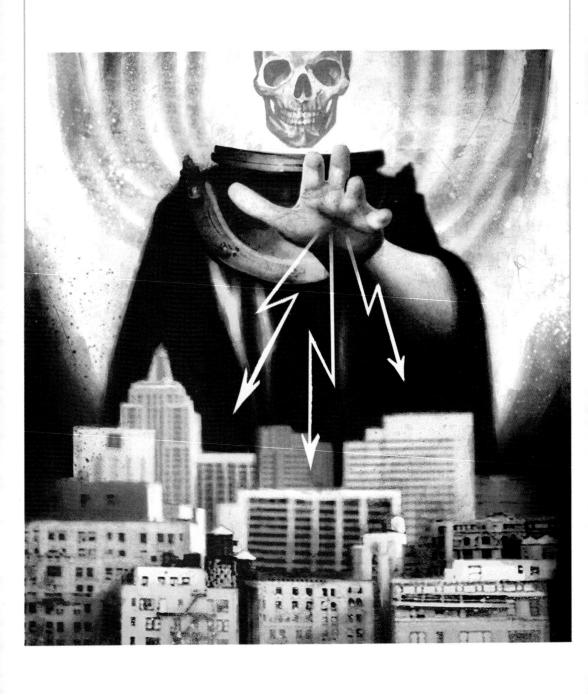